Disagreement, Deference, and Religious Commitment

Disagreement, Deference, and Religious Commitment

JOHN PITTARD

OXFORD
UNIVERSITY PRESS

OXFORD
UNIVERSITY PRESS

Oxford University Press is a department of the University of Oxford. It furthers
the University's objective of excellence in research, scholarship, and education
by publishing worldwide. Oxford is a registered trade mark of Oxford University
Press in the UK and certain other countries.

Published in the United States of America by Oxford University Press
198 Madison Avenue, New York, NY 10016, United States of America.

Library of Congress Cataloging-in-Publication Data

Names: Pittard, John, author.
Title: Disagreement, deference, and religious commitment / John Pittard.
Description: New York, NY : Oxford University Press, [2019] | Includes bibliographical references. |
Summary: "The striking extent of religious disagreement suggests that religious conviction is very often
the result of processes that do not reliably produce true beliefs. For this reason, many have argued that the
only rational response to religious disagreement is to adopt a religious skepticism that eschews confident
religious belief. This book contests this conclusion, explaining how it could be rational to maintain
confident religious (or irreligious) belief even in the face of persistent disagreement. Part One argues
against the commitment to rigorous epistemic impartiality that underlies the case for disagreement-
motivated religious skepticism, while also critiquing highly sanguine approaches to disagreement that
allow for an unproblematic privileging of one's first-person perspective. According to the position
defended in Part One, justified confidence in the face of religious disagreement is likely to require that one
have rational insight into reasons that favor one's outlook. It is argued that many of the rational insights
that are crucial to assessing religious outlooks are not achievable through analytical reasoning, but only
through having the right sort of emotional experiences. Part Two considers the implications for religious
commitment of accepting the impartiality requirement favored by 'disagreement skeptics.' Challenges
are raised to the assumption that a commitment to rigorous epistemic impartiality rules out confident
religious belief. But it is further argued that such a commitment would likely make it irrational to pursue
one's favored form of religious life and might lead to normative uncertainty that would prevent rational
engagement in any religious or irreligious way of life whatsoever"—Provided by publisher.
Identifiers: LCCN 2019021280 | ISBN 9780190051815 (hardback) | ISBN 9780197766514 (paperback)
ISBN 9780190051822 (epdf) | ISBN 9780190051839 (ebook)
Subjects: LCSH: Belief and doubt. | Knowledge, Theory of (Religion) |
Skepticism. | Religion—Philosophy.
Classification: LCC BD215 .P58 2019 | DDC 218—dc23
LC record available at https://lccn.loc.gov/2019021280

Paperback printed by Marquis Book Printing, Canada

To my parents

Contents

Acknowledgments

This book is about the challenge that systematic and pervasive religious disagreement poses to confident religious (or irreligious) commitment. I have been seriously engaged with philosophical questions about disagreement since 2005, when I first encountered Thomas Kelly's seminal article "The Epistemic Significance of Disagreement." In 2006, I began graduate school at Yale with the intention of writing a dissertation in the epistemology of disagreement. I did so, submitting my dissertation in 2013. In 2015, I began working in earnest on this book. Throughout this journey, I've been helped in my thinking and work on disagreement by a great many teachers, friends, students, and family members. I want to thank them here, recognizing that I am no doubt forgetting some who have helped in important ways.

Keith DeRose influenced me significantly during my graduate work at Yale, both through the classes he taught and also as a generous and incisive dissertation advisor. He also read drafts of multiple parts of this book and provided valuable suggestions. John Hare was another important teacher and advisor during my time as a graduate student. Since I joined him on the faculty of Yale Divinity School, he has continued to be a supportive mentor and advisor. My colleague and friend Daniel Greco read drafts of every chapter and provided great feedback that was as supportive and helpful as it was challenging and incisive. I am immensely grateful for his help.

Others who have helped me by reading or discussing parts of the book or preceding essays include Alex Arnold, Emad Atiq, Matthew Benton, Michael Bergmann, Tomas Bogardus, Lara Buchak, Isaac Choi, David Christensen, Michael Della Rocca, Katherine Dormandy, Kent Dunnington, Adam Eitel, Tamar Gendler, Clifton Granby, Daniel Immerman, Klaas Kraay, Dustin Locke, Jonathan Matheson, Jack Sanchez, Miriam Schoenfield, Sun-Joo Shin, Fred Simmons, Jason Stanley, Bart Streumer, Zoltan Szabo, Josh Thurow, Michael Titelbaum, Matthew Vermaire, Bruno Whittle, and Alex Worsnip. The book also owes much to the detailed criticisms and suggestions of multiple anonymous referees. I'm grateful to students in multiple seminars where I have taught on disagreement and related material. Teaching really is one of the best ways to learn, especially when students are as perceptive, inquisitive, and creative as those I've been blessed to interact with.

Special thanks are due to Nathan Dowell, who served as my research assistant in the summers of 2018 and 2019. Nathan offered detailed editorial feedback, making multiple suggestions on nearly every page of the manuscript. The writing has benefited significantly from his careful work. He also later helped to produce the index.

I am very grateful to Peter Ohlin at Oxford University Press for his support of this work. I also extend sincere thanks to Madeleine Freeman and others at Oxford University Press who helped shepherd this work to publication, to project manager Asish Krishna, and to Martha Ramsey for her work as copyeditor.

My thinking has been challenged and sharpened by engaging with audience members at various venues where I've presented work related to the present volume. Some of the ideas and arguments that are featured in chapter 2 were presented at the 2011 Purdue Summer Seminar on Perceptual, Moral, and Religious Skepticism, organized by Michael Bergmann. A predecessor of chapter 3 was presented in 2014 at the Philosophy of Religion Colloquium at Yale and at the Defeat and Religious Epistemology Workshop at Oxford University (part of the New Insights and Directions for Religious Epistemology project). Essays that became the basis for material in chapters 4 and 5 were presented at a symposium of the 2015 congress of the Canadian Philosophical Association in Ottawa, at the Summer Research Retreat on Moral Epistemology and Moral Psychology hosted in 2015 by the Prindle Institute for Ethics at DePauw University, and at the Arguing Religion conference hosted in 2017 by Fondazione Bruno Kessler in Trento. An initial version of chapter 6 was delivered as a lecture at the University of Texas, San Antonio, in 2016. Much of chapter 7 was presented in 2018 at the Chapel Hill Normativity Workshop at the University of North Carolina.

I'm grateful to the publishers of the following articles for granting me permission to include material from them in this book:

"Fundamental Disagreements and the Limits of Instrumentalism," *Synthese*, forthcoming (published online 2018), https://doi.org/10.1007/s11229-018-1691-1.

"Religious Disagreement," in *The Internet Encyclopedia of Philosophy*, ISSN 2161-0002, https://www.iep.utm.edu/rel-disa/.

"Resolute Conciliationism," *Philosophical Quarterly* 65, no. 260 (2015): 442–463.

Finally, I want to thank my family. Alicia, my wife, has supported and helped me in an untold number of ways. She's read drafts of many sections, and her detailed feedback has helped me to be a better writer. She's solo parented three kids many days, evenings, and weekends to give me time to devote to this project. She's celebrated the triumphs along the way, big and small. And she's believed in me through all of the setbacks. I am so thankful.

My children, Thomas, Camille, and Samantha, besides being a source of joy and delight, have shown much patience and understanding when my work has imposed on our time together as a family. Thankfully, I've been able to join them in many adventures, and I hope that a great many more lie ahead.

My parents, each in their distinctive ways, have been models for me of the commitment to seeking after truth and living in its light. With immense gratitude, I dedicate this book to them.

Disagreement, Deference, and Religious Commitment

Introduction

1.1 Topic and Approach

This book explores the challenge that disagreement poses to the rationality of confident religious (or irreligious) commitment. I won't try to give a precise account of what commitments count as being *religious* (or irreligious), but you surely qualify as having such a commitment if you take a confident stance on any of the following questions. When confronted with arresting natural beauty, is it appropriate to feel gratitude? When a loved one has died, should you strive for an attitude of stoic acceptance, hope for eventual reunion, or frankly confront the tragic absurdity of permanent separation? Was the universe created by God? If so, does every event conform to the divine plan for creation, or might the universe unfold in ways that God neither expected nor desired? Was the Buddha enlightened? Is Jesus God incarnate? Was Muhammad God's prophet?

Answer any of these "religious" questions, and you will find yourself in disagreement with many people who appear to be as informed and thoughtful as yourself but who adopt some opposing view. The striking extent of religious disagreement, and its frequent persistence in the face of dialogue, raises worries about the reasonability of taking a stand on religious questions, whether one's stance is religious or explicitly irreligious. The challenge that religious disagreement poses to religious *belief* may initially be expressed as follows.[1] If you have good reason for thinking it likely that the mental processes that have produced some specific belief of yours are processes that do not reliably lead to true belief, then it is not reasonable for you to confidently persist in that belief. To use language commonly employed by epistemologists, good evidence that your belief in proposition *p* has been produced and maintained by unreliable processes constitutes a *defeater* for that belief, meaning that such evidence undermines whatever

---

[1] In chapter 7, I will consider how disagreement may also pose a challenge to the rationality of religious commitments that do not involve confident religious belief.

initial justification the belief may have had. And facts about religious disagreement give you good reason to think that your beliefs on controversial religious questions are the product of unreliable processes.

In support of this last claim, note first that the fact that there is so much disagreement over religious questions means that a good deal of people affirm answers to these questions that are false; and this in turn strongly suggests that in a large portion of cases, the processes that give rise to beliefs on religious matters are not reliable, or at least they are not reliable when directed toward religious questions. And it is unlikely that a more favorable verdict will be reached when one looks specifically at the process or processes that lie behind some particular religious or irreligious belief of *yours*. Whether that belief is the product of philosophical reasoning, trust in the testimony of others, "mystical" experience, or some combination of these or other processes, there are no doubt many others who have arrived at contrary religious views by means of relevantly similar processes. It seems, then, that consideration of the nature and scope of religious disagreement gives you strong reason to think that the processes that lie behind your religious or irreligious beliefs are unreliable. Since you have good reason to think this, it is not reasonable to remain confident on religious matters.

The argument just rehearsed is overly hasty, and I will refine and strengthen it in due course. But even if there are steps in the argument that deserve philosophical scrutiny, I hope that it is evident that there is a troubling worry here. One can plausibly maintain that humankind in its present incarnation is quite good at forming true beliefs in those domains of inquiry that are characterized by significant consensus, including mathematics, most areas of science, and to a significant extent even morality (despite a number of prominent areas of moral contention). But human beings clearly are *not* reliably good at forming true beliefs with respect to religious questions.[2] Having acknowledged this, would not continued confidence in one's own religious opinions amount to little more than unwarranted epistemic hubris? Given that even the most intelligent and thoughtful of those who devote themselves to religious questions are, taken as a whole, highly unreliable, isn't the only reasonable stance one of *religious skepticism* that refuses to confidently answer any central religious question?

---

[2] One might contest this generalization by noting that the majority of human beings do agree on *some* religious questions, for example the existence of God. So perhaps human beings are, taken as a whole, epistemically reliable on some religious matters. This important suggestion will receive significant attention in chapter 6.

Grappling with these questions is the central task of this book. Questions about the epistemic significance of religious disagreement cannot, of course, be separated from questions concerning the significance of disagreement more generally, and a good deal of this book is concerned with developing a fully general theory of the rational significance of disagreement. I defend a principled middle way between extreme "conciliatory" approaches to disagreement that are committed to rigorous epistemic impartiality and highly sanguine approaches that allow for an unproblematic privileging of one's first-person perspective. Identifying this middle way requires distinguishing between two kinds of impartiality: agent impartiality (which I endorse) and reasons impartiality (which I oppose). According to the position I defend, it can be rational to maintain confident belief in the face of disagreement with others who appear to be equally qualified, but this is likely to require that one have genuine insight into the greater rational merits of one's outlook.

Deciding on a general approach to disagreement will not by itself settle the question of how one ought to respond to religious controversy. Rather, one's general approach to disagreement will determine an agenda of questions that must be answered in order to determine the epistemic implications of religious disagreement. This book pursues two such agendas, each arising from a different approach to disagreement. The first approach I will consider is the one I endorse—an approach that does not require the most rigorous form of epistemic impartiality. The second approach I will consider is one that *does* require this rigorous form of epistemic impartiality. While I oppose this second approach, I do not have a fully decisive argument against it. For this reason, it is worth exploring what bearing it has on religious commitment.

If my favored approach is correct, then how a person should respond to religious disagreement will significantly depend on whether that person's views on religious matters are genuinely insightful. In considering whether it is plausible that a given person has insight on religious matters, I will need to address questions about the character of religious insight and about the role that religious experiences might play in the acquisition of such insight.

If the second and more deferential approach to disagreement is correct, then a key question is whether there is some "doxastic stance" on religious matters that has the best claim to being the stance of impartiality (where a "doxastic stance" encompasses attitudes of belief as well as of skepticism). As I will show, answering this question requires that one address vexing questions about the sources of religious bias and the kinds of qualifications that are most important in assessing religious claims. Another key question is whether someone who pursues epistemic impartiality could nonetheless rationally maintain a robust form of religious commitment that does not require holding controversial religious beliefs.

As this summary of agenda items should make clear, a cursory application of some disagreement framework to the religious domain will not be sufficient. A proper assessment of the challenge posed by religious disagreement must substantively engage with central questions in the epistemology of disagreement and with several important questions in the epistemology of religious belief. I aim to make significant progress on both of these fronts in this book.

This is a book by an epistemologist for epistemologists, but not *only* for epistemologists. Or at least not only for *professional* epistemologists. If there is any topic that can motivate the layperson to wade into thorny epistemological questions, disagreement is surely one of them. Unlike Cartesian skeptical scenarios involving lifelike dreams or deceptive demons, possibilities that raise difficult epistemological questions but generally do not occasion real doubt about one's epistemic standing, disagreement frequently does lead to genuine worry and loss of confidence. When those worries concern not only some isolated beliefs but one's entire moral, philosophical, or religious outlook, epistemological questions gain an uncommon urgency. With this in mind, I have tried to write a book that is approachable enough to be useful to nonspecialists who may not be steeped in the specialized vocabulary of contemporary epistemology.

I.2 Overview of Chapters and Reading Guide

Here is where the argument is headed. In part I, I argue against the epistemic impartiality requirement that undergirds the strongest argument for disagreement-motivated religious skepticism. I commend instead a rationalist approach to disagreement that does not rule out confident religious (or irreligious) belief even in the face of pervasive and systematic religious disagreement. Chapter 1 begins by clarifying the focus of the book, which may be called the "higher-order argument for disagreement-motivated religious skepticism." I then show that a viable version of this higher-order argument must posit three constraints on the factors that may justifiably ground epistemic self-trust in the face of religious disagreement. These constraints are an "internal reason constraint," an "agent impartiality constraint," and a "reasons impartiality constraint." The position I develop and defend in part I is a rationalist position that endorses the internal reason and agent impartiality constraints but rejects the reasons impartiality constraint.

As a first step in arguing against a reasons impartiality requirement, I turn in chapter 2 to two very different arguments for some sort of reasons impartiality constraint, one from David Christensen (who is focused on disagreement in general) and one from John Schellenberg (whose focus is religious disagreement in particular). I argue that neither argument is successful.

In chapter 3, I develop and defend an approach to disagreement that rejects the strong epistemic impartiality requirement endorsed by "strong conciliationists." The central tenet of the "weak conciliationism" that I defend is a requirement that I call "instrumentalism." Instrumentalism supplies a basis for demanding conciliatory requirements in disagreements that are rationally superficial, but does *not* support similarly demanding conciliatory requirements in fundamental disagreements that are the result of divergent epistemic starting points. I argue that the radical impartiality requirement of strong conciliationism, which *does* issue demanding conciliatory prescriptions in fundamental disputes, is unmotivated in light of the explanatory power of instrumentalism. One should therefore affirm a weak conciliationism that allows for the possibility of reasonable confidence in the face fundamental disagreements with highly qualified disputants.

Weak conciliationism rejects any sort of sweeping epistemic impartiality requirement. Nevertheless, weak conciliationism does not itself supply an account of when it is rationally acceptable to adopt "partisan" epistemic starting points that do not accord with epistemic impartiality. My general position on disagreement is therefore not complete until the weak conciliationism I defend in chapter 3 is combined with a theory of "partisan justification." Developing such a theory is the task of chapter 4. According to the rationalist account of partisan justification that I defend, justified religious belief in the face of religious disagreement is likely to require that one have *rational insight* into the greater rational merits of one's own religious outlook. In assigning this significance to rational insight, I stand opposed to the most prominent approach to religious epistemology of the last thirty to forty years, the tradition of "reformed epistemology" that was most forcefully promulgated by Alvin Plantinga and William Alston. I argue that the religious epistemologies of Plantinga and Alston, which deemphasize the significance of rational insight and rational assessment, do not have the resources to meet the higher-order challenge posed by religious disagreement.

Chapter 5 considers further what implications rationalist weak conciliationism has for religious belief. Initially, the rationalist position I endorse may seem to imply that justified religious belief is a philosophical accomplishment reserved only for those blessed with a great deal of analytical sophistication. The view might also seem to imply that personal religious experience plays at best a minor role in accounting for the rationality of religious belief. But I argue that these alleged implications follow from my view only if one presupposes an "austere rationalism" that sees all rational insight as a product of (ostensibly) dispassionate analytical faculties. I urge that such a view be rejected in favor of an "affective rationalism" that emphasizes the essential role played by the emotions in facilitating insight into evaluative questions.

Throughout chapters 1–5, which make up part I, my aim is to oppose a reasons impartiality requirement and to commend a rationalist approach to disagreement that does not rule out confident religious (or irreligious) belief. While I think that the discussion in part I puts the strong conciliationist who supports reasons impartiality on the defensive, I concede that I do not have a knockdown argument that shows strong conciliationism to be hopelessly misguided. For this reason, I am not content merely to argue against epistemic impartiality. In part II, I accept for sake of discussion that strong conciliationism is correct and consider what the implications of this supposition are for religious commitment.

The central claim of chapter 6 (the first chapter of part II) is that epistemic impartiality in the religious domain is elusive. The first reason for this has to do with a vexing self-undermining challenge that confronts conciliatory approaches to disagreement. I consider various ways that the conciliationist might respond to this self-undermining problem, and I argue that a viable response to the problem is unlikely to be compatible with a commitment to full epistemic impartiality in the religious domain. The second reason why epistemic impartiality proves elusive in the religious domain is that the most plausible methods for identifying an impartial doxastic stance on religious matters will require that one take a stand on various questions that are themselves implicated in religious controversy. In particular, one must take a stand on questions concerning the importance of various epistemic credentials in the religious domain and concerning the degree to which various factors bias people's religious thinking. These questions cannot be settled in a religiously impartial way. Because it is extremely unclear how the strong conciliationist should proceed in light of the elusiveness of impartiality, I contend that it is far from obvious that the commitment to epistemic impartiality vindicates religious skepticism.

Even if strong conciliationism *does* require religious skepticism, some have suggested that one can maintain robust religious commitment while conforming to the prescriptions of strong conciliationism. This is thought to be possible because there are forms of religious commitment where one can be committed to an outlook without believing in it. In chapter 7, I present arguments that challenge the view that such "nondoxastic" religious commitment is a rational option for someone who conforms to strong conciliationism. The most radical argument that I defend concludes that conformity to strong conciliationism makes rational decision-making in the religious domain impossible. If this argument is right, then the strong conciliationist cannot rationally engage in any religious *or* irreligious way of life.

I end this introduction with brief reading plans for different sorts of readers of this book. Many readers, I hope, will be keenly interested both in the general epistemology of disagreement and in the epistemology of religious belief. The entire book should be of interest to such readers.

To readers interested in the epistemology of disagreement but less interested in religious belief in particular, I offer a caveat and a suggested reading plan. The caveat is that some sections that are focused on religious belief also have significant relevance to more general issues and questions in the epistemology of disagreement. There is reason to think that the general discussion of disagreement would profit significantly from more serious engagement with the messy reality of religious disagreement. To be sure, the highly idealized cases of two-person disagreement that have been the focus of much of the disagreement literature are helpful since they allow one to isolate variables of epistemic significance. But attending to the real-world example of religious disagreement presents opportunities to clarify various disagreement policies and surfaces challenges to those policies that are obscured in idealized examples.

That being said, here is a suggested reading plan for those who want to focus on general issues in the epistemology of disagreement while passing over most of the material more particularly focused on religious disagreement. Look at chapter 1, sections 1.4 and 1.6, for orientation to some key commitments of the "disagreement skeptic." Then read chapter 2, sections 2.1–4; chapter 3; chapter 4, sections 4.1–4; chapter 6, sections 6.1–2; and chapter 7 (perhaps skipping section 7.1).

To readers primarily interested in issues pertaining to religious commitment, I encourage you to read the whole book. The general approach to disagreement that I defend informs the sections focused on religion. And I've worked hard to make the more technical epistemological arguments accessible to a broad philosophical audience. That being said, here is a reading plan that emphasizes those sections most relevant to religious belief and religious commitment: chapter 1; chapter 2, sections 2.5–6; chapter 3; chapter 4; chapter 5; chapter 6, sections 6.4–10; and chapter 7, up through section 7.1. Chapter 3 is not focused on religious belief, but I've included it in this reading plan since it is so crucial to much of the discussion that follows.

PART I
AGAINST IMPARTIALITY

1

Disagreement-Motivated Religious Skepticism and the Commitment to Impartiality

In a short passage in *The Methods of Ethics*, nineteenth-century moral philosopher Henry Sidgwick argues that "an indispensable negative condition" of the certainty of some belief is the absence of disagreement among those "experts" who are most qualified to assess the matter.[1] Sidgwick reasons as follows:

> For if I find any of my judgments, intuitive or inferential, in direct conflict with a judgment of some other mind, there must be error somewhere: and if I have no more reason to suspect error in the other mind than in my own, reflective comparison between the two judgments necessarily reduces me temporarily to a state of neutrality. And though the total result in my mind is not exactly suspense of judgment, but an alteration and conflict between positive affirmation by one act of thought and the neutrality that is the result of another, it is obviously something very different from scientific certitude.[2]

This argument nicely encapsulates the sort of reasoning that many have advanced in support of disagreement-motivated religious skepticism. The fact of systematic religious disagreement implies that many people are in significant error on religious matters. Since (it is alleged) no one has good reason to think that the error lies with her disputants rather than with herself, one should, in the words of Sidgwick, be reduced to a state of "neutrality."

Sidgwick himself does not exactly say that neutrality is the ideal response to expert disagreement. His description suggests that such disagreement

---

[1] Henry Sidgwick, *The Methods of Ethics*, 7th ed. (London: Macmillan, 1907), 342.
[2] Sidgwick, *The Methods of Ethics*.

brings about a sort of double-mindedness: thinking through the disputed issue for himself inclines him to affirm a particular view, while consideration of others' opinions inclines him toward a state of neutrality in which judgment is suspended. While Sidgwick clearly thinks that *certainty* in the face of expert disagreement is inappropriate, he does not go so far as to condemn any belief whatsoever on controversial matters.

But many writing on religious disagreement *do* take this further step, arguing that the appropriate response to pervasive disagreement is a *religious skepticism* that refrains from holding any controversial religious views. According to these disagreement skeptics, trusting that one's own religious community has gotten things right would be rationally arbitrary, given that the epistemic credentials of one's own community are no more impressive than the credentials of other communities with opposing viewpoints.

Sidgwick makes the conditional claim that one should be inclined toward neutrality on a disputed matter *if* one has no more reason to think that the error lies with the other side of the dispute rather than with one's own side. But might not some significant number of religious believers have good reason to think that the error lies with their disputants rather than with themselves? Disagreement skeptics answer this question in the negative: those who are reasonably informed about the facts of religious disagreement lack any sufficient reason for thinking that they are more likely than their disputants to have arrived at religious truth. This is the key claim in the argument for disagreement-motivated religious skepticism (as I will argue shortly).

The central thesis of this chapter is that a viable defense of this claim requires one to affirm that any legitimate responses to religious disagreement must exhibit a very demanding form of *epistemic impartiality*. Arguments for disagreement-motivated religious skepticism do not always explicitly invoke impartiality requirements, but these arguments are not plausible unless such requirements are taken for granted.

The chapter proceeds as follows. In section 1.1, I will clarify the particular challenge posed by religious disagreement that is the focus of this book, as some worries posed by religious disagreement will not be treated here. Subsequent sections then give a more precise characterization of the argument for disagreement-motivated religious skepticism and identify the central epistemological commitments that drive the argument. These commitments involve two distinct sorts of impartiality requirements that the disagreement skeptic must endorse if the argument for disagreement-motivated religious skepticism is to succeed. Later chapters provide a critical evaluation of these impartiality requirements.

1.1 First-Order and Higher-Order Challenges of Religious Disagreement

Religious disagreement presents distinct sorts of challenges to religious belief, and it will be useful to distinguish between these various challenges and to indicate which one is the principal concern of this book. To begin with, religious disagreement may cause one to be aware of arguments against one's religious (or irreligious) outlook. (Here, and throughout the book, labels like "religious view" and "religious belief" will typically be used to refer to *all* beliefs that take a stand on religious questions, including explicitly *irreligious* beliefs such as the belief that there is no God.) But while these new challenges might be encountered in the context of religious disagreement, the challenges themselves will often be independent of the fact of religious disagreement: the arguments would be no less worrying if they were identified in the context of private reflection.

My focus in this book is a challenge posed by the very fact of religious disagreement. But my focus is more specifically the *higher-order* challenge posed by such disagreement. Importantly, there are two distinct sorts of challenges that the fact of religious disagreement might present to a given religious belief: a "first-order" challenge and a "higher-order" challenge. Understanding the distinction between first-order and higher-order challenges is essential to adequately grasping the topic.

In the epistemological literature on disagreement, a contrast is frequently drawn between first-order and higher-order evidence. First-order evidence for or against some proposition p "directly" bears on the question of whether p. By contrast, higher-order evidence for or against p does not directly bear on the question of whether p but directly bears on the question of whether one has rationally and reliably assessed the first-order evidence for or against p.[3] To illustrate the distinction, consider the case of Detective, who has

---

[3] This characterization of first-order and higher-order evidence is similar to the way these types of evidence are characterized in David Christensen, "Higher-Order Evidence," *Philosophy and Phenomenological Research* 81, no. 1 (2010): 185; Paulina Sliwa and Sophie Horowitz, "Respecting All the Evidence," *Philosophical Studies* 172, no. 11 (2015): 2836; and Maria Lasonen-Aarnio, "Higher-Order Evidence and the Limits of Defeat," *Philosophy and Phenomenological Research* 88, no. 2 (2014): 315.

stayed up all night studying the evidence bearing on a particular crime.[4] At the end of the lengthy process of sifting the evidence, Detective judges that it is very likely that Lefty, rather than Righty, committed the crime. When she calls Lieutenant to share her conclusion, Lieutenant asks whether Detective has stayed up all night, and informs Detective that every time Detective has stayed up all night in the past, her reasoning has been atrocious and unreliable (despite its seeming to Detective that nothing is amiss). I'll call this fact that Detective has a bad track record after all-nighters UNRELIABLE. According to many epistemologists, upon learning UNRELIABLE, Detective ought to become significantly less confident that Lefty committed the crime.[5] But UNRELIABLE does not directly bear on the question of whether Lefty committed the crime in the same way that the evidence Detective stayed up examining does. It is not as though UNRELIABLE is more to be expected if Righty committed the crime than if Lefty committed the crime: someone who had a full night's sleep before examining the evidence inspected by Detective could dismiss UNRELIABLE as evidentially irrelevant. If UNRELIABLE gives Detective reason to doubt the Lefty hypothesis, it is only because UNRELIABLE is higher-order evidence that raises doubts about *any* conclusion that Detective might have reached after an all-nighter.

Facts about religious disagreement may pose first-order or higher-order evidential worries for religious belief (or both). Suppose that religious outlook *O1* suggests a view of human nature according to which persistent religious disagreement is to be expected, while religious outlook *O2* suggests a view of human nature according to which persistent religious disagreement would be very surprising (though not impossible). Given this supposition, persistent religious disagreement would constitute first-order evidence in favor of *O1* over *O2*. But the facts about religious disagreement may constitute higher-order evidence against *either* of these religious views if these facts raise worries about the rationality of one's religious views or the reliability of the process by which one's religious beliefs have been formed. Alternatively, one can imagine a situation where widespread religious agreement on the truth of *O1* provides higher-order support of *O1* (by boosting

---

[4] The case is from Andrew Rotondo, "Undermining, Circularity, and Disagreement," *Synthese* 190, no. 3 (2013): 563–584.

[5] For a defense of this sort of verdict, see Christensen, "Higher-Order Evidence." There are some who argue that Detective should not reduce confidence if she in fact assessed the first-order evidence correctly. For example, see Lasonen-Aarnio, "Higher-Order Evidence and the Limits of Defeat"; Michael G. Titelbaum, "Rationality's Fixed Point (Or: In Defense of Right Reason)," *Oxford Studies in Epistemology* 5 (2015): 253–294.

one's confidence in the general reliability of religious belief formation) even though religious agreement is unexpected given *O1* and thus counts as first-order evidence against it. The first-order significance of religious disagreement is thus distinct from its higher-order significance.

Arguments that appeal to religious disagreement in order to challenge religious belief may point to religious disagreement as first-order evidence against some religious outlook, or they may point to religious disagreement as higher-order evidence. The first type of argument I will call a "first-order argument" (or a "first-order challenge"), and the second type of argument I will call a "higher-order argument" (or a "higher-order challenge").

An example of an argument in the philosophy of religion that makes claims about the first-order significance of religious disagreement is the argument from divine hiddenness. This argument against theism begins by noting that according to most theists, the highest good for a human being is to be in a loving relationship with God. Many theists also claim that since God loves all human beings, God desires to be in a loving relationship with each human person. Since the lack of belief that God exists is a barrier to the sort of loving relationship that God desires, one has reason to think that should God exist, God would make God's existence evident to all. The fact that many intelligent and thoughtful people fail to believe in God (including many people who indicate they would like to believe in God if it were possible for them to do so) is evidence that God has not made God's existence very evident, contrary to what theism might lead one to expect. Thus, extensive and pervasive disagreement over whether God exists is claimed to be evidence against theism.

This argument is clearly a first-order rather than higher-order challenge to theistic belief. Even if religious disagreement did not pose a higher-order challenge to the theist, the fact of significant and persistent disagreement over theism could still be first-order evidence against theism. For example, suppose a theist somehow knew that she and her fellow theists were in possession of more evidence than nontheists. In this case, disagreement over theism might not give her any reason for questioning whether or not she has made some error in her assessment of the evidence. Even so, the fact that many reject theism (due to lack of information) would constitute evidence against theism since prevalent disbelief is more to be expected given nontheism than it is given theism.

As the argument from divine hiddenness illustrates, first-order challenges are directed toward a specific religious perspective and not to religious belief generally. A first-order challenge directed against the belief in religious proposition *r* claims of some observed disagreement concerning *r* that such a disagreement is more likely to occur given ~*r* (i.e., not-*r*) than it is given *r*. Making this comparative claim requires attending to the particular claims of *r* as well as to the implications of the leading alternatives to *r* (i.e., the viewpoints that together make up ~*r*). And a first-order argument *against r* will at the same time be an argument *in favor* of the religious belief ~*r*.

Higher-order arguments, however, are not typically directed toward one particular outlook. Rather, the claim is that disagreement casts suspicion on the epistemic processes that are operative in the religious domain. Such suspicion may raise questions about *any* religious belief, at least if it is held with a high enough degree of confidence. The same higher-order argument against someone's belief *r* could also call into question excessive confidence in ~*r*. The force of such an argument is to move someone toward *greater skepticism* rather than moving someone away from one particular view and toward a particular alternative.

Because arguments concerning the first-order significance of disagreement are focused on one first-order evidential factor among many, these arguments, even if successful, will not typically show that some religious outlook is rationally unacceptable. For example, no matter how much religious disagreement may evidentially support atheism over theism, there could be other evidential factors that provide even greater support to theism over atheism. Unless theism *entails* that there is no religious disagreement, then a first-order argument from religious disagreement will at most point to one factor that needs to be taken into consideration alongside numerous other evidential factors.

Higher-order arguments, on the other hand, often claim to more or less settle whether a given belief is reasonable. Because disagreement casts suspicion on one's assessment of various evidential factors, it is often thought that disagreement is not merely one evidential factor to be weighed with many others. Rather, it is evidence that should prevent one from putting much stock in one's weighing of first-order evidential factors. According to the more ambitious sort of higher-order challenge that is the focus of this book, the appropriate response to religious disagreement is to give up one's contested views on religious matters, however well-supported those views might be when considering only first-order evidence.

1.2 Introducing the Master Argument
for Disagreement-Motivated Religious Skepticism

Having clarified the higher-order challenge that is to be my focus, it is time to characterize the argument for disagreement-motivated religious skepticism and to discern the argument's central commitments. Here is an initial sketch of the argument. Suppose that you are a religious believer who is informed about the nature and extent of religious disagreement. In light of what you know about religious disagreement, you can see that human beings are highly unreliable in the religious domain, and that this collective unreliability applies even among thoughtful and informed people. Given your knowledge of the collective unreliability on religious matters of those who are otherwise epistemically qualified, you have justification for believing that *you* are reliable on religious matters only if you have justification for believing that your degree of reliability is significantly higher than the collective reliability of otherwise qualified people. But you do not have justification for believing that your degree of reliability is significantly higher than the collective reliability of those who are otherwise qualified. So you do not have justification for believing that you are reliable on religious matters. But you are justified in maintaining confident religious beliefs only if you have justification for believing that you are reliable on religious matters. Therefore, you are not justified in maintaining confident religious beliefs.

The argument just sketched involves premises about what claims you have "justification" to believe. Since the justification of religious belief in the face of disagreement is a central topic in this book, I should say a bit about the meaning of "justification" (and cognate terms) in this context. The kind of justification that is in view is *epistemic* justification. Beliefs that are epistemically justified satisfy certain epistemic evaluative standards (as opposed to, say, *moral* standards, or standards concerned with pragmatic utility). Such beliefs possess the sort of epistemically good-making features that make it appropriate to judge a belief as rational, reasonable, or (if other conditions are met) an instance of knowledge. Whether someone's belief is *justified* is not a matter of whether or not that belief is true but a matter of whether in this particular case the believer is believing in a way that accords with the relevant norms and standards of right believing. Cases where justification is clearly lacking include cases where a belief is based on obviously fallacious reasoning and cases where a belief is sustained by wish fulfillment despite overwhelming evidence against the believed proposition.

When one inquires about the justificatory status of a subject's belief that *p*, one is asking about what is often called *doxastic* justification. But one can also reasonably ask whether a subject *has* justification to believe that *p*, whether or not the subject has this belief. This latter question concerns what is called *propositional* justification. Roughly, if *p* is propositionally justified for subject *S* at time *t*, then *S* has reasons at *t* that are sufficient to confer doxastic justification on a belief that *p* at time *t*, so long as this belief is based on those reasons in the appropriate way.[6] One may adopt doxastic attitudes other than beliefs toward a proposition, such as the attitudes of disbelief or agnosticism or a more precise attitude like having a particular confidence level or "credence." These attitudes may also have, or fail to have, doxastic justification, and one can have propositional justification to adopt such attitudes.

I should also say something about the relationship between the language of "justification" and the language of "rationality" that features prominently in this book, since these are not perfectly substitutable. Persons are often described as being rational or as being irrational, but a rational person is not aptly described as being "justified," nor an irrational person as being "unjustified": a person may be justified or unjustified *in holding a particular belief*, but a person is not normally described as being justified or unjustified *full stop*.[7] Similarly, procedures of modifying and updating beliefs are frequently described as rational or irrational, but not as justified or unjustified (though of course one might or might not be justified in one's belief about a certain procedure).

Despite these and other differences between the notions of justification and rationality, in this book I use the modifiers "rational" and "justified" more or less interchangeably when these notions are applied to *beliefs*. Even if justification is a more demanding notion than rationality, most disagreement skeptics think that confident belief in the face of suitably qualified disagreement is *irrational* (and therefore unjustified). Since in this context the question of justification hinges on the question of rationality, there is no harm in equating justified and rational belief.

I'll now return to the argument for disagreement-motivated religious skepticism that was sketched above in order to characterize this argument more precisely. I will focus on a generic subject *S* and assume that *S* is a

---

[6] Providing a characterization of the relationship between doxastic and propositional justification that is free from apparent counterexamples proves difficult. For a helpful discussion, see John Turri, "On the Relationship between Propositional and Doxastic Justification," *Philosophy and Phenomenological Research* 80, no. 2 (2010): 312–326.

[7] Robert Audi, *Rationality and Religious Commitment* (Oxford: Oxford University Press, 2011), 24–25.

religious believer who is well-informed about the nature and extent of religious disagreement:

The Master Argument for Disagreement-Motivated Religious Skepticism

1. *S*'s religious outlook is justified only if *S* has justification for believing that most of her religious beliefs are the result of a reliable process.
2. In light of *S*'s knowledge of systematic religious disagreement, *S* should believe that the processes that (otherwise) epistemically qualified people rely on to form religious beliefs are, *taken as a whole*, very unreliable.
3. *S* lacks justification for believing that her process of religious belief formation is significantly more reliable than the collective reliability of the processes that (otherwise) epistemically qualified people use to form religious beliefs.
4. If (2) and (3), then *S* lacks justification for believing that most of her religious beliefs are the result of a reliable process.
5. Thus, *S* lacks justification for believing that most of her religious beliefs are the result of a reliable process. (From [2], [3], and [4].)
6. Therefore, *S*'s religious outlook is not justified. (From [1] and [5].)

I call this the "master argument" since an argument with this basic structure can be discerned in many defenses of disagreement-motivated religious skepticism, including defenses by John Hick, John Schellenberg, Philip Kitcher, and Sanford Goldberg.[8] Those who endorse this sort of argument I will call "disagreement skeptics." It should nevertheless be kept in mind that for purposes of this book, the disagreement skeptic is someone who advocates *religious* skepticism as the appropriate response to *religious* disagreement in particular. Such a view may or may not be combined with a more general conciliatory position on disagreement.

Among the disagreement skeptics who endorse the master argument, there are different views on what qualifies (for purposes of the argument)

---

[8] John Hick, "The Epistemological Challenge of Religious Pluralism," *Faith and Philosophy* 14, no. 3 (1997): 277–286; J. L. Schellenberg, *The Wisdom to Doubt: A Justification of Religious Skepticism* (Ithaca: Cornell University Press, 2007); Philip Kitcher, *Life after Faith: The Case for Secular Humanism* (New Haven: Yale University Press, 2014); Sanford Goldberg, "Does Externalist Epistemology Rationalize Religious Commitment?," in *Religious Faith and Intellectual Virtue*, ed. Timothy O'Connor and Laura Frances Callahan (Oxford: Oxford University Press, 2014), 279–298.

as a "religious outlook," resulting in different views on the scope of the argument. In Kitcher's hands, the master argument targets only outlooks that are *conventionally* religious. Kitcher does not think that the argument threatens his secular atheism. In Hick's hands, the master argument targets the detailed and specific doctrinal claims of various religions but does not target the bare affirmation of some transcendent reality that is a source of salvation. Others who endorse the argument understand it to have a wider scope, so that all religious outlooks (including *irreligious* outlooks, such as secular atheism) are equally called into question.[9] Whether restrictions in the argument's scope are well-motivated is a question I take up later in this chapter.

Premises (1)–(3) are the argument's philosophically substantive claims. (If one had precise definitions for "significantly more reliable" and "very unreliable," premise [4] would follow from fairly modest coherence requirements; premises [5] and [6] are logically entailed by the earlier premises.) Much of the discussion in this book could be characterized as an assessment of the merits of premise (3), which essentially holds that a religious believer does not have justification for believing that her own group is highly *exceptional* in its reliability on religious matters. Before launching into a discussion of this premise, which is the lynchpin of the argument, some preliminary clarifying remarks are in order, with special attention to premises (1) and (2).

Because the argument relies on claims about what S can and cannot justifiably think about the reliability of various belief-forming processes (those employed by others and those employed by herself), it is necessary to briefly address a thorny problem that afflicts discussions of the epistemic reliability of a given belief-producing process. The problem arises from three facts: (1) reliability is a feature that pertains to process *types* rather than to a process *tokens* (where a token process is a concrete instantiation of a process type); (2) any given token process instantiates many different process types (types that apply at different levels of generality); and (3) a given token process of belief formation typically instantiates both reliable and unreliable process types.

To illustrate, consider the example of a second-grade student who has not properly learned long subtraction and who as a result incorrectly answers most of the long subtraction questions on a quiz administered in class. Perhaps the student knows that when a digit on top is smaller than the digit on the bottom that is to be subtracted from it, the student should write a one

[9] For example, see Richard Feldman, "Reasonable Religious Disagreements," in *Philosophers without Gods: Meditations on Atheism and the Secular Life*, ed. Louise M. Antony (Oxford: Oxford University Press, 2007), 194–214.

in front of the top digit (changing a 2 into 12, for example), but he doesn't understand that he should also *subtract* 1 from the next digit over. (So in solving 175 – 108, he would arrive at the answer 77 instead of 67.) Consider some belief concerning a question on the quiz that the student arrives at by applying his faulty subtraction procedure. Did the student form this belief by means of a reliable process? Well, the process by which the student answered the question instantiated many different process types, some of which were reliable and some of which were not. Here's one process type that was operative: believing what seems true after thinking through matters carefully. *That* process might very well be highly reliable if most of the reflective beliefs the student forms are true, even though this process frequently leads to an incorrect view when it is applied to long subtraction. If one considers a narrower process type that was also instantiated—for example, arriving at a view on a subtraction problem by employing the student's faulty method of long subtraction—then one might find that the process type is not reliable. (After all, the student misses most long subtraction questions.) On the other hand an even narrower process type instantiated by the token process might be reliable. Suppose that the student's belief concerned the answer to the problem 186 – 135. His mistaken procedure for long subtraction would not lead to a wrong answer in this case, since in this case there is no need to "borrow" a 1 from the next number. And the process of "subtracting using the student's procedure in cases when there is no need to borrow any 1s" might very well be a reliable process. The lesson is that there is often no single answer to the question of whether a token process is reliable, since the process instantiates types at different levels of generality, some of which are reliable and some of which are not.

This fact that there is frequently no unique way to determine the reliability of a token belief-forming process is what drives the well-known "generality problem" for reliabilist theories of justification.[10] Reliabilist theories of justification hold that whether I am justified in holding a certain belief significantly depends on the reliability of the process by which my belief was formed. However, a reliabilist theory cannot plausibly say that a belief is justified if one of the instantiated process types is reliable; nor can it plausibly say that a belief is unjustified if one of the instantiated process types is unreliable. Recall that the second-grade student employs a broad process that is reliable

---

[10] For a discussion of the generality problem for reliabilism, see Earl Conee and Richard Feldman, *Evidentialism: Essays in Epistemology* (Oxford: Oxford University Press, 2004), chap. 6.

(namely, basing beliefs on careful thought). And when there is no need to borrow 1s, he employs a reliable narrow process. Nevertheless, he does not seem justified in either case. To see that a belief is not unjustified merely because the process producing it instantiates an unreliable type, consider the following example. A fifth-grade teacher sits at his classroom desk and averages his students' scores for their quiz on long division. In calculating this average, the teacher himself relies on long division and thus employs the process of "forming a belief using long division in this fifth-grade classroom." Unsurprisingly, this is not a very reliable process, since this process is most often used by fifth graders who are not very good at long division. But this does not show that the teacher is not justified in believing the result that he has carefully and skillfully calculated. As these examples help to show, a viable reliabilist theory of justification must give a principled account of which process types are relevant for assessing a belief's justification. This difficult task is the generality problem for reliabilism.

The master argument outlined above appears to face its own sort of generality problem.[11] The general idea behind premise (1) is that for S's belief that p to be justified, it must be the case that S has justification for believing that S's belief that p is the result of a reliable process. This suggests that if S learned that her belief that p was *not* the product of a reliable process, this knowledge would constitute a *defeater* that undercuts whatever justification S may have enjoyed in believing that p. The problem, however, is that the realization that one's belief that p is formed using an unreliable process type does not always give one a defeater for that belief. Consider the fifth-grade teacher: he knows that his calculation of the class average employed an unreliable process type, but his belief is not thereby defeated. So the process type or types that are relevant to (1) must be clarified: which process types must S have justification to believe reliable if S's religious outlook is to be justified? And it is not only (1) that needs to be clarified. Premises (2) and (3) are also plausible only if they implicitly concern process types at the relevant level of generality.

The relevant level of generality is somewhat clarified if the master argument is understood as being focused on processes of *religious* belief formation specifically, even if such processes are instances of broader process types that are not restricted to the religious domain. When the argument

---

[11] The generality problem for norms governing situation of disagreement is identified and discussed in Robert Pasnau, "Veiled Disagreement," *Journal of Philosophy* 111, no. 11 (2014): 608–630.

is understood in this way, (2) is rather uncontroversial: in light of systematic religious disagreement, it is clear that the processes people use to form religious beliefs are not collectively reliable in their application to religious questions. Since the reliability of a broad process type cannot save one from worries raised by the unreliability of a strictly narrower process type, there is no harm in taking the argument to be focused on processes as they apply to the religious domain.

Interpreting the master argument as being focused on religious belief-forming processes specifically helps to address the generality problem, but it certainly does not resolve it. Consider a (perhaps unrealistic) case of a Christian who acknowledges that the process by which she formed and maintains her Christian belief is one of "believing whatever one's parents have taught one to believe about religion." Would this person's Christian beliefs be defeated when she learns that this process is highly unreliable? This remains unclear, since it still hasn't been settled whether her justification depends on her ability to affirm the reliability of her process at this particular level of generality. Perhaps her justification on religious matters does not require her to be justified in trusting this generic process but instead requires only that she be justified in affirming the reliability of "believing what *Christian* parents say about religious matters." So the question remains: in order for S to be justified in maintaining her religious outlook, exactly which of the (broader and narrower) process types are the ones that she must have justification to believe to be reliable? Fortunately, as I will show, the impartiality requirements that disagreement skeptics appeal to in arguing for premise (3) of the master argument *also* supply them with an answer to this question about the level of generality that is relevant to premise (1). So I will set aside this generality problem until my discussion of premise (3).

Another worry about (1) is that it looks suspiciously like a certain type of "metajustification" requirement that most epistemologists reject, and for understandable reasons. Consider a metajustification requirement that says that S's belief that p is justified only if S *justifiably believes* that her belief that p is the result of a reliable process. As Alston and others have argued, such a requirement implausibly implies that justified belief is possible only for those who are sophisticated enough to form metalevel beliefs about the reliability of their belief-forming processes. And requirements of this sort also lead to a vicious regress, since a justified belief that p must be accompanied by a justified metalevel belief that the belief that p is reliably formed, and this latter belief must be accompanied by a justified meta-metalevel belief that the metalevel belief is reliably formed, and so on.[12]

Crucially, premise (1) does not succumb to these problems, since it does not require S to actually form a favorable belief about the reliability of S's process of religious belief formation but requires only that S have justification for such a metalevel belief. The requirement is one of *propositional* justification, which has to do with whether a proposition is supported by S's evidence and reasons, rather than a *doxastic* requirement that is concerned with S's actual beliefs.[13] For this reason, (1) clearly avoids a vicious regress. And, plausibly, (1) applies even to someone who is not sophisticated enough to form metalevel beliefs about the reliability of his first-level beliefs. A child who cannot yet form such metalevel beliefs, perhaps because he has not yet grasped the relevant notion of reliability, may still be said to have justification for such beliefs. It's just that the child needs to achieve a greater degree of cognitive sophistication before he can appropriately respond to the reasons that are already available to him. In any case, even if (1) fails to apply to those who lack the requisite sophistication, this is no comfort to the typical person who *is* capable of reflecting on the reliability of the processes that produce his or her religious beliefs.

When (1) is properly distinguished from doxastic metalevel requirements and is understood as applying only to process types at the relevant level of generality, (1) does seem highly plausible. If I do not have justification to believe of some cognitive process that it is reliable (whether that process be vision, memory, mathematical calculation, some combination of processes, or whatever), then the natural conclusion is that I am not justified in trusting the outputs of that process. Someone who denies this presumably must allow that someone could justifiably combine a belief in p with doubt about the reliability of the process producing that belief. But it looks positively irrational to believe "*p*, but the cognitive process producing my belief that *p* is unreliable"; and the belief that "*p*, but it is an open question whether the cognitive process producing my belief that *p* is reliable" also appears to be irrational.[14]

[12] William P. Alston, "Level-Confusions in Epistemology," *Midwest Studies in Philosophy* 5, no. 1 (1980): 135–150.

[13] For an argument that a metalevel propositional justification requirement avoids the charges commonly brought against metalevel doxastic requirements, see Declan Smithies, "Moore's Paradox and the Accessibility of Justification," *Philosophy and Phenomenological Research* 85, no. 2 (2012): 273–300.

[14] For a forceful development of this sort of argument, see Smithies. It is Smithies who suggests that an attitude of withholding belief on the matter of *p* could be expressed by the assertion that "it is an open question whether *p*" ("Moore's Paradox and the Accessibility of Justification," 282).

Because these combinations of attitudes are both rationally objectionable, one should conclude that someone justifiably believes that p only if he has justification to believe that the process producing this belief is reliable.

There are some philosophers who deny this interlevel coherence requirement.[15] If these philosophers are right, then there may be reasons to reject disagreement-higher-motivated religious skepticism beyond the reasons I will explore, which are all reasons for rejecting (3). For purposes of this discussion, I accept the requirement that a justified believer must have justification to affirm his or her reliability. Premise (1) merely extends this requirement to S's entire religious outlook, where S's "religious outlook" is to be understand as a perspective constituted by S's core religious convictions. The premise assumes (reasonably enough) that for S's religious outlook to be justified, the majority of the beliefs that make up that outlook must be justified. On the assumption that any individual belief is justified only if S has justification for believing that it is the product of a reliable process, it would seem that the outlook as a whole is justified only if S has justification for believing that most of the individual beliefs are the product of a reliable process.

Perhaps there is room for quibbling with the statement of premise (1), but I will accept (1) and focus critical attention elsewhere—on (3) in particular. But first, some commentary on premise (2). Philosophers who argue that disagreement has significant skeptical force do not hold that it is the mere fact of disagreement that is epistemically worrying. My four-year-old daughter maintains with great conviction that staying up long past her bedtime to finish a movie will not result in any adverse effects the following day. I disagree, of course, and no philosopher would fault me for remaining unmoved in the face of her persistent disagreement.

What is worrying is not disagreement per se but disagreement with those who appear to be qualified to assess the matter under dispute. This is one reason why the disagreement literature focuses significantly on disagreements between apparent *epistemic peers*.[16] The notion of epistemic peerhood is characterized somewhat differently by different thinkers. But as I will use the term, two people qualify as epistemic peers with respect to p just in case their epistemic credentials with respect to p are equally strong. This

---

[15] For examples of philosophers who would deny principles like (1), see Allen Coates, "Rational Epistemic Akrasia," *American Philosophical Quarterly* 49, no. 2 (2012): 113–124; and Lasonen-Aarnio, "Higher-Order Evidence and the Limits of Defeat." For criticisms of these views, see Sophie Horowitz, "Epistemic Akrasia," *Noûs* 48, no. 4 (2014): 718–744.

[16] The term "epistemic peer" was coined by Gary Gutting in *Religious Belief and Religious Skepticism* (Notre Dame: University of Notre Dame Press, 1982).

strength should be understood as taking into account *all* of the dimensions of epistemic evaluation that bear on the reliability of one's judgment, including facts about the quality and quantity of one's evidence as well as facts about one's ability to respond to that evidence in a rational and unbiased manner. In a disagreement with someone whom I rightly take to be my epistemic inferior with respect to the disputed matter, my stronger epistemic credentials give me a reason to think my disputant is more likely than me to have made an error. In a disagreement with an acknowledged epistemic peer or superior on the other hand, comparing epistemic credentials does not give me any reason to be more suspicious of my disputant than of myself. The evidential force of a disagreement is positively correlated with the strength of the epistemic credentials of one's disputant.

Religious disagreement with those known to be significantly less epistemically credentialed would not pose significant higher-order worries. For this reason, premise (2) focuses on those religious believers who are "otherwise" epistemically qualified, by which I mean those who prove themselves to be sophisticated, careful, informed, and judicious thinkers *outside the religious domain*.[17] The argument supposes (and rightly, I believe) that even this epistemically qualified group fails to exhibit anything approaching religious consensus.

One might wonder why premise (2) focuses on those who are *otherwise* epistemically qualified rather than focusing instead on those who are qualified in the religious domain. The premise that there is disagreement (and unreliability) among those who are epistemically qualified on religious matters would, if granted, be a more promising claim on which to build a skeptical argument. But that claim is much more contentious than premise (2). This is because the question of what qualifies someone to reliably assess religious questions is itself a question that is significantly contested. It is incontestable that there is substantial religious disagreement among those who are highly informed about religion and who have thought long and hard about the answers to central religious questions. But according to many religious views, more than this is needed in order to qualify as a reliable and trustworthy judge of religious matters. Theravada Buddhists, for example, maintain that in order to have adequate insight into the nonexistence of any personal self, one must engage in a rigorous and disciplined path of

---

[17] In focusing on disagreement with those who are "otherwise" qualified, I follow Goldberg ("Does Externalist Epistemology Rationalize Religious Commitment?").

meditation. Is there substantial religious disagreement among those who not only have pursued the requisite meditative disciplines but have done so with the right motives and proper spirit and have enjoyed the sort of experience that according to Buddhists conveys insight into the truth of nonself? There is no uncontestable answer to this question, especially since the character of others' experiences is not open to examination.

I will say more in chapter 6 about the significance of the fact that religious believers disagree not just on first-order religious questions (whether there is a God, whether people are reincarnated, etc.) but also on what intellectual virtues, practices, insights, and other factors are required in order to reliably assess religious questions. For now, it suffices to note that a premise that asserted that there is substantial disagreement among those who are truly qualified to assess religious questions would beg the question against many theories of religious epistemic credentials. Of course, one could *argue* for a certain theory of religious epistemic credentials and then go on to note that there is disagreement among those who are credentialed according to this theory. But such an argument would require that one argue against religious perspectives that support an opposing theory of epistemic credentials. And this would require giving a *first-order* argument for one (or more) religious perspectives and against others. In other words, this approach would first have to show that certain religious views are (probably) false before issuing a higher-order challenge to the religious views that remain on the table.

My question, though, is whether disagreement poses a *distinctively higher-order* challenge to confident religious belief, one that could have force against any religious position even if first-order challenges fell short. And a distinctively higher-order challenge would need to avoid premises that straightforwardly take a stand on controversial religious questions. Such a challenge must instead characterize the facts about disagreement in a religiously neutral way and then show why, in light of these facts and certain principles of higher-order epistemic defeat, one ought to give up confident religious belief. This is why premise (2) merely affirms that there is substantial evidence of unreliability among the *otherwise* epistemically qualified, something that any informed religious believer should be able to affirm.

One might be skeptical about the possibility of developing an argument for disagreement-motivated religious skepticism that is in fact religiously neutral, since the epistemic principles presupposed by the argument may prove to be in direct tension with some religious views. This worry will receive attention in chapter 6. For now, I merely note that even if a religiously neutral argument proves to be unattainable, there is still value in developing an argument for religious skepticism that is *distinctively epistemological.* Issuing a universal challenge to religious beliefs on epistemological grounds is a distinctive approach that merits exploring, even if the epistemic principles that drive the challenge turn out to be contestable on religious grounds.

1.3 The Master Argument's Critical Premise

As I've indicated, I affirm premises (1) and (2) of the master argument, at least when these premises are understood to be focused on processes at the relevant level of generality. The discussion from here on will primarily be focused on the plausibility of (3). To smooth my discussion of this premise, I'll introduce the following label for the proposition that, according to (3), S does *not* have justification to believe:

> SUPERIOR: S's process of religious belief formation is significantly more reliable than the collective reliability of the processes that (otherwise) epistemically qualified people use to form religious beliefs.

Using this label, the critical third premise, which I will call "EQUAL ESTIMATED RELIABILITY," can be formulated as follows:

> EQUAL ESTIMATED RELIABILITY: S lacks justification for believing SUPERIOR.

This premise does not assert that the reliability of S's process is *in fact* equal to the collective reliability of the processes employed by otherwise qualified people. The claim is only that S does not have justification for believing that her process is significantly more reliable than the collective reliability of these processes. One way of expressing this idea is by saying that any *estimate* of her own reliability must at most be approximately equal to her estimate of the collective reliability of all the processes. So suppose there were three incompatible religious views, each with its own distinctive process of belief formation. Oversimplifying, imagine that S knows that one of these processes is perfectly reliable and that the other two are completely unreliable. If one measures reliability on a scale from 0 to 1 (with 0 being complete unreliability and 1 being perfect reliability), then the average reliability of these processes would be 1/3. EQUAL ESTIMATED RELIABILITY says that in this situation, S is not justified in thinking that her process is especially likely to be the one that is perfectly reliable; this implies that any estimate of her own reliability should not significantly exceed 1/3, which is her estimate of the overall reliability of (otherwise) epistemically qualified people on religious matters.

At the most basic level, the argument for EQUAL ESTIMATED RELIABILITY may be characterized as follows. S has justification for believing SUPERIOR only if S has a good reason for this belief. (In this context, a "good reason" means a good *all-things-considered* reason.) But, say disagreement skeptics, S does not have a good reason for believing SUPERIOR. Therefore, S lacks justification for believing SUPERIOR (which is, of course, to say that EQUAL ESTIMATED RELIABILITY is true).

While the claim that justification for believing SUPERIOR requires having a good reason for this belief may strike many as obviously correct, the claim that S lacks any such reason stands in obvious need of defense. What is the basis for this claim? Here, the disagreement skeptic appeals to an alleged parity between the reasons for believing SUPERIOR and the reasons for believing any number of competing claims that ascribe superior reliability not to S but to one or more of S's religious disputants. In light of this parity, it is claimed that a belief in SUPERIOR would be rationally arbitrary and thus unjustified.

Here is Philip Kitcher's defense of the relevant parity claim:

> The religious convictions of many contemporary believers are formed in very much the same ways. Often the faithful are born into a religious tradition whose lore they absorb in early childhood and continue to accept throughout their lives; sometimes, when the surrounding society contains adherents of a different doctrine, acquaintance with a rival religion prompts conversion, and a shift of allegiance. In either case, however, religious believers rely on a tradition they take to have carefully preserved insights once vouchsafed to privileged witnesses in a remote past. Because that pattern is so prevalent in undergirding the religious beliefs of the present, it is very hard to declare that one of the traditions has a special status, or even that a manageable few have transmitted truth about the transcendent. The beliefs of each tradition stand on much the same footing: complete symmetry prevails.[18]

---

[18] Kitcher, *Life after Faith*, 8.

On Kitcher's view, the reason for accepting EQUAL ESTIMATED RELIABILITY is that S's process of religious belief formation is relevantly like the competing processes employed by S's religious disputants. And given the symmetry that characterizes these processes, believing of any one in particular that it alone is reliable would be irrational.

John Hick similarly appeals to epistemic parity between processes of religious belief formation in order to defend EQUAL ESTIMATED RELIABILITY. Hick asserts that a viable defense of the rationality of religious belief must appeal to the rationality of basing religious belief on religious experience. He then argues that facts about religious diversity and disagreement defeat presumptive trust in one's religious experiences. First, Hick claims that the fact of religious disagreement shows that "if only *one* of the many belief-systems based upon religious experience can be true, it follows that *religious experience generally produces false beliefs,* and that it is thus a generally *unreliable* basis for belief formation."[19] This claim is more or less premise (2) of the master argument. A believer can reconcile premise (2) with the claim that he is reliable in the religious domain if he believes that his process is an exception to the general fact of religious unreliability. But Hick maintains that "whilst it is possible that the doxastic practice of one's own community constitutes the sole exception to a general rule [of unreliability], the claim that this is so can only appear arbitrary and unjustified unless it is supported by good arguments."[20] Might a good argument be forthcoming? For example, might the Christian identify reasons to put greater trust in the development of Christian belief and doctrine than in the processes accounting for non-Christian beliefs? Hick does not think so, and his reason is that "the other great world faiths are as epistemically well based as Christianity; and also that they seem, when judged by their fruits, to be morally on a par with Christianity."[21] Like Kitcher, Hick thinks that there is epistemic parity in the processes giving rise to religious beliefs (and also in their moral fruits), at least when it comes to the "great world faiths." And in light of this parity, trust in a particular religion is thought to be unreasonable.

It should be noted that Kitcher and Hick can be seen as proponents of the master argument only if one has a suitably restricted understanding of the "religious outlooks" that the argument calls into question. Kitcher and Hick do not think that *any* controversial view on religious matters is defeated by

[19] Hick, "The Epistemological Challenge of Religious Pluralism," 278.
[20] Hick, "The Epistemological Challenge of Religious Pluralism," 278.
[21] Hick, "The Epistemological Challenge of Religious Pluralism," 279.

the reality of disagreement, since they both appeal to the epistemic challenge posed by disagreement in order to motivate their particular perspective. In Kitcher's case, the perspective that is left standing is secular atheism. In Hick's case, the perspective that remains viable in light of religious disagreement is a position he labels "religious pluralism." According to Hick's religious pluralism, the world's "great" religions are products of encounters with that transcendent reality that is the source of salvation, and the doctrinal teachings of these different religions are all equally limited and inadequate attempts to understand these encounters through culturally conditioned conceptual frames.[22]

Can Kitcher and Hick plausibly maintain that religious disagreement defeats the justification of conventional religious belief while denying that religious disagreement similarly undercuts their own position? I will return to this question later in this chapter. I turn now to the task of critiquing and refining this sort of parity argument that is advanced by Kitcher, Hick, and several others.

1.4 The Striped Dress, and Two Commitments of the Disagreement Skeptic

The parity argument for EQUAL ESTIMATED RELIABILITY maintains that because S and her religious disputants form religious beliefs in ways that are rationally on a par, S lacks reason to believe SUPERIOR and therefore lacks justification for believing that proposition. I suspect that many readers will immediately take issue with the suggestion that the various processes of religious belief formation are rationally on a par. Even if Kitcher's broad-brushed characterization of religious belief formation accurately describes how nearly everyone arrives at their religious convictions, a more fine-grained characterization of religious belief-forming processes will reveal differences in the processes employed by representative atheists, Jews, Hindus, Buddhists, and so on. And some of these differences might introduce significant asymmetries in the epistemic merits of these processes. Until one has identified a reason to

---

[22] John Hick, *An Interpretation of Religion: Human Responses to the Transcendent*, 2nd ed. (New Haven: Yale University Press, 2004). Another argument for disagreement-motivated religious skepticism that appeals to similarities in the processes of religious belief formation may be found in Goldberg, "Does Externalist Epistemology Rationalize Religious Commitment?"

dismiss this possibility, it seems that there is little reason to suppose that "the beliefs of each tradition stand on much the same footing," as Kitcher insists.

This is a powerful criticism of the sort of broad-brush symmetry argument advanced by Kitcher and Hick, a criticism that will ultimately require the disagreement skeptic to take a more nuanced argumentative approach. But before pursuing this criticism further, I want to consider two other challenges that could be raised against the broad-brush symmetry argument. Considering these challenges will help to identify two crucial commitments that lie behind the higher-order argument for disagreement-motivated skepticism.

It will be useful to shift focus away from religious disagreement for the moment, and to consider a case of disagreement where it's clear that the belief-forming processes involved are epistemically on a par in all discernible respects. Consider a (briefly) famous real-life example.[23] In February 2015, there was an explosion of attention (on social media and then in major news sources) given to a particular photograph of a particular dress—one worn by a mother at her daughter's recent wedding. Of those who saw the photograph online, a sizeable minority saw the striped dress as clearly being blue and black, while the majority saw it as clearly being white and gold. Most found themselves completely unable to experience the photograph in a way that made the alternative viewpoint visually plausible. Neither side had any reason (aside from the disagreement) to suspect that something was amiss in their processing of the visual data. The dress was later revealed to be blue and black. But before this fact was known, there were no discernible differences in the belief-forming processes used by the two sides that would give one any reason to trust one group more than the other. Later reporting suggested that subjects may have perceived the colors differently in part because of different assumptions that were being made at the level of unconscious visual processing, assumptions about the ambient lighting at the time of the photograph. Physiological differences, especially differences in the number of blue light cones, may also have played a role. But at the conscious level, subjects were not reasoning from such assumptions; they were simply looking at the photo and forming judgments that aligned with how things appeared to them.

---

[23] See Jonathan Mahler, "The White and Gold (No, Blue and Black!) Dress That Melted the Internet," *New York Times*, February 27, 2015.

For the sake of discussion, imagine that subsequent research confirmed that those who see the dress as blue and black are more reliable interpreters of visual color data than those who see it as white and gold. For example, suppose that staring at computer screens for long periods of time causes some people to lose functionality in some of their blue light cones, a slight loss of function that explains the incorrect judgment about the dress's color. Now consider the epistemic situation of someone—call him Vince—who sees the dress as blue and black, who is aware of the controversy concerning the dress's colors. Is a belief in the blue/black hypothesis justified for Vince at a time before the color of the dress has been confirmed and before anyone has an understanding of the reasons for the disagreement?

An argument analogous to that sketched in the last section supports a negative verdict: however reliable human beings may typically be in their color judgments, Vince knows that they are not collectively reliable when it comes to interpreting the colors of the dress. And given the remarkable symmetry that characterizes this disagreement (i.e., both camps appear to be equally trustworthy, and there are no discernible differences between the belief-forming processes operative in the two camps), Vince's reasons for trusting his own side of the disagreement are no better than his reasons for trusting the other side. Vince therefore lacks a good all-things-considered reason for thinking that he has arrived at his belief in a reliable way and is therefore not justified in believing that his belief is reliably formed. For this reason, his belief about the colors is not justified.

I find this symmetry argument quite convincing. Nonetheless, there are two approaches to epistemic justification that, if taken seriously, might challenge the judgment that the dress case is symmetrical in all respects that are relevant to an epistemic evaluation of Vince's blue/black belief. The first is an *externalist* account of epistemic justification, and the second is an *agent-centered* account of justification. Both accounts could be used to resist conciliatory requirements even in disagreements like the dress case, and briefly examining them will help to identify two important commitments of the disagreement skeptic.

1.4.1 An Internal Reason Constraint

Externalist accounts of justification stand in opposition to "internalist" accounts of justification. According to internalists, whether someone's belief that p is justified depends only on reasons and evidence that are internally accessible to that person, which is to say reasons and evidence that are discernible from that person's cognitive perspective.[24] On this view, "external" factors that affect a subject's cognitive reliability but that are not internally discernible can make no difference to whether or not a given belief of that subject is justified. Since the number and health of a person's light cones are not matters that are internally discernible, an internalist would deny that such factors can directly affect the justificatory status of that person's perceptual beliefs. (Of course, damage to one's eyes could indirectly affect one's justification by causing one to receive accessible evidence of such damage.) Against internalists, externalists hold that purely external factors *can* make a difference to whether or not someone is justified. So the externalist might hold that one's justification in trusting one's vision depends at least in part on external factors concerning the reliability and functioning of one's vision.

As I've been imagining the disagreement concerning the dress, there is perfect symmetry with respect to the internal factors but *not* with respect to the external factors: those who see the dress as blue/black have better functioning light cones and are more reliable in their color vision. So it is in principle open to the externalist to argue that Vince continues to have justification for the blue/black belief even after he acknowledges that the disagreement over the dress is characterized by perfect symmetry with respect to the internally discernible reasons.

Similarly, the externalist could hold that even if all processes of religious belief formation are on a par with respect to the *internally discernible* reasons one has for trusting those processes, *external* factors could perhaps help to justify someone in believing that she is reliable in the religious domain. For example, suppose that S and those who share her beliefs do in fact form their religious beliefs in a reliable way (and in a way that accords with how people are "supposed" to think about religious matters). This could perhaps help to justify S's self-trust even though S's internally discernible grounds for self-trust are acknowledged to be no stronger than her disputants' internal grounds for self-trust.

---

[24] There are different ways of characterizing internalism, and corresponding to the different ways of characterizing internalism are differing versions of externalism. The internalist thesis offered here is a form of what is called "access internalism," since it says that the justification of beliefs depends only on factors that are cognitively "accessible" or "discernible." This is stronger than "mentalism," which says that the justification of some proposition depends only on facts about what mental states the agent has, but without positing that all such facts are accessible.

Like many others, I find this kind of appeal to externalism to be quite implausible in the dress case. Whether this sort of externalist maneuver is more plausible in the case of religious disagreement is a matter I will address in chapter 4. At present, however, my aim is to identify the commitments of the disagreement skeptic. The disagreement skeptic must deny that external factors (such as the reliability of S's process of religious belief formation) could help to justify S in believing that her process of religious belief formation is more reliable than competing processes. The disagreement skeptic is therefore committed to affirming something like the following:

INTERNAL REASON CONSTRAINT: S has justification for believing SUPERIOR only if S has a good *internal* reason for believing SUPERIOR.

For my purposes, for S to have a good "internal" reason for believing SUPERIOR is for S to have a reason that gives S justification to believe SUPERIOR and that does not depend for its justificatory adequacy on any purely external factor that distinguishes S from her disputants. INTERNAL REASON CONSTRAINT implies that there can be no scenario where S's reasons for self-trust and her disputant's reasons for self-trust are internally symmetrical, but where only S has justification for self-trust. For such a possibility to be realized, the adequacy of S's reasons for self-trust in the face of disagreement could not be accounted for by the internal merits of those reasons, or even by the internal merits of those reasons combined with external factors that S and her disputant share in common; rather, the adequacy of the reasons would have to depend at least in part on some advantage S has over her disputant that is not internally accessible. And this is what INTERNAL REASON CONSTRAINT rules out.

It is important to note that I am not claiming that the disagreement skeptic must altogether oppose externalism about epistemic justification. INTERNAL REASON CONSTRAINT merely implies that external factors separating S from her disputants cannot make a difference to whether S is justified in trusting her own religious belief-forming process in the face of disagreement. One way to defend this would, of course, be to argue against externalism with respect to justification. But one could also argue that even if externalism is true, it cannot account for justification in disagreements characterized by internal symmetry. For example, an externalist could maintain that S's reliability and proper functioning in the religious domain helps to justify S in having *species-level* trust in the religious domain, and that this species-level trust, if not defeated, accounts for the initial justification of S's self-trust in the religious domain. Once S learns that the species is not in fact reliable on religious matters, the basis for S's self-trust would be undermined, and the external fact of S's reliability would no longer help to justify S's religious confidence.

1.4.2 An Agent Impartiality Constraint

There is a second asymmetry in the dress case that might bear on the question of whether Vince has justification for believing that the dress is blue and black. The disagreement about the dress is symmetrical in all relevant respects that are internally discernible *and that can be described from a third-person perspective*. But if one considers the situation from Vince's first-person perspective, there is a notable asymmetry that some epistemologists would deem significant. Vince can truthfully make the following first-person affirmation: "upon looking at the photo, it seems *to me* that the dress is blue and black." Vince cannot, of course, truthfully assert that it seems to him that the dress is white and gold. Thus, from Vince's first-person perspective, there is something special about the blue/black visual "seeming" that distinguishes this seeming from the (internally similar) white/gold seeming experienced by others. The blue/black seeming is Vince's; the white/gold seeming is not. Is this asymmetry of rational significance? The answer arguably depends on whether or not all epistemic norms are *agent-neutral* or whether at least some norms are *agent-centered*.

An agent-centered epistemic norm, as defined by Michael Huemer, is "an epistemological principle requiring agents to assign different evidential value to their own experiences or other epistemically relevant states from the value they should assign to the qualitatively similar states of someone else."[25] If there are agent-centered norms, then rationality is irreducibly *first-personal* or *perspectival*. For example, the evidential significance (to me) of the fact that it seems to me that promise-breaking is wrong may not be exhausted by the evidential significance of the third-person fact that it seems to *someone relevantly like me* (in intellectual credentials, epistemic track record, and so on) that promise-breaking is wrong. On such a view, the rational significance of the "mineness" of some moral seeming of mine cannot be fully

---

[25] Michael Huemer, "Epistemological Egoism and Agent-Centered Norms," in *Evidentialism and Its Discontents*, ed. Trent Dougherty (Oxford: Oxford University Press, 2011), 17.

explained by the fact that I know more third-person facts about myself and my experiences (including third-person facts about this very moral seeming) than I can possibly know about other people and their experiences.

If there are agent-centered norms, then the fact that the dress example exhibits rational symmetry from the third-person perspective does not straightforwardly support the conclusion that matters are rationally symmetrical from Vince's perspective. Assessed from a third-person perspective, the fact that it appears to Vince that the dress is blue and black is no more significant than the fact that the dress appears to some other person to be white and gold. From Vince's perspective, however, his own seemings and doxastic inclinations may be of special rational significance. Vince may acknowledge that he can offer no *agent-neutral* reasons in favor of trusting how things appear to him more than how things appear to some other person. Nevertheless, the agent-centered conception of rationality allows for the possibility that the fact that the dress appears blue and black *to Vince* makes Vince justified in trusting the blue/black interpretation to a degree that outstrips what would be reasonable when assessing matters from a third-person perspective. On the agent-centered conception of rationality, the *having* of an experience is itself a source of epistemic weight.

Someone who is partial toward her own reasoning, doxastic inclinations, or experiential evidence for reasons that are irreducibly first-personal exhibits what may be called *agent partiality*. It is important to distinguish agent partiality from forms of self-favoring that arise when there is an asymmetry of third-person, agent-neutral reasons and where this asymmetry is explained by the limitations that result from inhabiting a particular first-person perspective.[26] Suppose that I am walking in the countryside and come across a tranquil pond on which floats a lone swan. No other animals are visible. As a gentleman passes by on the path, I comment on the stateliness of the swan. "That's no swan," says the man, "Swans are white, and larger. That small brown bird is a duck." Even if I knew that the man wasn't joking, and that one of us was experiencing some sort of hallucination, I would not trust the man's judgment as much as my own. But this partiality toward myself need not indicate agent partiality. In support of

---

[26] For explorations of the bearing that evidential asymmetries arising from one's first-person perspective have on disagreement, see Jennifer Lackey, "What Should We Do When We Disagree?," *Oxford Studies in Epistemology* 2 (2010): 277; David Christensen, "Disagreement, Question-Begging and Epistemic Self-Criticism," *Philosophers' Imprint* 11, no. 6 (2011): 9–10; and John Pittard, "Disagreement, Reliability, and Resilience," *Synthese* 194, no. 11 (2017): 4399–4401.

my self-trust, I could cite as reasons for trusting myself various facts that, if known by a third party, would also give that third party reason to trust my perspective. These reasons include the fact that I have never been aware of having experienced a hallucination, that I have never taken mind-altering drugs, that I am not unusually tired, and so on. Because I do not know that facts such as these are true of the stranger before me, I should give more weight to my own perspective.

Suppose, however, that the stranger insisted in conversation that all of these facts are true of him also. In telling me these things, he would not succeed in providing me with reasons for trusting him that perfectly counterbalance the reasons I have for trusting myself. For example, when I affirm that I have never taken mind-altering drugs, I know that I am being sincere. When he affirms this, I am not certain whether he is sincere. While this sort of asymmetry is caused by the limitations of my first-person perspective, it is still an asymmetry in my *agent-neutral* reasons. The fact that someone has not taken mind-altering drugs is a reason that counts in favor of trusting that person, whether or not I happen to be that person. The fact that someone insists with apparent sincerity that he has not taken such drugs is *also* an agent-neutral reason for trusting that person; but this latter reason is not as strong as the former reason.

Returning to the question of the justification of S's religious beliefs, the significance of an agent-centered theory of rationality is quite clear. Suppose the correct theory of rationality is an agent-centered theory that licenses a significant degree of agent partiality. In this case, S might be justified in favoring her own process of religious belief formation even if she acknowledges that religious disagreement exhibits third-person rational symmetry. The disagreement skeptic needs to deny that first-person reasons can have this sort of epistemic weight and is therefore committed to some premise like the following:

AGENT IMPARTIALITY CONSTRAINT: S has a good internal reason for believing SUPERIOR only if S has a good *agent-neutral* internal reason for believing SUPERIOR.

My aim at present is not to assess AGENT IMPARTIALITY CONSTRAINT but merely to establish that the disagreement skeptic is committed to it. I will assess the constraint in chapter 4.

1.5 Does Religious Disagreement Exhibit Internal, Third-Person Rational Symmetry?

The critical third premise of the master argument, EQUAL ESTIMATED RELIABILITY, says that S does not have justification for believing SUPERIOR. Suppose one grants that S has justification for believing SUPERIOR only if S has a good internal agent-neutral reason to believe SUPERIOR. Kitcher and Hick think that S lacks such a reason because her disputants have arrived at their religious outlooks using processes that are symmetrical to, and rationally on a par with, S's own process of religious belief formation. Being aware of this symmetry, S has no reason to trust her own process more than any one of the processes employed by her disputants. In this section, I argue that this simplistic, broad-brush symmetry argument for EQUAL ESTIMATED RELIABILITY is inadequate. Moreover, any adequate defense of the symmetry claim would involve significant first-order argumentation, thereby undermining the higher-order character of the disagreement skeptic's argument.

There are at least two sorts of agent-neutral reasons that one might have for thinking that one religious belief-forming process is more likely to be reliable than some competitor process. First, there might be differences in the intrinsic features of the two processes that would provide a reason for putting more trust in one process than in the other. Second, if the beliefs that arise as *outputs* of one process are more reasonable and plausible than the beliefs arising from the competing process, this might provide a reason to think that the process outputting plausible beliefs is the more likely of the two to be reliable.

Consider first the possibility that the features intrinsic to various processes of religious belief formation might supply a reason to trust some of these processes more than others. Suppose all instances of religious belief formation conform to some broad process type that is highly unreliable. Nonetheless, when one considers a more fine-grained way of characterizing token processes of religious belief formation, one might find grounds for trusting some processes over others. Recall the example of the fifth-grade teacher. His belief about the class average is formed on the basis of a broad process type that he knows to be highly unreliable. But when one considers a narrower characterization of his process (one that specifies that the person doing the calculation is a skilled math teacher rather than a fifth grader), one has ample reason to think that his belief is reliably formed. Similarly, the religious believer may base her epistemic self-trust in a high estimation of the reliability of some narrower process that she also employs.

Kitcher does go a small way toward consideration of narrower process types. He considers the possibility that "thoughtful religious people" might suppose that the symmetry between religions is broken by the fact that their religious beliefs are grounded in testimony that has been critically assessed and supported by a rigorous and sophisticated tradition of natural theology (i.e., philosophical exploration of questions concerning the existence and nature of God).[27] As Kitcher rightly notes, the mere fact that one's religious beliefs have the backing of some sophisticated tradition of metaphysical theorizing does not justify trusting one's own process above all competitors. This is because there are numerous religious traditions that have conflicting outlooks and that nonetheless have a "well-articulated intellectual tradition."[28] One could simply reformulate the master argument so that instead of focusing on all religious believers who are (otherwise) epistemically qualified, it focused on all religious believers who are (otherwise) epistemically qualified and whose processes of religious belief formation involve reliance on a sophisticated philosophical tradition. Because systematic religious disagreement is also found in this narrower group of people, the master argument that is reformulated to focus on this narrower group would still reach the same skeptical conclusion without any loss of plausibility.

Merely differentiating between processes that make use of sophisticated philosophy and those that do not does not give one a reason to trust in any single religious group above the rest. But it is possible that one will discover a reason to trust in a particular religious group when one differentiates the philosophical credentials of religious traditions in a more fine-grained way or when one considers some other dimension along which the processes of religious belief formation differ.[29] For example, among the processes that

---

[27] Kitcher, *Life after Faith*, 8–9.

[28] Kitcher, *Life after Faith*, 8–9.

[29] The appeal to particular features of one's narrow process type in order to justify putting significant more trust in one's own process need not involve an appeal to natural theology (or metaphysical theorizing more broadly). Some religious thinkers contend that giving significant influence to explicit metaphysical theorizing renders religious belief formation *less* reliable: such thinkers think that explicit appeals to metaphysical argumentation distort divine revelation by requiring theological beliefs to conform to the expectations of cognitively limited and culturally conditioned beings. (For example, see Karl Barth's essay "No!" written in response to Emil Brunner's defense of the legitimate place of natural theology in Christian thought. Brunner's piece and Barth's reply are collected together in *Natural Theology* [Eugene: Wipf and Stock, 2002].) Someone who shares this suspicion of metaphysical reflection in the religious domain might still be able to point to certain distinctive features of her process of belief formation that she thinks supply a reason to trust it more than the competing processes.

assign a role to sophisticated philosophical reflection, one obviously has more reason to trust those process that are shaped by *strong* philosophical arguments, ones that start from reasonable starting points and that reach conclusions on the basis of a sensible methodology. A narrower, more fine-grained characterization of a belief-forming process may go beyond noting whether or not philosophical reflection is given a role and may take into account the operative philosophical presuppositions and inferential principles. When processes are assessed at this level of granularity, one might find reason to trust the process or processes of one community in particular.

Might one persuasively argue that processes of religious belief formation exhibit rational parity even when one differentiates those processes according to the specific kinds of philosophical arguments that are employed? Probably not. It does not seem especially likely that the philosophical arguments supporting various divergent religious outlooks are comparable in strength. Unless one is altogether skeptical about assessments of the comparative strength of philosophical arguments, then one should expect that when the philosophical credentials of religious belief-forming processes are compared, not all processes will be on equal footing.

Of course, it is *possible* that even when the cogency of philosophical reasoning is taken into account, multiple processes from two or more divergent religious outlooks are tied as the most trustworthy. Or, even if there is no exact tie at the top, the degree of approximate parity could be sufficient to make a high degree of trust in any one process unjustified.[30] But disagreement skeptics have not given any reason to think that this possibility holds. Moreover, there are other discriminating factors beyond quality of philosophical argumentation that might further winnow the field and allow one to identify a clear "winner." For example, one might judge that a religious community is more likely to employ a reliable process if it can point to reasonably credible accounts of miracles that serve to vindicate the authority of their founding prophets. (Alternatively, if one thinks that miraculous accounts are inevitably suspect, one might think that a community that does *not* make miracle claims is more likely to employ a reliable belief-forming process.)

---

[30] *Approximate* parity between S's outlook and another outlook with significantly divergent views is all that is needed in order to defend EQUAL ESTIMATED RELIABILITY. Despite the name I am using for that premise, the premise only asserts that S is not justified in thinking that her process is *significantly* more reliable than the collective reliability of competing processes. And given approximate epistemic parity between two or more competing processes, it seems that the estimated reliability of any one of these processes should not greatly outstrip the collective reliability of those processes that are approximately on a par.

And among those communities that offer reasonably credible accounts of miracles, there would likely be further evidential criteria that could be used to distinguish between more and less plausible miracle accounts. When one takes into account the many factors that might bear on the trustworthiness of processes of religious belief formation, it is not incredible to think that one could reasonably identify one religious group as the group that is more likely than any other (and perhaps more likely than not) to have formed religious beliefs in a reliable way.

I said above that there are two sorts of agent-neutral reasons one might have for thinking that one religious belief-forming process is more reliable than another: first, factors that are intrinsic to the (narrow) process types might provide a reason for putting greater trust in a particular process; and second, the *outputs* of the processes might provide a reason to trust one process more than the other. Even granting that two processes are rationally on a par as far as their intrinsic features are concerned, one might have reason to trust one of those processes more if the beliefs that the process produces are more plausible than the beliefs produced by the competing process. To get a sense of this second sort of reason, consider again the dress case. Imagine that before anyone turned up information on the actual dress, you learned that a pattern of white and gold stripes was a much more common pattern on recent dresses than one of blue and black stripes. This information would give you a reason to think that those who saw the dress as white and gold were relying on a more reliable interpretive process than those who saw the dress as blue and black. Even though the processes were relevantly indistinguishable in terms of their phenomenology and the degree of conviction they inspired, differences in the probability of the propositions supported by the processes would give you reason to favor one of the two competing processes.

Similarly, differences in the plausibility of the religious outlooks supported by various processes of belief formation could provide a reason to think that some processes of religious belief formation are more likely to be reliable than others. If processes are judged not only according to their intrinsic features but also according to the rational plausibility of their outputs, there is even less reason to suppose that there is approximate parity among the most credible processes of religious belief formation.

I have not shown that an evaluation of the credibility of various processes will vindicate any one religious outlook. It is still possible that a careful evaluation of the credibility of different processes would result in an approximate tie at the top between processes that support significantly opposed religious outlooks. My main point is that to motivate EQUAL ESTI-MATED RELIABILITY by appealing to putative epistemic parity between religions (as Kitcher and Hick do), it is insufficient to merely note symmetries in broad process types. One would need to show that "symmetry prevails" even when process types are compared at a fine-grained level and even when the plausibility of various religious views is taken into consideration. Needless to say, mounting such an argument would be quite an undertaking. And it is not something that disagreement skeptics have attempted in any serious way.

Importantly, even if such a case for rational parity *was* provided, this would not yield the sort of argument for disagreement-motivated religious skepticism that most disagreement skeptics are seeking. For an argument which did the difficult work of establishing rational parity among the various belief-forming processes would cease to be a distinctively *epistemological* argument, one that is unencumbered by controversial metaphysical claims. The above discussion shows that a serious argument for rational parity would need to wade deeply into metaphysical arguments in order to show that no religious outlook enjoys a decisive advantage with respect to its fundamental plausibility or the quality of arguments that support the outlook. One would need to take a stand on the significance of *first-order* evidence in order to then argue that disagreement constitutes evidence that requires religious skepticism. While a principle of higher-order defeat could still play a role in such an argument, such an argument would not exemplify a purely higher-order approach.

The question of this book, however, is whether facts about disagreement give one a reason for religious doubt that is independent of the various arguments that directly challenge one's first-order reasoning on religious matters. To show that disagreement provides such an independent reason for religious doubt, one must identify a higher-order argument that does not rely on controversial views about the merits of various instances of first-order religious reasoning, but that appeals only to noncontroversial facts about religious disagreement and to epistemological principles governing higher-order defeat. For the master argument to provide this, there must be some way of defending EQUAL ESTIMATED RELIABILITY without arguing for the rational parity of religious belief-forming processes.

1.6 Reasons Impartiality

At this point, the prospects for identifying a viable and purely *higher-order* argument for disagreement-motivated religious skepticism may appear to be dim. The religious believer may respond to the broad-brush symmetry argument by noting features of his *narrow* belief-forming process that distinguish it from others and make it worthier of trust. In particular, he might allege that the reasoning supporting his religious outlook has greater cogency and power than the arguments offered in support of other outlooks. In attempting to counter this claim, the disagreement skeptic would sacrifice the higher-order character of her argument.

In order to pursue a purely higher-order argument, the disagreement skeptic must insist that S cannot legitimately base her self-trust on a controversial assessment of first-order religious reasoning, *even if this assessment happens to be correct.* An attempt to ground self-trust in the merits of one's religious reasoning must be ruled out on *epistemological grounds*, rather than on grounds that concern the substantive merits of the reasoning itself.

Many philosophers writing on disagreement defend the sort of principle that the disagreement skeptic needs for such a higher-order argument. These philosophers argue that when disagreement has raised a worry about the adequacy of one's reasoning about some disputed matter, one cannot legitimately appeal to that reasoning when deciding how much to trust to put in oneself and in one's disputants. On this view, any legitimate reason for trusting oneself more than one's disputant must be a *non-question-begging* reason that could be compelling to someone irrespective of his view on the contested issue. The requirement that disagreements be assessed from a nonpartisan, dispute-neutral standpoint is explicitly endorsed by many advocates of so-called conciliatory views. Conciliationist Robert Pasnau describes the requirement this way:

> What we want, it seems, is for parties to a dispute to be able to consider everything about the dispute, on down to the most precise details that might be relevant, but somehow without begging the question in favor of the truth of their own views. . . . My suggestion is that we borrow a page from political theory and consider cases of peer disagreement from behind a veil of ignorance. In that spirit, let us imagine ourselves informed about all the factual circumstances of the situation—what is agreed upon, what is contested, what the opposing arguments are, what the credences [i.e., confidence

levels] are of the contending parties—but without knowing *who we are* in the dispute. To say that we would not know who we are means more than that we would be blocked from knowing certain autobiographical facts. It means as well that we would know neither where we stand on the proposition in dispute, nor on any other relevant propositions that are contested by the two sides. We would recognize that one of the parties takes *p* to be highly likely and regards *p* as supported by strong evidence, but we would also recognize that the other party thinks none of these things. We ourselves would enter imaginatively into a state of neutrality on such questions, setting aside our intuitions in one direction or the other.[31]

John Rawls famously held that the principles of social justice should be determined by considering what sort of laws and social structures a rational individual would endorse from behind a "veil of ignorance." From this standpoint, one does not know what social location one will occupy or what substantive conception of the good life one will endorse. Pasnau similarly suggests that the proper response to disagreement is one that would be endorsed by someone who stands behind another sort of veil of ignorance, one that involves ignorance of one's location in the dispute and also an absence of any rational commitments or inclinations that are implicated in the disagreement. Importantly, assessing a disagreement from behind this veil would block appeals not only to agent-centered considerations but also to any agent-neutral reasons whose rational significance is contested by the parties to the dispute.

This sort of impartiality constraint is exactly what the disagreement skeptic needs in order to block attempts to justify religious self-trust by appealing to features of one's narrow process type, and to block such attempts without entering into controversial first-order argumentation. Consider, for example, a Christian who points to what she takes to be compelling evidence for Jesus's resurrection as a reason to think that Christian belief formation is likely to be significantly more reliable than processes that give rise to beliefs opposed to Christianity. Presumably, a reflective Muslim not only would dispute whether Jesus was in fact resurrected but also would dispute the Christian's assessment of the strength of the evidence for the resurrection. Since the strength of this evidence would be a matter of contention, facts about the strength of the evidence would not supply a dispute-independent reason.

---

[31] Pasnau, "Veiled Disagreement," 624.

Appealing to an anti-question-begging constraint of the sort endorsed by Pasnau and other conciliationists allows one to give an argument for EQUAL ESTI-MATED RELIABILTY that is much more promising than the broad-brush symmetry argument considered earlier. The argument could be formulated as follows:

The Impartiality Argument for EQUAL ESTIMATED RELIABILITY

INTERNAL REASON CONSTRAINT: S has justification for believing SUPE-RIOR only if S has a good *internal* reason for believing SUPERIOR.

AGENT IMPARTIALITY CONSTRAINT: S has a good internal reason for believing SUPERIOR only if S has a good *agent-neutral* internal reason for believing SUPERIOR.

REASONS IMPARTIALITY CONSTRAINT: S has a good agent-neutral internal reason for believing SUPERIOR only if S has a good *dispute-independent* agent-neutral internal reason for believing SUPERIOR.

NO INDEPENDENT REASON: S does not have a good dispute-independent agent-neutral internal reason for believing SUPERIOR.

Therefore, S does not have justification for believing SUPERIOR. (In other words, EQUAL ESTIMATED RELIABILTY is correct.)

This argument does not assert that each major world religion is as epistemically well-based as any other (Hick) or that "complete symmetry prevails" among processes of forming and maintaining religious beliefs (Kitcher). In place of such ambitious (and questionable) theses, the impartiality argument holds that there is symmetry when one looks to those (agent-neutral and internal) considerations that are *dispute-independent*. It is further claimed that any reason that justifies S in believing SUPERIOR must come from this class of dispute-independent considerations. Combining the master argument with the impartiality argument for EQUAL ESTIMATED RELIABILITY appears to yield a purely higher-order argument for religious skepticism, one that does not presuppose any particular view on metaphysical questions (or moral or aesthetic questions) that are subject to religious dispute. In principle, it seems that this argument could be affirmed even by someone who has cogent first-order arguments for his religious view, who is unpersuaded by critiques of these arguments, and who is rightly unconvinced by arguments for alternative outlooks.

Appealing to REASONS IMPARTIALITY CONSTRAINT allows the disagreement skeptic to avoid the most obvious shortcomings of the broad-brush symmetry argument. But is REASONS IMPARTIALITY CONSTRAINT plausible?

What reasons may be offered in its favor? I take up these questions in the next two chapters, where I present and critique multiple arguments for reasons impartiality. But before I begin that discussion, there are two loose ends from earlier in this chapter that I am now in a position to tie up.

The first loose end is the generality problem facing the master argument for disagreement-motivated religious skepticism. Premise (1) of this argument says that S's religious outlook is justified only if S has justification for believing that most of her religious beliefs are the result of a reliable process. As explained earlier, (1) is plausible only if understood as a requirement that pertains to the process type (or types) at the relevant level of generality. I already identified an upper limit on how generic or broad the relevant process can be when I noted that the master argument should be understood as an argument focused on processes of specifically *religious* belief formation, even if such processes are domain-specific versions of broader processes. But, as noted earlier, this clarification does not address the question of whether S's epistemic self-trust can be tied to trust in arbitrarily narrow processes. Even if S acknowledges that "trusting one's parents about religious matters" is an unreliable process, can she dismiss any worries this raises by noting that her self-trust is tied to her trust in the more specific process of "trusting what one's *Christian* parents say about religious matters"? For (1) to be a requirement with any teeth, there must be some principled limit on when one can legitimately appeal to some highly specific feature of one's belief-forming process.

As Pasnau has argued, the reasons impartiality requirement provides the disagreement skeptic with a principled way of identifying which of the specific features of S's belief-forming process are ones that can legitimately ground self-trust in the face of disagreement.[32] Since a reasons impartiality constraint forbids S to base her self-trust on factors whose epistemic significance is religiously contentious, S's epistemic self-trust must be tied to a process that can be characterized without mention of any factors whose epistemic benefit is religiously controversial. Obviously, "trusting what one's Christian parents say about religious matters" does not pass this test, since only those who accepted Christian beliefs would have reason to think that it is epistemically advantageous to trust *Christian* parents in particular. According to Pasnau, when S is attempting to estimate the reliability of herself and her interlocutors, in order to ascertain how much weight she should

---

[32] Pasnau, "Veiled Disagreement."

give to her own view and to the views of others, she should take into account *all* the epistemically relevant details of the various belief-forming processes *except* those factors whose epistemic significance cannot be determined in a dispute-neutral manner.

If it is granted that one's reliability assessment should be responsive only to factors that can be appreciated from an impartial standpoint, then it would initially appear that there are strong reasons to adopt religious skepticism. For it is plausible that no religious believer can point to features of her belief-forming process that supply an agent-neutral and *dispute-independent* reason for putting much greater trust in her beliefs than in the beliefs of all her disputants.

The second loose end I can profitably address now is whether either Kitcher or Hick is justified in restricting the scope of his skeptical arguments so that his own views (secular atheism in Kitcher's case and "religious pluralism" in Hick's case) escape unscathed. Kitcher and Hick rightly note that a certain broad process type (relying uncritically on religious tradition or on religious experience) is unreliable; and since neither Kitcher nor Hick relies on that process, their particular beliefs are not threatened by its unreliability. But as I've shown, someone who acknowledges that her belief is the result of an unreliable broad process may remain justified if he has good reason to think that the belief in question is also the result of a narrow process that *is* reliable. In order for Kitcher and Hick to give conventional religious believers a reason to abandon their religious outlook in favor of Kitcher's or Hick's position, they would need to show that conventional religious believers cannot reasonably dismiss disagreement worries by appealing to some feature of their narrow process that makes that process worthy of greater trust. How could they show that such appeals to narrow features of one's process fail? One approach would be to consider each feature that the religious believer might plausibly appeal to (including the supposed merits of various arguments for the believer's religious outlook) and to convincingly argue that the feature in question should not inspire much trust. A second approach would be to rule out such appeals as illegitimate on the grounds that they are question-begging and inadequately impartial. This second approach seems to be what Kitcher and Hick implicitly have in mind, since they do not begin to offer the detailed first-order arguments that the first approach would require.

But if Kitcher and Hick do implicitly rely on some sort of reasons impartiality requirement, then it is doubtful that they can reasonably stand by their own favored position. A robust epistemic impartiality requirement would seem to undercut secular atheism and religious pluralism as much as any other religious position.[33] A belief in atheism or pluralism is also produced by a broad process type that is unreliable—namely, the process of forming beliefs on religious questions after careful reflections on all of one's evidence. While Kitcher or Hick may have reason to think that their narrow process is reliable, the reasons they might give in favor of thinking this would no doubt be controversial and contested by those with other perspectives. Appealing to features of their narrow process would therefore violate the requirement of epistemic impartiality. At least initially, it seems that a rigorous impartiality requirement can be employed in the service of sweeping religious skepticism but not in the service of any particular religious (or irreligious) view.[34]

---

[33] Bogardus advances a similar *tu quoque* argument against Kitcher in "The Problem of Contingency for Religious Belief," *Faith and Philosophy* 30, no. 4 (2013): 371–392.

[34] Chapter 6 challenges the initially plausible view that a robust impartiality requirement supports religious skepticism. As I argue, it is difficult to argue of *any* stance on religious matters, *including that of religious skepticism*, that it is the stance that best comports with epistemic impartiality.

2

Demotivating Reasons Impartiality

Chapter 1 argued that the most promising higher-order argument for disagreement-motivated religious skepticism appeals to both an agent impartiality constraint and a reasons impartiality constraint. Philosophers arguing in favor of epistemic impartiality often do not distinguish between these two sorts of constraints in order to consider their individual merits. This is unfortunate since, when one *does* distinguish between agent impartiality and reasons impartiality, one finds reason to endorse the former and to reject the latter. Or so I will argue in Part I of this book. This chapter looks at two prominent (and very different) arguments for epistemic impartiality and considers whether either argument adequately motivates a reasons impartiality requirement. The first argument is one offered by David Christensen (whose primary focus is disagreement more generally), and the second by John Schellenberg (who is focused on religious disagreement in particular). I will argue that when these arguments are subjected to careful scrutiny, the initial case for reasons impartiality proves to be much weaker than many have supposed.

2.1 Christensen's Case for INDEPENDENCE

The motivations for affirming REASONS IMPARTIALITY CONSTRAINT are perhaps less immediately apparent than the motivations for either INTERNAL REASON CONSTRAINT or AGENT IMPARTIALITY CONSTRAINT. The case for the latter two constraints is easily appreciated when one considers the striped dress example. While the blue/black contingent may have processed the visual data in a more reliable way, it nonetheless seems that members of this group should not have been any more confident than members of the white/ gold group. In this context, at least, external facts concerning de facto reliability do not seem to make it reasonable for someone to put more trust in his own belief-forming process. Similarly, it seems that it would not be rational for me to favor my belief about the color of the dress for the agent-centered reason that it seems *to me* that the dress is such and such color. Of course, there may be important differences between the dress case and a case of religious disagreement that make it inappropriate to extrapolate from one case to the other. For this reason, I do not take the dress case to show that INTERNAL REASON CONSTRAINT and AGENT IMPARTIALITY CONSTRAINT are correct, and I will give more attention to these premises in chapter 4. Nonetheless, the dress case does supply a powerful initial motivation for these two constraints.

Does the dress case similarly motivate REASONS IMPARTIALITY CONSTRAINT? It seems not. When attending only to internal, agent-neutral considerations, there do not appear to be any considerations (contested or otherwise) that would account for the rationality of someone's believing that his belief about the dress is correct. It is not as though the blue/black thesis has greater or lesser antecedent probability than the white/gold thesis; nor do the blue/black believers reason in some manner that is distinct from the manner of the white/gold believers. What is needed to motivate a proscription of reasons partiality is a case where there *is* an internal, agent-neutral reason that favors one side of the dispute but where it is clear that this reason cannot legitimately ground epistemic self-trust since it is contested by the disputants.

In search of such a case, I'll turn to the most prominent recent argument in favor of reasons impartiality, an argument developed by David Christensen. Christensen defends the following principle:

INDEPENDENCE: In evaluating the epistemic credentials of another's expressed belief about *p*, in order to determine how (or whether) to modify my own belief about *p*, I should do so in a way that doesn't rely on the reasoning behind my initial belief about *p*.[1]

According to Christensen, INDEPENDENCE provides the basis for diagnosing what is wrong with "blatantly question-begging" dismissals of the worries raised by a disagreement.[2] INDEPENDENCE, he writes, "attempts to capture what would be wrong with a *p*-believer saying, e.g., 'Well, so-and-so disagrees with me about *p*. But since *p* is true, she's wrong about *p*. So however reliable she may generally be, I needn't take her disagreement about *p*

---

[1] Christensen discusses and defends INDEPENDENCE in several different places. This particular formulation is from "Disagreement, Question-Begging and Epistemic Self-Criticism," *Philosophers' Imprint* 11, no. 6 (2011), 2.

[2] Christensen, "Disagreement, Question-Begging and Epistemic Self-Criticism."

as any reason at all to question my belief.'" In support of INDEPENDENCE, Christensen presents his now classic restaurant case.[3] In the example, two individuals who are sharing a dinner at a restaurant with several friends both calculate in their heads what each person's share of the total bill is. They agree to add 20% of the posttax total for the tip and to split the check evenly among all the members of the party. Both friends do this sort of calculation often and know that the other person is no more or less reliable than they are. They usually agree on the answer in such cases. But in those instances when they do reach different answers, neither of them has proven more likely than the other to be the one who has made an error. While nothing is out of the ordinary in this case (neither friend is especially distracted or extra alert, for example), upon finishing their mental calculations they discover that their answers differ: one has arrived at an answer of $43, and the other at $45.

Christensen's claim about the motivation for INDEPENDENCE, when translated to this example, is that INDEPENDENCE is intended to explain why it would be wrong for one of the friends to respond to this case by reasoning as follows:

QUICK DISMISSAL: "Since my friend fails to see that the facts support an answer of $43, I have good reason for thinking that, contrary to my expectations, she is not (at least at this moment) a reliable judge of the question we are disputing; therefore, her disagreement gives me no reason at all to question my answer."

Clearly, the reasoning expressed by QUICK DISMISSAL is dubious. It seems, moreover, that it would be unreasonable for either friend to be significantly more confident in her or his own answer than in the other's answer. INDEPENDENCE gives a principled explanation for these verdicts: responses like QUICK DISMISSAL are illegitimate because they presuppose the very correctness of the reasoning that has been called into question; and the two answers should be given approximately equal weight since neither friend has a dispute-independent basis for putting more trust in his or her own answer than in the answer of his or her friend.

Initially, it looks like Christensen's restaurant case might motivate a reasons impartiality requirement even if the dress case does not. In the dress case,

---

[3] My description of the case is adapted from David Christensen, "Epistemology of Disagreement: The Good News," *Philosophical Review* 116, no. 2 (2007): 187–217.

the "reasoning" of both sides (which involves little more than trusting the outputs of some visual processing faculty) is equivalent. But in the restaurant case, one side has reasoned incorrectly and (one can suppose) one side has reasoned correctly. Nonetheless, it strongly seems that this fact does not justify the friend with the true belief in maintaining a high degree of confidence. Despite the fact that one friend is in a more rational position than the other, the friend who is correct should still give equal weight to both answers. She cannot appeal to her contested yet superior mathematical reasoning in order to justify trusting herself more than her friend. INDEPENDENCE explains why such an appeal would be illegitimate: the friend cannot rely on such reasoning because it is contested and thus unacceptably *question-begging*.

I'll call this argument for INDEPENDENCE the "restaurant argument." This argument describes a straightforward case of disagreement where nearly everyone is likely to agree that QUICK DISMISSAL is illegitimate and that the friends should give approximately equal weight to the opposing views. It is then claimed that one should accept INDEPENDENCE since it offers a principled explanation of these verdicts.

The fact that INDEPENDENCE can explain the commonsense verdicts in the restaurant case provides a strong reason for accepting INDEPENDENCE only if there are no other explanations of these verdicts that are at least as plausible as INDEPENDENCE. I will argue that one can explain these verdicts without appealing to a reasons impartiality principle like INDEPENDENCE. The verdicts can be explained in terms of plausible epistemic norms that are far less radical than INDEPENDENCE, and that one has reason to accept quite apart from any issues related to disagreement. After spelling out these alternative explanations, I will consider whether there are other cases of disagreement where an equal weight verdict is intuitive and where INDEPENDENCE would indeed be needed to explain such a verdict.

2.2 Diagnosing QUICK DISMISSAL without Appealing to INDEPENDENCE

Christensen suggests that one reason for affirming INDEPENDENCE is its ability to capture what is wrong with blatantly question-begging responses such as QUICK DISMISSAL. In this section, I show that one can explain the illegitimacy of QUICK DISMISSAL without appealing to any impartiality constraint such as INDEPENDENCE. (In the next section I will take on the somewhat more ambitious task of explaining the equal weight verdict without any appeal to INDEPENDENCE.) The illegitimacy of QUICK DISMISSAL can be fully explained by standard Bayesian epistemology together with the (eminently plausible) claim that neither friend should be *maximally* confident in the correctness of her answer before learning of the disagreement. Since one can coherently affirm these two claims without affirming INDEPENDENCE, the latter principle is not needed to diagnose what is wrong with QUICK DISMISSAL.

2.2.1 Introduction to Bayesian Epistemology

Before showing how Bayesianism adequately accounts for the illegitimacy of QUICK DISMISSAL, I will briefly introduce the Bayesian framework. These brief introductory remarks will be pertinent to other parts of the book as well, since at many points in the book I adopt a Bayesian approach.

Much of so-called traditional epistemology is concerned with the justification of *beliefs*. In some cases where I do not have justification for believing that p, I have justification for disbelieving that p, which simply amounts to believing the negation of p. In other cases, though, I may lack justification to believe that p and also lack justification to believe that $\sim p$. For example, I am not justified in believing of an upcoming toss of a coin (that is known to be fair) that it will land heads, nor am I justified in believing that it will *not* land heads; in this case, a withholding of judgment is justified. Traditional discussions of epistemic justification are primarily concerned with these three "doxastic attitudes": belief, disbelief, and withholding judgment. But it seems that the doxastic state of a typical human person cannot be adequately described if these are the only doxastic attitudes referenced. Among the propositions believed by an agent, some will be believed with greater confidence than others; likewise, an agent may assign various degrees of plausibility to propositions that are neither believed nor disbelieved. Adequately representing these varying confidence levels requires one to invoke a much more fine-grained range of doxastic attitudes. This is provided by the *credence* framework of contemporary formal epistemology, which represents a subject's confidence in the truth of some proposition with a precise credence value that may take on any value between 0 (representing certainty of falsehood) and 1 (representing certainty of truth).[4]

---

[4] Those who affirm that people have credences (or at least some set of fine-grained attitudes that

Where traditional epistemology is concerned with the rational requirements that pertain to belief, formal epistemology is concerned with the rational requirements that pertain to credences and conditional credences. My credence for p is my (unconditional) confidence in p, whereas my credence for p *conditional on* q represents how likely I take p to be on the supposition that q holds. To illustrate, suppose that the star of my hometown basketball team has the flu. Because I think it unlikely that she will quickly recover from her illness, my credence that my team will win tomorrow's game might be quite low. Nonetheless, I might think that in the event that she *does* recover and play in tomorrow's game, my team will likely prevail. In other words, my credence for victory *conditional* on the star recovering and playing in the game might be quite high. If C is my credence function, $C(p)$ is used to designate my unconditional credence for p, and $C(p \mid q)$ designates my credence for p conditional on q (which I will sometimes refer to as my conditional credence for p given q, or my conditional credence for p on the supposition that q).

Bayesianism is the consensus framework of formal epistemology, and it provides the best theory of how one's credences for various propositions ought to shift in light of new evidence. The first core tenet of standard Bayesianism is that one's credences should be probabilistically coherent.[5] This means that the credence function of a rational agent will be a probability function with outputs that satisfy the standard axioms of probability. In addition to this synchronic constraint of probabilistic coherence, standard Bayesianism posits a diachronic constraint that requires that upon learning new information, credences be updated by a process of conditionalization. The standard requirement of conditionalization pertains to a "learning episode," where a subject who starts with a credence for E (for "evidence") greater than 0 but less than 1 then learns that E is the case (without simultaneously learning or forgetting anything else), resulting in the subject assigning E a credence of 1. Conditionalization says that in such a situation, the subject's

the credence framework imperfectly models) are not thereby committed to holding that the coarse-grained attitude of belief is a fiction. Nor are they committed to holding that beliefs are in some sense "reducible" to credences, so that if you already knew some agent's credence values, you would not gain further information about her doxastic state by being told what her beliefs are. Some proponents of a credence framework *do* hold one or the other of these views about beliefs, but many do not.

[5] My characterization of Bayesianism owes much to James M. Joyce, "Bayesianism," in *The Oxford Handbook of Rationality*, ed. Alfred R. Mele and Piers Rawling (Oxford: Oxford University Press, 2004), 132–155; and James M. Joyce, "How Probabilities Reflect Evidence," *Philosophical Perspectives* 19, no. 1 (2005): 153–178.

new credence for some proposition p should be equal to the conditional credence for p given E that the subject had just *before* learning E. So if C_{Old} is a subject's credence function just before a learning episode of the relevant sort, and if C_{New} is the subject's credence function just after becoming certain of E, then conditionalization says that the following equality should hold:

$$\text{Conditionalization: } C_{New}(p) = C_{Old}(p|E)$$

Going back to the sports example, suppose that my credence for a victory tomorrow is 0.25, but my credence for victory conditional on the full recovery of the team's star is 0.8. I now learn that the star *has* fully recovered and will play in the game (and I learn nothing else). According to conditionalization, my new (*unconditional*) credence for victory ought to be 0.8.

The diachronic constraint of conditionalization is more useful and illuminating when it is combined with a *synchronic* rational constraint on the value of $C_{Old}(p \mid E)$. It is clear on reflection that $C(A \mid B)$ rationally ought to be equal to the ratio $C(A \text{ and } B) / C(B)$, provided that these unconditional credences are defined and $C(B) > 0$.[6] For example, if my credence that the sick basketball star will fully recover before the game is 0.2 and my credence that she will fully recover before the game and her team will win is 0.16, then coherence requires me to have a conditional credence of 0.8 for her team winning the game conditional on her fully recovering before the game. After all, of the 0.2 credence assigned to her recovery, 80% of this (i.e., 0.16) is assigned to the hypothesis that her team wins the game. Given this constraint on conditional credence and the constraint of probabilistic coherence, it can easily be shown that one's credences should conform to Bayes's theorem:

$$\text{Bayes's theorem: } C(p|E) = C(E|p) \times C(p) / C(E)$$

$$\left[\text{provided that } C(E) > 0\right]$$

---

[6] Some philosophers define the conditional probability $P(A \mid B)$ as being equal to the ratio of P $(A \text{ and } B) / P(B)$, provided that $P(B) > 0$. Alan Hájek has persuasively argued that this ratio is not a viable *definition* or *analysis* of conditional probability. See Hájek, "What Conditional Probability Could Not Be," *Synthese* 137, no. 3 (2003): 273–323. But even Hájek agrees that $P(A \mid B)$ is rationally constrained to be $P(A \text{ and } B) / P(B)$ in contexts where these unconditional probabilities are precisely defined and $P(B) > 0$.

Employing Bayes's theorem in conjunction with conditionalization can make it much easier in practice to determine how credences ought to be updated in light of new evidence. The reason for this is that the rational values for $C(E|p)$, $C(p)$, and $C(E)$ are often much more evident than the rational value for $C(p|E)$. Bayes's theorem allows one to calculate the latter value using values that are more readily determined.

2.2.2 A Bayesian Explanation of the Illegitimacy of QUICK DISMISSAL

I'll now consider what Bayesianism says about the restaurant case.[7] Suppose that Dave is the friend who arrived at the answer \$43. Let p stand for the proposition that this answer is correct, let D (for "disagreement") stand for the proposition that Dave's friend has arrived at an answer different than \$43, and let C be Dave's credence function just before learning whether or not his friend agrees. Bayesians say that some piece of evidence *disconfirms* some proposition if and only if conditionalizing on that evidence causes one's credence in that proposition to go down. Conversely, when conditionalizing on some bit of evidence causes one's credence in a proposition to go up, the evidence is said to *confirm* that proposition. According to Bayesian confirmation theory, in cases where $\sim p$ and D are both epistemic possibilities for Dave (so that Dave's credences for $\sim p$ and for D are both positive), evidence D disconfirms proposition p if and only if before learning D, Dave's conditional credence for D given p is less than his conditional credence for D given $\sim p$. In other words, if on Dave's view D is more likely on the supposition that $\sim p$ than it is on the supposition that p, then upon learning

---

[7] There is a worry about my applying the Bayesian framework to Christensen's restaurant case. Bayes's theorem is a constraint on probabilistically coherent credence distributions. But someone who is uncertain about the answer to a math problem is not probabilistically coherent. Thus, one cannot prove that Bayes's theorem expresses a legitimate rational constraint in this case. So there is a theoretical concern here to which I do not have a fully worked out response. (For one early attempt at meeting this challenge that strikes me as quite plausible, see Daniel Garber, "Old Evidence and Logical Omniscience in Bayesian Confirmation Theory," *Minnesota Studies in the Philosophy of Science* 10 [1983]: 99–131.) But I still maintain that Bayesian conditionalization is applicable in this case. Imagine a similar case where what is disputed is not a math problem but the number of marbles in a jar (which two friends have each counted). It would be *very* strange if the principles of confirmation theory that govern disagreement in this case were different from the principles that govern disagreement in the restaurant case. The epistemically relevant features do not vary across the two cases. So if Bayesian conditionalization applies in the marble case (and why wouldn't it, since the hypothesis under consideration is not a logical or mathematical truth?), then one should expect that it will apply in calculation disagreements as well.

D he should reduce his credence for p (assuming he has not at same time learned something else besides D that is evidentially relevant). This principle follows from conditionalization and the synchronic constraints on credences discussed above.

What this means is that if one can explain why (1) D should be an epistemic possibility for Dave, why (2) $\sim p$ should be an epistemic possibility for Dave, and why (3) it should be the case that $C(D \mid p) < C(D \mid \sim p)$, then the explanations of (1)–(3), together with the explanation of the Bayesian diachronic and synchronic requirements, will collectively explain why Dave should take D to be evidence against p. And it seems clear that one *can* explain (1)–(3), and that one can do so without invoking any principle like IN-DEPENDENCE (and without invoking any principle that somehow implies that INDEPENDENCE is correct).

Starting with (1), it is clear that Dave's credence for D should be positive. Dave knows that his friend is not perfectly reliable, and thus that D has a nonzero probability (whether or not Dave's answer is correct). Skipping over (2) for the moment, it is also obvious that $C(D \mid p)$ should be less than $C(D \mid \sim p)$ (given that D and $\sim p$ are both epistemic possibilities). Since it is given in the example that Dave knows his friend to be highly reliable, Dave should think it fairly likely that his friend has arrived at the right answer, whether that answer be $43 or something else. So on the supposition that p is true, then it is quite probable that Dave's friend has arrived at an answer of $43, and thus quite likely that D is false. And on the supposition that p is *false*, it is quite probable that Dave's friend has arrived at the right answer, which is *not* $43, in which case it is quite probable that D is true. In other words, if Dave is reasonable, $C(D \mid p) < C(D \mid \sim p)$. Obviously, it is not necessary to invoke INDEPENDENCE to explain this requirement of reasonability.

Now I'll turn to (2), the claim that Dave's initial credence for $\sim p$ should be positive. Here, matters are a bit more delicate. It seems clear that (2) is *true*: given Dave's knowledge that he sometimes makes mistakes in complex mental calculations, maximal certainty in p would be unreasonable, in which case Dave ought to have a positive credence for $\sim p$. Moreover, the truth of (2) can be appreciated whether or not one accepts INDEPENDENCE. Nonetheless, an advocate of INDEPENDENCE *might* insist (and not without some plausibility) that the truth of (2) cannot be satisfactorily *explained* apart from INDEPENDENCE. So even if one can explain the illegitimacy of QUICK DISMISSAL by appealing to claims (1)–(3) and to Bayesian confirmation theory, it might be that claim (2), one element of this explanation, is itself explained by INDEPENDENCE (or perhaps by some closely-related principle that itself implies INDEPENDENCE). In this case, the *full* account of why QUICK DISMISSAL is epistemically inappropriate could not be given without invoking INDEPENDENCE or some related principle that implies it.

Why might one think that INDEPENDENCE (or some principle that implies it) is needed to explain the truth of (2)?[8] Well, first note that if Dave's belief that *p* is correct, then Dave's evidence (i.e., the fact that the total bill is such and such value) *entails p*. If Dave correctly calculated each person's share and thus appreciates this entailment relation, then there is something a bit puzzling about his assigning a credence to *p* that is less than 1. After all, Dave sees that his evidence *guarantees* the truth of *p*. Presumably, Dave's less-than-perfect confidence in *p* is a response to the higher-order evidence concerning his reliability, including his good but less-than-perfect track record. But the evidence constituted by Dave's track record cannot be weighed against the mathematical evidence in any straightforward sense. The mathematical evidence guarantees the truth of *p whatever Dave's track record may be*. So it can seem that if Dave were to proportion his credence to the strength of his mathematical evidence, a credence of 1 would be required. This line of thinking may lead one to conclude that one cannot simultaneously maintain *both* that Dave's credence should be less than 1 *and* that he should proportion his credence in a way that fully reflects the strength of his first-order mathematical evidence. Even though he *has* this mathematical evidence available to him, in determining his credence it seems that he must, in the words of Christensen, "*put aside* or *bracket off*" the mathematical reasoning that supports assigning *p* a credence of 1.[9] Doing this requires that Dave assess the trustworthiness of his mathematical reasoning in a manner that is *independent* of the specific mathematical reasoning whose trustworthiness is being assessed. This would involve giving weight to the hypothetical perspective of someone who has not gone through the calculation itself (and who perhaps does not even know the total on the bill) but who does know that Dave reached an answer of $43, that Dave is highly but not perfectly reliable in these sorts of situations, that Dave is not unusually distracted at the moment, and so on. But to give weight to this perspective (in order to arrive at a less than maximal credence for

---

[8] The argument sketched in this paragraph draws heavily from David Christensen, "Higher-Order Evidence," *Philosophy and Phenomenological Research* 81, no. 1 (May 2010): 185–215. Christensen, however, would probably stop short of saying that a good explanation of (2) commits one to INDEPENDENCE.

[9] Christensen, "Higher-Order Evidence," 195.

p) is to give weight to a perspective that is *dispute-independent* inasmuch as it does not rely on the mathematical reasoning that would be contested by someone who arrived at a different answer.

So it seems that a full account of why Dave should be less than maximally confident in p before the disagreement leads one to affirm that Dave should be evaluating matters from a dispute-independent perspective. The advocate of INDEPENDENCE might therefore insist that it only superficially *appears* that one can explain the illegitimacy of QUICK DISMISSAL without reference to IN-DEPENDENCE. On closer inspection, it appears that INDEPENDENCE plays a crucial role in explaining why Dave should not be maximally confident in p, a fact that crucially figures in the Bayesian account of why QUICK DISMISSAL is unreasonable.

As it stands, this attempt to uncover a commitment to INDEPENDENCE beneath the Bayesian critique of QUICK DISMISSAL is overly hasty. First, even if one accepts the "bracketing" explanation of why Dave should be less than maximally certain that p, all one needs to affirm is that Dave should give at least *some* weight to a perspective that brackets the mathematical reasoning (and that is therefore dispute-independent). If Dave gives any weight at all to this dispute-independent perspective, he will have a nonmaximal credence for p, allowing one to go forward with the Bayesian explanation of QUICK DISMISSAL's flaws. But INDEPENDENCE does not merely say that *some* weight should be given to a dispute-independent perspective. It at least appears to require that one's response to the disagreement be settled on grounds that are *entirely* dispute-independent, such that full weight is given to the impartial vantage point and no weight is given to partisan reasoning. Christensen himself acknowledges that one can deny the "strong independence principles" he has advocated (principles that require assessing a disagreement in a way that is *fully* independent of one's contested reasoning) while nonetheless accepting that someone in Dave's situation is required to *partially* "bracket" his (potentially contested) reasoning.[10] Endorsing bracketing of this sort does not immediately commit one to INDEPENDENCE, at least not if INDE-PENDENCE is interpreted in a way that would support reasonably demanding conciliatory policies.

Second, it may be possible to explain the requirement that Dave be less than maximally certain without appealing to bracketing at all. A bracketing requirement could explain why Dave is less than maximally confident in p

---

[10] Christensen, "Higher-Order Evidence," 196.

even though he sees that his evidence entails p, but perhaps in this case Dave does not see that his evidence entails p. Or, if he does see that his evidence entails p, perhaps he only dimly or imperfectly sees this, and perhaps one's confidence in propositions that are entailed by one's evidence should be proportionate to the clarity with which one sees the relevant entailment relations. If this is right, then it might be possible to explain why Dave should have a credence for p that is less than 1 without maintaining that Dave is giving some weight to a dispute-independent perspective. Dave's *own* perspective would support a nonmaximal credence because that perspective lacks full clarity. A full defense of this position would require confronting several difficult questions about the nature of rational insight and the degrees of clarity that characterize various insights. My intention is not to develop this position at present but merely to gesture toward an approach that might vindicate nonmaximal confidence in p without relying on the idea that Dave ought to give weight to an impartial perspective.

It seems, then, that INDEPENDENCE is not needed to explain why "blatantly question-begging" responses to disagreement like QUICK DISMISSAL are illegitimate. But most philosophers who discuss the restaurant case judge not only that QUICK DISMISSAL is illegitimate but also that the proper response is for Dave to give approximately equal weight to his friend's answer, so that his subsequent credences for the two answers are approximately the same. Is there a good explanation of this equal weight verdict that does not appeal to an impartiality requirement like INDEPENDENCE? In the next section, I argue that there is.

2.3 Explaining the Equal Weight Verdict without Appealing to INDEPENDENCE

I contend that in the restaurant case, an internal reason constraint and an agent impartiality constraint are sufficient to explain why Dave is rationally required to give his friend's answer as much weight as his own. There is no need to posit a reasons impartiality requirement like INDEPENDENCE. The key feature of the restaurant case that makes it unnecessary to appeal to INDEPENDENCE in order to explain an equal weight verdict is the fact that (on any realistic way of imagining the case) Dave has forgotten some of the details of his mathematical reasoning by the time he has arrived at his answer. His mathematical reasoning is therefore not entirely accessible from his current cognitive perspective, and this allows one to explain (without appealing to any reasons impartiality requirement) why that reasoning cannot justify self-trust in the face of disagreement.

Consider Dave's situation after he has arrived at his answer but before learning of the disagreement. Suppose that p (the proposition that Dave's answer of $43 is correct) is true and that his high credence for p is the result of cogent mathematical reasoning. All but the most radical skeptics would allow that he is rationally justified in having a high credence for p. But what accounts for the justification of his confidence in p? A natural response might be that his confidence in p is justified because it is the product of cogent mathematical reasoning. But this response may be problematic from the perspective of someone who is an internalist about rational justification. A normal human being who engages in a complex multistep mathematical calculation typically does not retain a clear memory of the reasoning employed at each step. Success in a multistep calculation problem requires one to remember the *result* of a step long enough to employ that result in the next step and to keep track of what steps need to be performed and where one is in the process. Success does not require maintaining conscious awareness of the reasoning employed at each step. Even if it were possible for creatures with humans' cognitive limitations to maintain such awareness, attempting to do so would likely compete with mental resources required for the present step, slowing down the calculation process tremendously. So it is not surprising that people typically forget the details of the reasoning at a given step as soon as that step is completed.

Suppose the posttax total for 7 people is $250.95 and Dave calculates the total share for each person when tipping 20% on the posttax total. Dave will likely attend carefully to one step (e.g., adding 20% to the total) and then forget the detailed reasoning of this step while retaining the *result* for use in the next step (e.g., dividing this result by 7). This means that when he arrives at his answer of $43 and forms a high credence for this answer, the cogency of the reasoning that led to this answer is not a factor that is *internally discernible*. And since traditional internalism about epistemic justification says that the factors that account for justification must be internally accessible or discernible (as discussed in chapter 1), there is reason to think that the traditional internalist should not affirm that the cogency of Dave's mathematical reasoning explains why he is justified.

Granted, internalism does not require that justifying factors be internally *discerned* but only that they be internally *discernible* to the subject. And it might be suggested that the cogency of Dave's (forgotten) mathematical reasoning *is* internally discernible, since if he were to do the calculation again (proceeding in just the same manner) he would discern the cogency of each bit of reasoning as he performed it. However, even if one granted that the cogency of *each step* in Dave's reasoning is internally discernible, it arguably does not follow that the cogency of his reasoning *as a whole* is itself internally discernible. Plausibly, discerning the latter fact requires appreciating the cogency of the *entire line of reasoning* all at once. In addition, it is clear that at least *many* internalists (if not all) would resist stretching the notion of internal "discernibility" in a way that would recognize Dave's forgotten reasoning as discernible. It is true that many internalists allow that some factors count as discernible even though the subject does not presently have conscious awareness of them. But not just any possible object of awareness will count as being discernible in the relevant sense. While Dave might be able through certain mental operations to once again put himself in a position to discern the cogency of the reasoning that led to his answer, it does seem natural to say that *from his present perspective*, the cogency of this reasoning is not discernible. By going through the mental calculations once more in order to see the cogency of his reasoning, Dave arguably moves to a new cognitive perspective that is not identical to the perspective occupied just before learning of the disagreement. This suggests that on at least some natural ways of understanding internalism, Dave's justification immediately prior to the disagreement cannot be due to an appreciation of the cogency of his reasoning. And this conclusion is sufficient for my argument that internalism (on at least some natural construals) can help to explain the equal weight requirement without invoking a reasons impartiality requirement.

Before describing how internalism can provide such an explanation, I should note that my full explanation of why equal weighting is appropriate in the restaurant case will not come until the next chapter. There, I develop a fully general approach to disagreement that applies not only to symmetrical "peer disagreements" like the restaurant case (where the apparent epistemic qualifications are equal) but also to disagreements with asymmetric epistemic credentials. But in a symmetric example like the restaurant case, one can offer an intuitive explanation of the equal weight verdict without appealing to the formal policy I defend in the next chapter.

If the internalist holds that Dave's confidence in p is not justified in virtue of the cogency of the reasoning that led him to this belief (since that cogency is not presently discernible), then what *does* justify his confidence before learning of the disagreement? Presumably, his confidence is justified by his beliefs (perhaps occurrent, perhaps merely dispositional) that he carefully calculated his answer and that when he carefully calculates in this sort of situation he is quite reliable. In addition, if Dave can see without any exact calculation that $43 is a reasonable answer, one that it is at least "in the ballpark" of the correct value, then this also would be a justifying factor.

Once one takes the cogency of Dave's calculation off of the table as a potential justifier, then the same sort of factors that justify Dave in thinking that $43 is correct could also justify his friend in thinking that $45 is correct. When Dave learns of his friend's disagreement, he learns that his friend, who is equally reliable in this sort of situation, carefully calculated her answer and arrived at an answer of $45. And if a "gut check" does not favor Dave's answer, in other words if Dave judges that $45 is on its face as plausible an answer as $43, then all of the cognitively accessible evidential factors that support believing $43 will be counterbalanced by relevantly similar evidential factors that support $45. Of course, matters are not symmetric with respect to agent-centered, first-person facts. Dave can affirm "*I* arrived at an answer of $43," and he cannot similarly affirm this of the answer $45. But if one rejects agent-centered norms and holds that first-person asymmetries are rationally irrelevant, then there will be symmetry of evidential support: all of the factors that justify confidence in the answer $43 are equally matched by factors that justify confidence in the answer $45. Since in the face of this symmetry it would be rationally arbitrary to favor either answer, Dave should give equal weight to the two answers.

Internalism (or at least some natural ways of construing internalism) and a rejection of agent partiality are collectively sufficient to explain why equal weighting is required in the restaurant case. It is therefore unnecessary to appeal to a reasons impartiality requirement like INDEPENDENCE. The reason why it would be wrong for Dave to appeal to the cogency of his mathematical reasoning is arguably *not* that this would be question-begging but that the cogency of this reasoning is no longer cognitively discernible and therefore cannot be a determinant of justification.

2.4 Can the Restaurant Argument
for INDEPENDENCE be Repaired?

There is an obvious way to try to improve on the restaurant argument in order to avoid the objection developed in the previous section. What is required is a disagreement case where it is clear that equal weighting is appropriate (even when one has reasoned correctly and one's interlocutor has not) and where this verdict cannot be explained by internalism and an agent impartiality constraint. Such a case must be one where the disputants' reasoning remains accessible and open to assessment in the face of disagreement. If such a case could be found, then Christensen's basic approach to motivating IN-DEPENDENCE could be rehabilitated. But I am not aware that there is such a case. To be sure, there are many cases where the subject's contested reasoning remains cognitively accessible throughout the disagreement, but I am not aware of such a case where it is also relatively obvious that equal weighting is the correct response. This is not to say that in such cases equal weighting is obviously *wrong* but only that I do not know of a case of this sort where it is obviously *right*.

As one step toward evaluating the prospects of rehabilitating Christensen's basic strategy for motivating INDEPENDENCE, I turn to a case where the subjects' reasoning remains consciously accessible as they assess the disagreement's epistemic significance. Consider the case of MULTIVERSE, as follows.

MULTIVERSE: Joy and Lynne like to talk metaphysics, though they know very little about the opinions of professional philosophers. While they don't always agree on the matters they discuss, they both have good reason for thinking that their reliability on metaphysical matters is approximately the same. One day in conversation Joy and Lynne stumble into a debate concerning the plausibility of the thesis that the realm of space and time inhabited by humans is but one universe of an infinite number of universes that are causally, spatially, and temporally disconnected from one another (so that no universe bears any spatial, temporal, or causal relations to any other). Call this thesis INFINITE UNIVERSES. Lynne assigns INFINITE UNIVERSES a credence of approximately 0. On her view, the very notion of spatiotemporally disconnected universes is probably nonsensical and incoherent. While this notion may not be straightforwardly contradictory (just as the notion of a highest prime number or of something's moving diagonally in time are not straightforwardly contradictory), Lynne thinks that her inability to positively picture spatiotemporally disconnected universes (i.e., her inability to see such a scenario before her "mind's eye") is good evidence that INFINITE UNIVERSES is not a genuine metaphysical possibility. Her credence that it *is* a genuine metaphysical possibility is, let's say, 0.05. But even on the supposition that it *is* possible for there to be spatiotemporally disconnected universes, Lynne thinks that the probability that there are an infinite number is infinitesimal. On her view, simpler hypotheses should be favored over complex hypotheses (all else being equal), and for this reason the probability of a cosmological theory is inversely correlated with the number of universes it postulates. So "infinity" is the *least* probable possibility for the number of universes.

Joy, it turns out, sees matters quite differently. While she acknowledges that she cannot "picture" spatiotemporally disconnected worlds (how, after all, could one picture the *absence* of a spatial or temporal relation between two things), she thinks that this inability is not good evidence that the notion is incoherent. Since Joy sees no reason for thinking that one spacetime must pervade all of reality, and since INFINITE UNIVERSES appears to her to have prima facie credibility, her credence that INFINITE UNIVERSES is metaphysically possible is 0.95. Moreover, her conditional credence for INFINITE UNIVERSES, given that this idea is a coherent possibility, is much higher than Lynne's. While Joy acknowledges that simpler hypotheses should be judged more probable than complex ones (all else being equal), it seems to her that the sort of simplicity that is relevant to epistemic probability has more to do with avoiding "arbitrary" aspects of a theory and less to do with minimizing postulated entities. Since an infinite number of universes would be the logical outcome if there is some sort of unchecked cosmic impetus toward maximality, Joy thinks that INFINITE UNIVERSES is simple in the relevant sense. Thus, INFINITE UNIVERSES is *vastly* more probable than the hypothesis that there are 105 universes, for example, or even the hypothesis that there are 5. Her conditional credence for INFINITE UNIVERSES, given the coherence of the thesis, is 0.2.

Joy and Lynne share their reasoning as best as they can. While they are unable to articulate explicit theories of conceivability (and how it bears on possibility) or of simplicity (as it bears on theory selection), they do their best to express the bases for their conflicting assessments of INFINITE UNIVERSES. But even when both have conveyed their reasoning to the best of their abilities, neither is at all persuaded by the reasoning of the other. It seems to Joy that the weight Lynne puts on "picturing" a scenario is unreasonable and that her way of assessing simplicity is wrongheaded. But Lynne is equally confident that Joy's way of thinking about these matters is highly misguided.

When Joy and Lynne are assessing the epistemic significance of their disagreement, they know precisely where their reasoning diverges and why they disagree. Because their reasoning is present to them and assessable, an internalist view of justification does not rule out the possibility that Joy and Lynne's response to the disagreement should depend (at least in part) on the cogency of their different ways of reasoning about INFINITE UNIVERSES. In this respect, MULTIVERSE is quite different from the restaurant case. Since internalism could not be used to explain an equal weight verdict in MULTIVERSE, explaining such a verdict would presumably require positing a reasons impartiality requirement like INDEPENDENCE.

Related to this first difference between MULTIVERSE and the restaurant case is a second difference that is worth noting. Because Lynne's and Joy's reasons are consciously present and actively shape their current perspective, one should not expect that either of them will acknowledge that their divergent views are in some sense equally plausible. In the restaurant case, both friends might acknowledge that the answers $43 and $45 both look equally plausible in light of the "gut check" reasoning that is cognitively accessible from their present position. According to the approach to disagreement that I develop and defend in the next two chapters, these differences between the two cases may have significant bearing on the degree of conciliation that is appropriate.

What responses in MULTIVERSE would accord with a reasons impartiality constraint like INDEPENDENCE? Presumably, responding in a dispute-neutral way would require Joy and Lynne to give approximately equal weight to each of their credences concerning the metaphysical possibility of INFINITE UNIVERSES (so that their new credence that INFINITE UNIVERSES is a genuine metaphysical possibility would be approximately 0.5). They would also give approximately equal weight to each of their *conditional* credences for INFINITE UNIVERSES, given that the hypothesis is genuinely possible (so that their new conditional credence would be approximately 0.1). Following this procedure would lead Joy to reduce her credence for INFINITE UNIVERSES from 0.19 (= 0.95 · 0.2) to approximately 0.05 (= 0.5 · 0.1) and would lead Lynne to *increase* her credence from approximately 0 to approximately 0.05.

Is it the judgment of common sense that this sort of equal weight response is rationally required? I have not conducted any sort of poll. Nonetheless, I highly doubt that there will be any sort of consensus that favors an equal weight verdict in MULTIVERSE. In my own case, at least, the pull toward an equal weight verdict is dramatically stronger in the restaurant case than in MULTIVERSE. While I am strongly inclined to judge that Lynne and Joy should become less confident in the wake of their disagreement, I am not inclined to judge that equal weighting is required. In the restaurant case, equal weighting appears to be the only principled response, since (I am inclined to say) neither thinker has any reason to think that he or she is the one who has reasoned correctly. But in MULTIVERSE, it seems that if one of the thinkers has some degree of insight into the correctness of her way of thinking about the matter (and/or some degree of insight into the wrongness of her friend's way of thinking about the matter), then she thereby *does* have reason to put more trust in her own view on the matter.

While I think that it is clear that the pull toward an equal weight verdict diminishes when one considers a case like MULTIVERSE, I am not claiming that the equal weight verdict is obviously incorrect in this case. At this point, my claim is more modest: because it is far from clear that an equal weight response is appropriate in a case like MULTIVERSE, the case for INDEPENDENCE is significantly less compelling once one corrects for the problem afflicting Christensen's restaurant argument. In chapters 3 and 4, I will undertake the more ambitious task of offering a positive argument against the equal weight response in MULTIVERSE and similar examples.

2.5 Schellenberg on Impartiality and the Aims of Inquiry

I now turn to an argument for epistemic impartiality developed by John Schellenberg.[11] His argument occurs in a context where he is arguing against the rationality of appealing to religious experience as a way of supporting religious belief in the face of religious disagreement. But as I will show, the epistemic principles Schellenberg defends have implications not just for appeals to religious experience but also for other ways of defending religious beliefs.

---

[11] J. L. Schellenberg, *The Wisdom to Doubt: A Justification of Religious Skepticism* (Ithaca: Cornell University Press, 2007).

2.5.1 Schellenberg's Commitment to Reasons Impartiality

Schellenberg's defense of epistemic impartiality (and of religious skepticism) is developed in critical conversation with William Alston's attempt to meet the epistemic challenge of religious pluralism in Alston's groundbreaking book *Perceiving God*. To adequately present Schellenberg's argument, it will be necessary to introduce some useful notions from Alston's work. The central questions of *Perceiving God* are, first, whether apparent perceptual experiences of God can confer prima facie epistemic justification on belief in God's existence, and second, whether this prima facie justification can stand in the face of supposed defeaters (and thus become *ultima facie* justification). Alston defends affirmative answers to both questions. In mounting his defense, he compares the merits of forming beliefs about God in response to "mystical" experiences with the merits of other "doxastic practices." A "doxastic practice" is "the exercise of a system or constellation of belief-forming habits or mechanisms, each realizing a function that yields beliefs with a certain kind of content from inputs of a certain type."[12] To simplify somewhat, one can think of doxastic practices as processes of belief formation. The components of a doxastic practice are not limited only to the processes that produce a belief (or an inclination to believe something), but may also include an "overrider system" that weakens or blocks beliefs that have prima facie support from the practice but that conflict with one's other beliefs or fail some other test of adequacy.[13] According to Alston, a person's doxastic state is the product of many such practices, including inferential, sensory, introspective, and memory-based practices (among others).

In some cases, the reliability of one doxastic practice can be established by means of one or more other practices (on the assumption that the reliability of the latter practices is not in question). For example, the reliability of forming beliefs by means of *hearing* could, in many cases, be established by means of vision. My belief that my wife is in the living room, based on my hearing her speak to me from there, is visually confirmed when I enter the living room and see her. But a key claim of Alston is that the reliability of many broad doxastic practices cannot be *independently* confirmed—that is, confirmed in a manner that utilizes other doxastic practices but *not* the

---

[12] William P. Alston, *Perceiving God: The Epistemology of Religious Experience* (Ithaca: Cornell University Press, 1991), 155.
[13] Alston, *Perceiving God*, 159.

practice whose reliability is under consideration. So suppose I ask my friend to give me evidence that his memory is not wholly unreliable (and perhaps unreliable in a systematically deceptive way that leads him into thinking that it has been reliable in the past). And suppose he answers by telling me that in the vast majority of occasions when he has checked to make sure that his memory is accurate, it has been. For example, when he has looked up a phone number to double-check his memory of it, he has nearly always found his memory to be accurate. Clearly, this reasoning fails to offer independent grounds for trusting in memory. In arguing that his memory is not wholly unreliable, he has appealed to beliefs that are themselves the product of memory. If my friend did not implicitly trust that his memory was not wholly unreliable (perhaps in a systematic and deceptive way), then he would have no reason to accept the veracity of the premises to which he has appealed. Thus, his argument suffers from what Alston calls *epistemic circularity*. An argument for the reliability of some belief-producing faculty is epistemically circular when one's belief in one or more of the premises in the argument depends on that very faculty.[14] Such an argument presupposes the truth of the conclusion rather than establishing it.

Adapting terminology from Alston, say that some doxastic practice of mine is *basic* if and only if I do not have good evidence (or even evidence I merely take to be good) for the reliability of the practice that is not epistemically circular.[15] On Alston's view, humans employ many doxastic practices that cannot be shown to be reliable without epistemic circularity and that therefore qualify as basic. As I showed earlier, the practice of forming beliefs

---

[14] The concept of epistemic circularity was originally developed in William P. Alston, "Epistemic Circularity," *Philosophy and Phenomenological Research* 47, no. 1 (September 1986): 1–30. While the term is Alston's, my characterization of epistemic circularity is adapted from Michael Bergmann, "Epistemic Circularity: Malignant and Benign," *Philosophy and Phenomenological Research* 69, no. 3 (2004): 710. See also Alston, *Perceiving God*, 108.

[15] Alston defines a basic "belief source" in the following way: "O is an (epistemologically) basic source of belief = df. Any (otherwise) cogent argument for the reliability of O will use premises drawn from O." (Alston, "Epistemic Circularity," 8.) While I am indebted to Alston for the notion of a basic belief source or basic doxastic practice, I think that his definition results in some sources being labeled as "basic" that ought to be excluded from the category and some sources being labeled as "nonbasic" that ought to be thought of as basic. First, suppose that subject S trusts belief source O on the basis of some non-epistemically circular argument that she *takes* to be cogent but that in fact is not. In fact, there are no cogent non-epistemically circular arguments for the reliability of O. Alston's definition implies that O is basic, but this does not seem appropriate since S's trust is based on independent reasons for trusting O that *appear* to S to be sufficient. Second, consider the case where there is some excellent, non-epistemically circular argument for the reliability of O, where S is not even dimly aware of this argument, and where S employs O despite thinking that there is no cogent, non-epistemically circular argument in favor of O. Clearly, O qualifies as being basic for S in this case, given that S's trust in O is not independently grounded. But Alston's definition—which is not relativized to a particular individual—categorizes O as nonbasic.

by memory is one such basic doxastic practice. Forming beliefs in response to hearing (or any other individual sense modality) may not be a basic practice, since other sense modalities can be used to corroborate such beliefs. Alston nevertheless thinks that the broader practice of forming beliefs on the basis of sense perception *is* basic.[16] He argues extensively for the claim that any argument for the reliability of sense perception is either a bad argument or is epistemically circular since it relies, at least implicitly, on perception.[17]

In arguing that sense perception (and many other noncontroversial practices) are not susceptible to noncircular support, Alston aims to defuse one of the principal charges brought against the doxastic practices particular to a given religion such as Christianity. Alston characterizes the Christian doxastic practice as one that gives prominent place to putative perceptions of God and that also employs various checks and overrider systems (including agreement with central teachings of scripture and Christian tradition). Alston allows that there is no non–epistemically circular way of establishing the reliability of this practice. Many conclude from this that it must be irrational to rely on the practice. Alston's counter to this charge is that many of the most trusted doxastic practices, including sense perception, are basic and thus not susceptible to noncircular justification. If one is unwilling to be a radical skeptic and stop trusting sense perception, one cannot consistently hold that the Christian doxastic practice should be rejected for the mere reason that its reliability cannot be independently established.

Alston might succeed in showing that religious doxastic practices should not be dismissed simply because they are not susceptible to noncircular justification. But this, of course, does not entail that one is justified in relying on religious doxastic practices. Alston recognizes this and attempts to rule out other reasons for thinking that religious doxastic practices are all unworthy of trust. Alston's full argument on behalf of religious doxastic practices is not my focus here. What is important, rather, is to understand the core epistemological picture painted by Alston, a picture Schellenberg takes for granted in his argument for epistemic impartiality and religious skepticism. The picture is one where everyone employs a variety of broad doxastic practices

---

[16] Given the way I have defined basic practices, Alston should be understood as arguing that sense perception *ought* to be basic (if employed at all), since if one rightly evaluated the arguments for its reliability one would see that there is no cogent argument that is not epistemically circular. Of course, some people might trust sense perception on the basis of some non–epistemically circular argument that is not cogent, and according to my definition sense perception would not be a basic practice for such people.

[17] Alston, *Perceiving God*, chap. 3.

that are basic since they lack support that is not epistemically circular. These doxastic practices may exhibit significant *self-support*, a feature that is perhaps not a trivial accomplishment. (One can, after all, imagine a situation where a doxastic practice is unreliable by its own lights: for example, if I seem to remember checking my memory a number of times and finding out on nearly every occasion that my memory beliefs were mistaken.) But these various doxastic practices cannot be confirmed by some independent and overarching practice that is epistemically superior.

Suppose I have before me a list of those basic doxastic practices that I am inclined to use and trust, at least before entertaining any critical questions about the reliability of any of these practices. Which of these practices are worthy of trust even after sober reflection on the sort of skeptical worries epistemologists entertain? Alston and Schellenberg defend very different answers to this question. In brief, Alston is rather liberal in his views about which of these practices can be rationally trusted. He argues that it is *practically* rational to affirm the reliability of a *socially established* doxastic practice as long as it has not been shown to be unreliable (for example, by generating internally incoherent beliefs, or by conflicting with the outputs of some more firmly entrenched practice).[18] Since Alston is not my focus at present, I will not discuss here what he means by "practical" rationality. I simply note that he thinks it is epistemically respectable for religious believers to rely on the religious doxastic practices of their communities as long as doing so does not involve them in any sort of incoherence. Furthermore, such trust can be perfectly rational even if the believer knows that her religious views are inconsistent with the outputs of alternative (and equally coherent and rational) religious doxastic practices.[19] So Alston explicitly opposes any requirement of epistemic impartiality.

Schellenberg contends that Alston is far too permissive in his views on which doxastic practices one can presumptively trust as reliable in the absence of external confirmation from some independent (and epistemically unassailable) doxastic practice. According to Schellenberg, the only practices that should be treated as "innocent until proven guilty" are those that are both *universal* among human beings (or at least nearly so) and *unavoidable*.[20] Any other doxastic practice must be shown to be reliable before it is rational to rely on it. It would appear that the various doxastic practices

---

[18] Alston, *Perceiving God*, chap. 4.
[19] Alston, *Perceiving God*, 274–376.
[20] Schellenberg, *The Wisdom to Doubt*, 169–175.

that produce and sustain the religious outlook of some religious community are neither universal nor unavoidable. Such practices are not universal, as is shown by the diversity of incompatible approaches to religious belief formation. Nor are such practices unavoidable, as is demonstrated by the great number of people who abandon their religious faith after critical reflection. Schellenberg's criteria thus appear to exclude such religious doxastic practices from being worthy of presumptive trust. In contrast, practices of relying on memory, sense perception, introspection, and certain sorts of inductive and deductive inference are nearly universal and are practically unavoidable. While the rationality of relying on such a doxastic practice could be defeated (for example, if it produced outputs that were sufficiently incoherent or that were in significant tension with the outputs of an equally trustworthy practice), Schellenberg holds that this kind of doxastic practice can be trusted without independent evidence of its reliability.

I'll hold off for a moment on presenting Schellenberg's reasons for thinking that default trust should be extended to all and only those practices that are universal and unavoidable. First, I want to justify my claim that by endorsing these criteria of universality and unavoidability, Schellenberg commits himself to a very demanding reasons impartiality requirement. The key point here is that if some line of reasoning is not dispute-neutral, then any doxastic practice that involves accepting that line of reasoning will not be universal. Suppose I believe that p on the basis of evidence E and reasoning $r1$. And suppose that $r1$ is not dispute-neutral, since even if my disputants and I had the same evidence and fully disclosed our reasoning concerning p, some of my disputants would reject $r1$ even as I continue to accept it. In this case, my doxastic practice that involves accepting $r1$ is not universal. So according to Schellenberg's criteria, this doxastic practice is not worthy of default trust.

Of course, it might be that my acceptance of $r1$ is not the output of a practice that I trust by default but is instead the output of a practice that I have independent reasons for trusting. For example, my belief in the reliability of the doxastic practice that leads me to accept $r1$ might be based on an independent line of reasoning $r2$. If $r2$ would be universally accepted by those who hear and understand it (and who share my evidence), then a doxastic practice that involves accepting $r2$ might be worthy of default trust (according to Schellenberg's view). But on the assumption that $r2$ would be universally accepted by those who share evidence E, then when considering the *entirety* of my reasoning that grounds my belief that p, it turns out that my grounds are dispute-neutral after all. For my disputants would accept $r2$ (upon understanding *r2*), which would in turn lead them to accept *r1* and thus *p*. So, while Schellenberg's criteria would not rule out my justifiably believing that *p* in this case, neither would an epistemic impartiality requirement.

But suppose that the entirety of my grounds for *p* fails to be dispute-neutral, so that the chain of my reasons for accepting *p* does not "bottom out" with some line of reasoning that would be accepted by my disputants (even if I fully shared my evidence and adequately communicated my reasoning). In this case, I will be conferring default trust on a doxastic practice that is not universal and will thus violate Schellenberg's criteria.

One worry about my argument that Schellenberg is committed to epistemic impartiality is that it relies on the assumption that doxastic practices can be individuated as narrowly (or broadly) as one wants. And one might worry that the narrow way in which I characterize doxastic practices in the argument is not what Schellenberg has in mind, and that my argument therefore does not fairly characterize his position. I claim in the foregoing argument that if *E* is my evidence and I believe that *p* on the basis of reasoning *r1*, then I employ a doxastic practice that involves accepting *r1* when *E* is one's evidence and *r1* is adequately understood. But suppose that in fact I am employing a "permissive" doxastic practice that permits someone with evidence *E* to either accept *r1* or reject *r1*. In this case, one cannot infer from the fact that my disputants reject *r1* that they are employing a different doxastic practice. Perhaps they are employing the same doxastic practice, but in their case the same practice has a different output.

My response to this suggestion is that the claim that my disputants and I are employing the same permissive practice in assessing *r1* is compatible with the claim that my disputants and I are also relying on different doxastic practices. Though my disputants and I may be employing the same broad, coarse-grained practices, the narrow, fine-grained processes that we employ will differ. Since practices may be characterized at different levels of generality, I could accurately be characterized as employing a permissive doxastic practice that does not take a stance on *r1* while *at the same time* employing a more narrowly construed practice that is committed to *r1*'s acceptance.

But now the worry about my argument comes into clear focus: my argument assumes that doxastic practices may be individuated as narrowly as one wants, but this assumption is arguably not faithful to the notion of a doxastic practice that Schellenberg is appropriating from Alston. The doxastic practices Alston speaks of are typically quite broad groupings of belief-forming mechanisms, including such broad mechanisms as sense perception, memory-based belief formation, and so on. Even when he considers more narrowly individuated belief-forming practices (such as religion-specific doxastic practices), these are still reasonably broad. If practices should be individuated using broad criteria, then perhaps one should not conclude that two people who share evidence but disagree about some bit of reasoning thereby rely on different doxastic practices. So perhaps there is room for Schellenberg to advocate a strong universality condition for presumptive innocence while allowing that competent thinkers with equivalent evidence can reasonably stand by their views in the face of significant disagreement.

Schellenberg does not address the question of how broadly or narrowly one should individuate doxastic practices when applying the criteria of universality and unavoidability, so I cannot claim in certain terms that he is committed to a strong form of reasons impartiality. Nonetheless, I think that it is not uncharitable to think that Schellenberg would endorse the conclusion that his conditions impose a reasons impartiality constraint. For starters, Alston, the source of the notion of a "doxastic practice," acknowledges that there can be significant flexibility in how one individuates practices. He writes: "there is no one uniquely right way to group mechanisms into practices. A doxastic practice has only 'conceptual' reality. It proves convenient for one or another theoretical purpose to group particular mechanisms into larger aggregations, but a 'practice' is not something with an objective reality that constrains us to do the grouping in a certain way."[21] In line with this view, it can be assumed that Schellenberg's criteria for presumptive innocence apply to both narrow and broad practices unless there is a well-motivated reason for restricting those criteria. And Schellenberg's arguments for the criteria, to be discussed shortly, seem to pertain to narrow practices as much as to broad practices.

As far as I can tell, Schellenberg *should* be prepared to follow his arguments all the way to an endorsement of a fully general reasons impartiality constraint. In any case, his argument for the universality criterion constitutes an interesting way of motivating a strong reasons impartiality requirement. This way of motivating reasons impartiality deserves careful attention whether or not Schellenberg would count himself as an advocate of reasons impartiality requirements.

---

[21] Alston, *Perceiving God*, 165.

2.5.2 The Doxastic Minimalism Argument

I turn now to Schellenberg's reasons for thinking that presumptive innocence should be granted only to those doxastic practices that are universal
and unavoidable. Keeping in mind that Schellenberg's defense of these criteria occurs in a context where he is arguing against presumptive trust in
beliefs arising out of "mystical" experiences, here is his opening case for
these criteria:

> Although we must utilize some practice to get going in inquiry, there
> is clearly still a question as to which one(s). It seems natural and
> appropriate—and has seemed so to others on whom Alston draws, like
> Thomas Reid—to go with what is universal and unavoidable here, and thus
> to restrict ourselves, at least initially, to such practices as those we call sen-
> sory, introspective, memorial, and (rationally) intuitive. But how can we
> prevent this restriction from being arbitrary? I would argue that it is *pre-
> cisely because of* the requirements of an investigative stance and an inves-
> tigative aim that it is non-arbitrary. If we really are would-be investigators,
> concerned for the truth and seeking understanding, then we will ascribe
> epistemic innocence—even an initial innocence—*only where we have to:*
> assuming that we have to pick certain belief-forming practices as innocent
> until proven guilty to get started, we will still pick only what we have to
> pick, in order to minimize the extent to which non-inquiry-based factors
> influence the direction of inquiry. (After all, if we are inquirers, we want as
> much as possible of what we believe and do to be *grounded* in inquiry: as
> the principles of justification I have been utilizing have it, we want suffi-
> cient and overall good *evidence*.)[22]

In this initial (and partial) defense of the criteria of universality and unavoidability, Schellenberg argues for what he later labels "doxastic minimalism."[23] The key idea of doxastic minimalism is that one should minimize
the role that default trust plays in one's cognitive life. For this reason, one
should seek to minimize the number of *basic* (i.e., presumptively innocent)
doxastic practices one employs. Since one cannot *establish* the reliability
of basic doxastic practices, and since (according to Schellenberg) genuine

[22] Schellenberg, *The Wisdom to Doubt*, 170.
[23] Schellenberg, *The Wisdom to Doubt*, 173.

inquirers aim to believe only what is established, one should rely on as few basic practices as possible.

It is easy to see how doxastic minimalism could lead to the conclusion that default trust should be limited to those practices that are *unavoidable*. Where a practice can be avoided, one ought to exercise the unsparing axe of the doxastic minimalist. But where a practice is genuinely unavoidable, furthering the minimalist aim is impossible and one can hardly be faulted for continuing to trust it. But why should doxastic minimalism also require that default trust be further restricted to doxastic practices that are *universal*? If one finds oneself with some basic doxastic practice that is unavoidable (for oneself) but not universal, why isn't one rationally entitled to trust this practice? As an example, consider someone in colonial America who was raised to believe that chattel slavery is morally abhorrent and who simply cannot get rid of this belief even after discovering that the belief is not universally shared.[24] Is this person's unavoidable belief in the wrongness of slavery irrational because it is the product of a nonuniversal doxastic practice?

Unfortunately, Schellenberg does not address the possibility of an individually unavoidable but nonuniversal basic doxastic practice. Indeed, he does not even explicitly spell out what he means by "universal" and "unavoidable" in this context. But according to one initially plausible way of understanding Schellenberg's reasoning quoted above, he should be prepared to admit the reasonability of extending default trust to a nonuniversal but individually unavoidable practice. On this interpretation, the key premises that ground his criteria for presumptive innocence are doxastic minimalism and a "rationally ought implies can" principle. Doxastic minimalism says that adopting an initially skeptical attitude toward doxastic practices is epistemically good (since this restrains the influence of default trust). The "rationally ought implies can" principle says that one rationally ought to adopt an initially skeptical attitude toward a practice only if one *can* do so. In the moral domain, it is often claimed that an action cannot be morally required of one if one is unable to perform it; the "rationally ought implies can" principle carries this principle over to the rational domain and asserts that one cannot be *rationally* required to adopt an attitude that one is unable to adopt.

[24] This example, which seems to reveal an embarrassing implication of epistemic impartiality requirements, is inspired by an example of Plantinga in *Warranted Christian Belief* (New York: Oxford University Press, 2000), 450.

If this principle is presupposed by Schellenberg, then it seems that he should concede that the antislavery belief in my example is justified, even though it is not based on a universal doxastic practice.

Because a "rationally ought implies can" principle does not comport with Schellenberg's insistence on the "universality" condition for presumptive innocence, there is reason to doubt that he means to rely on this principle. In his discussion following the passage quoted above, he gestures toward a principle that is *somewhat* similar to the "rationally ought implies can" but that supports the universality condition. Throughout his discussion, Schellenberg seems concerned with what is unavoidable for people *as human inquirers* and not with what may or may not be unavoidable for some particular individual. Consider, for example, the following passage.

> One might want to say, as intimated above, that universality and unavoidability are required because only where they are present is one forced by the human cognitive condition to go along: we would like to substantiate more fully even such belief-forming practices if we could, but because we cannot, and because to do so is a necessary condition of arriving at any truth and understanding that might be possible for us, we concede defeat and settle for what is basically a naked assumption instead.
>
> But there is something else here too, already suggested by all this talk of what we "want," which puts things in a somewhat different perspective. Because we find ourselves unable to *not* form and revise beliefs on the basis of sense perception, introspection, memory, and rational intuition, a certain basic picture of the world has been generated involving birth and conscious experience and physical objects and relations with other conscious beings and the reality of things past and death and also the appropriateness of *valuation* (presupposed by the humblest desires, and sanctioned by intuition). This picture appears to be our common inheritance. It becomes part of the very fabric of a human being, affecting one's sense of identity and of connectedness to others and of value and thus also of the appropriate goals, *including intellectual goals.* What we can see here—and some of what Alston says about the psychological and social establishment of our basic belief-forming practices is in accord with this—is that we are not independent, truth-registering machines that care not what the truth is and would question everything if we could, but rather deeply *human* inquirers, whose humanity and the basic picture

with which it is intertwined do much to shape the nature of our inquiring impulse.[25]

Schellenberg reveals that he is concerned for what is exigent in virtue of a person's *humanity* (rather than in virtue of his or her particular upbringing, for example). This may suggest a view according to which the rational norms that pertain to some subject are sensitive to the capacities and limitations of her *species* or the *general kind* of being that she is, rather than being sensitive only to her more particular capacities and limitations.

Such a view is not without some plausibility. Suppose that some adult human being is torn between the view that $2 + 1 = 3$ and the view that $2 + 1 = 4$ (assigning equal credence to both possibilities). People are likely to judge that this stance is irrational even if they know that it is absolutely unavoidable for her (perhaps due to some strange bit of irreversible neural programming). But if some adult human being thinks that the hundredth digit of pi is just as likely to be odd as it is even, people are likely to judge that this uncertainty is perfectly rational. This is true even if people know that for some alien species the value of the one-hundredth digit of pi would be as transparently obvious as the value of "2 + 1" is to humans. In these examples, mathematical uncertainty that results from the limitations of the human species is rationally acceptable, while mathematical uncertainty that arises from some idiosyncratic constraint may be judged irrational.

If Schellenberg is relying on the idea that rational obligations are limited by species-level limitations (and perhaps species-level investigative interests as well) but not by more particular limitations (or community-specific investigative interests), then one can better understand how he arrives at the criterion of universality. The presupposition of his argument may be that "rationally ought implies *humanly* possible." If doubting some doxastic practice is not humanly possible, then one is not required to doubt it. But if my inability to doubt some doxastic practice is particular to me or my particular group, then this does not exempt me from the skeptical prescriptions of doxastic minimalism.

On this reading of Schellenberg, the unavoidable doxastic practices are to be understood as those that are *humanly* unavoidable. Unavoidability therefore entails universality. This means that Schellenberg has really offered only

---

[25] Schellenberg, *The Wisdom to Doubt*, 172–173.

one criterion for presumptive innocence. The fact that my suggested reading collapses Schellenberg's two criteria into one is not, I think, a significant count against my interpretation. The language of "universality" is not otiose since it serves to clarify the sort of unavoidability that Schellenberg is really interested in.

Taking a step back from exegesis of Schellenberg, here is one interesting argument for reasons impartiality that I think he means to advocate, and that in any case is worthy of consideration. Inquirers who aim at truth should seek to minimize the influence of default trust on their doxastic states. Of course, completely eliminating default trust in any doxastic practices would result in the most radical sort of skepticism. But this radical skepticism need not concern human inquirers since complete elimination of default trust is humanly impossible. Normal human inquirers cannot avoid forming those beliefs that arise from sense perception, memory, basic inductive inferences, and so on. But how much further should we human beings extend default trust in the conduct of our doxastic lives? No further. While we cannot do anything about that trust that is endemic to our human situation (and thus have no obligations to extirpate humanly unavoidable doxastic practices), our interest in truth should constrain us from extending default trust beyond what is inevitable for creatures like us. Doxastic minimalism requires of a human inquirer that she build on a foundation of belief that, for someone with their evidence, is *humanly unavoidable* (at least after sufficiently careful consideration) and thus *uncontroversial*. If a particular belief of some individual is the product of reasoning that would continue to be significantly contested even after all of the relevant evidence and reasoning has been disclosed, then this belief is the product of a nonuniversal doxastic practice that is illegitimately taken to be presumptively innocent. Commitment to the truth requires the person to stop relying on the practice and to give up the belief in question.

Schellenberg is not alone in thinking that one should extend default trust only to those doxastic practices that are universal. Sanford Goldberg, for example, advances an argument that is reminiscent of Schellenberg when he explains why one should not extend default trust to processes of religious belief formation even if one is right to extend such trust to sense perception. Goldberg notes that perceptual processes differ from processes of religious belief formation in being "part of the human natural endowment," and he thinks this difference helps to explain why "no one is entitled to rely on any process of revelation [the term Goldberg uses for any process of religious belief formation] unless she has independent reasons to think that the process in question is in fact reliable (rather than one of the unreliable 'look-alikes,' as it were)."[26]

In addition to agreeing that those practices that are part of the natural human endowment should be privileged, Goldberg and Schellenberg both emphasize that inquirers have a legitimate interest in trusting enough practices to form a "rich system of justified belief,"[27] and to "get past the most general skepticism."[28] But neither thinker believes that this interest could help to exonerate religious belief. As Goldberg notes, "epistemic impoverishment is not the unavoidable consequence of a refusal to rely on revelation."[29]

In light of this additional emphasis on the importance of avoiding sweeping skepticism, perhaps Schellenberg could be understood as putting forward two independent considerations that can make it reasonable to extend default trust to a doxastic practice (and that therefore place boundaries on the extent of one's doxastic minimalism). First, extending default trust to a practice is reasonable when one is *compelled* to do so by human nature (this follows from the "rationally ought implies humanly possible" principle). Second, it is reasonable to extend default trust when failing to do so would result in general skepticism and severe epistemic impoverishment. Perhaps Schellenberg thinks that this second consideration does not justify any instances of default trust that would not already be justified by the first consideration. This might explain why he mentions it in passing and focuses most of his discussion on the universality and unavoidability criteria.

I'll call Schellenberg's argument for limiting default trust to unavoidable universal practices the "doxastic minimalism argument." It is now time to assess its merits. Drawing on William James, I will argue in the next section that Schellenberg's depiction of the aims of inquiry is impoverished and one-sided. A more adequate account of the aims of inquiry does not lead one to conclude that committed inquirers are doxastic minimalists. In addition, I will argue that the restrictions Schellenberg imposes on doxastic minimalism are epistemically arbitrary. There is no good reason for thinking that all and only those practices that are part of humans' natural inheritance should be exempt from the otherwise unsparing axe of the doxastic minimalist.

---

[26] Sanford Goldberg, "Does Externalist Epistemology Rationalize Religious Commitment?," in *Religious Faith and Intellectual Virtue*, ed. Timothy O'Connor and Laura Frances Callahan (Oxford: Oxford University Press, 2014), 293–294.

[27] Goldberg, "Does Externalist Epistemology Rationalize Religious Commitment?," 293.

[28] Schellenberg, *The Wisdom to Doubt*, 171.

[29] Goldberg, "Does Externalist Epistemology Rationalize Religious Commitment?," 293.

2.6 A Jamesian Critique of Schellenberg's
Doxastic Minimalism

For the moment, I will grant that one is justified in extending default trust to those doxastic practices that are humanly unavoidable and focus critical attention on Schellenberg's claim that no practices beyond this set should be treated as presumptively innocent. Schellenberg suggests that this doxastic minimalism is in keeping with the "investigative stance" since investigators who are "concerned for the truth" will want to "minimize the extent to which non-inquiry-based factors influence the direction of inquiry."[30] On Schellenberg's view, one should not (and cannot) completely eliminate the influence of "non-inquiry-based factors," since one must trust in universal and unavoidable doxastic practices whose reliability cannot be established by means of (independent) inquiry. But these practices do not supply answers to all of the questions that may be of interest. In order to arrive at views on questions that are controversial (and that would remain so even after evidence sharing), it would be necessary to employ additional doxastic practices that are *not* humanly unavoidable. Employing these practices would allow one to take a stance on controversial matters, thereby allowing one to fill out one's picture of the world. But doing this would also widen the influence of default trust on one's doxastic stance. And according to Schellenberg, the true investigator will never extend the scope of default trust in order to arrive at a more opinionated take on the world. Doing so would fail to show the regard for the truth that is essential to the investigative stance.

Curiously, Schellenberg does not here address William James's well-known contention that the investigator's concern for the truth consists of not one but two distinct (and often conflicting) aims: the aim of avoiding error and the aim of believing the truth.[31] When considering Schellenberg's account of investigative aims in light of James's important insight, Schellenberg's account looks implausibly one-sided. James notes that one can succeed in avoiding erroneous belief on some question by remaining agnostic and withholding belief altogether. But error avoidance is not the only good that human inquirers pursue in managing their opinions. They also seek to believe truths. And while being agnostic with respect to some question may guarantee that

---

[30] Schellenberg, *The Wisdom to Doubt*, 170.
[31] William James, *The Will to Believe and Other Essays in Popular Philosophy* (New York: Longmans, Green and Co., 1896), 17–18. William James does not receive an entry in the index of Schellenberg's *Wisdom to Doubt*.

one avoids erroneous belief, it also guarantees that one fails to believe the truth on the matter. Thus, it should not be assumed that the investigator who is concerned for the truth will remain agnostic on some question anytime the evidence is less than fully conclusive. Encompassed within a "concern for the truth" is the aim of holding true opinions as well as the aim of avoiding error, and there is no reason to assume that the latter must always trump the former. To the extent that one prioritizes the aim of believing the truth, it will be reasonable to rely on practices that produce beliefs in the place of agnosticism, even if the possibility of error is salient. Transposing James's insights into a credence framework, to the extent that one prioritizes being confident in truths, it will be reasonable to extend default trust to doxastic practices that lead one toward more confident and opinionated credences. And to the extent that one prioritizes avoidance of mistaken confidence in falsehoods, it will be reasonable to withhold default trust from such practices, leaving one instead with more tentative credence assignments (or perhaps in the case of some propositions, with no determinate credence assignment whatsoever).[32]

In holding that the committed investigator will (as far as possible) be a doxastic minimalist, Schellenberg presupposes without argument that the aim of error avoidance always trumps the aim of believing the truth. And this assumption is dubious. If forced to pick one of the epistemic aims identified by James as the aim that is most fundamental to human inquiry, there is good reason to choose the aim of believing the truth. The aim of error avoidance is not by itself sufficient to motivate inquiry since one could satisfy this aim merely by adopting a radical skepticism that is agnostic on every question. It seems that the impulse to investigate requires that at least some weight be given to the aim of believing the truth. Moreover, this aim is sufficient to give one reason to continue investigating as long as one recognizes that one's current beliefs may not be true.

Schellenberg's rationale for doxastic minimalism is unsound. Once it is allowed that committed inquirers may value believing the truth alongside error avoidance, there is no straightforward way of arguing from the aims of inquiry to the conclusion that extending default trust to an avoidable doxastic practice is always bad (or always good).

I've argued that aims of inquiry need not incline one toward doxastic minimalism. But suppose that I am wrong about this. Suppose that my

---

[32] Whether one can make sense of James's dual aims within a credence framework, and how best to do so, are difficult and controversial questions. I pass over this controversy here.

commitment to an investigative stance gives me a reason (though perhaps a defeasible one) to resist extending default trust to additional doxastic practices. Even granting this, Schellenberg's overall argument for withholding trust from religious doxastic practices is dubious. He acknowledges that one cannot be absolutely committed to doxastic minimalism, since withholding default trust from *every* doxastic practice would require radical skepticism (something Schellenberg assumes is not rationally required). So he proposes that those practices that are universal and humanly unavoidable are the sole exception to what is otherwise an unsparing doxastic minimalism. Against this position, I will argue the following. First, if one's reason for giving special treatment to universal and humanly unavoidable practices is the fact of their unavoidability, then one must admit that radical skepticism would be rationally required if it were possible, and that one's nonskeptical outlook is in a certain sense lamentable. And this concedes too much to the skeptic. Second, there is no principled basis for singling out universal and unavoidable practices other than the fact of their unavoidability. Thus, for someone who does not want to concede significant ground to the skeptic, there are no principled reasons for maintaining that the only practices that should be spared from doxastic minimalism are those that are universal and humanly unavoidable.

To advance my argument, it will be helpful to consider a hypothetical example where, due to advances in human cognitive manipulation, one or more of the doxastic practices Schellenberg endorses as presumptively innocent is no longer universal and unavoidable. I'll take as the focus of my example human beings' way of forming beliefs about whether other human beings are conscious—that is, whether they are creatures with subjectively felt experience (and are not organic "robots," or "zombies," to use philosophical parlance, who behave normally and represent themselves as having conscious sensations but in fact have no subjectively felt experiences).[33]

The practice of confidently attributing consciousness to just about any human being who talks (or communicates intelligibly in some other way) is about as universal and unavoidable as a doxastic practice can be. I'll refer to this practice as the "universal consciousness attribution" practice. This practice is almost certainly basic for a great many of the individuals who employ it. There are multiple reasons for affirming that the practice is typically

---

[33] In focusing on one's beliefs concerning the consciousness of others in order to cast religious belief in a favorable light, I am following a strategy pioneered by Alvin Plantinga in *God and Other Minds: A Study of the Rational Justification of Belief in God* (Ithaca: Cornell University Press, 1967).

basic. For starters, it does not seem that the belief in what may be called the "universal consciousness thesis" (the view that nearly all human beings who communicate are conscious) is a belief that is typically reached by way of inductive reasoning. To be sure, some philosophers have offered arguments for the thesis. Perhaps the argument with the most merit is an inductive argument that starts by noting that certain of one's behaviors are attended by certain subjective experiences (for example, wincing and exclaiming "Ouch!" is attended by the feeling of pain). This argument then concludes on the basis of induction that other beings exhibiting similar behaviors also have similar subjective experiences (and must therefore be conscious). Whether or not this argument is a strong one, it is doubtful that such sophisticated inductive reasoning is the basis for, say, a toddler's firm belief that her crying brother "feels bad." And even if inferential reasoning of this sort *does* occasion the belief of the toddler (and others), belief in the universal consciousness thesis does not seem to depend on continued endorsement of the sort of inferential reasoning in question. Certainly, many philosophers do not think that there is overwhelming inductive support for the universal consciousness thesis, yet they continue to be quite certain of the truth of the thesis.

I count myself among those who think that there are at best weak inductive reasons for believing in other conscious minds, reasons that are not sufficient in strength to justify my certainty regarding the universal consciousness thesis. Certain behaviors of mine (e.g., exclaiming "Ouch!" when I touch a hot pan) are invariably attended by certain subjective sensations (e.g., pain). Does this give me a strong reason for thinking that when another person manifests the same sorts of behavior, they have similar sensations (or at least *some* sort of subjective sensation)? Arguably, I am justified in extrapolating from my own case only to the extent that I am justified in thinking that there is no difference between me and the other person that might explain why the other person is not conscious even though I am. And since we humans presently lack any real understanding of why matter configured in certain ways should give rise to conscious experience, we do not have a firm grip on what sort of factors might make a difference as to whether or not an organism is conscious. We therefore cannot definitively establish *through argument* that there is no relevant difference between me and some other (apparently normal) individual that could account for why I am conscious and they are not. Perhaps consciousness is a fragile affair and it only "takes" in individuals who experienced conditions in early childhood that were "just right." Perhaps there is a loving God who sees to it that those who will experience lives of hardship and tragedy are not conscious. Perhaps consciousness typically flickers off sometime in late middle age (even while normal speech and behavior continues on). I don't believe any of these possibilities, of course, but I can hardly show that these possibilities (and countless other "limited consciousness" theses) are false.

Realizing this, I do not think that I have a compelling inductive basis for highly confident belief in the universal consciousness thesis. Nor do I think that I can in some other way provide independent confirmation of the reliability of universal consciousness attribution. Nonetheless, I am for all practical purposes certain that other human beings who intelligibly communicate are conscious. Since my beliefs on this matter are not dependent on validation by some other doxastic practice, it seems that my practice of universally attributing consciousness is basic. Clearly, I am not especially unusual in this regard. Most others who concede (rightly or wrongly) that there is no good independent reason to trust their consciousness attributions nonetheless remain fully confident in their beliefs attributing consciousness to others.

Since universal consciousness attribution is a universal and unavoidable practice, and since this practice is basic for at least a great many people, Schellenberg would presumably allow that one can justifiably extend default trust to the practice. But now I'll consider what he might say about a situation where the ability was developed to make this hitherto unavoidable practice *avoidable*. Suppose that some drug is developed that has the peculiar effect of blocking the otherwise irresistible inclination to attribute consciousness to other communicating human beings. The drug does not make people inclined to *deny* that others are conscious but merely removes people's natural bias in favor of attributing conscious to others. Someone who has taken the drug typically finds that she is, at least initially, highly unsure about whether any particular person is conscious. Some who have taken the drug go on to form opinions on how far consciousness extends, though these opinions are based on controversial philosophical or scientific arguments and do not often lead to certainty on the matter. Suppose also that there is significant variation in the opinions reached by those who have taken the drug and who are left to form their views on the basis of philosophical and/or scientific argument alone. Some do ultimately endorse the universal consciousness thesis; others hold that consciousness is the privilege only of some select group (the highly intelligent, for example, or God's "elect," or nonpsychopaths); others remain skeptical and refrain from endorsing any single view.

While this sort of hypothetical scenario is far-fetched, there is no reason to think that it is impossible. It is therefore entirely fair to consider what responses Schellenberg might commend in the envisioned scenario, in order to see whether there are plausible responses that can be reconciled with his doxastic minimalism argument. So I'll consider what he might say to the question of whether someone who is committed to what Schellenberg calls the "investigative stance" ought to take the hypothetical drug (assuming there are no other relevant consequences to taking it). I will argue that any answer Schellenberg might give poses a problem for his views on presumptive trust.

First, consider the possibility that Schellenberg would endorse taking the drug. His rationale for adopting this position would presumably be that those who are truly committed to the investigative stance should ascribe initial epistemic innocence "only where we have to . . . in order to minimize the extent to which non-inquiry-based factors influence the direction of inquiry." Though without the drug people cannot help attributing consciousness to normal human beings (and doing so for reasons that are independent of any serious inquiry), the development of the drug would eliminate this necessity. Taking the drug would allow people to further reduce the influence played by default trust, and Schellenberg seems to view the reduction of such influence as an improvement in humans' epistemic condition. While taking the drug would lead the honest inquirer to skepticism about the prevalence of consciousness among other human beings, so be it. As she does in the domain of religion, the truly committed investigator is willing to embrace skeptical positions when doxastic minimalism requires it.

If this is the response that is in fact implied by Schellenberg's position, then many will take this implication to be sufficient reason for rejecting his position. He may not require that people *presently* be skeptical about the prevalence of other conscious minds. But any view that would endorse such skepticism in the event that it became a legitimate possibility is a view that departs significantly from common sense. Most would view skepticism about the prevalence of consciousness among human beings not as an epistemic improvement but as some sort of disability or insanity.

Furthermore, the claim that people should take the drug should it become available is in deep tension with the view that people are *currently* rationally justified in confidently believing the universal consciousness thesis. If people presently know that they should take the drug should it be developed, then they can presently see that their beliefs concerning consciousness suffer from an epistemic deficiency that should be remedied if given the opportunity. So if Schellenberg would endorse taking the drug, then he should already view people's belief in the universal consciousness thesis as a presently unavoidable but nonetheless rationally deficient commitment. Granted, without access to the hypothetical drug a person perhaps cannot be *blamed* for maintaining this epistemically deficient belief. This may very well be an instance of blameless irrationality, as in other instances where someone is "trapped" in unreasonable and groundless belief. Nonetheless, it seems that the proper attitude toward these beliefs (of someone who would endorse taking the drug) is disappointed resignation, not cheerful acceptance. The beliefs should be viewed as presently groundless and irrational, however unavoidable they may be.

If Schellenberg endorsed taking the hypothetical drug, then his position would collapse into a fairly radical form of skepticism. Of course, a brave few may be prepared to embrace this result. But an epistemological outlook that supports this sort of skepticism does not give one reason to think that that there is some special problem facing one's *controversial* beliefs. On such an outlook, controversial beliefs, including one's religious beliefs, would be in the same problematic position as a great many uncontroversial beliefs, including the belief in the universal consciousness thesis and many commonsense moral beliefs. Since I am interested in whether disagreement defeats religious beliefs that might otherwise be justified, I can set aside positions that imply that many noncontroversial beliefs of common sense are epistemically deficient.

I now turn to Schellenberg's other alternative: to deny that taking the drug would be epistemically desirable. I suspect that this second alternative would more likely be his actual position, since it is easy to see that the first position slides into a sort of radical skepticism that he seems keen to avoid. I will argue that there is no plausible way for Schellenberg to defend this response while simultaneously insisting that default trust should be limited to practices that are universal and unavoidable.

How might Schellenberg defend the epistemic acceptability of *not* taking the "consciousness skepticism" drug while *also* endorsing a doxastic minimalism that aims to minimize the influence of default trust? I see three possibilities, all of which find some support in Schellenberg's discussion.

First, Schellenberg might justify not taking the drug by appealing to the genuine need to "get past the most general skepticism."[34] There are, I grant, doxastic practices that must be trusted in order to avoid pervasive

[34] Schellenberg, *The Wisdom to Doubt*, 171.

skepticism, such as sense perception and memory. But skepticism with re-spect to the prevalence of other conscious minds certainly does not come close to any sort of "general" skepticism. So the interest in avoiding sweeping skepticism does not provide any reason to look favorably on the practice of universal consciousness attribution. Perhaps Schellenberg could allow that people have a legitimate interest in avoiding not just general skepticism but also narrower forms of skepticism in specific domains. But it's not clear why an opposition to narrow forms of skepticism would vindicate trust in uni-versal consciousness attribution (even in the event that this process became avoidable) but would not vindicate trust in one's process of religious belief formation.

Second, Schellenberg might defend not taking the drug by arguing that humans have special epistemic reason to trust those practices that are part of their *natural* inheritance, even if what is natural ceases being unavoid-able. This position may be implied when Schellenberg approvingly notes that people are not "independent, truth-registering machines" but are in-stead "deeply *human* inquirers" whose intellectual aims are deeply shaped by humans' "common inheritance." Why, though, should what is natural be es-pecially deserving of people's trust? To be sure, one might provide arguments for why evolved doxastic practices common to human beings are likely to be epistemically reliable. But it is doubtful that such an argument will be convincing for every natural doxastic practice. In particular, there is some reason to think that whether or not belief in the universal consciousness thesis is true, this belief would be advantageous for individuals and social groups and thus favored by natural selection. The belief that others are con-scious promotes care and respect for others, which is good for the family and larger social units. So even if universal consciousness attribution is worthy of default trust on account of its naturalness, this basis for default trust would presumably be defeated once someone realized that there is in this case no non-question-begging reason to think that natural selection favors epistemic reliability. In short, I see no reason for thinking that the "naturalness" of people's consciousness attributions is of any epistemic significance.

Third, Schellenberg might argue that consciousness skepticism should be resisted for "practical" rather than epistemic reasons. Roughly speaking, *ep-istemic* reasons for or against believing that *p* are considerations that bear on the question of whether *p* is probable or plausible. In contrast, *practical* reasons for believing that *p* do not bear on the question of whether *p* is plau-sible or probable. Instead, they bear on the question of whether it would in some way be good or useful to believe that *p* (for example, because the belief is morally required, or because it helps in the pursuit of some goal). Many philosophers appeal to broadly practical concerns when attempting to explain the reasonableness of trusting some basic doxastic practice or cognitive faculty.[35] And if there are any doxastic practices that people are justified in trusting on the basis of practical reasons, then there is good reason to think that people's practice of attributing consciousness to other normal human beings is one such practice. Quite plausibly, doubts about the consciousness of some individual would severely threaten people's degree of concern for the individual and motivation to treat that person with moral respect. Taking a drug that might lead me to doubt the universal consciousness thesis would therefore be to court moral disaster. This consideration might justify people continuing to trust the practice of universal consciousness attribution even if that practice ceases to be unavoidable. In the case of religious belief on the other hand the moral stakes may not be so high. Thus, the differences in the practical stakes might explain why one should exempt universal consciousness attribution from the requirements of doxastic minimalism even though one should not extend a similar exemption to religious doxastic practices.

The initial problem with the position just sketched is that many religious believers insist that a great deal rides on whether someone holds the correct religious beliefs. Many Buddhists maintain that seeing through the illusion of the self is the key to escaping suffering and the self-centeredness that inhibits moral compassion. On this view, to stop trusting those insights that ground the no-self view would be to invite unhappiness and selfishness. Many theists hold that the greatest fulfillment comes from a loving relationship with the world's creator and that full realization of this relationship requires believing in the reality of such a creator and understanding something of the creator's good intentions for humankind. From this perspective, abandoning belief in God's existence in the name of doxastic minimalism would cheat people (at least for a time) of the intimate relationship with God wherein human beings may find ultimate fulfillment. Even if the religious believer were to acknowledge that religious unbelief is *less* disastrous than not believing the universal consciousness thesis, the believer may still think that religious unbelief is highly costly. And if both kinds of unbelief would result in significant

---

[35] See, for example, Alston, *Perceiving God*, 168; Crispin Wright, "Warrant for Nothing (and Foundations for Free)?," *Aristotelian Society Supplementary Volume* 78, no. 1 (2004): 167–212; David Enoch and Joshua Schechter, "How Are Basic Belief-Forming Methods Justified?," *Philosophy and Phenomenological Research* 76, no. 3 (2008): 547–579.

existential and/or moral costs, then there is no principled basis for exempting one practice from doxastic minimalism but not the other.

Schellenberg explicitly contests the suggestion that the practical benefits of religious belief are significant enough to justify such belief in the absence of independent epistemic support.[36] A key contention in his argument is that the benefits that allegedly result from having religious *belief* can just as easily be attained by having religious *faith*. According to Schellenberg's view of faith, having faith that some religious outlook is true does not require *believing* the central tenets of that outlook. More strongly, Schellenberg holds that having faith that p is *incompatible* with believing that p. On Schellenberg's understanding of propositional faith, a person who has faith that p neither believes that p nor its negation but nonetheless imaginatively represents the world to himself as including the state of affairs that p.[37] And he does this "tenaciously and persistently."[38] He then voluntarily "assents" to this representation, an assent that, among other things, involves taking that representation for granted for purposes of practical deliberation. Faith, then, is a kind of operational assumption that is actively imagined to be true. If such faith is a realistic possibility for people, and if its benefits rival or surpass the benefits of belief, then one should probably agree with Schellenberg that religious belief is not justified on account of its practical benefits.

I've identified, then, one way that Schellenberg might *affirm* the reasonability of extending default trust to people's practice of universal consciousness attribution while *rejecting* the reasonability of extending default trust to religious doxastic practices. He could appeal to practical considerations to justify giving default trust to universal consciousness attribution while arguing that people lack practical reasons to trust religious doxastic practices. People lack such reasons because the practical benefits of religious belief are just as easily attained by means of religious faith.

There are at least two problems with this attempt to draw a principled distinction between trusting the practice of universal consciousness attribution and trusting some religious doxastic practice. First, there is ample room to doubt Schellenberg's suggestion that faith, as he understands it, is a viable means of capturing the benefits that attend religious belief. Even if someone

---

[36] Schellenberg, *The Wisdom to Doubt*, chap. 6.

[37] Propositional faith is an attitude toward propositions, and not the faith attitude that one has toward persons or entities (as in the case of Mary's faith in God or Paul's faith in divine justice).

[38] Schellenberg, *The Wisdom to Doubt*, 315–316. Schellenberg describes faith as an imaginative exercise (123).

with nondoxastic faith could heroically achieve the same level of religious commitment as someone who is truly *convinced* of the truth of her religious outlook, much of importance could still be lacking. For example, could a religious Jew genuinely rejoice over who God is, over what God has done for the world and for the Jewish people, and over what God has promised to do while failing to believe that God has acted as the scriptures claim, or even that God exists? It is doubtful that one can rejoice over facts that one does not believe. For theists who think that an ideal relationship with God involves rejoicing over truths about God, faith of the sort envisaged by Schellenberg may appear to be a poor substitute for religious belief.[39]

Second, if one grants that nondoxastic faith in some religious outlook is as beneficial as believing that outlook, then one should also expect that nondoxastic faith in the universal consciousness thesis succeeds in capturing all of the benefits that result from believing that thesis. It therefore appears arbitrary to insist that one should, for moral reasons, refrain from taking a consciousness skepticism drug while also insisting that religious belief cannot similarly be justified on practical grounds.

In sum, there are reasons to question both Schellenberg's doxastic minimalism *and* the nature of the restrictions he places on doxastic minimalism. His argument for doxastic minimalism is predicated on an implausibly narrow understanding of the aims of human inquiry. And even if one endorses the impulse toward doxastic minimalism, there is reason to question Schellenberg's proposal that all and only humanly unavoidable doxastic practices are exempt from the strictures of doxastic minimalism. First, if one holds that the unavoidable practices are exempt precisely *because* they are unavoidable, then one should concede that many noncontroversial belief-forming practices (like universal consciousness attribution) are epistemically deficient and should be given up in the event that this becomes possible. Such a position is implausibly skeptical and also undermines the view that there is a special problem facing beliefs that are controversial. Second, there does not appear to be something that the unavoidable practices have in common (other than their unavoidability) that could explain why only they (and not avoidable practices like those in the religious domain) are properly exempted from doxastic minimalism.

---

[39] This is not to deny that some valuable goods may be available only to the believer with nondoxastic faith. Because it is more difficult to maintain religious commitment without belief, the religious person who does not believe arguably has opportunities to practice and cultivate virtues that are not available to the believer.

In this chapter, I have critiqued two prominent arguments for epistemic impartiality that could provide the basis for a defense of REASONS IMPARTIALITY CONSTRAINT: Christensen's restaurant argument and Schellenberg's doxastic minimalism argument. Two additional arguments for reasons impartiality will receive attention in the next chapter. But my primary aims in that chapter are constructive rather than critical. I articulate and defend an approach to disagreement that rejects radical epistemic impartiality requirements but still vindicates commonsense conciliatory requirements. With this policy at hand, I will be in a position to articulate the conditions under which religious confidence could be reasonable in the face of systematic disagreement.

3

From Impartiality to Instrumentalism

In many cases of disagreement, the best explanation for the divergence of opinion is that the disputants do not have access to the same evidence. It is uncontroversial that in a large portion of such cases, the evidence supplied by the disagreement gives one or more parties to the dispute a reason to adjust their credence on the disputed matter. In some cases, when you reasonably infer that the other party lacks some decisive piece of evidence that you yourself possess, it may be reasonable to remain steadfast upon learning of a disagreement. In a great many other cases, where it is uncertain who possesses an evidential advantage (and to what degree) both parties should revise their credences in the direction of the other party. Matters are much more controversial when one turns to cases where interlocutors have fully disclosed their evidence and reasoning that bears on p (to the extent that is possible) yet continue to have opposing views on the plausibility of p. When disagreement does not indicate a straightforward evidential disparity (since the relevant evidence has been disclosed), does disagreement still provide a reason for doxastic revision? *Conciliationism*, as I will use the term, is the view that in contexts of full disclosure, disagreement with qualified thinkers typically constitutes a reason to reduce confidence in one's views to a nontrivial extent, *even if one has rightly responded to one's first-order evidence.* Any view that denies conciliationism may be called a *steadfast view.* These definitions are obviously quite vague, but they are serviceable as broad characterizations of two popular and opposed positions in the disagreement debate.

The most prominent conciliatory position is the *equal weight view*. According to the equal weight view, if *dispute-independent* considerations support equal estimates of your disputant's reliability concerning p and your own reliability concerning p, then the weight you assign to your disputant's opinion regarding p should be equal to the weight you assign to your own opinion.[1] (Here, your "opinion" should be understood as the view that you

[1] The equal weight view was so named by Adam Elga in "Reflection and Disagreement," *Noûs* 41, no. 3 (2007): 478–502. I am not, however, using his particular formulation of the view. Some conciliationists maintain that for it to be appropriate to equally weight my and my disputant's

would have on the basis of first-order considerations alone, prior to any adjustments in response to higher-order worries raised by the disagreement.) I argued in the last chapter that one of the most prominent arguments for the equal weight view—Christensen's restaurant argument—does not succeed. In this chapter, I begin by looking at another argument for the equal weight view. This argument says that the rational response to disagreements arising from different ways of reasoning can be modeled after the rational response to disagreements arising from inconsistent readouts on different instruments (like thermometers, watches, and so on).[2] According to the argument, just as it would be irrational for me to place more confidence in readouts of my thermometer than in the readouts of someone else's thermometer that is known to be just as reliable, it would also be irrational to place more confidence in my reasoning (and in the resultant judgments) than in the reasoning and judgments of some other thinker whom I estimate to be my epistemic peer.

In the opening sections of this chapter, I argue that the instrument model does not support a demanding epistemic impartiality requirement like that imposed by the equal weight view. The instrument model supports demanding conciliatory requirements in superficial disagreements but does *not* ground similarly demanding requirements in fundamental disagreements that are driven by differences in epistemic starting points. Building on this result, I argue that a "strong conciliationism" that *would* support equal weight verdicts in fundamental peer disagreements is unmotivated and implausible. I defend a "weak conciliationism" that rejects sweeping epistemic impartiality requirements while fully respecting the instrument model.

In the penultimate section, I address two important objections to the weak conciliationism that I favor. The first of these objections, adapted from an

---

views, I need *sufficiently strong* dispute-independent reasons for equally estimating my reliability and the reliability of my disputant. See, for example, David Christensen, "Disagreement, Question-Begging and Epistemic Self-Criticism," *Philosophers' Imprint* 11, no. 6 (2011): 1–22; and Katia Vavova, "Moral Disagreement and Moral Skepticism," *Philosophical Perspectives* 28, no. 1 (2014): 302–333. For my purposes, this more qualified position still counts as one version of the equal weight view.

[2] Analogies involving thermometers or other instruments are common in discussions of conciliatory views. See, e.g., David Christensen, "Epistemology of Disagreement: The Good News," *Philosophical Review* 116, no. 2 (2007): 187–217; Tomas Bogardus, "A Vindication of the Equal-Weight View," *Episteme* 6, no. 3 (2009): 324–335; Roger White, "On Treating Oneself and Others as Thermometers," *Episteme* 6, no. 3 (2009): 233–250; Thomas Kelly, "Peer Disagreement and Higher Order Evidence," in *Disagreement*, ed. Richard Feldman and Ted A. Warfield (Oxford: Oxford University Press, 2010), 111–174; David Enoch, "Not Just a Truthometer: Taking Oneself Seriously (but Not Too Seriously) in Cases of Peer Disagreement," *Mind* 119, no. 476 (2010): 953–997; and Clayton Littlejohn, "Disagreement and Defeat," in *Disagreement and Skepticism*, ed. Diego E. Machuca (New York: Routledge, 2013), 169–192.

argument by Miriam Schoenfield, claims that following weak conciliationism has a lower expected "accuracy" than following a "strong" conciliatory policy that is rigorously impartial. This accuracy argument captures what I think is the most significant worry for views like mine that dispense with stringent impartiality constraints. The second objection holds that the instrument model, when pushed far enough, can be used to support the requirement of rigorous epistemic impartiality.

3.1 The Equal Weight View and Instrumentalism

Suppose that on the basis of the readout on my thermometer, I form the belief that it is 61 degrees Fahrenheit. I then learn that you believe that it is 59 degrees because this is the readout on your equally reliable thermometer. Clearly, without some reason for thinking that my thermometer is likely to be more reliable than yours, it would be irrational for me to persist in my original belief. Similarly, say advocates of the equal weight view, I should not trust my own judgments, which one can think of as the "readouts" of my *cognitive* instrument, any more than the judgments of some other person that I take to be equally epistemically reliable. So if after some process of reasoning I arrive at the view that *p* and then learn that an apparent epistemic peer has (after a similar process of reasoning) arrived at an equally confident belief that ~*p*, I ought to assign just as much weight to my peer's judgment as to my own. Privileging my own judgment in contexts of peer disagreement would amount to a sort of epistemic egotism that is no more rational than privileging the readouts on my thermometer simply because it is *mine*.

Though some proponents of the equal weight view do not explicitly appeal to instrument analogies in making the case for their position, I will argue that the equal weight view is plausible only if it is combined with the view that, in a wide range of cases, one ought to adopt an "instrumentalist" stance toward one's own cognitive faculties. On this view, which I will call *instrumentalism*, one should, ideally and *to the extent possible*, treat the deliverances of one's cognitive faculties like readouts of a complex instrument, so that the degree to which one trusts those readouts should be "calibrated" with beliefs about one's cognitive reliability.[3] In this section, I characterize instrumentalism

---

[3] Some readers might reasonably worry that instrumentalism is subject to a vicious regress. If my confidence in *p* ought to be calibrated with my estimated reliability on the matter, what about the

and argue that proponents of the equal weight view have good reason to affirm it. In the next sections, I will argue that while instrumentalism can help
to explain why demanding conciliatory requirements apply in superficial
disagreements, it does not support demanding conciliatory requirements in
fundamental disagreements.

To get a feel for instrumentalism, consider the following case.[4] Horse
A and Horse B are neck and neck as they approach the finish line in a thrilling
race. I see that Horse A beats Horse B by a nose. Suppose that, while I correctly judged the result in this case, I know that my accuracy in judging races
this close is only 90%. According to instrumentalism, I should not add the
fact that Horse A won by a nose to my stock of known evidence, even though
this is in fact what I witnessed. For this would be to trust the deliverances of
my cognitive faculties absolutely, rather than treating them like the readouts
of an instrument that is imperfectly reliable. My evidence should instead be
construed as *its seeming to me (with such and such degree of clarity, and in a
state of such and such degree of alertness, etc.), that Horse A won by a nose.*
I then arrive at my credence for a Horse A victory by conditionalizing on this
evidence, and this will result in credences that are properly calibrated with
my beliefs about my cognitive reliability. Assuming that it is antecedently no
more or less likely that Horse A will win than Horse B, my final credence for
a Horse A victory will simply be 0.9, which is equal to my accuracy rate in
judging races that are this close.[5]

As illustrated by the horse race example, the instrumentalist conditionalizes
on the evidence supplied by the "readouts" of her cognitive faculties. These
readouts include such things as perceptual seemings, intuitions, conclusions
reached by mathematical calculation, and inclinations to adopt certain

---

calibration of this reliability estimate itself? Shouldn't it also be calibrated with my estimated reliability in estimating my reliability with respect to p? If so, then it seems that an infinite regress is required, since every reliability estimate would have to be calibrated with a further reliability estimate.
I will develop the basis for addressing this kind of regress worry in section 3, where I argue that instrumentalism is limited in scope because it does not apply to one's epistemic starting points.

[4] Adapted from Elga, "Reflection and Disagreement."

[5] Let A stand for the proposition that Horse A won the race, SA stand for the proposition that it
seems to me that Horse A won by a nose, and C be my credence function prior to learning SA but after
I see that the race is coming down to the wire and that *some* horse will win by a nose. Since I know
that I reach an accurate judgment in races this close 90% of the time (regardless of which horse wins),
$C(SA \mid A) = 0.9$. Given the assumption that I have no reason to think that a Horse A victory is more or
less likely in a close race than a Horse B victory, $C(A) = 0.5$. And since I do not think I am more likely
to seem to see a Horse A victory than a Horse B victory, $C(SA) = 0.5$. Bayes's theorem requires that
$C(A \mid SA) = C(SA \mid A) \cdot C(A) / C(SA)$. Substituting, one gets $C(A \mid SA) = 0.9$.

doxastic attitudes (such as a certain credence, or the attitude of belief). Rather than uncritically following such doxastic inclinations, the instrumentalist seeks as far as possible to treat these inclinations as pieces of evidence that are more or less reliable indicators of the truth. Conditionalizing on this evidence results in credences that are properly "calibrated" with the subject's estimate of her reliability.

A number of philosophers have defended policies that are similar to instrumentalism; these include Roush's "calibration," Schoenfield's "calibrationism," Sliwa and Horowitz's "Evidential Calibration," and Christensen's "Idealized Thermometer Model."[6] White critically discusses another such policy under the label "Calibration Rule."[7] But while these policies take inspiration from a rational approach to instruments, I will argue in the next section that many of these proposals obscure a crucial feature of how rational agents assimilate instrumental readouts.

Unlike the equal weight view, instrumentalism is not a thesis about what to do in situations of disagreement. Rather, it is a view about the stance I should take toward my doxastic inclinations (and other cognitive "readouts") *before* any disagreeing parties are on the scene. Nonetheless, there is good reason for thinking that the equal weight view is reasonable only if instrumentalism is correct. The reason for this is that the prescriptions of the equal weight view can be made to align with the requirements of Bayesian conditionalization only if one's predisagreement credences conform to the requirements of instrumentalism.[8] To see this, suppose that Beth is with me at the horse race, and that I know that she is exactly as accurate as I am in judging close races (i.e., 90%). After I judge that Horse A won by a nose, Beth reports that it looked to her like Horse B edged out Horse A. The prescription of the equal weight view in this case of symmetrical peer disagreement is clear: my credence for

[6] See Sherrilyn Roush, "Second Guessing: A Self-Help Manual," *Episteme* 6, no. 3 (2009): 251–268; Miriam Schoenfield, "A Dilemma for Calibrationism," *Philosophy and Phenomenological Research* 91, no. 2 (2015): 425–455; Miriam Schoenfield, "An Accuracy Based Approach to Higher Order Evidence," *Philosophical and Phenomenological Research* 96 (2018): 690–715; Paulina Sliwa and Sophie Horowitz, "Respecting All the Evidence," *Philosophical Studies* 172, no. 11 (2015): 2835–2858; and David Christensen, "Disagreement, Drugs, Etc.: From Accuracy to Akrasia," *Episteme* 13, no. 4 (2016): 392–422.

[7] White, "On Treating Oneself and Others as Thermometers."

[8] This result was shown by White ("On Treating Oneself and Others as Thermometers," 239), who shows that the sort of "splitting the difference" prescribed by the equal weight view aligns with the requirements of conditionalization only if one also conforms to a principle he calls the "Calibration Rule." White argues that the Calibration Rule is quite implausible, though White's target is a naïve principle that differs from the instrumentalism I advocate here. I discuss this naïve form of instrumentalism in section 3.3.

a Horse A victory ought to move to 0.5. But Beth's report is also a piece of evidence that could be handled by the standard conditionalization framework. This framework would have me treat this evidence just as I would treat the readout of some instrument with 90% accuracy. Will conditionalization lead me to the same 0.5 credence that is prescribed by the equal weight view? Only if my predisagreement credence is 0.9, which is the credence required by instrumentalism.[9] Not surprisingly, if before the disagreement I give my own visual impression more evidential weight than it deserves according to instrumentalism, conditionalizing on the evidence of Beth's opinion will not result in my giving equal weight to our respective views.

The prescriptions of the equal weight view align with conditionalization only if one's predisagreement credences conform to instrumentalism. This means that the proponent of the equal weight view should also endorse the predisagreement credences prescribed by instrumentalism. For if the equal weight view were offered as a *competitor* to conditionalization in simple disagreements like this one, then it would be implausible. An agent who was committed to following the equal weight view in circumstances where doing so departed from conditionalization would be susceptible to a "dutch book" strategy in which a "bookie" offers a series of bets to the agent that the agent views as fair (at the time the bet is made) but that *guarantees* monetary loss for the agent and gain for the bookie.[10]

An agent who violated conditionalization while following the equal weight view would also violate a highly plausible "epistemic reflection" requirement. Intuitively, one's current credences should "reflect" one's expectations concerning the credences of one's future self, at least if one knows that one's future self will be just as rational as one's present self, will possess evidence one does not currently possess, and will not lack any evidence that

---

[9] Let A stand for the proposition that Horse A won the race, and D (for "disagreement") stand for the proposition that Beth judges that Horse B won the race. According to the equal weight view, my credence for A after learning of the disagreement should be 0.5. Reaching this by conditionalizing on D would require that, before the disagreement, $C(A \mid D) = 0.5$. This, together with Bayes's theorem and the law of total probability, requires that $0.5 = C(D \mid A) \cdot C(A) / [C(A) \cdot C(D \mid A) + (1 - C(A)) \cdot C(D \mid \sim A)]$. Since I know Beth's accuracy is 0.9 no matter which horse wins, I know that $C(D \mid A) = 0.1$ and $C(D \mid \sim A) = 0.9$. Making these substitutions gives $0.5 = 0.1 \cdot C(A) / [C(A) \cdot 0.1 + (1 - C(A)) \cdot 0.9]$, and solving for $C(A)$ gives $C(A) = 0.9$. So the equal weight view is compatible with conditionalization only if *before* learning of the disagreement I already have an instrumentalist attitude toward my own judgment that Horse A won the race.

[10] For an overview of the "diachronic dutch book argument" against any policy that departs from conditionalization in a determinate and predictable way, see Alan Hájek, "Dutch Book Arguments," in *The Handbook of Rational and Social Choice*, ed. Paul Anand, Prasanta K. Pattanaik, and Clemens Puppe (Oxford: Oxford University Press, 2009), 173–195.

one currently possesses.[11] So in the foregoing example, imagine that I am virtually certain that Horse A won (assigning this proposition a credence of 0.9999999) yet am committed to adopting the equal weight credence of 0.5 in the event that I learn that Beth disagrees. I assign this disagreement a credence of approximately 0.1 (since I think that Beth is only 90% reliable). In this case, I will have a credence for a Horse A victory of 0.9999999, even though I know that the expected value of my credence a few moments from now when I have learned Beth's view (and am therefore more informed) is only 0.95 (approximately). Intuitively, it is not rational to exhibit this sort of mismatch between my present confidence and my expectations concerning the confidence of a future self who is strictly more informed and no less rational than myself.

In light of the irrational outcomes that follow from a departure from conditionalization, reasonable proponents of the equal weight view should affirm that in at least a wide range of cases—cases that are relevantly like the horse race case—one's predisagreement credences ought to align with the recommendations of instrumentalism.

The argument just rehearsed does not quite get to the conclusion that proponents of the equal weight view should affirm instrumentalism.[12] Even if the proponent of the equal weight view endorses the predisagreement credences recommended by instrumentalism in paradigm examples of disagreement like the horse race case, she could conceivably deny that instrumentalism supplies the correct explanation for why these predisagreement credences are required. Granting that my predisagreement credence for a Horse A victory ought to be 0.9, perhaps the reason for this is *not* that I should adopt the credence reached by conditionalizing on the evidence supplied by the "readouts" of my cognitive faculties. But I see no viable explanation for why my predisagreement credence ought to take this value other than the one supplied by instrumentalism. And since instrumentalism is in

---

[11] The reflection principle originally formulated by Bas van Fraassen, "Belief and the Will," *Journal of Philosophy* 81, no. 5 (1984): 244), states that an agent's current credence for *p* should "reflect" her expected future credence for *p*; more precisely, her conditional credence for *p given* that at some future time her credence for *p* will be *r* ought to be *r*. While reflection is subject to well-known counterexamples, these counterexamples do not raise doubts about the applicability of the reflection requirement in contexts where I know that in the future my epistemic position with respect to *p* will in every respect be at least as strong as my current epistemic position with respect to *p*. (This is argued in R. Briggs, "Distorted Reflection," *Philosophical Review* 118, no. 1 [2009]: 59–85.) The violation of reflection that would result from following the equal weight view when it departs from conditionalization could easily be in contexts where I know that my future self will be in an epistemically superior position and thus where the reflection requirement holds.

[12] Thanks to an anonymous referee for pointing this out.

keeping with the way many advocates of the equal weight view speak about cognitive self-trust, I conclude that proponents of the equal weight view have good reason to affirm instrumentalism. In arguing this, my purpose is *not* to saddle proponents of the equal weight view with some view I find objectionable. I accept instrumentalism, which is a central component of the weak conciliationism I will defend below (though I do criticize a naïve form of instrumentalism in the next section). Rather, my aim is to show that the instrumentalist principle affirmed by weak conciliationism should not be viewed with suspicion by the proponents of the equal weight view. It is a principle that they should already endorse.

3.2 Prior Probability and Instrumental Trust

In the previous section, I argued that proponents of conciliatory views like the equal weight view should affirm the correctness of instrumentalism, at least in a wide range of cases. In this section and the next, I argue that instrumentalism (together with conditionalization) rationalizes demanding conciliatory requirements in superficial but not in fundamental disagreements. I have characterized instrumentalism as the view that one ought to treat the deliverances of one's cognitive faculties like instrumental readouts *to the extent possible*. This last qualification is crucial since, as I will argue in this section, it is impossible to adopt a thoroughgoing instrumentalist stance that treats *all* of one's doxastic attitudes like instrumental readouts. Instrumentalism is necessarily limited in scope. In the next section, I show why these limits lead to different implications for fundamental and superficial disagreements.

The first step toward appreciating the limits of instrumentalism is to note that the degree to which one ought to trust some instrument on a given occasion is a function of both the instrument's reliability *and* the prior probability of the "claim" made by the instrument.[13] Suppose I awake one morning in tropical Panama City (where temperatures are consistently warm all year) and look out my window and see that my hitherto reliable thermometer says it is a frigid 20 degrees Fahrenheit. Even if I know that the thermometer is accurate 99.99% of the time, my credence that it is 20 degrees will surely be

---

[13] White's discussion ("On Treating Oneself and Others as Thermometers," 241) is the basis of the following example of the thermometer in Panama City.

much lower than 0.9999! Likewise with cognitive instruments: the degree to which I should trust some deliverance of my cognitive faculties depends on my assessment of my cognitive reliability *and* on my prior credence for the proposition that the deliverance supports. So suppose that in the horse race example above, I know that Horse A and Horse B have raced hundreds of times and that while the races are *always* a photo finish, Horse A wins 80% of the time. If this is the case, then when it appears to me that Horse A wins, my credence for a Horse A victory should be greater than 0.9 even though the probability that I will correctly judge any given race is 0.9. Conversely, if it appeared to me that Horse B won, my credence for a Horse B victory should be *less* than 0.9.[14] Just as with the thermometer in Panama City, I have more reason to trust readouts that support a proposition that is antecedently probable than readouts that support a proposition that is antecedently improbable.

Epistemologists who argue that one's credences should be "calibrated" with one's reliability estimates typically fail to note the role that priors play in determining how much one should trust a given doxastic inclination. As a result, the policies these epistemologists advocate could understandably be interpreted as naïve forms of instrumentalism that ignore prior probabilities. Consider, for example, the following principles, the first defended by Schoenfield and the second defended by Sliwa and Horowitz:

Calibrationism: If, independently of the first order reasoning in question, your expected degree of reliability concerning whether p at time t is *r*, *r* is the credence that it is rational for you to adopt at t.[15]

Evidential Calibration: When one's evidence favors P over ~P, one's credence in P should equal the expected reliability of one's educated guess that P.[16]

---

[14] This can be shown using Bayes's theorem, but here is an intuitive way of justifying this claim. Out of 100 races, I'd expect that Horse A would win about 80 times, and that in about 72 of these races I'd correctly judge that Horse A won and in about 8 of these races incorrectly judge that Horse B won. I'd also expect Horse B to win about 20 times, and that in about 18 of these races I'd correctly judge that Horse B won and in about 2 races I'd incorrectly judge that Horse A won. Thus, the proportion of judgments in favor of Horse A that I expect to be correct is 0.97 (72/74), and the proportion of judgments in favor of Horse B that I expect to be correct is 0.69 (18/26).

[15] Schoenfield, "A Dilemma for Calibrationism," 428. In the article just cited, Schoenfield considers challenges to calibrationism without explicitly rejecting or endorsing the principle; but she defends calibrationism in "An Accuracy Based Approach to Higher Order Evidence."

[16] Sliwa and Horowitz, "Respecting All the Evidence," 2843.

While there are arguably some important differences in the formulation of these principles, both principles require that the credence assigned to one's view on p be equal to an independent estimate of one's reliability on the matter. (Evidential Calibration does not explicitly say that the reliability estimate must be based on considerations independent of one's view on p, but Sliwa and Horowitz later clarify that this is what they have in mind.)[17] Sliwa and Horowitz's explanation of what they mean by "expected reliability" is similar to Schoenfield's explanation of "expected degree of reliability." Sliwa and Horowitz explain that "the *reliability* of your guess is the probability that you will assign the highest credence to the option that is *true*—it is the probability that you would get the answer right, if you had to choose," and the *expected* reliability is simply the rational "weighted average of different possibilities for how reliable you could be, as assessed by your own lights."[18]

Given one way of interpreting this explanation of "expected reliability," these policies would lead to the wrong result in the variation of the horse race example just described. I know that in any given race, the probability that I will assign the highest credence to the correct claim about which horse won is 0.9. If 0.9 counts as my "expected degree of reliability" or "expected reliability," then calibrationism/Evidential Calibration would imply that when I correctly judge that Horse A won the race, my credence for a Horse A victory should be 0.9. This credence is clearly mistaken, however. It is true that my "educated guesses" are right 90% of the time. But because the prior probability of a Horse A win is 80%, I know that *when I judge that Horse A wins, I am right 97% of the time.*[19] So my credence in this situation should be 0.97.

As the above example shows, on one natural interpretation of "expected reliability," policies like calibrationism and Evidential Calibration turn out to be naïve instrumentalist procedures that ignore the role of prior probabilities. But there is an alternative way of thinking about reliability that takes prior probabilities into account. If one uses this conception of reliability when applying these calibration policies, then they will deliver the correct verdict in the horse race case. Since in the horse race case the antecedent probability that I will judge a race correctly is 90% (whichever horse in fact wins), one could reasonably say that my reliability is 90%, whatever my judgment may be. But one might instead suggest that my reliability should take

[17] "Respecting All the Evidence," 2844 n. 14.
[18] "Respecting All the Evidence," 2844. Cf. Schoenfield's description of "expected degree of reliability" ("A Dilemma for Calibrationism," 426).
[19] See note 14.

into account the specific content of my judgment and the prior probability of the view I judge to be correct. On this way of understanding reliability, it is not my general propensity to judge correctly that is relevant but rather the probability that I am right *given that I have arrived at such and such judgment*. So I would count as 97% reliable on occasions when I judge that Horse A won, and only 69% reliable when I judge that Horse B won. I'll call this notion of reliability *readout reliability*. Readout reliability can be calculated using the very process of conditionalization I am advocating, a calculation that makes use of the value that *I* am calling "reliability." By using readout reliability, the calibration policies get the correct result.

Whatever notion of reliability proponents of policies like calibrationism and Evidential Calibration may have in mind, their discussion of examples used to motivate these policies often overlooks, or at least obscures, how prior probabilities should affect one's confidence in a particular judgment. It is useful to consider different ways of filling in the details of one of these examples in order to illustrate just how critical it is to take prior probabilities into account. Consider the following case (adapted from Elga) that Schoenfield uses to motivate calibrationism.

HYPOXIA: Aisha is flying her airplane on a bright Monday morning, wondering whether she has enough gasoline to fly to Hawaii. Upon looking at the dials, gauges and maps, she obtains some first order evidence E, which she knows strongly supports (say to degree 0.99) either that she has enough gas (G) or that she does not have enough gas (~G). Aisha does some complex calculations and concludes G, which is, in fact, what E supports. But she then gains some higher order evidence: she realizes that she is flying at an altitude that puts her at great risk for hypoxia, a condition that impairs one's reasoning capacities. Aisha knows that pilots who do the kind of reasoning that she just did, and who are flying at her current altitude, only reach the correct conclusion 50% of the time.[20]

According to Schoenfield, the calibrationist thinks that Aisha's credence should be 0.5, a verdict Schoenfield thinks "has a great deal of intuitive plausibility."[21] But this verdict follows from Schoenfield's description of the case

[20] Schoenfield, "An Accuracy Based Approach to Higher Order Evidence," 690–691. The case is adapted from Adam Elga, "Lucky to Be Rational," unpublished paper presented at the Bellingham Summer Philosophy Conference, 2008, www.princeton.edu/~adame/papers/bellingham-lucky.pdf.

[21] Schoenfield, "An Accuracy Based Approach to Higher Order Evidence," 691.

only if one understands calibrationism to be using "reliability" in a more conventional way that does not take the prior probability of the judgment into account. If one understood calibrationism to be relying on the notion of *readout* reliability, then one would lack any basis for concluding that the calibrationist thinks that Aisha's credence should be 0.5. For Aisha's readout reliability depends on the prior probability of G, and HYPOXIA gives us no information about this prior probability.[22] Suppose that Aisha is piloting a routine cargo flight from Los Angeles to Honolulu. On a whim, with no special reason for concern, she decides to confirm that her airplane has adequate fuel. If *this* is how one fills out the relevant details, then Aisha's readout reliability (upon judging G) should be *much* higher than 0.5, since it is incredibly unlikely that she took off with inadequate fuel. Or, if one imagines that Aisha is flying a small prop plane in Florida, her readout reliability (upon judging G) is incredibly low. As these elaborations of the example show, a naïve instrumentalist approach that ignored the role of priors would frequently lead to absurd results.

I've suggested that discussions of calibration policies have suffered from a lack of explicit attention to the role prior probabilities play in modulating the degree to which one should trust various doxastic inclinations. And when one *does* attend to this role played by prior probabilities, one finds reason for questioning a very common way of understanding the equal weight view. The equal weight view is often described as requiring one to "split the difference" with epistemic peers by adopting a credence halfway between the two predisagreement credences.[23] But splitting the difference generally does *not* accord with how epistemic peers treat discrepancies between equally reliable instruments. Splitting the difference in a peer disagreement is a reasonable response that accords with instrumentalism only in the special circumstances where one's prior credence distribution favors neither one's own view nor the view of one's peer.[24]

---

[22] The same sort of criticism applies to Sliwa and Horowitz's discussion of the case they call "CALCULATION" ("Respecting All the Evidence," 2836–2844).

[23] For example, see Christensen, "Epistemology of Disagreement," 203; Enoch, "Not Just a Truthometer," 994; Stewart Cohen, "A Defense of the (Almost) Equal Weight View," in *The Epistemology of Disagreement: New Essays,* ed. David Christensen and Jennifer Lackey (Oxford: Oxford University Press, 2013), 100; and Brandon Carey and Jonathan Matheson, "How Skeptical Is the Equal Weight View?," in *Disagreement and Skepticism,* ed. Diego E. Machuca (New York: Routledge, 2013), 132.

[24] Maria Lasonen-Aarnio has advanced a similar argument against splitting the difference in "Disagreement and Evidential Attenuation," *Noûs* 47, no. 4 (2013): 767–794.

To illustrate this point, I'll continue with the horse race example where Beth and I know that Horse A wins 80% of the close races. I know that in very close horse races, I correctly judge the result 90% of the time. So when it seems to me on the basis of my visual impressions that Horse A won the race by a nose, an experience that many philosophers would refer to as a visual "seeming," instrumentalism says to treat this seeming as the readout of an instrument with an accuracy rate of 90%. Conditionalizing on the fact of this seeming, as instrumentalism recommends, leads to a credence for a Horse A victory of approximately 0.97. When Beth watches the same race and thinks that she has observed Horse B win, conditionalizing on her visual seeming will lead her to a credence of approximately 0.69 for a Horse B victory and a credence of 0.31 for a Horse A victory. Upon learning of the disagreement, "splitting the difference" would result in Beth and I having a credence for a Horse A victory of approximately 0.64. But conditionalizing on the evidence of the other person's opinion would not lead Beth and me to this halfway point. It would instead lead both of us to a credence of 0.8, which was our original credence before updating on the perceptual evidence.[25] As this example makes clear, instrumentalism does *not* support an equal weight view that gives equal weight to the *credences* of epistemic peers (except in special cases). While instrumentalism supports the idea that I should treat myself and my peer as equally reliable instruments, the claim of one "instrument" may be accorded more trust than the other if that claim more closely aligns with what is taken to be antecedently probable.

The advocate of the equal weight view could reasonably respond to these points *not* by giving up the equal weight view but by acknowledging that the equal weight view should not be understood as requiring that peers split the difference. After all, as long as the equal weight view requires that disputing peers converge on a single credence, and as long as the prescribed credence depends only on what the initial views are and not on who holds which view, then there is a significant sense in which the disputants are giving one another equal weight. In the horse race case just discussed, Beth and I could have swapped positions (so that I judged that Horse B won and she that Horse A won), and would still have converged on a credence for a Horse

---

[25] Again, let A stand for the proposition that Horse A won the race and D (for "disagreement") stand for the proposition that Beth judges that Horse B won the race. If C is my credence function after seeming to see Horse A win but before learning of the disagreement, using Bayes's theorem and the law of total probability, my credence after the disagreement should be $C(D \mid A) \cdot C(A) / [C(A) \cdot C(D \mid A) + (1 - C(A)) \cdot C(D \mid {\sim}A)]$, which is equal to $0.1 \cdot 0.973 / (0.973 \cdot 0.1 + 0.028 \cdot 0.9)$, or 0.8.

A victory of 0.8. There is still impartiality since both of us will converge on the same value irrespective of whose initial credence happens to be the one that is closest to the point of convergence.

Even if instrumentalism does not support a "split the difference" approach to all peer disagreements, one might think that instrumentalism (together with conditionalization) *will* require convergence on the same credence (as it does in the horse race example) and will to that extent vindicate the equal weight view. If two disputants aim to treat their views as readouts of equally reliable instruments, it would seem that there can be no explanation for any lingering divergence after they have fully shared all of their evidence. But I will now argue that this supposition is mistaken. A further implication of the role played by priors in determining instrumental trust is that instrumentalism is necessarily limited in scope and less self-critical than it might have seemed.[26] As I will explain, one cannot adopt an instrumentalist stance toward one's most fundamental epistemic starting points. As a result, the combination of instrumentalism and conditionalization does not have the same demanding conciliatory implications for fundamental disagreements that it has for superficial disagreements.

3.3 Instrumentalism and Fundamental Disagreements

When following instrumentalism in order to determine how much to trust some "readout" of my cognitive faculties that bear on p, I must conditionalize on the evidence supplied by this readout. This process of conditionalization requires me to make use of my prior credence for p. So while instrumentalism involves detaching myself from some of my doxastic inclinations regarding p in order to critically assess the evidential worth of those inclinations, instrumentalism does *not* involve my taking a critical stance toward *all* of my doxastic attitudes toward p. If I conditionalize in the way that instrumentalism recommends, I take for granted the rationality of my prior credence for p in order to critically evaluate the evidential import of subsequent doxastic

---

[26] Enoch also argues for the impossibility of a thoroughly instrumentalist perspective. (See "Not Just a Truthometer," 961–965.) By giving a formal account of instrumentalism, I aim to characterize more precisely why instrumentalism is limited in scope and which doxastic inclinations can and cannot be treated in an instrumentalist fashion.

inclinations toward p. Thus, I cannot adopt an instrumentalist stance toward all of my doxastic attitudes simultaneously.

However, not only am I unable to adopt an instrumentalist stance toward all of my doxastic attitudes simultaneously but also there are some attitudes that cannot be treated in an instrumentalist way *at all*. In particular, I am unable to adopt an instrumentalist view of my most fundamental rational starting points. Adopting an instrumentalist attitude toward some doxastic attitude or inclination involves treating that attitude or inclination as a "readout" of a complicated instrument and then conditionalizing on that readout evidence from an antecedent perspective *that is not itself informed by the readout*. So this process requires that I have some antecedent perspective that is not informed by the very readout being treated instrumentally. But if the "readout" in question is my most fundamental attitude regarding the plausibility of p, what Bayesians sometimes refer to as my "ur-prior" for p, then clearly I have no perspective on p that is antecedent to the readout. Suppose that c is my ur-prior for p. Since c represents my most fundamental view on the plausibility of p, there is no antecedent perspective on p from which I can view the fact of my having ur-prior c as *merely* a piece of evidence upon which to conditionalize. If I wanted to conditionalize on the fact of my having ur-prior c, I would have to make use of c itself as the starting position from which the process of updating on evidence proceeds. Because such conditionalization would require that I employ c as my prior credence in the relevant calculation, this process would simply presuppose that a starting perspective constituted by c is rational. At this most fundamental level, the attempt to follow instrumentalism would cease to be a way of detaching myself from my doxastic attitudes in order to evaluate them critically.

We never face this problem when assimilating the evidence provided by instruments like thermometers: when deciding how much to trust the readout of some thermometer, we can always make use of some antecedent expectations that are not themselves informed by the readout in question. But once we turn to the instrument in our own heads, there is no guarantee that every readout can be weighed in light of our antecedent expectations. Some of those readouts simply *are* our antecedent expectations! Our assimilation of instrumental readouts therefore cannot give us a model for how we ought to approach our most fundamental rational attitudes. At the level of ur-priors, instrumentalism fails to apply.[27]

---

[27] Because instrumentalism does not apply at the level of ur-priors, certain sorts of regress worries are avoided. When I have a doxastic inclination or "readout" that bears on p, arriving at my final

I am now in a position to show why instrumentalism (combined with a commitment to conditionalize on disagreement evidence) will not always require convergence in peer disagreements. Divergence is possible even given a commitment to instrumentalism because a thoroughly instrumentalist treatment of one's own attitudes is impossible. If I disagree with you about the *fundamental* plausibility of *p*, so that we have two different ur-priors for *p*, I cannot treat both of these ur-priors in a purely instrumentalist way. Suppose that I have a high ur-prior for *p* and you have a low ur-prior. I am able to gauge the trustworthiness of your ur-prior by making use of an antecedent perspective on *p*'s plausibility, a perspective that is independent of your ur-prior. But I cannot gauge the trustworthiness of my *own* ur-prior by making use of an antecedent perspective on *p* that is independent of *that* ur-prior. If I make use of my antecedent perspective in order to gauge which ur-prior is most likely to be trustworthy, then I will be relying on a perspective that is shaped by one of the two ur-priors in question. Such a process is inevitably self-favoring.[28] And, of course, your attempt to gauge the trustworthiness of our ur-priors using your own antecedent perspective would be equally self-favoring. Thus, a commitment to instrumentalism will not bring about convergence in disagreements that are fundamental, since it is precisely at this fundamental level where a purely instrumentalist posture toward one's own doxastic attitudes cannot be maintained.[29]

In disagreements that are merely superficial (like the horse race case, or disagreements arising from calculation error), instrumentalism requires that I assess the views of myself and my disputant from an antecedent perspective that

credence *c* for *p* by an application of instrumentalism requires that I make use of some antecedent credence for *p*, which one can label *c1*, and an estimate *r* of the reliability of the relevant sort of doxastic inclination. One might reasonably ask whether *c1* and *r* should also be determined by an application of instrumentalism. If the answer is yes, then it would seem that an infinite regress looms. But as should now be clear, the answer will not always be yes. When one pushes back to an ur-prior (or an "ur" reliability estimate), instrumentalism does not apply, and this sort of regress is blocked.

[28] For a similar argument, see Lasonen-Aarnio, "Disagreement and Evidential Attenuation," 773.

[29] A certain sort of coherentist might be skeptical of the idealized Bayesian picture that is presupposed here, according to which one's credences are the product of one's empirical evidence and fundamental preevidential plausibility assessments—one's ur-priors. Perhaps any doxastic inclination toward *p* can be critically evaluated from some standpoint that includes a credence for *p* and that, *for purposes of evaluating that particular doxastic inclination*, counts as being rationally prior to the inclination. In this case, no disagreement would count as being fundamental (since there would be no attitudes that uniquely qualify as one's epistemic starting points), and the process of instrumentalizing could go on indefinitely. Nonetheless, the key point holds: because there is no guarantee that two disputants who continue to treat more and more attitudes in an instrumentalist fashion will eventually land on a common prior for *p*, a common commitment to instrumentalism will not guarantee convergence in credences.

happens to be shared and is thus dispute-neutral. In fundamental disagreements, however, a commitment to instrumentalism does not result in a dispute-neutral evaluation since there is no antecedent perspective that both disputants share and that can supply a dispute-neutral vantage point for assessing the disagreement.

3.4 Beyond Instrumentalism to Independence?

I've argued that the instrument model does not support an impartiality requirement that would require convergence in fundamental disagreements with full disclosure. Of course, this does not show that there is no plausible "strong" conciliatory view that includes some sort of impartiality or independence requirement that requires convergence in both superficial and fundamental disagreements. Even if a demanding epistemic impartiality requirement cannot be motivated by the instrument model, it still may be correct. But I will now argue that such a strong conciliatory policy is less plausible than a weak conciliatory policy that affirms instrumentalism and rejects highly demanding impartiality constraints. In this section, I give more precise characterizations of weak and strong conciliationism and illustrate their different approaches to fundamental disagreements. Then, in following sections, I will offer reasons to prefer weak conciliationism.

The *weak conciliationism* that I advocate affirms the following commitments:

> *Instrumentalism*: One should, *ideally* and *to the extent possible*, treat the deliverances of one's cognitive faculties that bear on p like readouts of a complex instrument, conditionalizing on the evidence supplied by such readouts using one's expected reliability *and* a prior credence for p that is rationally antecedent to the readouts in question.

> *Conditionalization*: One should conditionalize on information about the views of one's disputants, treating their views like the readouts of a complex instrument.

In addition to affirming instrumentalism and conditionalization, weak conciliationism denies any sort of sweeping impartiality requirement that would require convergence of credences in all (or nearly all) fundamental disputes with full disclosure between apparent epistemic peers. In affirming instrumentalism, weak conciliationism does require that one view one's doxastic inclinations with some critical distance (when possible). But the instrumentalist stance is not the stance of impartiality. The vantage point you occupy in order to assess the trustworthiness of some doxastic inclination of yours that bears on p is still *your* perspective, one that includes your own antecedent perspective on p's plausibility. Thus, when the ur-priors that constitute your fundamental perspective differ from the ur-priors of your disputant, weak conciliationism will not guarantee convergence of opinion. A policy that required convergence in such disputes while respecting instrumentalism and conditionalization would have to include an impartiality constraint on the ur-priors that serve as the starting point for conditionalization.

To articulate such an impartiality constraint, one can look to a "calibration" policy along the lines of the proposals endorsed by Schoenfield, Sliwa and Horowitz, and Christensen. I earlier said that one could understandably interpret these proposals as recommending a naïve instrumentalist procedure that ignores prior probabilities. But a subject who uses such a procedure to determine the trustworthiness of his *most fundamental* plausibility assessment of p cannot be accused of naïvely ignoring the prior probability of p. For an agent does not have any view on p's probability that is rationally prior to her fundamental plausibility assessment. Thus, while a calibration policy that ignores priors would be implausible if offered as a fully general requirement, such a policy might nonetheless be plausible if reformulated as a constraint applying only to ur-priors.

One can, then, understand *strong conciliationism* as the view that affirms instrumentalism and conditionalization (as I've argued any plausible "equal weight" approach should) but that also adds an additional independence constraint on ur-priors. One may characterize this constraint as follows:

> *Fundamental Calibration*: If you are inclined on the basis of first-order considerations to assign to p an ur-prior c (where c is greater than 0.5), then your ur-prior for p should be equal to your *independent* reliability estimate for someone who is relevantly similar and who is inclined to assign to p or to ~p an ur-prior c.[30]

---

[30] Fundamental calibration bears obvious similarities to calibrationism and evidential calibration. In requiring that the agent use a reliability estimate for someone "relevantly similar" (in dispute-neutral respects), fundamental calibration is perhaps most similar to the "Idealized Thermometer Model" in Christensen, "Disagreement, Drugs, Etc.," 409.

Some explanatory commentary will be helpful here. Your *independent* relia-bility estimate is the assessment of expected reliability that you would reach on the basis of what one might call "p-neutral considerations." P-neutral considerations are those considerations whose force can be appreciated in-dependently of any particular view on p and independently of any particular opinion regarding the merits of (potentially controversial) lines of reasoning that might be offered in support of p or its negation. P-neutral reasons may include such factors as whether someone has a good epistemic track record in the relevant domain, how confident that person feels in his view on p, how much care he took in forming his view, whether there are nonrational factors that may bias his reasoning about p, facts about his intelligence and educa-tion, and other factors whose import can be appreciated irrespective of one's particular stance on p. Examples of considerations that would *not* count as p-neutral include the fact that some view on p is self-evidently true or the fact that some particular argument for p (which is potentially controversial) is unassailable.

By tying an agent's ur-prior for p to a p-neutral reliability assessment, fun-damental calibration ensures that she exhibits what I have called reasons impartiality. Because fundamental calibration also ties one's ur-prior to a re-liability estimate for someone who is *relevantly similar*, fundamental calibra-tion also imposes agent impartiality. For example, fundamental calibration does not allow me to highly estimate my reliability with respect to p for the reason that everyone should exhibit default self-trust. The value of *self*-trust does not give me a reason to trust some *other* person who is relevantly like me with respect to her epistemic credentials.

A concrete example will help provide a clearer sense of how weak and strong conciliationism differ in their handling of fundamental disagreements. Suppose that Roger is told that he is about to be presented with some meta-physical thesis p that he has never before considered. Roger is not told in advance the content of p or any specific details about the way he will reason about p, though he is given information that would enable him to arrive at an informed independent estimate of his reliability on the matter.[31] Before Roger is presented with the content of p, he is asked to consider a number of

---

[31] Of course, since Roger does not yet know what the content of p is, Roger is not in a position to determine with confidence what considerations count as p-neutral. But as I am imagining the ex-ample, Roger knows that the people feeding him information to arrive at a reliability estimate *do* know what p is, and they ensure that the evidential significance of the information they provide to Roger (for purposes of arriving at a reliability assessment) is information whose significance can be appreciated independently of one's stance on p.

doxastic responses that someone relevantly like him (in p-neutral respects) might have after learning the content of the proposition and reflecting on its plausibility. For each of these possible doxastic responses, Roger estimates the reliability of someone relevantly like himself *conditional on their responding in the envisioned way*. For example, Roger might estimate the reliability of someone's view on p given that (1) she is relevantly like Roger in p-neutral respects (e.g., similar educational background, similar degree of intelligence, similar amount of time and care put into assessing p, and so on) and (2) upon thinking about p for a couple of minutes, she is inclined (on the basis of first-order considerations alone) to assign her view on p an ur-prior of 0.99. Imagining Roger arriving at these reliability estimates before he knows the content of p or the details of his reasoning about p allows one to have a firmer grasp of the sorts of considerations that could legitimately inform Roger's p-neutral reliability estimates.

Now suppose that after Roger has arrived at these p-neutral reliability estimates, he learns the content of p and has a chance to reflect on its plausibility. Here is the thesis Roger is asked to consider:

ONE WAY: For any objects A and B, if A is the cause of B's coming to exist for the first time, then it is *not* the case that B is the cause of A's coming to exist for the first time.

After reflecting on ONE WAY for two minutes, Roger is strongly inclined on the basis of first-order considerations to believe it and to assign it an ur-prior of 0.99. (To be clear, this is the initial credence he is inclined to adopt *before* taking into account higher-order worries about any tendencies toward overconfidence or underconfidence on such matters.) As it happens, this exact response is one of the many doxastic responses Roger considered before learning the content of p. Suppose that Roger estimated that someone who responds in this way and who is like him in p-neutral respects is 0.9 reliable with respect to p. Finally, after Roger has formed his initial credence for ONE WAY, Roger presents the thesis to Fiona, who Roger knows is relevantly like himself in all p-neutral respects. After reflecting on ONE WAY for two minutes, Fiona is strongly inclined to believe that ONE WAY is false and to assign the *negation* of ONE WAY an ur-prior of 0.99.

With this idealized example in place, one can clearly illustrate the different approaches of strong and weak conciliationism. Consider Roger's doxastic state after reflecting on ONE WAY and being inclined to assign it a credence of 0.99, but before he learns Fiona's view on ONE WAY. According to strong conciliationism, Roger should at this juncture assign ONE WAY an ur-prior of 0.9, his p-neutral estimate of his reliability in his present circumstances. Then, when he learns that his epistemic peer Fiona is inclined toward an equally confident ur-prior for the opposite view, Roger should conditionalize on this fact. Since Roger thinks that someone relevantly like himself (and Fiona) is 0.9 reliable in the relevant circumstances, the evidential weight of Fiona's judgment will exactly counterbalance Roger's predisagreement confidence. Conditionalizing on Fiona's judgment will therefore result in a final credence of 0.5.

Now compare how weak conciliationism handles the case. Roger has no view on the plausibility of ONE WAY that is rationally antecedent to his inclination toward an ur-prior of 0.99. It is thus not possible for Roger to treat the inclination toward this ur-prior in the manner that he would treat an instrumental readout. As I have emphasized, the degree to which one ought to trust an instrumental readout that supports p depends *both* on the reliability of the instrument *and* on the antecedent plausibility of p. When there is no antecedent plausibility assessment, instrumentalism does not apply. Thus, by the lights of weak conciliationism, Roger is free to adopt an ur-prior for ONE WAY of 0.99. Of course, Roger *is* capable of treating Fiona's doxastic stance like an instrumental readout (since Roger has a stance on ONE WAY that is rationally antecedent to the evidence supplied by her view). If Roger starts with an ur-prior of 0.99 and then conditionalizes on Fiona's high initial credence that ONE WAY is false—a readout Roger takes to be 0.9 reliable—then Roger will arrive at an updated credence for ONE WAY of approximately 0.917.[32] In a fundamental disagreement of this sort, weak conciliationism can prove significantly less demanding than strong conciliationism.

Having spelled out the difference between weak and strong conciliationism in a concrete (even if highly idealized) example, I can now present my case against strong conciliationism and the independence requirement it imposes on ur-priors.

---

[32] Suppose that before Roger learns Fiona's view, he learns that she is inclined to assign an ur-prior of 0.99 to her view (whatever it is). Presumably, this information should not change Roger's confidence, so his credence for p should remain 0.99. Next, Roger learns D, which stands for the proposition that Fiona judges that ONE WAY is false. Using Bayes's theorem and the law of total probability, one knows that prior to learning D, Roger should satisfy the following: C (ONE WAY | D) = C (D | ONE WAY) · C (ONE WAY) / [C (ONE WAY) · C (D | ONE WAY) + C (~ONE WAY) · C (D | ~ONE WAY))]. Because Roger expects that Fiona is 90% reliable in the present circumstances, one knows that C (D | ONE WAY) = 0.1 and C (D | ~ONE WAY) = 0.9. Substituting, one gets C (ONE WAY | D) = 0.1 · 0.99 / (0.99 · 0.1 + 0.01 · 0.9) ≈ 0.917.

3.5 The Explanatory Power of Weak Conciliationism

The principal argumentative strategy for strong conciliatory views that feature an independence requirement (such as fundamental calibration) begins by focusing on easy "toy" cases where it is fairly obvious that equal-weighting is the right thing to do. These cases include Elga's horse race case and Christensen's bill tabulation case. In the latter, discussed in the previous chapter, two equally qualified individuals do some complicated math in their heads, and one arrives at the answer 43 and the other at 45. The commonsense response in these cases is to split the difference, giving equal weight to both views. Strong conciliationists maintain that the lesson one should draw from such cases is that one's response to the disagreement cannot appeal to contested first-order reasoning (since such reasoning would not favor giving both sides equal weight). Instead, one's response to the disagreement must be based on p-neutral considerations alone. Strong conciliationists then argue that the independence requirement motivated by these "easy" cases of disagreement also applies in "hard" cases that involve, for example, philosophical, moral, or religious disagreement. Granted, some strong conciliationists suggest that the weight that must be given to an independent evaluation diminishes in certain contexts. Where there is at best an impoverished base of p-neutral considerations on which to base one's independent reliability estimates, less weight should be given to independent considerations.[33] Still, in hard disagreements where one has a rich set of p-neutral considerations that can be used to compare expected reliability, the independence requirement can be as stringent as it is in mundane cases like Christensen's bill tabulation case.[34]

Once one has appreciated the explanatory power of instrumentalism, this attempt to argue for an independence requirement by appealing to toy cases like Elga's horse race case and Christensen's bill tabulation case must be judged a failure. For the weak conciliationist can explain the same intuitive equal weight verdicts in these cases without any appeal to an independence

---

[33] Christensen, "Disagreement, Question-Begging and Epistemic Self-Criticism"; and Vavova, "Moral Disagreement and Moral Skepticism." I criticize this variation in the next section.

[34] Christensen, for example, concedes that in many philosophical controversies, the base of p-neutral considerations is robust enough to give him a "strong, dispute-independent reason to think that those who disagree with [him] are as well-informed, and as likely to have reasoned correctly from their evidence, as those who agree with [him]." "Disagreement and Public Controversy," in *Essays in Collective Epistemology*, ed. Jennifer Lackey (New York: Oxford University Press, 2015), 147.

requirement.[35] Weak conciliationism can explain these equal weight verdicts because, in the easy cases I've offered for consideration, there is a single antecedent perspective that would be shared by any reasonable person. More specifically, reasonable people would agree (or at least very nearly agree) on the comparative antecedent probability of the competing views and on the reliability of the parties to the dispute. And when there is a shared antecedent perspective, an evaluation of the dispute from one's own antecedent perspective also happens to be a dispute-neutral evaluation.

To see this, consider first the horse race case. Clearly, no reasonable person would think that the *fundamental* plausibility of a Horse A victory differs from that of a Horse B victory. In addition, given robust track record data where each disputant has correctly judged 90% of the races, the disputants should enter the race with very similar estimates of their own reliability. This is true even if the *fundamental* reliability estimates built into their ur-priors were self-favoring and not impartial. So on any natural way of filling out the details of this sort of case, the case will be one of merely superficial disagreement. And weak conciliationism and strong conciliationism deliver the same result in cases of merely superficial disagreement.

Similarly, in Christensen's case involving complex mental math, a person of normal mathematical abilities will not think (prior to calculating) that an answer of 43 is significantly more or less plausible than an answer of 45. Thus, if the disputants are reasonable, their antecedent perspectives will be relevantly the same, or nearly so. They will both think that the prior probability that 43 is the correct answer is approximately the same as the prior probability that 45 is the correct answer. Moreover, given robust track record information, they will enter the disagreement with reliability estimates that are nearly equal. Hence, this is again a case of merely superficial disagreement, one where evaluating the matter from one's own antecedent perspective (as weak conciliationism requires) happens to be equivalent to evaluating the matter from a dispute-independent perspective (as strong conciliationism requires).

---

[35] One might protest that instrumentalism is a kind of independence requirement in that it requires that nonfundamental doxastic inclinations be treated as evidence and assessed from a vantage point that is antecedent to, and thus *rationally independent of*, the readouts in question. While it is true that instrumentalism can in this sense be understood as an independence requirement, it is not an impartiality requirement. The perspective one occupies in order to assess one's nonfundamental inclinations is *one's own* antecedent perspective. This perspective could include controversial views on the fundamental plausibility of disputed propositions. It could also include a favorable fundamental estimate of one's own reliability that could not be motivated on impartial grounds, a possibility I discuss in the next section.

Weak conciliationism delivers the same verdicts as strong conciliationism in the easy cases of disagreement that have been the focus of so much of the disagreement literature. These cases, then, cannot be used to motivate the standard sort of independence requirement, one that requires epistemic impartiality. Moreover, one cannot generalize from these easy cases to hard cases like those involving religious or moral disagreement. As I will argue in chapter 5, many disagreements in such domains are at least partly driven by opposing assessments of the fundamental plausibility of the contested views. If that is right, and if weak conciliationism is correct, then the equal weighting and convergence of opinion required in easy cases may not be required in many of the hard cases.

3.6 Independence and the Scope of Partisan Justification

Having attempted to undercut the most prominent arguments for dispute-independence requirements like fundamental calibration, I turn now to a more positive argument against such requirements. I will argue that the strong conciliationist must grant that at least some ur-priors are justified on "partisan" grounds, and that once partisan justification is admitted, there is no principled way of delimiting partisan justification so that it applies only to some narrow class of fundamental commitments. So one is not in general required to determine the value of one's ur-priors on impartial grounds.

Suppose that subject S has a high ur-prior for $p1$. According to fundamental calibration, for S to be justified in having this high ur-prior for $p1$, she must have a high $p1$-neutral estimate of her reliability with respect to $p1$. This high $p1$-neutral estimate of her $p1$-reliability will in turn depend on her having high ur-priors for other propositions (in particular, propositions that bear on the reliability of people relevantly like S when they are assessing propositions relevantly like $p1$). Let $p2$ be one of the propositions for which S must have a high ur-prior in order to have a high $p1$-neutral estimate of her $p1$-reliability. According to fundamental calibration, S is justified in having this high ur-prior for $p2$ only if she has a high $p2$-neutral estimate of her reliability in assessing the plausibility of $p2$. Applying the logic just rehearsed, this favorable reliability assessment will require S to have a high ur-prior for some further proposition, $p3$. Moreover, S's high ur-prior for $p3$ must be independent not only of her stance on $p2$ but also of her stance on $p1$. (Otherwise, S's supposedly $p1$-neutral assessment of her $p1$ reliability would turn out not to be $p1$-neutral after all, since it would depend on a high ur-prior for $p2$, which in turn would depend on confidence in $p1$.) Since the requirements of fundamental calibration do not stop at $p3$, an infinite regress looms. For S to be justified in having a high ur-prior for $p1$, S must have a high ur-prior for every member of an infinite hierarchy of propositions, each of which helps to justify S's favorable estimate of her reliability with respect to the proposition at the next level down in the hierarchy.

Moreover, as one ascends this hierarchy, S's rational basis for each ur-prior must be entirely independent of her rational basis for her high ur-priors for propositions lower in the hierarchy. For example, suppose that $p2$ is a proposition that denies some skeptical hypothesis pertaining to S's reasoning about $p1$. The nonskeptical reasoning that accounts for S's confidence in $p2$ must play no role in explaining S's confidence in proposition $p3$ that denies some skeptical hypothesis pertaining to S's reasoning about $p2$, and so on. S would have to deny an infinite number of skeptical scenarios, all for reasons that are entirely independent of one another! It is implausible to hold that one's justification depends on the availability of this sort of infinite hierarchy of independent reasons. Therefore, the strong conciliationist must allow that one can sometimes be justified in having a high initial credence for some proposition p without having any impartial reasons for highly estimating one's reliability on the matter.

It will be useful to have a label for this kind of justification that does not depend on impartial grounds. Say that S's high initial credence for p has *partisan justification* if and only if S is justified in having this high initial credence for p and a credence this high cannot be justified on the basis of third-person, p-neutral reasons for trusting S's reliability with respect to p. Defined in this way, partisan justification is simply that kind of justification that one could not have if fundamental calibration was a genuine and fully general requirement. Roughly, fundamental calibration says that justified ur-priors must have impartial grounds, whereas partisan justification is the justification enjoyed by ur-priors that *lack* impartial grounds. So fundamental calibration (taken as an exceptionless requirement) is the denial of partisan justification. To avoid confusion, I should emphasize that in this context I do not intend the label *partisan* to be derogatory. Someone who affirms the possibility of partisan justification does not thereby support ur-priors that are in some way prejudiced, arbitrary, or groundless. Rather, she simply affirms that ur-priors can be justified at least partly on grounds that do not satisfy the strong conciliationist's standards of impartiality.

The regress argument sketched above shows that the strong conciliationist who wants to avoid radical skepticism must allow that one sometimes has partisan justification, and that fundamental calibration is therefore not an exceptionless requirement. But since the strong conciliationist thinks that one's confidence levels typically should conform to an impartiality require-ment like fundamental calibration, she must also hold that partisan justifica-tion is very limited in scope. But once the existence of partisan justification is admitted, what is the principled reason for thinking that only some narrow class of doxastic commitments enjoys a significant degree of partisan justifi-cation? Why should one think that the partisan justification that applies to some beliefs fails to apply to Roger's assessment of ONE WAY and to other contexts where one allegedly ought to follow fundamental calibration? I will raise doubts about the ability of strong conciliationism to give a plausible an-swer to these questions.

The regress argument shows that people sometimes enjoy partisan justi-fication (assuming they are not required to be radical skeptics), but it does not say which beliefs might benefit from such partisan justification. To sharpen the challenge to the strong conciliationist, it will be helpful to iden-tify two examples where it would seem that partisan justification must be admitted. The first is one's belief that one is not systematically unreliable. It seems that I can have no p-neutral grounds for highly estimating my relia-bility with respect to the proposition that I am not systematically unreliable. For if I am neutral on the question of whether I am systematically unreli-able, then I should presumably not be confident in my evaluation of any piece of reasoning, including reasoning that allegedly supports a high estimate of my reliability with respect to the question of whether I am systematically unreliable.

Second, it would seem that the strong conciliationist must allow that she has partisan justification to have a high initial credence for strong conciliationism itself. Conciliationism is a controversial position, one that is challenged by a significant portion of philosophers who write on disagreement. In light of this expert disagreement over conciliationism, strong conciliationists do not have a good impartial reason to think that they are reliable in their assess-ment of strong conciliationism. Because strong conciliationism lacks the kind of impartial support that the theory says is normally required for jus-tified belief, many would say that strong conciliationism impugns itself and cannot be rationally believed.[36] But as I will argue in chapter 6, there may be principled reasons why conciliatory policies should not issue the normal conciliatory prescriptions in disagreements over conciliationism itself. If this is right, then conciliatory views may not be self-undermining. Even so, if a conciliatory view is to be justified in the present context, then it must be justified on grounds that fail to be impartial. Whatever narrow theory of partisan justification is affirmed by strong conciliationist, it should be one that helps to explain how the belief in strong conciliationism could be justified in the absence of impartial support.

Is there a principled reason for thinking that partisan justification is limited only to some narrow class of propositions, a class that presumably includes denials of radical skeptical hypotheses and the affirmation of conciliationism? When one turns to some of the main accounts of partisan justification, there is no clear reason for supposing that partisan justification is extremely limited in scope.

Consider, for example, a *rationalist* account of partisan justification. According to this account (which will receive more attention in the next chapter), you are sometimes justified in confidently believing that p in virtue of having *rational insight* into the truth or epistemic probability of p, or into the cogency of some argument that entails or strongly supports p. This rational insight justifies your confidence even if you have no independent reason for thinking that you are reliable in the relevant domain. For example, it is plausible that one's epistemic confidence with respect to simple arithmetic is based on the character of one's mathematical insight and not on some reasoning about one's reliability that is neutral regarding basic arithmetical claims. Granted, in many contexts whatever insight is possessed will be less "clear and distinct" (to invoke Cartesian terminology) than in the domain of simple arithmetic. Nonetheless, perhaps even lesser degrees of insight could help to justify a reliability estimate that is higher than that which could be justified on p-neutral grounds.

If one allows for the possibility of rationalist partisan justification, then it is doubtful that the scope of partisan justification is as narrow as the strong conciliationist maintains. For example, couldn't Roger enjoy rational insight that gives him partisan justification for a high ur-prior for ONE WAY? Might it be the case that many people have rationalist partisan justification for their

---

[36] See, for example, Jason Decker, "Conciliation and Self-Incrimination," *Erkenntnis* 79, no. 5 (2014): 1099–1134.

controversial moral, religious, or philosophical beliefs? The challenge posed by these questions is made even more acute for a strong conciliationist who appeals to rationalist grounds to explain how conciliationists are justified in their confidence for conciliationism (despite the absence of impartial support).[37] Strong conciliationism is hardly a view that is *obviously* correct. If strong conciliationism can enjoy rationalist partisan justification, why not many other controversial theories?

Consider next a *practical account* of partisan justification. Many philosophers have appealed to practical reasons to explain how a person can be justified in dismissing radical skepticism.[38] According to this account, your justification for believing that your cognitive faculties are on the whole reliable stems from the fact that robust epistemic self-trust is required in order to rationally engage in important intellectual and deliberative projects. If this kind of practical consideration grounds the reasonability of epistemic self-trust, then it is doubtful that one is typically required to conform to an impartiality requirement like fundamental calibration. In order for me to rationally pursue my intellectual aims, it may be necessary for me to believe that my faculties are on the whole reliable. But it is not necessary for me to believe that *your* faculties are reliable. Even if there are no differences between us that would justify some neutral third party in trusting my faculties more than yours, the fact that *I* must use *my* faculties gives me a special first-person reason to affirm my own reliability. This reason is not counterbalanced by any similar sort of reason for me to believe that you are reliable. Thus, there is no reason to expect that my estimate of my own reliability with respect to *p* must be equal to my estimate of the reliability of some other person who is relevantly similar to me in *p*-neutral respects, as fundamental calibration requires.

---

[37] A maneuver along these lines is pursued in Bogardus, "A Vindication of the Equal-Weight View." Bogardus argues that the equal weight view does not self-undermine because (1) it does not apply to propositions that one can directly "see" by rational intuition to be true, and (2) the equal weight view is one such proposition. Because Bogardus carves out this significant class of exceptions to the prescriptions of the equal weight view, his policy is arguably closer in spirit to weak conciliationism than to strong conciliationism.

[38] Some examples include Wright's "strategic account of entitlement," "entitlement of cognitive project," and "entitlement to rational deliberation"; Enoch and Schechter's "pragmatic account of justification"; and Alston's defense of the practical rationality of trusting in socially established doxastic practices. (See Crispin Wright, "Warrant for Nothing (and Foundations for Free)?," *Aristotelian Society Supplementary Volume* 78, no. 1 (2004): 167–212; David Enoch and Joshua Schechter, "How Are Basic Belief-Forming Methods Justified?," *Philosophy and Phenomenological Research* 76, no. 3 (2008): 547–579; and William P. Alston, *Perceiving God: The Epistemology of Religious Experience* [Ithaca: Cornell University Press, 1991].) Note that the rationalist and practical accounts of partisan justification need not be competitors. They could both be correct.

Some epistemologists contest this claim that the practical account justifies a strong asymmetry in the level of self-trust and trust of others. Perhaps practical reasons provide more *immediate* support to self-trust than to other-trust. Nonetheless, it is argued that *once a subject affirms that she is reliable*, this belief together with some sort of "treat like cases alike" principle rationally requires placing the same degree of trust in others who are relevantly similar.[39] I happily concede that it would be objectionably arbitrary for subject $S1$ to weight his high ur-prior for p more heavily than the low ur-prior of a disputant $S2$ whom $S1$ takes to be "relevantly similar" to himself. But this concession is not enough to vindicate fundamental calibration. To do that, one would need to show that $S1$ ought to acknowledge $S2$ as "relevantly similar" anytime it appears that $S1$ and $S2$ are on a par with respect to the accessible p-neutral considerations. And why should $S1$ think that relevant similarity is entirely determined by p-neutral considerations?

According to the rationalist position I will defend in the next chapter, whether $S1$ should count $S2$ as relevantly similar will ultimately depend on the discernible rational merits of $S1$'s position and $S2$'s position. Since the rational merits of these positions cannot be assessed in a dispute-neutral way, this view does not support the idea that relevant similarity must be determined in an impartial manner. But even if someone rejects this rationalist approach to determining relevant similarity, it does not follow that relevant similarity should be determined on the basis of p-neutral considerations. For example, $S1$ might think that his reliability with respect to p is not grounded in some broad cognitive process that is also employed by those who reject p. He might instead think that his reliability is due to some narrow process that favors a high credence for p and that is therefore not employed by those who reject p (however similar they may be in p-neutral respects). $S1$ might think that someone qualifies as relevantly similar only if she employs this narrow process. Absent some further reason to think that relevant similarity must be assessed from an impartial perspective, one cannot appeal to a "treat like cases alike" principle in order to show that partisan justification has narrow scope.[40]

---

[39] Linda Trinkaus Zagzebski, *Epistemic Authority: A Theory of Trust, Authority, and Autonomy in Belief* (Oxford: Oxford University Press, 2012), 55–56.

[40] For a similar argument against attempts to motivate a very strong degree of other-trust by appealing to self-trust, see Elizabeth Fricker, "Epistemic Trust in Oneself and Others—An Argument from Analogy?," in *Religious Faith and Intellectual Virtue*, ed. Laura Frances Callahan and Timothy O'Connor (Oxford: Oxford University Press, 2014), 174–203.

Of course, certain background beliefs might make *S1* confident that *if* he is reliable with respect to *p*, then his reliability is accounted for in terms of available *p*-neutral considerations. In this case, the discovery of significant disagreement over *p* among those who are like *S1* with respect to *p*-neutral considerations might lead *S1* to conclude that he is not reliable with respect to *p*. Thus, his view on the matter would be defeated. Alternatively, conditionalizing on robust track record data might result in *S1* estimating his own reliability at (approximately) the same level as *S2*'s, even if *S1*'s fundamental reliability estimates were self-favoring. Nonetheless, the practical account of partisan justification does not (any more than the rationalist account) supply a principled reason for thinking that in all (or most) domains it is rationally *required* that *S1*'s reliability estimate for himself be equal to his estimate for those who are similar in *p*-neutral respects.

Christensen is one strong conciliationist who acknowledges that independence requirements are not absolute and offers an account of when significant partisan justification is and is not available. I close this section by considering whether this account successfully explains why, even though there is partisan justification, partisan justification is highly limited in scope. On Christensen's view, I am required to assess my reliability with respect to *p* in a *p*-neutral way only to the extent that I have a sufficiently rich and informative base of *p*-neutral considerations on which to base such an evaluation.[41] When I have a highly impoverished and uninformative base of *p*-neutral considerations, I can give less weight to the *p*-neutral reliability estimate.

Accommodating this suggestion requires weakening the fundamental calibration requirement. The revised view does not straightforwardly require that your ur-prior for *p* be equal to your independent reliability estimate of someone who is relevantly similar. Rather, it says that your ur-prior for *p* should *approach* this independent reliability estimate to the extent that this estimate is based on a sufficiently rich set of *p*-neutral considerations. Call this requirement *graded fundamental calibration*. By itself, graded fundamental calibration will not support the highly demanding conciliatory verdicts of the sort that Christensen endorses when he discusses real-world philosophical disagreements. To support these demanding conciliatory verdicts, one must add that in cases where you have a sufficiently rich set of *p*-neutral considerations, your ur-prior should be equal to your *p*-neutral

---

[41] Christensen, "Disagreement, Question-Begging and Epistemic Self-Criticism," 15–16.

reliability estimate, or at least very close to that estimate.[42] Call the latter claim the *swamping thesis* since it holds that *p*-neutral considerations, if not too impoverished, swamp partisan considerations. I will give the label *graded strong conciliationism* to the Christensen-inspired position that affirms both graded fundamental calibration and the swamping thesis.

It might seem that graded strong conciliationism provides a plausible way of affirming demanding impartiality requirements while acknowledging the reality of partisan justification. But further inspection reveals that the position is highly problematic. As I will argue, graded strong conciliationism requires that one either violate a highly plausible epistemic reflection requirement or shift one's expectations about future impartial considerations in ways that are not evidentially justified.

To illustrate the problem, consider the following permutation of the example involving Roger and ONE WAY. Suppose that Roger is told that he is about to be asked to evaluate some metaphysical claim randomly selected from a book called *Easy True/False Questions in Metaphysics*. Before the specific claim is revealed, a reliable and trustworthy source tells Roger the following facts. People with Roger's sort of education and intellectual background fall into one of two groups: the metaphysical whizzes and the metaphysical dummies. When the whizzes are presented with one of the metaphysical claims taken from the book, they always correctly judge its truth value. The dummies on the other hand do no better than chance. They feel just as confident as the whizzes, but for each question in the book, the probability that a dummy gets the right answer is only 50%. Unfortunately, the dummies aren't able to tell that they are dummies. When the dummies are informed about the two groups, they (like the whizzes) almost invariably think they are whizzes, at least until their dismal track records are revealed to them. (One can imagine that the metaphysical dummies aren't bad at *other* subjects; their dimwittedness is confined to metaphysics.) Finally, Roger is told that the percentage of people who are dummies is positive, but he is not told whether or not the percentage is significant.

Imagine that before Roger is shown the claim that he is to evaluate, he is asked to form his best guess about the percentage of people relevantly like him who are metaphysical whizzes and the percentage who are dummies. Roger has almost nothing to go on. He's hardly thought about metaphysics

---

[42] For an example of how Christensen suggests responding to real-world philosophical disagreement, see "Disagreement and Public Controversy," 147.

at all, and he has no idea how common it is for people to disagree about metaphysical matters. On a highly impoverished base of evidence, Roger's best guess is that of those relevantly like him, about 70% are whizzes and about 30% are dummies. Suppose that this is in fact the most rational estimated value of the actual percentages in light of Roger's extremely impoverished base of relevant evidence. Having arrived at this view, Roger is then presented with ONE WAY, the claim he is asked to evaluate. He evaluates the claim and is inclined to assign it a credence of 0.99. He is told that in one hour, he will be told the actual values for the percentages of people relevantly like him that are whizzes and dummies. But in the meantime, what credence for ONE WAY is permissible for Roger?

The strong conciliationist would say that Roger must set his credence in an impartial way. When relying only on reasons that are p-neutral and agent neutral, Roger's best guess is that there is a 70% chance that he's a whiz (in which case he's sure to be right about ONE WAY) and a 30% chance that he's a dummy (in which case his odds are no better than chance). So according to unqualified strong conciliationism, Roger's credence for ONE WAY should be $0.85 (= 0.70 \cdot 1 + 0.30 \cdot 0.5)$. But *graded* strong conciliationism is not nearly as stringent. Because Roger has almost no evidence to go on in guessing percentages of whizzes and dummies, the impartial grounds for estimating his reliability are very weak. And graded strong conciliationism says that when Roger has very weak impartial grounds for estimating his reliability, he can give significant weight to his first-order reasoning that is not p-neutral. So suppose that graded strong conciliationism permits Roger to adopt a credence of 0.95 for ONE WAY. And suppose that Roger is a graded strong conciliationist who does in fact adopt a credence of 0.95 for ONE WAY.

With this setup in place, I can now explain the problem for graded strong conciliationism. In an hour, Roger will be told the actual percentage of people like him who are whizzes and the actual percentage who are dummies. Since at that later time Roger will have very strong impartial grounds for estimating his reliability with respect to ONE WAY, he is committed to adopting a fully impartial credence when he learns the actual percentage values. More specifically, letting W stand for the percentage of whizzes (a value that will be revealed in an hour), Roger is committed to setting his credence for ONE WAY equal to $W \cdot 1 + (1 - W) \cdot 0.5$, which simplifies to $0.5W + 0.5$. But recall the highly plausible epistemic reflection principle discussed in section 3.1, which says that your current credence for p should not differ from the expected value of your credence for p at some future time t if you know that at

t you will be strictly more informed and just as rational as you are currently. This principle implies that Roger's *current* credence for ONE WAY should not differ from the expected value for $0.5W + 0.5$, the credence he will adopt in an hour. Thus, since Roger's current credence is 0.95, it should be the case that $0.95 = 0.5W_{exp} + 0.5$, where W_{exp} is the expected value for W. Solving, one gets $W_{exp} = 0.9$. In other words, if Roger satisfies epistemic reflection, then his current expected value for the actual percentage of whizzes is 0.9.

Here is the difficult question for the strong conciliationist: what evidence has Roger received that justifies increasing his expected value of W from 0.7 all the way to 0.9? One can stipulate that nothing about the content of ONE WAY has any bearing on the percentage of people who are whizzes. Even if Roger somehow learned that he is a whiz who has rightly assessed ONE WAY, such evidence would not normally justify such a large shift in Roger's expectations for W.[43] So it would seem that if Roger respects epistemic reflection, then his expectations about the content of the impartial evidence he will later acquire must shift in ways that are not evidentially justified and that cannot be supported by conditionalization. Or, if Roger does not shift his expectations for W in ways that are evidentially unjustified, then he will violate the epistemic reflection principle. In light of this unhappy result, graded strong conciliationism would appear to be an unprincipled and implausible policy.

I have argued that neither the rationalist nor the practical accounts of partisan justification give one a reason to think that partisan justification is limited in scope to some narrow class of commitments. Initially, it may seem that graded strong conciliationism provides a principled explanation as to why in many situations one lacks significant partisan justification. But this view proves to be highly problematic. Of course, there may be some account I have not yet considered that explains why partisan justification, while available in

---

[43] Suppose Roger received as a piece of evidence the fact that a randomly selected subject (namely, himself) is a whiz. Call this evidence E. It is true that one can construct prior credence distributions that support a value for W_{exp} of 0.7 before learning E and a value of 0.9 after conditionalizing on E. For example, Roger initially might have assigned a credence of 7/9 to $W = 0.9$ and a credence of 2/9 to $W = 0$. Learning that there is one whiz would then confirm with certainty $W = 0.9$. But there is no reason to suppose that Roger's credences for the possible values of W will be skewed in one of the ways that would give this result. Consider an overly simplified but more natural way of imagining Roger's initial situation, one where he starts with a credence function C that assigns the following values: C $(W = 0.95) = 1/3$, C $(W = 0.7) = 1/3$, and C $(W = 0.45) = 1/3$. If Roger started from this position and conditionalized on E, then his new credence function C_N would assign the following values: $C_N (W = 0.95) \approx 0.45$, $C_N (W = 0.7) \approx 0.33$, and $C_N (W = 0.45) \approx 0.21$. (I omit the straightforward Bayesian calculations.) In this scenario, updating on E would result in W_{exp} increasing from 0.7 to 0.76. As this example illustrates, even when one characterizes Roger's evidence in the most favorable terms, he is unlikely to have justification to increase his expected value for W from 0.7 all the way to 0.9.

some situations, is highly limited in scope. But I provisionally conclude that a substantial portion of one's ur-priors may enjoy some degree of partisan justification.

3.7 Two Objections to Weak Conciliationism

I now address two objections to weak conciliationism. The first objection claims that following weak conciliationism results in lower expected accuracy than following strong conciliationism, where expected accuracy is (roughly) a measure of how well some credence for p reflects the evidential probability of p. The second objection claims that if the instrumentalist approach is pushed far enough, instrumentalism ends up requiring the same epistemic impartiality that is explicitly required by fundamental calibration. According to this objection, the distinction between weak and strong conciliationism collapses.

3.7.1 The Inaccuracy Objection

To set up the objection, I'll again return to the original example of Roger and ONE WAY. In this version of the example, when Roger is told that he is about to be presented with some metaphysical thesis p, he is also told that half of those who are like him in relevant p-neutral respects are inclined toward a high ur-prior for p and half are inclined toward a low ur-prior for p. The inaccuracy objection is strongest as an objection to the combination of weak conciliationism and a purely rationalist account of partisan justification. So for sake of the argument, suppose that practical reasons for self-trust cannot give Roger partisan justification and that the only legitimate basis for trusting himself more than others like him will be if he has genuine rational insight into the truth or plausibility of the proposition in question. At the present juncture, Roger has not yet been told the content of the thesis and knows nothing about how he will reason on the matter. This means that he should think that it is only 50% probable that he will be inclined toward the correct view after learning the content of the thesis and reflecting on its plausibility. Finally, suppose that Roger knows that all those who reflect on p initially *take themselves* to have rational insight into the truth or plausibility of their position (whether or not they in fact do). As a result, those who follow weak conciliationism end up having fairly high credences for their views (0.7, say). By contrast, those who follow strong conciliationism ultimately adopt a credence for p of 0.5.

While Roger presently thinks that there is only a 0.5 chance that he will have the correct (first-order) view about p, he knows that following weak conciliationism will lead him to assign his view a credence of 0.7. In other words, he knows that following weak conciliationism will result in his confidence at some future time t being greater than the expected value of his reliability at t. On the other hand he knows that following strong conciliationism would result in his adopting a credence at t that is equal to the expected value of his reliability at t. It seems objectionable for Roger to follow an updating procedure that he knows will result in a credence that exceeds his expected reliability. Thus, it seems that he should reject weak conciliationism and follow strong conciliationism instead.

Schoenfield characterizes the issue here in terms of expected accuracy, where the accuracy of a credence function is a measure of how close it comes to the "omniscient" credence function that assigns 1s to all truths and 0s to all falsehoods.[44] The *expected* accuracy of a credence function can be measured in different ways, but measuring expected accuracy using "proper" scoring rules (such as the Brier score) gives the highest expected accuracy score to credences that match the evidential probability. Intuitively, credences should be accurate in this way. For example, if the probability of p on my evidence is 0.6, then my credence for p should be 0.6. In addition to considering the expected accuracy of a credence function, one can consider the expected accuracy of an update procedure. The expected accuracy of an update procedure is simply a weighted average of the expected accuracy of the future credence functions that could result from applying the procedure. And it can easily be shown that from Roger's present perspective, updating in accordance with strong conciliationism has a greater expected accuracy than updating in accordance with weak conciliationism.

The problem with this initial statement of the argument, as Schoenfield recognizes, is that which procedure is supported by considerations of expected accuracy depends on how one individuates the procedures to be considered. When Roger compares the broad procedure "follow weak conciliationism" with the broad procedure "follow strong conciliationism," the latter process has a higher expected accuracy than the former. But if

[44] Schoenfield, "An Accuracy Based Approach to Higher Order Evidence," 695.

Roger compares procedures that are individuated more narrowly, the procedure with the highest expected accuracy may well be one that involves following weak conciliationism. For example, suppose Roger compares the following procedures:

1. Follow weak conciliationism while reasoning rightly about p.
2. Follow weak conciliationism while reasoning poorly about p.
3. Follow strong conciliationism.

As long as Roger thinks that it is quite probable (more than 60%) that right reasoning will produce a true judgment about p, then procedure 1 will have a higher expected accuracy (as measured using the Brier Score) than either of the other two procedures.[45] So individuating the procedures this way leads to the conclusion that weak conciliationism is part of the superior procedure.

Now, one might be suspicious of any attempt to vindicate weak conciliationism by pointing to the high expected accuracy of procedure 1. After all, all weak conciliationists are *trying* to follow procedure 1. But half of them end up following procedure 2, the worst of the bunch, while wrongly thinking that they are following procedure 1. And Roger knows his chances are no better. According to Schoenfield, arguing against strong conciliationism by pointing to the superior expected accuracy of procedure 1 is a bit like absurdly arguing against evidentialism by appealing to the superior expected accuracy of the "truth procedure" that assigns a credence of 1 to all truths and a credence of 0 to all falsehoods.[46] While someone who successfully conforms to the truth procedure will have perfectly accurate credences, *trying* to follow the truth procedure is unlikely to meet with success. And the expected accuracy of *trying* to follow this procedure is lower than the expected accuracy of trying to adopt credences that reflect the strength of one's evidence. Schoenfield concludes that one should not choose between procedures by comparing the expected accuracy of *conforming* to the various procedures but should instead choose by comparing the expected accuracy

---

[45] Let r be the probability that right reasoning leads to a true first-order view on p. Recall my stipulation that weak conciliationists assign a credence of 0.7 to their first-order view. The *in*accuracy of a credence c for some true proposition as measured by the Brier score is $(1 - c)^2$. In this case, lower Brier scores are better. Using the Brier score, the expected inaccuracy score for procedure 1 is $r(1 - 0.7)^2 + (1 - r)(1 - 0.3)^2 = 0.49 - 0.4r$. The expected inaccuracy score for procedure 3, strong conciliationism, is $(1 - 0.5)^2 = 0.25$. So procedure 1 outperforms procedure 3 just in case $0.49 - 0.4r < 0.25$, or, in other words, anytime $r > 0.6$. Thus, if it is more than 60% probable that right reasoning leads to the correct judgment about p, then procedure 1 has a higher expected accuracy.

[46] "An Accuracy Based Approach to Higher Order Evidence," 692.

that results from *planning* to follow the various procedures.[47] The latter comparison allows one to take into account the possibility that one will fail in one's attempt to conform to a given procedure. If Roger takes Schoenfield's advice and compares the expected accuracy of planning to follow procedure 1 with the expected accuracy of planning to follow procedure 3, Roger will see that the latter plan has a greater expected accuracy and will therefore have good reason to be a strong conciliationist.

Against Schoenfield, however, I do not think that the rational standing of competing procedures can be settled by comparing the expected accuracy of plans to follow the various procedures. I believe the following example shows that something must be wrong with Schoenfield's "planning framework."[48] Veronica used to be a competitive soccer player. These days, she only plays soccer on rare occasions. But when she sleeps at night she still regularly *dreams* that she is playing soccer. When it occurs to Veronica in a soccer dream to consider whether or not she is dreaming, she invariably concludes that everything looks normal and is therefore inclined to be highly confident that she is awake. But in fact, things do *not* look normal in these dreams. When Veronica awakes and remembers her dream, she sees how silly it was for her to think that she was actually playing soccer. All sorts of crazy things happen in these dreams that any sober and normal awake person would recognize as "dreamlike." Sometimes, when Veronica is *actually* playing soccer, she also considers whether or not she is dreaming. Invariably, upon appreciating the normal vividness and coherence of her experience, she is inclined to be highly confident that she is awake. Suppose that Veronica knows that on 80% of the occasions when it seems to her that she is playing soccer, she is in fact asleep in her bed. Now, consider two procedures that Veronica might follow in moments where she is inclined to be confident that she is playing soccer. The "skeptical procedure" says to assign a credence of 0.2 to the proposition that Veronica is actually awake and playing soccer. The "attentive procedure" says to assign a high credence to the proposition that she is awake and playing soccer if and only if her experiences are vivid and coherent in the way that is typical for her when she is awake; otherwise, she should assign a low credence. Veronica knows that if she plans to follow the skeptical

---

[47] "An Accuracy Based Approach to Higher Order Evidence," 706–710.

[48] My example appeals to dreams and the fact that one can normally tell when one is not dreaming even though one often can't tell when one is dreaming. Roger White makes a similar appeal to dreams in arguing against views on higher-order defeat similar to the one advanced by Schoenfield. See "You Just Believe That Because . . . ," *Philosophical Perspectives* 24, no. 1 (2010): 603–604.

procedure, she will succeed in conforming to the skeptical procedure, even in her dreams. She also knows that if she plans to follow the attentive procedure, she will successfully conform to the attentive procedure only when she is awake.

Schoenfield's planning framework implies that Veronica should follow the skeptical procedure, since the plan to follow this procedure has a greater expected accuracy than the plan to follow the attentive procedure. But nearly everyone would acknowledge that when Veronica is awake and playing soccer, she is fully justified in being highly confident that she is indeed playing soccer. So the planning framework should be rejected. Now, I concede that if Veronica had the power to impose the skeptical procedure on her future self, this might be a rational thing to do, especially if the costs of error were high.[49] For example, suppose a mind-reading demon promised to steal $2,000 from Veronica every time she mistakenly believed that she was awake playing soccer. If there was a button she could push that would make her future self conform to the skeptical procedure, then it might be rational for her to push the button. But my question is not whether it would be rational for Veronica to force her future self to conform to some procedure. My question is what updating procedure is rational at the moment when it is time to apply one of the procedures.

Similarly, if Roger had the power to force his future self to conform to strong conciliationism, it might be rational for him to exercise this power. But my question is whether it is rational to conform to weak or strong conciliationism once it is time to apply one of these procedures. That is, I am asking what Roger should do after he has learned the content of the metaphysical thesis and has reflected on its plausibility. The dream example provides a strong reason for thinking that this question is not settled by the planning framework. The expected accuracy of *planning* to give more weight to the rational perspective on the metaphysical thesis in question is not very high. Still, this should not stop Roger from following procedure 1 and giving more weight to his view once he reflects on ONE WAY and has genuine rational insight into whether or not it is plausible.

Even if the dream example poses a grave problem for Schoenfield's planning framework, the example also poses some difficult questions for the

---

[49] White also endorses a view according to which it would be prudentially rational for Veronica to impose the skeptical procedure on her future self (if this were possible) even though when Veronica is awake and playing soccer, it would be rational for her to follow the attentive procedure. See White, "You Just Believe That Because," 603.

weak conciliationist. First, why is it not rational for one to try to follow the truth procedure (assigning a credence of 1 to all truths) even if it *is* rational for Veronica to try to follow the attentive procedure and for Roger to try to follow procedure 1? Here is a suggestion. Unlike the attentive procedure and procedure 1, the truth procedure requires one to assign credences that have a certain relationship with factors that may not be accessible to a fully rational agent. In many instances, the truth value of a proposition is not rationally accessible (unlike the proposition's degree of evidential support, at least given certain internalist ways of understanding evidence). This is obviously the case in situations where one's evidence is misleading. Given the rational inaccessibility of many truth values, successfully following the truth procedure would require one to make many rationally arbitrary decisions about when to assign a credence of 1 to a proposition that does not have evidential support. It would also require that one be very lucky in how these arbitrary decisions are made. And rationality cannot require credence assignments that would be rationally arbitrary. On the other hand whether the features of one's experience are normal in their coherence and vividness *is* a matter that is accessible to a fully rational agent. Likewise, whether some line of reasoning in support of ONE WAY is cogent is also a matter that is accessible to a fully rational agent. So the reason to reject the truth procedure does not apply to the attentive procedure or to procedure 1.

The second question poses a greater challenge to the weak conciliationist.[50] I have suggested that the cogency of some line of reasoning can be accessible to a rational agent (just as the coherence and vividness of Veronica's experience is accessible to her when she is awake). Given this, why not follow a nonconciliatory policy that says to reason correctly and then to remain entirely confident in one's reasoning no matter what one's epistemic peers (who have the same evidence) think about the matter? If Roger can see that his reasoning about ONE WAY is correct, can't he also see that the epistemically optimal outcome is to simply discount Fiona's view in the event that it conflicts with his own?

In addressing this question, the first thing to note is that if it is reasonable for Roger to adopt an ur-prior for ONE WAY that is less than 1, then the standard arguments for conditionalization can be used to support the view that Roger ought to reduce confidence when he learns of Fiona's

---

[50] I'm grateful to an anonymous referee for raising this challenge.

disagreement (assuming that the occurrence of her disagreement is more probable conditional on Roger being wrong than conditional on his being right). So the real challenge for the weak conciliationist is to explain why it could be reasonable for Roger to adopt an ur-prior lower than 1 in the first place, given that he is in a position to appreciate the cogency of some line of reasoning that ostensibly establishes the truth of ONE WAY. I must give an explanation here without invoking a demanding impartiality requirement like fundamental calibration. If I cannot, then it would seem that the only viable alternative to strong conciliationism is a "right reasons view," which says that if you are reasoning correctly you should not cede *any* ground in disagreements with interlocutors who are known to possess exactly the same evidence as yourself.[51]

In response, perhaps what is accessible to Roger is not the fact that he has reasoned rightly about ONE WAY but a fact pertaining to the degree and character of the insight that informs his thinking on the matter. Even if Roger is not in a position to know that he is following procedure 1, he might know that his procedure involves believing that p in response to genuine insight of a certain level of clarity and force. The fact that one's view is the product of genuine insight does not always guarantee that one's thinking on the matter is correct: one may correctly appreciate how certain considerations rationally support one's belief on some matter while mistakenly overestimating the evidential significance of those considerations; one may believe that p on the basis of insights that decisively support some proposition very closely related to p but not p itself (for example, one could imagine Roger believing ONE WAY on the basis of reasoning that correctly rules out circular *explanation* but not circular *causation*); or one might rightly perceive a significant tension between p and certain of one's core convictions while failing, through a lack of imagination, to identify an alternative system of beliefs that is highly plausible even though it includes p and rejects one or more of those core convictions. In light of such possibilities, someone with genuine insight can reasonably retain some doubt about the correctness of her reasoning while nonetheless estimating her reliability more highly than would be justified on the basis of purely dispute-neutral considerations.

---

[51] See Thomas Kelly, "The Epistemic Significance of Disagreement," *Oxford Studies in Epistemology* 1 (2005): 167–196; and Michael G. Titelbaum, "Rationality's Fixed Point (Or: In Defense of Right Reason)," *Oxford Studies in Epistemology* 5 (2015): 253–294.

3.7.2 Does Instrumentalism Amount to an Independence Requirement?

The last objection I will consider contests my contention that weak conciliationism differs significantly from strong conciliationism in its implications for deep disagreements in areas such as religion, morality, and philosophy. I suggested that many disagreements in these domains are driven by differing ur-priors, which I have glossed as "fundamental plausibility judgments." The present objection maintains that the sort of "fundamental" plausibility judgments I have in mind are not genuinely fundamental. Even if these plausibility judgments are *preevidential* (in that they do not take into account empirical information gained through experience), these judgments are not simply *given* but are the product of rational reflection on the content of these propositions. So, according to the objection, it therefore makes sense to ask about the attitude that one has toward a proposition *antecedent* to such reflection.

Presumably, prior to the sort of reflection that yields ur-priors (in my sense), one's credences should be determined by the application of some sort of "in-difference principle" that requires neutrality between competing views. Thus, if one wants to identify those doxastic attitudes that are *truly* fundamental, one must look behind one's ur-priors for some set of "indifference credences." Since these indifference credences are not informed by the reasoning that grounds one's ur-priors, they can provide an antecedent vantage point that would allow one to treat those ur-priors (or, more accurately, ur-prior inclinations) in an instrumentalist fashion. Moreover, because these indifference credences are antecedent to any reflection on the fundamental plausibility of various propositions, it is plausible that they would provide dispute-neutral common ground even in deep disagreements in religion, ethics, and so on. If disputants do start from a common set of indifference credences, then the instrumentalist framework would (when pushed far enough) amount to a sort of independence requirement that could bring about convergence in so-called fundamental disputes arising from opposed ur-priors.

There are several serious problems with the position just sketched. The most glaring problem is that one cannot on the basis of an indifference principle alone identify a uniquely correct initial credence distribution.[52]

---

[52] James M. Joyce, "A Defense of Imprecise Credences in Inference and Decision Making," *Philosophical Perspectives* 24, no. 1 (2010): 281–323; Christopher J. G. Meacham, "Impermissive Bayesianism," *Erkenntnis* 79, no. 6 (2014): 1185–1217.

The initial idea behind the indifference principle is that if I do not know of any evidence or other considerations bearing on the question of which of several disjoint hypotheses is true (or if I have not yet assessed whatever considerations are at my disposal), then I should be epistemically neutral between the hypotheses and assign the same credence to each. One can easily see why this initial statement of the principle is insufficient. Consider a race between Horse A, Horse B, and Horse C, where the rules guarantee exactly one winner. There are only two possibilities: (1) Horse A wins, or (2) Horse A does not win. According to the indifference principle as just characterized, my initial credence for the first possibility should be equal to my initial credence for the second possibility. But this is obviously not right. Not only is there an evident asymmetry between possibilities (1) and (2), but the same indifference principle would lead me to an inconsistent credence distribution if I had instead applied it to the following partitioning of the possibilities: (1) Horse A wins; (2) Horse B wins; or (3) Horse C wins. Clearly, the initial indifference principle needs to be amended so that it applies only when the menu of options is rightly constructed so that the hypotheses are on a par with one another in the relevant respects.

Unfortunately, an indifference principle that is amended in this way still cannot deliver a uniquely correct initial credence distribution. This is because in many contexts, there is no uncontroversial way to go about constructing the menu of possibilities toward which the indifference principle should be applied. Such a menu must partition the possibilities in such a way that the various possibilities exhibit the right sort of parity or symmetry. But hypotheses can be on par in one respect but not in others, and there can be disagreement about which sort of parity matters. The problem is powerfully illustrated by the example of the mystery cube.[53] I tell you that there is a factory that produces nothing but cubes. The cubes have various sizes, but none of them has a side length that is greater than 1 foot. I give you no other information about the purpose or nature of the cubes produced. Now I tell you that in the next room there is a cube that was produced in the factory. What is your credence that the side length of the cube is ½ foot or less? This might seem like an appropriate occasion for applying the indifference principle.

---

[53] "Mystery cube" examples trace their origin to the discussion of the "perfect cube factory" in Bas C. van Fraassen, *Laws and Symmetry* (Oxford: Oxford University Press, 1989), 303. But the challenge to the indifference principle illustrated by the example was originally developed by Joseph Bertrand in the nineteenth century.

There are two disjoint possibilities for the side length l: $0 < l \le$ ½ foot, and ½ foot $< l \le 1$ foot. Because both of these ranges are of equal magnitude (½ foot), the possibilities seem to be relevantly on a par. So in the absence of any other evidence to go on, it might seem that the rationally appropriate stance is to be indifferent between the two possibilities and to assign each possibility a credence of ½.

But note that the same cube factory could have been alternately described in the following way. There is a cube factory that produces cubes; the cubes have various sizes, but none of them has a volume greater than 1 cubic foot. Suppose that the factory was described in this way, and then you were asked your credence that the cube in the next room has a volume less than or equal to 1/8 cubic foot. Given this presentation of the same question, it might seem that your credence for this possibility should be 1/8. For there are 8 disjoint possibilities for the volume of the cube v: $0 < v \le$ 1/8 foot³, 1/8 foot³ $< v \le$ 2/8 foot³, and so on up to 7/8 foot³ $< v \le 1$ foot³. Because all of these ranges are equal in magnitude, they appear to be on par in the relevant respect. So proper application of the indifference principle would seem to require being indifferent toward these possibilities, assigning each one a credence of 1/8. But it is inconsistent to assign a credence of ½ to the possibility that $0 < l \le$ ½ foot while also assigning a credence of 1/8 to the possibility that $0 < v \le$ 1/8 foot³. For these are the *very same* possibility, alternately described. This example shows that even if one limits the application of the indifference principle to situations where the space of possibilities has been "evenly" partitioned into hypotheses that are seemingly on a par, the principle can lead to inconsistent results. For hypotheses that are on a par with respect to one dimension (magnitude of the range for side length, for instance) may not be on par with respect to other dimensions (for example, magnitude of the range for volume).[54]

This problem applies not just at the micro level of mystery cubes but also at the macro level of "worldviews." Consider how a Roman Catholic and an atheistic nihilist should go about identifying which indifference credences form the appropriate vantage point from which their disagreement should be assessed. Should they start with an "indifference" credence of 0.5 for Roman

---

[54] In the mystery cube case, one can easily identify an infinite number of parameters that could be used to partition the space of possibilities such that no two partitions yield consistent results when the indifference principle is applied. For example one could partition the possibilities evenly by side length, side area (l^2), volume (l^3), l^4, l^5, and so on, and none of these partitions would yield mutually consistent results when the indifference principle is applied.

Catholicism? Or a credence of 0.5 for theism? Or for nihilism? Or, perhaps they should start by adopting a stance of indifference with respect to some other question that indirectly bears on the dispute at hand. For example, perhaps they should evenly divide their credence between substance nihilism, substance monism, and substance pluralism; or between the principle of sufficient reason and its negation; or between realist and nonrealist views of evaluative facts. There is no coherent way of being "neutral" with respect to all of these questions, since they are not all orthogonal to each other. And which of these alternative ways of constructing an indifference credence distribution one chooses could significantly shape one's assessment of the antecedent probability of the disputants' respective views. Since there is no uncontroversial way of applying an indifference principle to arrive at an initial credence distribution, there is no reason to hope that such a principle will enable one to identify a dispute-neutral starting point.

Even if there were some unique and uncontroversial way of applying a principle of indifference, there is a further problem with the proposal under consideration. This proposal, recall, is that I should not uncritically endorse the ur-priors toward which I am inclined (after reflecting on the fundamental plausibility of various hypotheses). Instead, I should (ideally) treat my inclination toward these ur-priors as evidence and conditionalize on this evidence from the standpoint of my indifference credence distribution. Will this process lead me to move from my initial noncommittal stance (the one made up of indifference credences) to a more opinionated stance, one that at least somewhat resembles the ur-priors toward which I am inclined? It seems that this process will accomplish this only to the extent that I already believe that my fundamental plausibility judgments are reliable evidential indicators. And there is no reason to think that the "correct" indifference credences would assign a high credence to the proposition that my fundamental plausibility judgments are highly reliable. From the perspective constituted by the correct indifference credences, the fact that I strongly feel that torturing for fun is wrong, or that $1 + 1 = 2$, or that effects do not precede causes, may perhaps constitute only very weak evidence in favor of the proposition in question, or may not be considered confirming evidence at all. Thus, if the proposal is to avoid collapse into sweeping skepticism, it must be conceded that I should *not* start from a credal position that is "indifferent" across the board. Instead, my starting position must include a sufficiently confident belief in the evidential value of my fundamental plausibility judgments.

But avoiding skepticism does not require that I assign equal evidential value to *your* fundamental plausibility judgments, as I discussed in section 3.6. So even if I start from dispute-neutral indifference credences and then plug in credences about my reliability that are necessary to avoid skepticism, and then conditionalize on the "readouts" supplied by my plausibility judgments and by your plausibility judgments, there is no reason to think that I will end with a perspective that gives as much weight to your plausibility judgments as to my own. Someone who wants to appeal to indifference credences in order to show that instrumentalism requires dispute-independence must still provide a nonskeptical account of partisan justification that explains why I must trust others as much as I trust myself.

3.8 Conclusion

When one determines how much to trust some instrumental readout, one takes into consideration one's antecedent view on the reliability of the instrument *and* one's antecedent view on the plausibility of the "claim" made by the instrument. One can often approach the "readouts" of one's cognitive faculties in the same way. When I am inclined to believe some proposition p on the basis of memory, or on the basis of a perceptual seeming, or on the basis of a complex process of calculation, I can decide how much trust to put in such a readout by taking into consideration my expected epistemic reliability *and* my antecedent perspective on p's plausibility. This antecedent perspective serves as an independent check that modulates the degree to which I trust my doxastic inclinations. But my *fundamental* assessment of p's plausibility—that is, my inclination toward a certain ur-prior—cannot be treated in an instrumentalist fashion, since I have no rationally antecedent view on p's plausibility that could be used to gauge the trustworthiness of this ur-prior inclination.

According to weak conciliationism, in the absence of an antecedent vantage point that would allow me to treat my ur-prior inclinations in an instrumentalist fashion, it can be rationally permissible for me to adopt the ur-priors toward which I am inclined. Strong conciliationists on the other hand insist that all (or nearly all) of my ur-priors should be entirely determined by an impartial reliability estimate. I've argued that this fundamental calibration requirement is unmotivated. Contrary to what some seem to think, fundamental calibration is not a straightforward extension of the instrument model: the trust that a rational agent puts in some instrumental readout is never determined solely by the expected reliability of the instrument. Nor is fundamental calibration needed to explain commonsense conciliatory verdicts in the simple cases prominently featured in the disagreement literature. Finally, because fundamental calibration cannot be consistently applied to all ur-priors, the strong conciliationist must admit that some ur-priors enjoy partisan justification. And the strong conciliationist has not provided a good reason for thinking that partisan justification is extremely limited in scope.

Suppose that I am right and that weak conciliationism provides the correct account of how one should respond to disagreement. Does this mean that one can confidently maintain religious convictions in the face of significant disagreement? Not clearly, for three reasons. First, it is not clear that religious disagreements are in fact fundamental disagreements driven by partisan starting points. A significant strand in recent epistemology of religious belief, so-called reformed epistemology, points to perceptual and quasi-perceptual processes as an apt model for religious belief formation. As I will argue in the next chapter, this view of religious belief formation may be at odds with the notion that religious disagreements are rationally fundamental in a way that would alleviate the worries raised by religious disagreement.

Second, weak conciliationism is not committed to the view that one is *always* justified in having partisan starting points. It is open to the weak conciliationist to hold that some ur-priors should conform to fundamental calibration. Weak conciliationism affirms instrumentalism and conditionalization and denies that there is any sort of sweeping impartiality requirement that would require convergence of credences in all (or nearly all) fundamental disputes. Weak conciliationism thus denies that fundamental calibration is a fully general (or nearly general) requirement. But even if one often enjoys partisan justification, it could be that partisan justification is not available for all ur-priors. And where it is not available, fundamental calibration may apply. The next chapter will refine my weak conciliatory view by considering various positions on the nature and scope of partisan justification.

Third, even in disagreements that are fundamental and where one or more parties are justified in their partisan starting points, weak conciliationism can require nontrivial reduction in confidence. In any disagreement, superficial or fundamental, weak conciliationism requires one to conditionalize on information about the views of others. When you are not initially certain in your view and then learn that someone you take to be reliable disagrees with you, conditionalizing on this fact will lead you to reduce confidence in your opinion. So weak conciliationism is genuinely a form of *conciliationism*. Nonetheless, the conciliatory requirements in fundamental disagreements will often be considerably less demanding than those of strong conciliatory views that are committed to a sweeping epistemic impartiality requirement.[55]

---

[55] This chapter is a revised version of John Pittard, "Fundamental Disagreements and the Limits of Instrumentalism," *Synthese*, 2018, https://doi.org/10.1007/s11229-018-1691-1.

4

Partisan Justification and Religious Belief

The weak conciliationist and the strong conciliationist disagree on whether a person's ur-priors should, as a general matter, be impartial in the way that fundamental calibration requires. The weak conciliationist says that people often enjoy *partisan justification*—that is, justification for a high initial credence that exceeds the level of confidence that is supportable on impartial grounds. The strong conciliationist denies this and endorses fundamental calibration as a general requirement that applies to all (or at least nearly all) of a person's ur-priors.

While weak conciliationism denies that fundamental calibration is a *fully general* requirement (or even a *nearly* general requirement), the weak conciliationist need not affirm that partisan justification is always available. The weak conciliationist might hold that partisan justification is available only when certain conditions are met. Since weak conciliationism does not itself supply an account of partisan justification, it is not a complete theory of the epistemic significance of disagreement. To arrive at a complete theory, weak conciliationism must be combined with an account of partisan justification that specifies when such justification is available. Weak conciliationism therefore comes in different "strengths" depending on what theory of partisan justification is affirmed.

Suppose many religious disagreements are fundamental in that they are the result of one or more parties having partisan ur-priors. In this case, weak conciliationism *by itself* does not imply that the disputing parties should converge on a common credence. Nonetheless, a weak conciliationist who subscribes to a more restrictive account of partisan justification could push higher-order worries for religious belief by arguing that in many religious disagreements, the disputants are not entitled to their partisan epistemic starting points. One cannot simply assume that religious beliefs are included in the class of beliefs that can be justified on partisan grounds.

In this chapter, I identify the broad options for an account of partisan justification and argue for an exclusively "rationalist" account. This account says that partisan justification is grounded in rational insight and is not available in disagreements with acknowledged rational parity. As I will argue, this conclusion presents a challenge to those "reformed epistemologists" who defend religious belief by emphasizing similarities between religious belief formation and the formation of perceptual beliefs. The problem with assimilating religious belief formation to perceptual processes is that purely perceptual disagreements are *superficial* disagreements, or at least they *ought* to be superficial disagreements, given the lack of any insight into the greater rational plausibility of one's own perspective. And in disagreements that are (or ought to be) rationally superficial, some sort of "equal weight" response will often be rationally required.

4.1 Sources of Partisan Justification: The Options

While I briefly discussed two approaches to partisan justification in the previous chapter, in this section I provide a systematic account of the options for a theory of partisan justification. To facilitate the discussion, I'll focus on a case where I start with a high ur-prior for p that exceeds the level of confidence that could be justified on impartial grounds (i.e., grounds that are both agent-neutral and p-neutral). Against strong conciliationism, the weak conciliationist says that this partisan starting point could be justified. I'll suppose that it is. I then find myself in a disagreement with someone who starts with a low credence for p and who, on the basis of impartial considerations alone, would appear to be my epistemic peer on the matter. I conditionalize on the fact of this disagreement, as weak conciliationism requires. Because I started with a partisan initial credence, my updated credence will exceed the value that would be justified on purely impartial grounds.

As I argued in the previous chapter, the fact that I give more weight to my opinion about p than to my disputant's opinion does not imply that I take myself to be more reliable on the matter, at least on one common way of thinking about reliability. Even if I take two thermometers to be equally reliable, I can on a given occasion put more trust in one thermometer when it reports a temperature that is antecedently more plausible than the temperature reported by the other thermometer. Similarly, I might put more trust in my opinion about p not because I think that I am as a general matter more likely to arrive at the correct view than my disputant but only because I think that my actual judgment about p accords with what is antecedently plausible, while my disputant's judgment does not.

But there is another way of understanding one's "reliability" with respect to p, what I called "readout reliability" in the previous chapter, that takes into account information about the content of one's view on p and the reasoning behind that view as well as more general factors that bear on a person's reliability. When one has this narrower notion of reliability in view, then my credence for p should not differ from my estimate of my reliability on the matter. So the weak conciliationist who says that I can be justified in having a credence for p that exceeds what is supportable on impartial grounds must also allow that I can be justified in estimating my (readout) reliability as being higher than the (readout) reliability of my disputant even when I lack impartial grounds for such a self-favoring estimate.

What factor or factors could justify me in having this sort of self-favoring reliability assessment in a context where my impartial reasons for thinking that I am reliable are no stronger than my impartial reasons for thinking that my disputant is reliable? Different answers to this question correspond to different accounts of partisan justification. I'll sketch the possibilities.

First, one could affirm a *radically permissivist* account of partisan justification. According to this account, I can be justified in estimating my reliability (or my *disputant's* reliability!) to be significantly higher even in the complete absence of an epistemically relevant "symmetry breaker" that would support either of these rankings.[1] In the general epistemological literature, "permissivism" is the position that opposes the "uniqueness thesis," where the uniqueness thesis says that a given body of evidence rationalizes at most one doxastic attitude toward a given proposition.[2] One way to motivate permissivism is to consider situations where evidential reasoning requires that one weigh two rational criteria that support opposing theories and where it seems implausible that there is a uniquely correct way of weighing these opposing criteria. Consider, for example, a philosopher in ancient Persia who is a convinced atomist about the constitution of physical

---

[1] I take the terminology of a "symmetry breaker" from Jennifer Lackey, "A Justificationist View of Disagreement's Epistemic Significance," in *Social Epistemology*, ed. Adrian Haddock, Alan Millar, and Duncan Pritchard (Oxford: Oxford University Press, 2010), 298–325.

[2] There is a lively debate between proponents of the uniqueness thesis and those who endorse permissivism. For an early and vigorous defense of the uniqueness thesis, see Roger White, "Epistemic Permissiveness," *Philosophical Perspectives* 19, no. 1 (2005): 445–459. For a response to White that defends permissiveness and applies permissiveness to questions about the rationality of religious belief, see Miriam Schoenfield, "Permission to Believe: Why Permissivism Is True and What It Tells Us about Irrelevant Influences on Belief," *Noûs* 48, no. 2 (2014): 193–218.

reality and who reflects on the likelihood that there are more than four fundamental particle types. Simplicity considerations favor theories according to which there are few types, while theories that posit many particle types can more easily explain the diversity of material entities that the philosopher observes. The permissivist argues that there is no single rational way of weighing these competing considerations, and from this concludes that there are multiple doxastic attitudes that the philosopher may rationally adopt toward the theory that there are four or fewer particle types. For example, perhaps assigning this theory a credence of 0.5 would be perfectly rational, but so would assigning it a credence of 0.52. But note that in this case, the reasons favoring this theory are not perfectly symmetrical to reasons favoring the negation of the theory. There are reasons favoring each position, but they are reasons of different sorts. The radically permissivist account of partisan justification is *radical* in holding that an asymmetric reliability estimate could be rational even when there is no epistemically relevant asymmetry in the reasons I have for trusting myself and the reasons I have for trusting my disputant.

Suppose that radical permissivism is false or that, for some other reason specific to my situation, there must be some epistemically relevant symmetry breaker in order for me to be justified in having a self-favoring reliability assessment. Granting that such a symmetry breaker is needed, must I have a good *internal* reason for a self-favoring assessment? Those who say no affirm an *externalist* account of partisan justification. As you will recall from chapter 1, a good "internal" reason for trusting myself more than some other person is a reason that does not depend for its adequacy on my having some external advantage over the other person (i.e., an advantage that is not internally discernible). Externalists about partisan justification hold that purely external asymmetries can help to account for the rational justification of a self-favoring reliability assessment.

Next, suppose that the views on partisan justification identified above are wrong or that, for some other reason specific to my situation, I must have a good internal reason for a self-favoring reliability assessment in order for such an assessment to be justified. Granting that a good internal reason is required, must this reason also be *agent-neutral*? Proponents of an *agent-centered* account of partisan justification say no.[3] On their view, the epistemic

---

[3] Recall, from chapter 1, Huemer's definition of an agent-centered norm: "an epistemological principle requiring agents to assign different *evidential* value to their own experiences or other epistemically relevant states from the value they should assign to the qualitatively similar states of someone

significance of first-person facts about what seems true to *me* cannot be entirely captured by third-person facts that could have weight from an agent-neutral perspective. Thus, I may have good reason to put greater trust in myself than in my disputant even though I have no agent-neutral grounds for this preference. The practical account of partisan justification discussed in the previous chapter is one example of an agent-centered account.

Next, suppose that the foregoing views on partisan justification are all incorrect or that, for some other reason, I require a good agent-neutral internal reason in order to be justified in having a self-favoring reliability assessment. Granting this, it follows that partisan justification is a possibility for me only if a self-favoring reliability assessment can be justified on the basis of a good agent-neutral internal reason that is *not p*-neutral. (If the reason for my favorable assessment was an internal reason that was both agent-neutral and *p*-neutral, then this would not be an instance of *partisan* justification, since I would have fully impartial grounds for my reliability estimate.) Consider the position that says that in this situation, some partisan reason that is not *p*-neutral *could* justify a self-favoring reliability assessment. It will be helpful to further divide this position into two camps that give different answers to the question I will now pose. Suppose that my self-favoring reliability assessment is justified on the basis of an internal reason that is agent-neutral but partisan (because it fails to be *p*-neutral). Could my partisan reason justify this assessment even if I acknowledge that the partisan reasons I have for putting trust in myself do not have greater rational merit (in a way that I can discern) than my disputant's partisan reasons for putting greater trust in himself? Those who answer this question affirmatively endorse what I will call a *moderately permissivist* account of partisan justification. I will use the label *rationalist* for an account that gives a negative answer to this question (while affirming that partisan justification can stem from reasons that are not *p*-neutral).

Unlike radical permissivism, moderate permissivism does not deny that a symmetry breaker is needed in order for me to justifiably take myself (or my disputant) to be more reliable. But moderate permissivism does not require me to think that the symmetry-breaking reasons that favor putting more trust in myself have greater rational merit (in any way that I could discern) than any symmetry-breaking reasons that favor putting more trust in my disputant. The rationalist on the other hand endorses a more demanding

---

else." See Michael Huemer, "Epistemological Egoism and Agent-Centered Norms," in *Evidentialism and Its Discontents*, ed. Trent Dougherty (Oxford: Oxford University Press, 2011), 17.

requirement: my reasons for a self-favoring reliability assessment must also be reasons for thinking that my perspective is rationally stronger (in a way I can discern) than my disputant's perspective.

I've identified five accounts of partisan justification: a radically permissivist account, an externalist account, an agent-centered account, a moderately permissivist account, and a rationalist account. These accounts are collectively exhaustive, but they are not all mutually exclusive. (Only moderate permissivism and rationalism are mutually exclusive by definition.) For example, an externalist who affirms that external factors can contribute to partisan justification could also be a moderate permissivist or a rationalist. She would only need to hold that there are situations where externalist justification is not available but where a subject nonetheless has partisan justification on account of a good agent-neutral internal reason that is not p-neutral. There are multiple ways of combining the accounts I've identified, some of which look superficially plausible and others of which do not. I will not consider these combinations here, as my aim is to argue that only the rationalist account is tenable.

Each of the accounts I've identified presents a challenge to one of the commitments driving the higher-order argument for disagreement-motivated religious skepticism. As you will recall, the master argument introduced in chapter 1 asserts that subject S does not have justification for believing SUPERIOR. Again, SUPERIOR is the proposition that S's process of religious belief formation is significantly more reliable than the collective reliability of the processes that (otherwise) epistemically qualified people use to form religious beliefs. This claim that S lacks justification for believing SUPERIOR I labeled EQUAL ESTIMATED RELIABILITY. I argued that the most viable defense of EQUAL ESTIMATED RELIABILITY (that also preserves the aim of advancing a *higher-order* argument for religious skepticism) is an argument that appeals to the following four premises:

INTERNAL REASON CONSTRAINT: S has justification for believing SUPERIOR only if S has a good *internal* reason for believing SUPERIOR.

AGENT IMPARTIALITY CONSTRAINT: S has a good internal reason for believing SUPERIOR only if S has a good *agent-neutral* internal reason for believing SUPERIOR.

REASONS IMPARTIALITY CONSTRAINT: S has a good agent-neutral internal reason for believing SUPERIOR only if S has a good *dispute-independent* agent-neutral internal reason for believing SUPERIOR.

NO INDEPENDENT REASON: S does not have a good dispute-independent agent-neutral internal reason for believing SUPERIOR.

A radically permissivist account of partisan justification poses a challenge to INTERNAL REASON CONSTRAINT, since the radical permissivist denies that an asymmetric reliability estimate requires any sort of symmetry breaker that favors this assessment. Obviously, an externalist account also poses a challenge to INTERNAL REASON CONSTRAINT, since the externalist denies that a symmetry-breaking factor must be a good *internal* reason. An agent-centered account of partisan justification poses a challenge to AGENT IMPARTIALITY CONSTRAINT, which forbids significant agent partiality in the religious context. Finally, the moderately permissivist and rationalist accounts both pose a challenge to REASONS IMPARTIALITY CONSTRAINT.

4.2 Against Radically Permissivist, Externalist, and Agent-Centered Accounts of Partisan Justification

In this section, I argue against radically permissivist, externalist, and agent-centered accounts of partisan justification that could support continued confidence in religious disagreements with acknowledged internal rational symmetry (when evaluated from an agent-neutral perspective). My strategy is to present an example of religious disagreement where radically permissivist, externalist, agent-centered accounts support a self-favoring reliability estimate but where it is implausible to think that such an assessment is rational.

Here is the example. Kind Deity created a trusting species of intelligent creatures on Planet A and then chose some of these creatures to be prophets. Kind Deity interacted with these prophets and revealed important truths about morality and the purpose of creation. Among the things Kind Deity revealed was that the prophets were in communication with none other than Kind Deity herself, the creator of the world. Kind Deity also revealed that all of the creatures of Planet A would one day be blessed with an eternal afterlife of unending bliss. Up until now, the people of Planet A have believed these messages, because of their trusting attitude toward mystical experiences and toward prophetic utterances of those who have had such experiences. Kind Deity gave the inhabitants of Planet A this trusting attitude precisely so that they would come to believe the truth about religious matters. (Kind Deity has made sure that there are never any false prophets on Planet A, so that "trusting prophets on Planet A" is a highly reliable belief-forming practice.)

Around the time Kind Deity created Planet A, Kind Deity also created Planet B and gave all authority over Planet B to an angel that I'll call "Evil Angel." Kind Deity gave godlike powers to Evil Angel, though these powers were limited in their application to the realm of Planet B and its inhabitants. Kind Deity chooses never to interfere with Planet B, and Evil Angel lacks the power to interfere with the affairs of Planet A. Nevertheless, both beings have the power to observe the happenings on the other planet in great detail.

Here is what Evil Angel did with her opportunity. She created a people on Planet B just like the people Kind Deity created on Planet A, complete with their disposition to trust mystical experiences and prophetic utterances. But Evil Angel's purpose in creating such creatures was to lead them astray and to do so in a particularly sinister way. Evil Angel observed how Kind Deity interacted with the prophets on Planet A and then interacted in the same manner with the prophets on Planet B. If Kind Deity commanded in a booming voice from a thundercloud "Hear me, the maker of the universe!," Evil Angel mimicked this perfectly on Planet B. If Kind Deity softly spoke words of love to a prophet on Planet A, Evil Angel spoke in the same manner to a prophet on Planet B (despite the fact that Evil Angel felt no love in her heart). Evil Angel also made sure that the inhabitants of Planet B acquired the same sort of background evidence as those of Planet A. This meant that there would be no relevant differences between the planets in the evidential grounds for people trusting in their revelatory experiences. This copycat policy of course meant that Evil Angel declared on Planet B that the people on that planet could look forward to a blissful afterlife. But Evil Angel, who has authority over whether the creatures of Planet B will enjoy an afterlife, will see to it that none of the creatures of Planet B will experience postmortem existence. Evil Angel's entire aim is to perpetuate a great deception by misusing the actions and words of Kind Deity.

Now suppose that Kind Deity decides to tell the people of Planet A about the machinations of Evil Angel on Planet B. After visiting a prophet and sharing all about Evil Angel's scheme, Kind Deity attempts to reassure the prophet, saying: "Do not worry; it is true that there is a planet of people and prophets who have had similar revelatory experiences that are just as compelling and experientially equivalent to your own. But you here on this planet are the ones who are in communication with the loving creator of the universe, and you are the ones who really will enjoy eternal life. Of course, in the shortest of moments, Evil Angel will be saying to a prophet on *that* planet that there is another planet where an evil angel is carrying off a great deception. Evil Angel will then say the same reassuring words that I have just said to you. And whatever feeling of confidence you may feel is *experientially* no different from the confidence that will be felt by your counterpart on Planet B. But don't worry, *you* aren't being deceived, *he* is!"

I'll make three stipulations about the example. First, before Kind Deity revealed information about the machinations of Evil Angel, the prophets of Planet A were epistemically justified in believing the truths revealed to them, and the people of Planet A were justified in believing these truths on the basis of the prophets' testimony. Second, there are no differences in the phenomenal character of the experiences on the two planets that could explain why the inhabitants of Planet A but *not* Planet B are justified in believing what was told to the prophets. The experience of hearing from Kind Deity was no more impressive, assuring, or different in any other discernible way from the experience of hearing from Evil Angel. Finally, the inhabitants of Planet A and Planet B both succeed in learning that there is an Evil Angel on exactly one of the two planets behaving in the way described.

Epistemologically significant questions may be asked about the justificatory status of Planet A and Planet B believers during two periods of time: the period *before* the believers are told about the sinister actions of Evil Angel (supposedly occurring on the *other* planet) and the period *after* they are told about Evil Angel. With respect to the first period, internalists must affirm that the inhabitants of Planet B were equally justified in believing what they were told by Evil Angel (since there is internal parity in the situation between the two planets). Externalists may disagree with this verdict. While people on both planets may have confidence in the process undergirding their religious beliefs, only the people on Planet A arrive at their beliefs by means of reliable cognitive faculties that were designed with the aim of producing true beliefs. Externalism allows that such purely external differences can make a difference to epistemic justification.

For my purposes, however, I can set aside the question of the epistemic status of Planet B believers before learning of Evil Angel. My interest is in questions about the epistemic status of Planet A believers *after* learning about their supposedly deceived counterparts on a distant planet. After receiving this revelation, could Planet A believers remain justified in continuing to believe that they are in fact communicating with the loving creator of the universe who will bless them in the afterlife?

Consider the implications of different views on partisan justification for the question of how I should update my credences if I am a prophet on Planet A. Let A designate the proposition that *my* planet—Planet A—is the planet with which Kind Deity, who is entirely trustworthy, is communicating. And let B stand for the only other alternative: that Kind Deity is in communication with people on the other planet, so that I have been hearing from Evil Angel. Obviously, I have no agent-neutral and dispute-independent reason for thinking that I am more reliable than my counterpart on the other planet. So a strong conciliationist will say that in this situation, I ought to think that B is no more or less likely than A, and I should assign a credence of 0.5 to each of these possibilities. The same verdict will be given by the weak conciliationist who rejects radically permissivist, externalist, and agent-centered accounts of partisan justification (affirming only rationalism or moderate permissivism). Because there is internal, third-person rational parity between the two planets, the rationalist and the moderate permissivist will deny that there is any symmetry breaker that could constitute an all-things-considered reason for me to privilege A over B.

While I am unaware of anyone who advocates a radically permissivist account of partisan justification, radical permissivism would seem to imply both that a self-favoring reliability assessment is reasonable in this situation and that a *disputant*-favoring reliability assessment is reasonable.

Now consider an approach that accords with an agent-centered account of partisan justification. If such an account is correct, then when I as a prophet on Planet A lay out all of the third-person facts about my mystical experiences on Planet A and find that they are relevantly like the facts about the mystical experiences of my counterpart on Planet B, this need not entail that I should assign equal reliability estimates to myself and my counterpart. It may be that the first-person fact that these Planet A experiences are *my* experiences, ones that seem compelling *to me*, makes it rational for me to estimate my reliability as being higher than the reliability of my counterpart on Planet B. And if I do have a higher reliability estimate for myself, then when I conditionalize on facts about my mystical experiences (that support A) and facts about my counterpart's experiences (that support B), I will have a higher credence for A than for B. If agent-centered norms vindicate the self-trust of a prophet on Planet A, those norms will also vindicate the self-trust of a prophet on Planet B. My counterpart on Planet B has first-person reasons for trusting *his* experiences that are symmetrical to my first-person reasons for trusting *my* experiences.

It is plausible that I have a very strong practical reason to maintain confidence that I am on the fortunate planet that is governed by Kind Deity. The benefit of having a trusting relationship with my loving creator may greatly outweigh the costs of being "duped" and falling for the deception of Evil Angel.[4] However, this strong practical reason for continued confidence does not seem to make it rational to trust in the mystical experiences that happen to be my own. Given the perfect internal third-person symmetry, it seems irrational to be even slightly more confident in A than in B. Because a radically permissivist account of partisan justification and an agent-centered account both allow that I could reasonably give greater credence to A than to B, one has good reason to reject these accounts.

Some prominent externalist theories of epistemic justification may also support implausibly sanguine responses in the two planets example. Consider, for example, Michael Bergmann's "proper functionalist" account of justification. This account, which Bergmann qualifies as "a first approximation," is as follows:

> *Bergmann's account of justification*: S's belief B is justified if and only if (i) S does not take B to be defeated and (ii) the cognitive faculties producing B are (a) functioning properly, (b) truth-aimed and (c) reliable in the environments for which they were "designed."[5]

Crucially, S's belief B does not meet conditions (iia)–(iic) merely by having *good reasons* or *good evidence* for thinking that B was produced by properly functioning cognitive faculties that were designed to produce true beliefs (and that reliably succeed at this in the appropriate environment); rather, justification requires that these conditions are *in fact* met. This makes Bergmann's account externalist, since facts about the design aims for one's cognitive faculties will typically not be internally discernible (at least on the most natural ways of understanding internal discernibility).

---

[4] On weighing the benefit of true belief against risk of having a false belief and being duped, see William James, *The Will to Believe and Other Essays in Popular Philosophy* (New York: Longmans, Green and Co., 1896), 18–19.

[5] Michael Bergmann, *Justification without Awareness: A Defense of Epistemic Externalism* (Oxford: Oxford University Press, 2006), 133. Bergmann appropriates much of what Alvin Plantinga says about "warrant" in order to develop an account of justification.

Bergmann's account can be used to support the view that I (as a prophet on Planet A) could be justified in assigning a higher credence to hypothesis A than to hypothesis B, even if I am a weak conciliationist. For example, Kind Deity might design me with an inclination to have a higher reliability estimate for my process of "mystical perception" than for any similar process that leads to incompatible results. Or Kind Deity might design me to be more confident in hypothesis A than in hypothesis B (despite the apparent symmetry of these hypotheses). And Kind Deity might give me these inclinations for the purpose of preserving my *true* religious beliefs in the event that I learn of Evil Angel's scheme. Thus, my high ur-prior for A (which is higher than my ur-prior for B), and my self-favoring reliability estimate, could satisfy condition (ii).

Now, one might think that my most *fundamental* perspective on the plausibility of A and B (and on the reliability of myself and my counterpart on Planet B) would surely not be influenced by these self-favoring inclinations given to me by Kind Deity. Surely, I would be able to see, on the basis of some sort of "parity" or "indifference" reasoning, that A and B have the same fundamental plausibility and that I am no more or less likely to be reliable than my counterpart. If this was right, then I would have a perspective on my situation that is antecedent to the inclinations given to me by Kind Deity. From this perspective, I could treat the doxastic inclinations of both myself and my disputant in an instrumentalist fashion. And doing this would lead me to give equal weight to each of our perspectives.

While it is tempting to think that I must have an antecedent perspective that is not informed by the self-favoring inclinations given to me by Kind Deity, I think that this is a mistake. Kind Deity might design me so that I am not inclined to endorse "parity" or "indifference" reasoning in all cases like the present one. And Kind Deity could make it the case that in this particular instance, I judge the indifference reasoning to be somehow confused or inappropriate. If I were designed in this way, then the indifference reasoning would not constitute my antecedent perspective. The inbuilt inclinations to favor A, and to trust myself more than any similarly situated prophet, might constitute my most fundamental attitudes on these matters. If so, I would have no neutral antecedent perspective that would allow me to treat these self-favoring attitudes in an instrumentalist fashion.

Suppose Kind Deity designed me to be utterly unimpressed by the indifference reasoning that would assign equal probability to A and B. In this case, I would not take the parity of my situation and my counterpart's situation to constitute a defeater for my high initial credence for A or for my high estimate of my own reliability estimate. In other words, these self-favoring starting points could also satisfy condition (i) of Bergmann's account of justification. Since these self-favoring starting points could satisfy both conditions, Bergmann's account supports the conclusion that I could enjoy partisan justification in this example. (What about my counterpart on Planet B? It would seem that my counterpart would *not* enjoy partisan justification, even if he had all of the same self-favoring doxastic inclinations. Unlike *my* inclinations, which were provided with the aim of leading me to true beliefs, my counterpart's equivalent inclinations were supplied with the aim of leading him to believe falsehoods. So on the most natural way of understanding Bergmann's account, my counterpart's beliefs would fail to satisfy condition [iic].)

If I am right that accounts of justification like Bergmann's could vindicate steadfast confidence in the two planets example, then this is, in my view, sufficient reason to reject such accounts. It is absurd to think that in religious disagreements exhibiting such perfect (internal, agent-neutral) parity, complacent confidence may be justified. If Kind Deity supplied all of the relevant seemings so as to guarantee that believers on Planet A are untroubled by the parity between the two planets, this would ensure that Planet A believers have true religious beliefs. But by protecting Planet A believers from worry in this way, Kind Deity would have rendered Planet A believers irrational. Perhaps this particular instance of irrational confidence could be a seen as a benevolent gift since it would protect religious convictions that are both true and meaningful. But this would not make their confidence any less irrational.

It's crucial to emphasize that I am not using the two planets example in order to refute externalist theories of justification in general. Rather, my objection is only to externalist theories that license partisan reliability assessments in cases like the present one, where there is acknowledged rational parity between two disagreeing groups of equal numbers. Bergmann's account of justification has this implausible implication not simply because it is externalist, but because his externalist conditions are not conjoined with sufficiently demanding conditions of the sort recognized by the internalist. In particular, Bergmann's "defeat" condition (condition [i] of his account) is implausibly weak, even though it does impose one internalist constraint.

To explain and defend this diagnosis, consider the following example. Upon consulting a website that purports to display the first 10,000 digits of pi, I form the belief that the twentieth digit of pi (including the 3 before the decimal) is 4. The reporting of the website is my only basis for this belief. I am then told by an apparently trustworthy person that the website I consulted is a hoax. According to this person, mischievous MIT undergraduates created the website, and they displayed following 3.14 a list of 9,997 randomly generated digits. They then worked hard on promoting the website on search engines in order to contribute to worldwide havoc. As it turns out, none of this is true, and the site I consulted is completely accurate. Nonetheless, I believe the person's story about the hoax website.

Does my belief that the website is a hoax constitute a *defeater* for my belief that the twentieth digit of pi is 4? According to the notion of defeat that is in the background of Bergmann's account of justification, a defeater for belief B is, roughly, any belief or mental state the having of which renders continued belief in B epistemically unjustified.[6] And clearly my belief about the twentieth digit is no longer justified after coming to believe that the website is a hoax. So the latter belief is a defeater for the former belief.

But now consider whether Bergmann's account supports the conclusion that the belief that the website is a hoax is a defeater for my (initially justified) belief that the twentieth digit of pi is 4. According to condition (1) of Bergmann's account, if I *take* my new belief about the hoax to be a defeater, then my belief concerning the twentieth digit is indeed unjustified. But what if I do not take the new belief to be a defeater? Suppose I think: "Well, I know that my belief was formed on the basis of a highly unreliable website. But I'm still quite confident that the twentieth digit of pi is 4. Luckily for me, the website by chance displayed the correct digit in the twentieth place." No doubt Bergmann would diagnose this response as irrational and unjustified. But to support this diagnosis, he could not directly appeal to some *necessary* rational principle that forbids this particular sort of appeal to epistemic luck. No such principles are featured in his theory. Instead, he would have to claim that my confidence in the present circumstances is not a result of properly functioning cognitive faculties that are truth-aimed and reliable in the environments for which they were designed.

Now, I would agree with Bergmann that continued confidence in this situation would not be the result of properly functioning faculties. But I do not think that this is an adequate explanation of why continued confidence would be unjustified. For it is, it seems to me, a *necessary* fact that continued confidence in my evidential situation is unjustified. But it is at best a *contingent*

---

[6] Bergmann, *Justification without Awareness*, 154–159.

fact that such confidence would not accord with properly functioning faculties (that are truth-aimed and reliable in the appropriate environments). Suppose that I am designed by a God who, for whatever reason, really cares about my continuing to believe the truth about the value of the twentieth digit of pi in the event that I come to hold a true belief on the matter. As it happens, the twentieth digit of pi is 4. God has designed me so that if I ever come to believe that the twentieth digit of pi is 4 and then receive evidence that my source for this belief is untrustworthy, I will be completely unworried about this evidence and will confidently persist in my belief that the value of the twentieth digit is 4. In other words, God builds in an exception clause to the "evidential defeat" standards that God has presumably designed me to follow in other contexts.

Of course, Bergmann does not think that God has in fact designed me this way, so Bergmann does not think that my continued confidence in the example would be rationally justified. But God *could have* designed me in the envisioned way. Therefore, it seems that Bergmann must concede that my continued confidence in the exact same evidential situation *could* be rationally justified by the lights of his theory. And that seems to be the wrong result. Without any evidence that God or some epistemically benevolent force is guiding me to maintain my belief that the twentieth digit is 4, continued confidence in the imagined situation would, of necessity, be irrational. If God programmed me to maintain confidence anyway, this would amount to programming me to be *irrational* in such situations. Of course, this particular instance of irrationality would in a certain sense be epistemically beneficial, since it would help preserve a true belief. But beneficial irrationality is still irrationality.

Bergmann makes the standards of evidential defeat almost entirely dependent on the contingencies of one's design plan (whose details are not internally discernible). In doing so, Bergmann makes the standards of epistemic defeat—and, to a large extent, the standards of rational reflection as a whole—opaque. Rationality on this view amounts to doing what one is programmed to do, as long as one's programmer (whether a being like God or, in some figurative sense, evolution) has the proper aim and has done a good enough job. Of course, a programmer could program humans to respond to certain "rational standards" (coherence "requirements," principles of inductive reasoning, and so on). This would be an efficient way of giving humans quite reliable cognitive faculties. But the right sort of programmer *needn't* do this. She could build in exceptions that violate these "standards" when this would conduce to true beliefs, and she could do this without giving humans any evidence that these violations are epistemically beneficial. A perspective that contains all sorts of apparently ad hoc exceptions to general rational "principles" could, on Bergmann's account, qualify as fully rational.[7]

The idea that rationality could be so unprincipled is a radical one that I think should be rejected. If it is rejected, then a plausible account of epistemic justification would need to acknowledge a sufficiently rich set of necessary rational principles (perhaps in addition to some externalist conditions) that do not depend for their legitimacy on contingent facts (including facts about one's design plan). Those principles will, I submit, explain why continued confidence in the two planets example is irrational.

An agent-centered theory of justification that supports continued confidence in the two planets example is, in one sense, more plausible than an extremely externalist theory like Bergmann's. His externalism implies that the rationality of continued confidence in the two planets example depends on contingent external facts about one's design plan. This renders the requirements of rationality opaque. An agent-centered view that supports a steadfast response in the two planets example does not need to appeal to contingent external factors. On such a view, the requirements of rationality are not opaque, as they are for the extreme externalist. But even if some of the

[7] Bergmann is fully aware of the fact that his theory of justification makes it the case that the conditions of epistemic defeat are largely contingent. He sees this as an advantage to his account, rather than a count against it (*Justification without Awareness*, 173). Here's why. Suppose I have strong evidence for my belief that p, and then come to learn q and r. As it turns out, q and r entail that p is false, though for reasons that are subtle and unlikely to be noticed by any normal human being. Plausibly, it is not irrational for me to continue believing that p, in which case my knowledge of q and r does not constitute a defeater for my belief that p. But for some alien species who could easily see that q and r entail the negation of p, knowledge of q and r *would* constitute a defeater for the belief that p. Thus, it seems that the rational justification of some perspective that affirms p, q, and r is a contingent matter that depends on the powers of the cognizer. I agree that one can truly affirm that *given the human inability to see any conflict between* p *and the conjunction of* q *and* r, persisting in my belief that p (which still appears to me to have strong evidential support) is what I rationally ought to do. But I also think that one can truly affirm that I *ideally* ought to cease believing that p upon learning q and r. The requirements of this more idealized conception of rationality do not depend on contingent features of my cognitive powers. In the case involving p, q, and r, one could perhaps appeal to externalist facts about reliability in order to explain why it is the aliens, rather than human beings, who more closely approximate ideal rationality (even if in some more subjective sense there is no difference in the degree of rationality). Properly drawing inferences from the conjunction of q and r makes them more reliable (all else being equal) in their belief concerning p. But no purely external factor like reliability or my design plan could explain why my lack of concern about the website hoax belief moves me further away from the ideal: since this singular exception to my normal standards of defeat improves my reliability and accords with proper functioning (of reliable and truth-aimed faculties), I do not see any straightforward externalist explanation for why it is irrational for me to have this apparently arbitrary exception to the standards of defeat that apply in other contexts. To explain this, one needs to invoke some *necessary* principle of rational defeat that does not depend on contingent features of my design plan.

more implausible implications of extreme externalism are avoided, any view that vindicates continued confidence in the two planets example is on that count highly implausible and should be rejected.

This does not mean that agent-centered considerations play no role in the correct theory of justification. It simply means that a theory of justification that appeals to first-person, agent-centered considerations must be supplemented with rational principles that rule out agent-centered norms that support agent partiality in situations where there is acknowledged rational parity. Just as a viable externalist account must be enriched with a requirement that forbids confidence in the two planets example (whatever might be true about the design plan of the planets' inhabitants or about other external factors), a viable agent-centered account must also accommodate such a requirement.

4.3 Against Moderately Permissivist Accounts of Partisan Justification

Suppose it is conceded that in disagreements with acknowledged internal, third-person rational symmetry (as in the two planets example), partisan ur-priors and self-favoring reliability assessments are unjustified. To those interested in defending religious belief against skeptical worries posed by disagreement, this concession may at first seem rather innocuous. Contrived cases designed to be perfectly symmetrical would seem to have little if any direct bearing on actual situations of religious disagreement. Even if there is something rationally arbitrary about assigning a higher credence to A than to B (in the two planets example), there would seem to be nothing rationally arbitrary about having unequal credences for Mahayana Buddhism and orthodox Judaism, for example. Given the remarkable differences between the sorts of religious claims made by Mahayana Buddhists and orthodox Jews, there is no reason to think that having asymmetric credences for these positions falls afoul of some sort of nonarbitrariness constraint.

I grant that a disagreement between orthodox Jews and Mahayana Buddhists is a scenario quite dissimilar to the contrived two planets example. That being said, I think that one can build on the commonsense conciliatory verdict in the two planets example in order to motivate similarly demanding verdicts in cases that do not exhibit perfect rational symmetry. My suggestion is that introducing asymmetries between the rational factors that favor the competing perspectives does not lessen the conciliatory requirement un-less one is justified in taking oneself to have insight into the greater rational merits of one's own perspective. If this is right, then moderate permissivism is false. It is not enough to maintain self-trust on the basis of partisan rea-soning that favors one's own position. One must judge that the partisan rea-soning favoring one's own position is rationally stronger, in some discernible way, than the partisan reasoning favoring the position of one's disputant.

To motivate and explain this claim, I'll make the following revision to the two planets example. Kind Deity is telling me, a prophet on Planet A, about the sinister work of Evil Angel. Kind Deity also informs me that while for the most part Evil Angel has said the same things on Planet B that Kind Deity says on Planet A, there has been one exception. When Kind Deity revealed a few hundred years ago that the physical universe contains fewer than seven types of fundamental particles, Evil Angel deliberately lied and told the prophets on Planet B that the physical universe contains seven or more types of fundamental particles. Kind Deity then tells me that Evil Angel is presently telling the mystics on Planet B a similar story: Evil Angel is saying that when she truthfully revealed hundreds of years ago that the physical universe contains seven or more types of fundamental particles, the "Evil Angel" on the other planet deliberately lied and said that the physical universe contains fewer than seven types of fundamental particles. Unfortunately, on neither planet has science yielded much ev-idence that would help to confidently enumerate the number of funda-mental particle types.

With this revision of the case, one can no longer take it for granted that hypotheses A and B are perfectly on a par with respect to their rational standing. Let FEWER stand for the proposition that there are fewer than seven fundamental particle types and MORE for the proposition that there are seven or more of them. I know that A is true only if FEWER is true (and that B is true only if MORE is true) and that A and B are rationally on a par in other respects. It follows, then, that the respective plausibility of A and B will de-pend on the rational merits of FEWER and MORE. Suppose that I am inclined to think that FEWER is more probable. (Perhaps I think that the creator would favor a parsimonious physics with very few fundamental particle types, and I have a hunch that seven particle types are enough to account for the diverse physical phenomena that I observe around me.) Unfortunately, I learn from Kind Deity that while inhabitants of Planet A tend to agree with my assess-ment of FEWER and MORE, inhabitants of Planet B typically have the opposite assessment and judge MORE to have greater probability. (Perhaps they think that the creator would favor universes that exhibit diversity, even at the fundamental level.)

For the sake of discussion, suppose that the inhabitants of Planet A hold the rationally superior view, the view that would be held by an ideal rational agent who possessed the same limited base scientific evidence as is possessed by inhabitants of planets A and B. Given this stipulation, can one conclude that it would be reasonable for me to have a higher credence for A/FEWER than for B/MORE? I do not think so. Even if FEWER has greater rational support than MORE, my inclination to believe FEWER may not be responsive to the factors that account for the greater objective rational merit of this position. My doxastic inclination might be brute. Perhaps Kind Deity (or Evil Angel, for all I know) programmed me to be strongly inclined to believe that a good creator would favor fundamental parsimony but gave me this inclination without any understanding of why parsimony was better than fundamental diversity.

Arguably, if I recognize that my confidence is the product of brute inclination and that my counterparts on Planet B have an equally strong inclination toward the opposing view, it would be arbitrary for me to have a self-favoring reliability assessment. Since I am blind to the objective considerations that favor my view, such considerations cannot contribute to the doxastic justification of my belief. Continued self-trust would be unreasonable when I recognize that my disputants' perspective is no more nor less rational with respect to the *grasped* rational considerations.

If I had ur-priors of 0.5 for FEWER and for MORE, ur-priors that were rationally antecedent to my brute inclination to judge that FEWER is more plausible than MORE, then weak conciliationism would straightforwardly support full conciliation in this case. But as I am envisioning the revised two planets example, this is not the case. As I am imagining the case, I simply have no access to principled reasoning that would allow me to arrive at any view on the relative probability of FEWER and MORE. Thus, my brute inclination toward a high credence for FEWER really is my initial perspective on the matter. My support of a fully conciliatory prescription in this case therefore requires me to affirm that in cases of this sort, where one has brute inclination but no rational insight into the matter, fundamental calibration is appropriate. On this view, when you have a strong brute inclination to believe that p but know that you lack rational insight into the matter, your confidence in p should not exceed the estimated reliability of a similar person who has a perspective that is *subjectively* as rational as yours, and who forms a judgment on the basis of a similarly strong brute inclination.

4.4 For a Rationalist Account of Partisan Justification

The position on disagreement that I favor, which I label *rationalist weak conciliationism*, affirms weak conciliationism and holds that only a rationalist account of partisan justification is correct. In this section, I will argue for a rationalist account of partisan justification, the last of the five approaches sketched earlier in the chapter. My aim is not to decisively show that a rationalist account of partisan justification is correct. I merely hope to show that it has a good deal of intrinsic plausibility and that its verdicts in concrete cases are significantly more plausible than those of the accounts already discussed. Since anyone who rejects sweeping skepticism should acknowledge that one sometimes enjoys partisan justification (as argued in chapter 3) and since the rationalist account of partisan justification is the most plausible account on offer, one has good reason to affirm the rationalist account. This is so even if one does not yet have well-developed and fully satisfactory responses to all of the challenges that might be raised against this account.

In subsection 4.4.1, I develop and defend the notion of rational insight that is presupposed by a rationalist account of partisan justification. In subsection 4.4.2, I argue that having genuine rational insight into some matter can help to justify a degree of confidence that could not be supported on impartial grounds alone.

4.4.1 Rationalism

Rationalism, as I will use the term, is the thesis that one sometimes has a priori rational insight into the truth or plausibility of some proposition or into the cogency of some line of reasoning in support of a proposition. On a standard Bayesian framework, the a priori plausibility judgments of a rational agent are reflected in that agent's ur-priors. So within the Bayesian framework, rationalism amounts to the thesis that one's ur-priors are sometimes based, at least in part, on rational insight. Such rational insight might bear directly on a proposition's truth or plausibility before empirical evidence is taken into account, or it might bear on questions about how potential pieces of empirical evidence should affect one's confidence in a given proposition. Both sorts of insights can be reflected in an agent's ur-priors, which include unconditional as well as conditional credences.

"Insight" is a success term: someone whose thinking about some matter is muddled and utterly confused lacks genuine insight, even if she is convinced that her reasoning is cogent and insightful. Nonetheless, a false belief that p could still be supported by genuine insight—not insight into the truth of p, of course, but insight into the truth of one or more other propositions. One might have insight into considerations that rationally support p, even though these considerations are ultimately misleading; or one might have insight into the truth of some proposition that is very much like p and mistake this as being insight into p itself. Consider, for example, someone who thinks that "to the east of" is a transitive relation. While such a person obviously does not have insight into the transitivity of this relation, she might insightfully see that "to the east of" would be transitive on a model where the earth is flat.

Rational insight is not an output of any paradigmatically a posteriori process of empirical knowledge acquisition, such as sense perception, remembering the past, introspection, or drawing inferences from premises that are outputs of such a posteriori processes. Nonetheless, rational insight may depend, either contingently or necessarily, on one's having certain sorts of experiences. Typically, achieving insight requires that one undergo an experience of suitably attentive and logical reflection of the relevant sort. My attaining insight into the fact that there is no highest prime required an experience of thinking through a proof of this fact and grasping the cogency of the proof.[8] Insight may also require that one employ concepts that cannot be possessed apart from certain sorts of experiences. For example, rational insight into the fact that something cannot at the same time be entirely red and entirely green may require that one have the concept "red" and the concept "green," or at least the concept of a color, and visual experience may be required in order for one to possess these concepts.[9]

---

[8] David Bourget gives an account of the experience of mentally "grasping" something that comports well with the rationalist view I am defending here; "The Role of Consciousness in Grasping and Understanding," *Philosophy and Phenomenological Research* 95, no. 2 (2017): 285–318. Elijah Chudnoff describes how "rational intuition" of some truth may be partly constituted by imaginings, mental visualizations, and/or reflections. See Elijah Chudnoff, "What Intuitions Are Like," *Philosophy and Phenomenological Research* 82, no. 3 (2011): 625–654, and "The Nature of Intuitive Justification," *Philosophical Studies* 153, no. 2 (2011): 313–333.

[9] Laurence BonJour, *In Defense of Pure Reason* (Cambridge: Cambridge University Press, 1998), 9.

Crucially, rational insight is distinct from mere a priori intuition, at least if one understands having an intuition that p as requiring only that one has a nonsensory "intellectual seeming" that p is true (or perhaps that p is *necessarily* true), one that arises when one reflects on whether p.[10] A mere intuition that p could be *brute*: it could seem to me that p must be true without my having any understanding of why this is so, or any grasp of rational considerations that count in favor of p. In contrast, someone with insight into the truth of p sees something of *why* p is true, or at least appreciates the rational force of reasons that support p.[11] This appreciation of the reasons why p is true, or of the force of reasons that support p, is direct. It is not as though one's insight into the truth or plausibility of p is mediated by a feeling of confidence in p that serves as an indicator of p's truth or plausibility. While someone with insight may have such mediated knowledge, he also has something stronger: an immediate awareness of the rational force of considerations favoring p.

When one has insight into some matter, the fact that one has genuine insight is often internally discernible. Consider the proposition that if A is taller than B and B is taller than C, then A must be taller than C. Typically, one who reflects on this proposition will not only be convicted of its truth but will also be introspectively aware of having insight into the necessary truth of this proposition. If the insightful character of one's thought is internally discernible, as I have claimed, then it would seem that there must be epistemically relevant differences between the phenomenal character of insightful thinking and the phenomenal character of noninsightful thinking. If this is right, then insight is importantly different from sense perception. A hallucinatory experience could, at least in theory, have the same phenomenal character as an experience of veridical perception. For this reason, one's confidence in a perceptual belief should ideally be calibrated with an antecedent estimate of the reliability of the process of forming perceptual beliefs in response to sense impressions of the relevant phenomenal type.[12] But since the phenomenal character of insightful thought favorably distinguishes it from noninsightful

---

[10] Many characterizations of intuition do not require that they have insightful character. For example, see George Bealer, "On the Possibility of Philosophical Knowledge," *Philosophical Perspectives* 10 (1996): 5–6.

[11] BonJour, *In Defense of Pure Reason*, 108; Yuri Cath, "Evidence and Intuition," *Episteme* 9, no. 4 (2012): 311–328; and Ali Hasan, "In Defense of Rationalism about Abductive Inference," in *Best Explanations: New Essays on Inference to the Best Explanation*, ed. Kevin McCain and Ted Poston (Oxford: Oxford University Press, 2017), 162.

[12] Roger White, "Problems for Dogmatism," *Philosophical Studies* 131, no. 3 (2006): 525–557.

thought, there is less reason to think that one's confidence in response to insight should be constrained by an antecedent reliability estimate of some generic process that applies to both insightful and noninsightful thinking.[13] This line of thought will be developed further shortly.

What reason is there to affirm that people sometimes enjoy rational insight, as rationalism maintains? The strongest reason to affirm rationalism is one's own introspective awareness of having rational insight into various matters. Of course, in a context where rationalism is being defended against its critics, it would be question-begging to cite one's introspective awareness of rational insight as a reason to affirm rationalism. While a full defense of rationalism cannot be offered here, it is worth noting the most significant objections to rationalism and briefly sketching what may be said in reply. Two main worries motivate the rejection of rationalism.

First, rational insight is often dismissed as objectionably mysterious and unscientific. There is a ready scientific account of how the concrete features of a person's environment may exert causal influence on that person's cognitive apparatus. But it is far from clear how one could come to know abstract, nonempirical facts that pertain to, say, what is and is not logically or metaphysically possible, or to the plausibility of various propositions prior to empirical evidence. Since it would seem that such abstract facts do not causally interact with people or their environments, it is difficult to explain how one could manage to reliably form true beliefs on such matters.[14]

Second, it may be alleged that cases of apparent but nongenuine insight undercut the principal motivation for rationalism. I said that rationalism should be affirmed on the basis of introspective awareness of having rational insight into some matter. If one can be introspectively aware of having rational insight into some rational truth or into the rational force of reasons that support believing some proposition, then arguably one should be able to tell when one has such insight and when one does not. But sometimes a person is unable to discriminate between cases where she has genuine insight and cases where she does not. Someone who takes herself to have insight into the transitivity of the "to the east of" relation may be unable to see that her thinking is confused. So it seems that rational insight is not something

---

[13] Tomas Bogardus, "A Vindication of the Equal-Weight View," *Episteme* 6, no. 3 (2009): 324–335.

[14] This worry is developed in Paul Benacerraf, "Mathematical Truth," *Journal of Philosophy* 70, no. 19 (1973): 661–679; and Hartry H. Field, *Realism, Mathematics, and Modality* (New York: Blackwell, 1989). Similar worries are directed against Laurence BonJour's "moderate rationalism" in Paul Boghossian, "Inference and Insight," *Philosophy and Phenomenological Research* 63, no. 3 (2001): 635.

of which one is directly aware. And if one's awareness of rational insight is mediated by some feeling of insight, then obviously this feeling can sometimes be mistaken. Even when this feeling attends some belief that is true and appropriately formed, it may be that one's thinking fails to be genuinely insightful. Indeed, given the aforementioned mysterious character of rational insight, it may be argued that the most plausible position is one that rejects rationalism and denies that a person can have direct a priori access to rational truths or to the rational force of reasons.

How should the rationalist respond to the charge of mysteriousness? I think it is true that philosophers do not at present have a fully illuminating and perspicuous account of the nature of rational insight, or of how it is achievable.[15] But, as Laurence BonJour notes, this would constitute a severe worry for rationalism only if philosophers had perspicuous and illuminating accounts of the cognitive acts and states that are uncontroversially possible. And BonJour maintains that current scientific understanding sheds very little light on consciousness, qualia, conceptual thought, introspective awareness, and other cognitive acts.[16] The lack of an illuminating account of rational insight should not, says BonJour, lead philosophers to reject the existence of rational insight any more than their current inability to explain consciousness should lead them to conclude that consciousness does not exist. This response seems to me to be sensible: in light of the deep difficulties in accounting for some of the most basic features of mental reality (especially consciousness and the intentionality, or "aboutness," of many mental states), the mysteriousness of rational insight does not give sufficient reason to dismiss rational insight as illusory.

It is also worth noting that the "mysteriousness" objection applies not just to rationalism as I have defined it but also to other accounts of a priori knowledge that do not posit direct rational insight. Suppose that one does not have rational insight into the necessary transitivity of "taller than" but nonetheless knows in some indirect way (e.g., by means of some

---

[15] I note two similar proposals that do seem promising, though to my mind neither proposal dispels all of the mystery about rational insight. Elijah Chudnoff argues that subject S becomes aware of an abstract object when that object determines the phenomenal character of S's intuition experience by being part of the *principle of unity* that the material parts of that experience instantiate. On this proposal, one becomes aware of an abstract object not because the object causally affects us but because it partially constitutes one's phenomenal experience (as part of the form that unifies the elements of the experience). (Elijah Chudnoff, *Intuition* [Oxford: Oxford University Press, 2013], chap. 7.) Similarly, Bengson argues that a "successful" intuition that *p* is partly *constituted* by the fact that *p*. John Bengson, "Grasping the Third Realm," *Oxford Studies in Epistemology* 5 (2015): 27.

[16] Laurence BonJour, "Replies," *Philosophy and Phenomenological Research* 63, no. 3 (2001): 673–674.

appropriately produced brute intuition) that "taller than" is necessarily transitive. This fact about the necessary transitivity of "taller than" is not an empirical fact that is made true by the way the world happens to be but rather a modal fact that concerns all possible worlds. It seems, then, that one cannot come to know this fact merely by coming to know empirical facts about one's world. It is therefore very difficult to see how one could achieve cognitive "contact" with this modal fact in a way that would allow one to come to know it, whether or not this contact is direct or mediated by some sort of brute intuition. Someone who is unwilling to countenance any mysterious sorts of knowledge would therefore need to deny knowledge of such modal facts, whether or not that knowledge is grounded in rational insight. And denying such knowledge would amount to a quite radical skepticism that is, at least on its face, implausible.

Next, do cases of apparent but nongenuine insight undercut the motivation for rationalism? I do not think so. The objection holds that if one had direct introspective awareness of rational insight, then one would always be able to discriminate between cases where one has rational insight and cases where one does not. But there is reason to doubt the assumption underlying this premise, namely, that some type of state is directly apprehended only if one is always able to accurately determine whether such a state holds. Plausibly, the fact that I currently have visual impressions that are not uniformly black is a fact of which I am directly aware. But one can imagine a case where a devious neuro-scientist ensures that some subject has no visual impressions other than complete blackness while also causing that subject to confidently believe that she is having colorful and variegated visual impressions. While some may conclude on the basis of such possibilities that one does not in fact have direct access to the fact that one is experiencing variegated visual impressions, a less radical and more plausible response is to reject the assumption that one has direct awareness of some state only if one is infallible in one's beliefs about whether one is in such a state. Direct awareness of some state surely puts one in an epistemically privileged position with respect to beliefs about that state, but one needn't understand this epistemic privilege in terms of unqualified infallibility.

Declan Smithies gives an alternative account of the privileged epistemic position afforded by direct introspective access to certain mental states. Smithies defends the following thesis:

The introspective accessibility thesis: for some mental states M, necessarily, one is in M if and only if one has introspective justification to believe that one is in M and one thereby has an introspective way of knowing that one is in M.[17]

Assuming that having variegated visual impressions is among the introspectively accessible mental states, it follows from Smithies's view that having variegated visual impressions guarantees that one has propositional justification to believe, by means of introspection, that one has variegated visual impressions. Furthermore, *not* having variegated visual impressions guarantees that one does *not* have introspective justification to believe that one has variegated visual impressions. If the introspective accessibility thesis is correct, then introspection is in an important respect epistemically superior to perception. If an evil demon has caused me to undergo a realistic hallucination, I could have perceptual justification to believe that I see a tree nearby even though there is no tree nearby. And if I have strong (but misleading) evidence to believe that I am being deceived by an evil demon, then I may lack justification to believe that I am seeing a tree even when I look at a tree that is right before me. The connection between perceptual states and perceptual justification can break apart, whereas there is an unbreakable connection between introspectively accessible states and introspective justification for believing one is in the relevant state.

While the introspective accessibility thesis accounts for the privileged status of introspection, it does not imply that one is capable of achieving infallibility in one's beliefs about one's mental states. Rationally imperfect beings are sometimes unable to respond properly to the rational grounds that are accessible to them, and for this reason one is sometimes unable to form a doxastically justified belief in a proposition that one has justification to believe. In addition, one sometimes cannot help but form beliefs for which one lacks propositional justification. To cite an example from Smithies, an infant who feels pain has propositional justification for the belief that she is in pain but is unable to form this belief because she lacks the concept of pain. The person who continues to see in color but is programmed to believe that he is experiencing total blackness is unable to form the belief that he sees in color, but he nonetheless has evidence (his variegated visual impressions) that gives him propositional justification to believe that he sees in color. His

---

[17] Declan Smithies, "A Simple Theory of Introspection," in *Introspection and Consciousness*, ed. Declan Smithies and Daniel Stoljar (New York: Oxford University Press, 2012), 263.

inability to believe in a way that accords with his evidence constitutes a rational deficiency, blameless though it may be.

If the introspective accessibility thesis or some relevantly similar thesis is right, then the claim that one has direct introspective awareness of rational insight (or at least of certain species of rational insight) is fully compatible with the claim that one is sometimes mistaken in one's beliefs about when one does and does not have rational insight into some matter. Such mistakes exhibit a rational deficiency (and not just an unfortunate situation of insufficient or misleading evidence), since they involve improperly responding to the evidence that is introspectively available. The rational deficiencies exhibited on such occasions will frequently be quite subtle. As already mentioned, the person who takes himself to be introspectively aware of rational insight into the transitivity of "to the east of" may indeed form this belief in response to some rational insight, while misidentifying what it is exactly that he has insight into: for example, whether he has insight into the truth of the believed proposition, or insight into the truth of some similar proposition, or insight into the inconclusive support provided by the considerations he has in mind.

Beyond answering objections and appealing to one's awareness of insight, more can be said to articulate a positive case for rationalism. Here, I briefly sketch one argument that is aimed only at the epistemic internalist. The first premise is that the determinants of justification are *directly* discernible by the subject, and not discernible only in some indirect way. Consider some factor $F1$ that one cannot directly discern, and to which one has only indirect cognitive access by means of some distinct factor $F2$. It would seem that $F1$ is not truly available to reflection in the way that is required of those factors that determine what may be rationally believed.

The second premise is that rational cogency (of a belief, or more generally of some package of doxastic attitudes) is, in some cases, a determinant of justification. Recall the example where I come to believe on the basis of some website that the twentieth digit of pi is 4, only to later receive strong evidence that the website is a hoax, reporting random numbers after "3.14." Having received this evidence, and lacking any other grounds for my belief about the value of the twentieth digit, I can either give up this belief or retain it. Clearly, the former option is justified and the latter option is not. Moreover, the explanation for this is that the former option is rationally cogent while the latter is not. One cannot explain the difference in justification by appealing to what *seems* to me to be rational, since it would be irrational for me to retain the belief even if doing so seemed to me to be the uniquely rational response. (As described in subsection 4.4.2, I might be designed by God to view this as an unusual exception to the normal standards of evidential defeat, so that there is no sense in which maintaining the belief would *by my own lights* be irrational.) Thus, in some cases, rational cogency is itself a determinant of justification. One can conclude, then, that rational cogency is sometimes directly discernible. And to conclude this is to concede rationalism.

4.4.2 Rationalist Partisan Justification

Rationalism is highly controversial, and I do not pretend to have thoroughly rebutted the objections that may be brought against it. But I will now shift focus to the question of whether rational insight, supposing that it is achievable, may be a source of partisan justification. According to a rationalist account of partisan justification, a self-favoring (readout) reliability estimate can be justified in virtue of having rational insight into the truth or plausibility of one's outlook. Merely identifying a rational merit that is unique to one's own position is not enough to justify a self-favoring position, since one might also see rational merits unique to opposing views while lacking any insight into how these competing merits should be weighed. For insight to ground partisan justification, that insight must help supply an all-things-considered reason for thinking that one's own outlook is rationally stronger than the outlooks of one's disputants.

In considering the merits of the rationalist account of partisan justification, it will be helpful to have a concrete example in view. So consider the case of Sierra and Arjun, two classmates in a high school math class who are working together on a homework assignment that requires them to consider the Monty Hall problem. This problem concerns a game show where a contestant must choose from among three closed doors, behind one of which is a car and behind two of which are goats. The winning door has been randomly determined. After the contestant announces a choice, the show host (who knows where the car is) always opens one of the doors that the contestant did *not* select and reveals a goat. (If either of the doors not selected by the contestant could be opened to reveal a goat, then the host randomly chooses which of these doors to open.) The host then gives the contestant the choice between sticking with her original selection or changing her selection to the other door that remains closed. Sierra and Arjun's homework asks whether taking the offer to switch doors increases the chance of winning the car.

Like many who reflect on this problem, Arjun thinks (incorrectly) that there is no advantage to switching. He explains his reasoning this way: "suppose the contestant initially selects Door 1 and then the host reveals a goat behind Door 2. What the contestant learns from this revelation can be distilled to this: the car is either behind Door 1 or Door 3. That information supports assigning 0.5 probability to Door 1 and 0.5 probability to Door 3. The information that Door 1 was the contestant's original selection gives us no reason to think that Door 1 is more or less likely to be the winner than Door 3. So, one's chances are not helped by switching." Sierra reaches the opposite conclusion. She explains her reasoning as follows: "two-thirds of the time the contestant's initial selection will be a losing door behind which lies a goat; in such cases, the winning door will be the door that was *not* originally selected and that remains shut after the host reveals a goat. So, two-thirds of the time, switching doors results in winning the car. Staying put results in a win only a third of the time, when one's initial selection happened to be right. So switching is the better choice."

After explaining and debating their reasoning, Sierra and Arjun both feel that their original reasoning was stronger and more conclusive than the other's reasoning, though neither can pinpoint exactly where the other person's reasoning goes wrong. As each acknowledges, the impartial considerations in this case are on a par: both feel equally confident, both have equally good track records on math assignments, neither has some dispute-neutral reason for thinking his or her position is more likely to be correct, and so on.

I'll label the reasoning articulated by Arjun *RA* and the reasoning articulated by Sierra *RS*. And suppose that Sierra knows that exactly one of the following two propositions is true:

1. Arjun's reasoning *RA* is correct.
2. Sierra's reasoning *RS* is correct.

The rationalist account I endorse says that Sierra could be justified in assigning higher credence to (2) than to (1). While in this case Sierra has not identified the mistake in *RA*, she also does not see that *RA* is cogent. So the evident cogency of *RS*, together with her awareness of the fact that *RA* and *RS* cannot both be correct, gives her a reason to favor possibility (2). Note that if before the disagreement Sierra had an impartial credence for the proposition that *RS* is correct, then conditionalizing on the fact of Arjun's disagreement would result in an updated credence for (2) of 0.5. (Recall that there is perfect parity in the impartial considerations.) So, on the supposition that Sierra should conditionalize on the facts about the disagreement and that her final credence for (2) could justifiably exceed 0.5, it follows that Sierra's initial credence for (2) can justifiably exceed what would be justified on impartial grounds, and thus that she enjoys partisan justification.

Exactly how much confidence should Sierra have for (2) prior to learning of the disagreement? It seems that an ideally rational person would be fully confident in (2). And perhaps one can for this reason truly affirm that Sierra *ideally* ought to be fully confident in (2). But the question at hand is best understood as a question not about how much weight Sierra *ideally* ought to give to (2) but about how much weight she ought to give to (2) *given her rational abilities and limitations*. Even if it is granted that Sierra has genuine insight into the cogency of *RS*, it is likely that her insight will lack something of the "clarity" (for lack of a better term) that is characteristic of ideal rationality. Arguably, Sierra's initial degree of confidence should be sensitive to the degree of clarity of her insight, in which case she should not start with maximal confidence. If this is right, then Sierra's ur-prior should be less than 1 but greater than the value that could be supported on impartial grounds alone.

Why should one affirm a rationalist account of partisan justification? First, the rationalist account better comports with commonsense verdicts than the alternatives do. In the variations of the two planets case discussed earlier, anything less conciliatory than an equal weight response appears to exhibit an irrational form of partiality. Unlike other accounts of partisan justification, the rationalist account does not support a self-favoring response in any of these cases. When the rationalist account does support a self-favoring response, this verdict is independently plausible. For example, there is nothing counterintuitive or prima facie problematic with the judgment that Sierra should give at least somewhat more weight to her view, which is after all supported by clear and conclusive reasoning.

Second, the rationalist account better comports with commonsense views on the nature of rationality than do other accounts of partisan justification. Intuitively, it is rationally arbitrary to favor one of two competing views when there is no discernible symmetry breaker that supports the favored view (as the radically permissivist and externalist accounts allow). And it also seems objectionably arbitrary to favor some view merely because it accords with the seemings and inclinations that happen to be one's own (as the agent-centered account allows) or to favor some view for reason $R1$ while acknowledging that $R1$ is not discernibly stronger than reason $R2$ that supports an opposing view (as the moderately permissivist account allows). In contrast, there is nothing counterintuitive in claiming that how much weight one assigns to competing views should depend not only on the credentials of the proponents of the views but also on whether one view is supported by reasons that are discernibly stronger than the reasons supporting the other view.

While the rationalist account of partisan justification may enjoy more initial plausibility than other accounts, it does face objections. Schoenfield's "inaccuracy objection," discussed in chapter 3, captures what I think is one of the primary sources of discomfort with rationalist weak conciliationism. Consider again the case of Sierra and Arjun. Suppose that Sierra and Arjun have previously had scores of similar disagreements concerning math homework problems where both strongly felt that they had insight into the rational superiority of their views, and suppose Sierra knows that she reasoned correctly in only half of these cases. Given this, Sierra should think that the plan to respond to her disagreements with Arjun by giving more weight to the rationally cogent position is likely to succeed only half of the time. Why, then, would Sierra be justified in giving greater than 0.5 credence to her view on the Monty Hall problem? Can't she see that there is only a 50% chance that she is correct?

I will not recapitulate the discussion of this objection from chapter 3, where I argue (among other things) that Schoenfield's planning framework leads to absurd verdicts in examples like the one involving Veronica and her soccer dreams. Here, I will simply reinforce that discussion from a slightly different angle. Suppose Sierra is a rationalist weak conciliationist and that she continues to give more weight to her view on the Monty Hall problem after discussing the matter with Arjun. In responding this way, Sierra engages in the cognitive process of "giving more weight to the view that appears to me to be rationally cogent," a process Sierra knows is only 50% reliable in her disputes with Arjun. But Sierra also employs a narrow process type that is characterized by very specific features of the reasoning that she uses to arrive at her view on the Monty Hall problem. Sierra's insight into the cogency of her reasoning makes it possible for her to appreciate the reliability of this narrow process. But at the time just before Sierra thinks through the Monty Hall problem and discovers her disagreement with Arjun, Sierra could not know the relevant narrow process that she would employ in response to their next disagreement, and therefore has no reason to expect that she is more likely than Arjun to be correct in their next disagreement. The reasonability of a more steadfast response can be seen only in light of information that is available to Sierra only after she has thought through the disputed matter. It is tempting to think that Sierra's response to the disagreement should accord with the plan that she would endorse prior to thinking through the dispute question, before she has fallen under the influence of her particular doxastic inclinations on that question. But this antecedent standpoint is the less informed position, one that lacks access to crucial rational considerations that bear on the matter under dispute.

Similarly, when one prescinds from the details of specific disagreements and considers rationalist weak conciliationism abstractly, it is natural to focus one's epistemic evaluation on the generic and highly unreliable process of giving extra weight to those apparent insights that happen to be one's own. But such an evaluation focuses on processes at the wrong level of generality. Sierra's reasonability in giving extra weight to her apparent insight is derived from the intrinsic merits of the genuinely insightful reasoning she articulates. When one considers rationalist self-trust abstractly, one loses sight of the myriad first-order reasons that make such particular instances self-trust reasonable.

4.5 The False Hope of Reformed Epistemology

On the picture of partisan justification I have been defending, a religious believer can have partisan justification only if his insight into the rational merits of his position justifies him in thinking that his position is rationally stronger than the position of his disputants. External factors (such as the proper functioning of truth-aimed faculties) and agent-centered reasons (such as the practical importance of epistemic confidence) do not supply partisan justification, since it is objectionably arbitrary to show partiality to one of multiple perspectives that one takes to be on a par with respect to their internal rational merits. Even if agent-centered reasons do give one a reason to highly estimate one's own reliability, the requirement that one avoid rational arbitrariness converts any reason to highly estimate one's own reliability into a reason to highly estimate the reliability of all those whose perspective on the matter is rationally on a par with one's own. Rationality can exhibit partiality toward particular arguments and positions on the basis of their discernible rational merits, but rationality does not tolerate partiality toward particular agents.

My emphasis on rational insight as the only legitimate basis for partisan justification stands in direct tension with the most prominent approach to defending the rationality of religious belief over the last few decades. This is the approach of "reformed epistemology," an approach most powerfully developed in the work of Alvin Plantinga and William Alston. Reformed epistemologists argue that the epistemic rationality of religious belief (and Christian belief in particular) does not depend on one's having good evidence or strong inferential support for one's religious views. Oversimplifying somewhat, the primary argumentative strategy employed by reformed epistemologists is to point to some class of beliefs that are clearly justified despite the lack of strong inferential support and then to argue that religious beliefs could be justified in the same manner. If this sort of argument works, then one should give up the view that the epistemic standing of religious views depends on the strength of the arguments (whether philosophical, historical, scientific, or whatever) for those views. This result is taken to be salutary for at least two reasons. First, it may be thought that those arguments are not particularly strong. (At least this is Plantinga's assessment; Alston is more optimistic.)[18] Second, even if there are strong arguments, it is claimed that most believers are not able to rehearse them and do not believe on the basis of compelling arguments. So if one is interested in vindicating the epistemic standing of everyday believers, one presumably needs to show how their religious confidence could be justified in the absence of strong inferential support.

By deemphasizing the role of rational assessment in religious belief formation, perhaps reformed epistemologists have made it easier to affirm the *initial* justification of religious belief. If religious belief is not like a complicated scientific hypothesis that is inferred from various strands of evidence, then perhaps it is a mistake to judge the epistemic standing of a religious outlook on the basis of the arguments that can be advanced in favor of that outlook. Plausibly, noninferential beliefs must be assessed in a different manner. But even if deemphasizing rational assessment strengthens the

---

[18] Plantinga's pessimism regarding evidential arguments for Christian faith is defended in *Warranted Christian Belief* (New York: Oxford University Press, 2000), 271–280. Alston's more optimistic assessment is registered in *Perceiving God: The Epistemology of Religious Experience* (Ithaca: Cornell University Press, 1991), 270.

case for the *initial* justification of religious belief, it undercuts the attempt to defend the justification of religious belief in the face of defeater worries raised by systematic religious disagreement. When disagreeing parties appear equally qualified (when judged from a dispute-neutral standpoint), insight into the greater rational merits of one's own position is the symmetry breaker that is needed to justify continued confidence. But reformed epistemologists depict religious belief formation as a process where insight plays little to no role.

4.5.1   Alston

In support of my claim that reformed epistemology is largely powerless to defuse worries raised by disagreement, consider first Alston's account of Christian belief formation. Alston suggests that belief in God is typically a result of mystical experiences that, if veridical, amount to experiences of perceiving God.[19] Such perception is not typically *sensory*: God does not typically appear in the subject's visual field or speak to the subject in an audible voice. Nonetheless, in such episodes God makes God's presence *felt* in some perceptual but not sensory way. God not only presents Godself as present but may also be presented as expressing love to the subject, or as providing comfort, or as expressing judgment, or as communicating a particular message, and so on.

If Alston is right that mystical experiences are often relevantly like standard perceptual experiences (a conclusion he argues for at great length), then it is reasonable to think that mystical experiences may justify certain beliefs in a manner that is analogous to the way standard perceptual experiences justify beliefs. As discussed in chapter 2, Alston thinks that one cannot provide a good argument in support of the reliability of sense perception as a whole that does not itself in some way rely on the deliverances of sense perception. Nonetheless, almost everyone grants that beliefs formed by sense perception enjoy a very high degree of initial justification. Given that standard perceptual beliefs can be justified even without strong noncircular evidence for the reliability of sense perception, there is no reason to think that beliefs formed in response to "mystical perception" are justified only if there is strong noncircular evidence for the reliability of mystical perception. To insist that

---

[19] Alston, *Perceiving God*, chap. 1.

mystical perception must have good noncircular support without requiring this of standard perceptual beliefs would be to impose an arbitrary double standard.[20]

Even if Alston's argument wholly succeeds as a defense of the prima facie justification of religious beliefs formed in response to putative perceptual experiences, the assimilation of religious belief formation to perceptual belief formation intensifies the worries raised by religious disagreement. For disagreements arising purely from incompatible perceptual seemings are rationally superficial disagreements where there are no rationalist grounds for self-trust. According to rationalist weak conciliationism, one should respond to such disagreements in an impartial manner. Given full disclosure, this should lead to convergence on a common credence. For example, suppose I seem to see the pastor of my church get into the driver's seat of a nearby Ferrari and drive away, and I go on to form the belief that this has in fact taken place. This belief does not alter my judgment that, *antecedently* speaking, this is an extremely improbable state of affairs. Because the visual seeming leaves my fundamental plausibility assessment untouched, I can treat this seeming in an instrumentalist fashion. Now suppose my friend who also saw the episode shares that it was clear to her that he drove away in a Toyota, and I become convinced that one of us has experienced some sort of extremely realistic hallucination. Because the Toyota hypothesis is antecedently much more plausible than the Ferrari hypothesis, my friend and I should both converge on a very high credence for the Toyota hypothesis.

If mystical experiences are relevantly analogous to perceptual experiences, then one should expect that this sort of instrumentalist approach to disagreements will also be possible in the religious context. Suppose that a religious seeker who goes to a Catholic mass seems to perceive that God is present in some special way in the bread and wine that is being consumed in the Eucharist and on the basis of this experience becomes a Christian. He then meets a Muslim who reports having a powerful and convincing experience of (apparently) perceiving that God is present in a special way when the Koran is being read, an experience that prompted her conversion to Islam. If these putative perceptual experiences leave antecedent plausibility judgments intact, then nothing prevents the Christian and Muslim from treating their putative perceptual experiences in an instrumentalist fashion. And if the two believers agree in their antecedent plausibility judgments,

---

[20] Alston, *Perceiving God*, 249–250.

then they should converge on a common credence (assuming full disclosure of their evidence). Of course, differing assessments of the antecedent plausibility of their outlooks might prevent such convergence. But in this case, their continued divergence would be explained not by their alleged perceptual experiences but by their divergent assessments of rational plausibility antecedent to experiential evidence.

Disagreements arising from inconsistent sense impressions are often rationally shallow disagreements where rationalist weak conciliationism requires significant conciliation and convergence on a common credence. Since perceptual grounds are easily undercut by disagreement, Alston's emphasis on the perceptual character of religious belief would seem to intensify the worries that religious disagreement raises.

While Alston is open to the possibility that some religious believers may have insight into the greater rational merits of their outlook, he does not want to rely on this possibility in his defense of religious confidence in the face of controversy.[21] Instead, he explicitly appeals to agent-centered *practical* reasons for sticking with the "mystical practice" of the community of which one happens to be a member. It is rational, says Alston, to continue believing in a religious outlook that has been personally beneficial (in conferring purpose and facilitating positive moral transformation, for example) and that may be a conduit for relating to the divine.

Despite this appeal to agent-centered practical reasons, Alston concedes that in many instances of mundane perceptual disagreement, full conciliation is rationally required.[22] (His particular example involves conflicting reports from witnesses to a traffic accident.) So what distinguishes these mundane perceptual disagreements from the religious case that makes full conciliation appropriate in the former but not the latter? Alston identifies two differences he takes to be relevant. First, mundane perceptual disagreements concern particular beliefs, not the reliability of general perceptual practices. Thus, full conciliation in mundane cases does not require abandoning perceptual belief formation in an entire domain. Second, in mundane cases, one can often identify some neutral way of arbitrating the dispute. In the dress case, for example, one could (and people did) hunt down other sources of information that could confirm the dress's color. Given the possibility of such independent confirmation, Alston thinks that in mundane perceptual disagreements, it is

---

[21] Alston, *Perceiving God*, 270.
[22] Alston, *Perceiving God*, 271.

sensible to refrain from giving extra weight to the perceptual seemings that happen to be one's own. But in the religious case, it is plausible that there is no independent way of settling the dispute arising from contrary mystical experiences. Alston thinks that in light of this difference, "the sting is taken out of the inability of each of us to show that he is in an epistemically superior position. . . . To put the point most sharply, we have no idea what noncircular proof of the reliability of [Christian Mystical Perception] would look like, *even if it is as reliable as you please.* Hence why should we take the absence of such a proof to nullify, or even sharply diminish, the justification I have for my Christian M-beliefs?"[23] (M-beliefs, here, are those beliefs formed in response to mystical experiences, using the standards for assessing those experiences that are operative in the relevant religious community.)

Unfortunately for Alston's position, the two planets example gives one reason to question the significance of these differences between mundane perceptual disagreements and systematic perceptual disagreements occurring between religious communities.[24] In the two planets example, the "dispute" between Planet A and Planet B concerns not just isolated religious propositions but the trustworthiness of the source of all of their religious beliefs. Neutrality between the opposing views would require giving up confidence that one's religious community is in genuine relation with the loving creator of the universe. Moreover, given the symmetry of the situation (which one can imagine will persist until the extinction of the two planets), there is no imaginable independent avenue for settling the dispute. Assuming that one does not endorse confidence in the two planets example, then it seems that the distinctions Alston has pointed to do not have the epistemic significance he claims for them.

Alston *does* gesture toward the sort of factor that may indeed justify confidence in the face of disagreement, though in my judgment he has not rightly described this factor. Consider the following analogy offered by Alston:

> Suppose that there were a diversity of sense perceptual doxastic practices as diverse as forms of [mystical perception] are in fact. Suppose that in certain cultures there were a well established "Cartesian" practice of seeing what is

---

[23] Alston, *Perceiving God*, 272.

[24] In my criticisms of Alston's reasons for treating religious disagreement differently from perceptual disagreement, I am in significant agreement with criticisms raised by Sanford Goldberg, "Does Externalist Epistemology Rationalize Religious Commitment?," in *Religious Faith and Intellectual Virtue*, ed. Timothy O'Connor and Laura Frances Callahan (Oxford: Oxford University Press, 2014), 294–297.

visually perceived as an indefinitely extended medium that is more or less concentrated at various points, rather than, as in our "Aristotelian" practice, as made up of more or less discrete objects scattered about in space. In other cultures we find a "Whiteheadian" [sense perception] to be equally socially established; here the visual field is seen as made up of momentary events growing out of each other in a continuous process. Let's further suppose that each of these practices serves its practitioners equally well in their dealings with the environment. We may even suppose that each group has developed physical science, in its own terms, to about as high a pitch as the others. But suppose further that, in this imagined situation, we are as firmly wedded to our "Aristotelian" form of sense perception as we are in fact. The Cartesian and Whiteheadian *ausländer* seem utterly outlandish to us, and we find it difficult to take seriously the idea that they may be telling it like it is. Nevertheless, we can find no neutral grounds on which to argue effectively for the greater accuracy of our way of doing it. In such a situation would it be clear that it is irrational for us to continue to form perceptual beliefs in our "Aristotelian" way, given that the practice is proving itself by its fruits? It seems to me that quite the opposite is clear. In the absence of any external reason for supposing that one of the competing practices is more accurate than my own, the only rational course for me is to sit tight with the practice of which I am a master and which serves me so well in guiding my activity in the world. But our actual situation with regard to [Christian mystical perception] is precisely parallel to the one we have been imagining.[25]

What should the proponent of rationalist weak conciliationism say about this case? On the one hand such a rationalist does not affirm a reasons impartiality constraint. So the lack of "neutral grounds" does not rule out justified confidence. On the other hand the mere feeling of confidence, or the mere conviction that the other side is crazy, is not enough to justify partiality toward one's perspective. Nearly any possible belief, no matter how rationally deficient it may be, can be attended by a feeling of confidence or a conviction that contrary positions are crazy. These reactions may be mere brute inclinations. Of course, one's judgment that some view is crazy is often a result of appreciating rational deficiencies in the view. To the extent that one sympathizes with Alston's nonconciliatory verdict in the case of conflicting

---

[25] Alston, *Perceiving God*, 273–274.

sensory practices, it may in part be because one imagines that one's sense that the competing view is outlandish is born of some insight into the greater rational plausibility of the "Aristotelian" perspective. If Alston stipulated that there was no such insight, just feelings of confidence on all sides, then I do not think his judgment concerning the case would be especially plausible.

Perhaps Alston himself is thinking of this as a case where one does indeed have legitimate insight into the greater rational merits of one's position but is unable to articulate this insight or to present it in a way that would move those who are gripped by the other views. But in this case the lesson of the example would seem to be that continued religious confidence may be reasonable when one has insight into the greater rational plausibility of one's religious outlook. And this does not help to support Alston's larger argument, which seeks to vindicate religious belief by downplaying the role of rational assessment and emphasizing in its place perceptual processes that are essentially nonrational (which is not to say *irrational*). That argument is ultimately unconvincing. Perceiving that p typically does not affect my assessment of p's preevidential plausibility, nor does it give me some insight into the rational deficiency of views that deny p. Perceptual experiences therefore do not typically transmit to the subject the epistemic resources that are needed to resist epistemic defeat in the face of disagreement.

4.5.2   Plantinga

I'll now turn to Plantinga's account of the formation of Christian belief to see if his religious epistemology is better equipped to address the concerns raised by disagreement. Plantinga contends that Christian belief is not typically a conclusion one reaches by way of inferential reasoning but is a "basic" belief one simply finds oneself having as a result of the Holy Spirit's gracious activity in the right sort of circumstances.[26] Basic beliefs are simply beliefs that are not inferentially grounded; they are, rather, starting points for inference. So, for example, one might hear the gospel preached and, as a result of the work of the Holy Spirit, find oneself believing that the preached message is true. Is this inclination the product of some sort of rational insight into the fundamental plausibility of Christian teachings? It is not entirely clear (to me, at least) how Plantinga would answer this question, but in general

---

[26] Plantinga, *Warranted Christian Belief*, 249–252.

his discussion does not seem to support the view that the acquisition of faith involves the experience of such insight. The new believer may view her past self as *mistaken*, but it's not clear that she will view her past self as *confused*, or even as insufficiently insightful.

There are, in fact, passages where Plantinga comes close to reveling in the improbability of Christian teaching, as though to emphasize that the conviction of faith is not the result of a more sober assessment of Christianity's plausibility. Rather, faith involves confidence in doctrines that the believer can *presently* recognize to be improbable in light of his evidence. Here is Plantinga:

> What is being taught, after all, is not something that chimes straightforwardly with our ordinary experience. It isn't like an account of an ancient war, or of the cruelty of the Athenians to the Melians, or of the overweening pride of some ancient despot. That sort of thing would be easy enough to believe. What we have instead, however, is the claim that a certain human being—Jesus of Nazareth—is also, astonishingly, the unique divine Son of God who has existed from eternity. Furthermore, this man died, which is not uncommon, but then three days later rose from the dead, which is uncommon indeed. Still further, it is by way of his atoning suffering and death and resurrection that we are justified, that our sins are forgiven, and that we may have life and have it more abundantly. *This* is heavy stuff indeed, and the mere fact that some ancient authors believed it would certainly be insufficient for a sensible conviction on our part.[27]

This view that the Christian story is antecedently quite implausible need not undercut the case for the *initial* justification of Christian belief. Think back to the example of my seeing my pastor get into a Ferrari and drive away. Antecedently, this is quite implausible. But as long as I highly estimate my reliability in forming beliefs on the basis of visual seemings, then I am justified in being highly confident that what I seem to have seen has indeed taken place. Similarly, the Christian could have a very high reliability estimate for beliefs formed in response to his basic doxastic inclinations. If he does, then when he finds himself with such an inclination to believe (without inferential grounds) some antecedently implausible Christian claim, he can justifiably be confident in that claim.

---

[27] Plantinga, *Warranted Christian Belief*, 270.

But while antecedent improbability does not pose a great barrier to *initial* justification, it can prove lethal once one learns of disagreement. Once I learn that my friend takes herself to have seen a Toyota and not a Ferrari, I should become quite confident that my friend saw correctly and I did not. Similarly, if Christian claims are antecedently improbable (like the Ferrari episode), then Christian belief will be highly susceptible to defeat when Christians encounter believers in other religions who are also responding to some sort of basic doxastic inclination.

The foregoing quotation from Plantinga suggests that when a Christian finds herself with the convictions of faith, this is not a result of having insight into the plausibility of Christian teaching. The basic doxastic inclination described by Plantinga may therefore leave one's antecedent plausibility assessments largely untouched. That means that it should be possible for the Christian to occupy a vantage point that is rationally antecedent to the newly acquired doxastic inclination in order to treat that inclination in an instrumentalist fashion. And Plantinga hasn't given us a reason for thinking that such an exercise will inevitably have an outcome that is favorable to Christian belief.

Even though Plantinga does not characterize Christian belief formation as a perceptual process, the same worries that plagued Alston's account apply here. The basic doxastic inclination that God grants the believer may not bring insight into the plausibility of Christian teaching (or into the rational cogency of some line of reasoning that supports this teaching). If it does not, then Christian belief will be rationally superficial in a way that leaves it vulnerable to defeat in the context of disagreement. To the extent that reformed epistemologists downplay the role of rational assessment in religious belief, they leave one no reason for thinking that contemporary religious believers are in a better epistemic position than the religious believers in the two planets example.

5

Affective Rationalism
and Religious Insight

In chapters 3 and 4, I developed and defended rationalist weak conciliationism. According to this view, confident religious belief is likely be justified only to the extent that one has insight that justifies thinking that one's own religious outlook is rationally stronger (in a way that one can discern) than the outlooks of one's disputants. Many may understand this to imply that justified religious belief is a philosophical accomplishment reserved only for those who can out-argue their opponents. The rationalist position may also seem to imply that personal religious experience plays at best a minor role in accounting for the rationality of religious belief in a religiously plural context. But in this chapter, I aim to resist these implications. The brand of rationalism I endorse is an "affective rationalism" that emphasizes the essential role played by emotional experiences in facilitating certain sorts of insights, insights that are religiously important and that are not available only to the analytically sophisticated. This broader understanding of rational insight allows one to see why a rationalist account of partisan justification need not marginalize personal religious experience as epistemically insignificant. Affective rationalism is offered as a compelling alternative to both the antirationalism of certain reformed epistemologists and the austere, highly intellectualist rationalism characteristic of contemporary natural theology.

5.1 Religious Experience Marginalized?

I suggested in the previous chapter that the religious epistemologies developed by Plantinga and Alston do not provide a good reason for thinking that religious confidence can withstand the threat posed by widespread and persistent disagreement. The seemings that result from the gift of faith or from perceptual encounters with God could be brute inclinations that do not yield insight into the greater rational merits of one's own religious position. In this case, it is perfectly possible that adherents of other faiths have relevantly similar seemings that are equally convincing. If such rational parity is acknowledged, then the rationalist weak conciliationism I favor will forbid significant confidence in one's own religious outlook.

One might think that if the view I have sketched is correct, then the fact that two believers have had very different religious experiences cannot help to explain why one or both of these believers may rationally persist in their opposing views in the face of disagreement. Disagreements driven by religious experiences would seem to be rationally superficial disagreements where rationalist weak conciliationism requires convergence of the disputing parties' credences. But there are at least two reasons why it might be mistaken to infer from my account that religious experience plays an insignificant role in supporting religious belief in contexts of controversy.

First, religious believers have a more complete and direct knowledge of the qualities of their own experiences than they can have of someone else's experiences. Because of this, many religious disagreements will fall far short of meeting the "full disclosure" assumption that has been operating in the background of this discussion. It is plausible that in many instances of what is called "religious experience," the epistemically relevant features of the experience cannot be fully and adequately communicated to others. Suppose that someone in desperate straits cries out to God for help and immediately experiences a peace that seems in its profundity to be a divine gift rather than a purely natural phenomenon. Could someone who believes in God partly on the basis of such experience fully disclose his reasons for belief? He could, of course, report having such an experience and describe the belief changes that seemed appropriate in its wake. However, the epistemic significance of the experience may significantly depend on subjective aspects of the experience whose qualities cannot be adequately communicated by means of verbal testimony.[1] If two parties to a religious disagreement cannot communicate the significant aspects of their experience, then the disagreement will not be analogous to a situation where one observes contrary readouts on two instruments. A better analogy might be a situation where one clearly sees the readout on one instrument but only has some suggestive clues about the readout on the second instrument.

The fact that people are unable to communicate the relevant features of many religious experiences does not by itself lessen the epistemic threat

[1] William James, *The Varieties of Religious Experience* (New York: Random House, 1902), 371.

posed by disagreement.[2] Consider a disagreement between a Buddhist and a Muslim who both appeal to distinctive sorts of experiences in justifying their contested religious beliefs. It is true that the Muslim does not herself experience the same sort of ineffable experiences that ground the Buddhist's belief in, say, the doctrine of nonself. Nonetheless, the Buddhist can tell the Muslim of his experiences, and he can describe the doxastic responses that seem to him appropriate in light of the experiences. If the Muslim has initial trust in the Buddhist as a reliable interpreter of experience, then it seems that the Buddhist's belief in nonself constitutes evidence that his experiences supply good evidence for this doctrine. Furthermore, evidence that there is good evidence for p is often itself evidence for p.[3] Hence, the Buddhist's belief in response to the reported experience may serve as a piece of proxy evidence that stands in for the experience itself. Since this proxy evidence *is* available to the Muslim, it seems that the incommunicability of the Buddhist's experience does not prevent that experience from having indirect evidential weight for the Muslim. And a symmetrical story can be told as to why the Muslim's report of mystical experiences and her doxastic response can serve as proxy evidence that can be appreciated by the Buddhist. Assuming that both attach comparable weight to their experiences and have responded with equal conviction, there may be no good reason for either thinker to maintain that his or her own experience should be given more evidential weight than the inaccessible experience of the trustworthy interlocutor.

This being said, there can be situations where the limitations imposed by one's first-person perspective help to explain why one has justification to give more weight to one's own religious experience than to equally powerful experiences of others. Consider the case of some religious believer who has had a mystical experience of arresting intensity and profundity. He then attempts to convey the significance of this experience using fairly extreme language, only to discover that believers from opposing standpoints use similarly extreme language to convey the apparent significance of their own mystical experiences. Suppose the religious believer thinks that it is quite plausible that people would use similarly extreme vocabulary even if their experiences were much less profound and compelling than his own.

---

[2] J. L. Schellenberg, *The Wisdom to Doubt: A Justification of Religious Skepticism* (Ithaca: Cornell University Press, 2007), 182–183; Stefan Reining, "Peerhood in Deep Religious Disagreements," *Religious Studies* 52, no. 3 (2016): 403–419.

[3] Richard Feldman, "Reasonable Religious Disagreements," in *Philosophers without Gods: Meditations on Atheism and the Secular Life*, ed. Louise M. Antony (Oxford: Oxford University Press, 2007), 206–209.

And suppose he can easily entertain the possibility of others having less compelling experiences than his own but cannot easily entertain the possibility of others having experiences that are more compelling than his own. Given these stipulations, he might be reasonable in believing that his own experience is evidentially more significant than the experiences of his disputants (despite the fact that these experiences are similarly described). In such a situation, religious belief that is grounded in surprisingly powerful experiences might be reasonably held in the face of religious disagreement even if multiple sides cite similar "powerful" religious experiences in explaining their views (and even if the disputants' perspectives were in fact equally impressive). In light of this sort of possibility, the failure of the "full disclosure" condition that results from privileged access to one's own experiences may in some cases help to ameliorate the worries raised by disagreement.

There is a second and more important reason why rationalist weak conciliationism may not inevitably assign religious experience a marginal epistemic role: religious experiences may sometimes be rationally deep in a way that perceptual or memorial experiences are not. While perceptual experiences typically leave one's fundamental plausibility assessments untouched, there are also experiences of *insight* that bring about changes at this fundamental level. In a perceptual experience, one may discover that what is intrinsically implausible is nonetheless true; in an *insightful* experience on the other hand one's views on what is intrinsically plausible undergo a rational improvement. Some proposition that *seemed* intrinsically implausible may, after gaining further insight on the matter, come to seem intrinsically plausible.[4] In the wake of such an experience, one's previous fundamental perspective looks to be deficient in insight or gripped by some error.

Perhaps some of the experiences focused on by Alston or Plantinga could be understood *not* primarily as perceptual or quasi-perceptual experiences but as experiences of apparent insight that change how the experiencer assesses the fundamental plausibility of some religious proposition. Indeed, while in some passages Plantinga seems to spurn the idea that the conviction of faith is precipitated by an experience of insight into Christianity's plausibility, some of his remarks could be taken to suggest the opposite conclusion.

---

[4] Less dramatic shifts in one's plausibility judgments are also possible, of course. Instead of viewing as plausible what was previously viewed as implausible, one might merely view some proposition as a bit more plausible or implausible than one previously thought.

Consider this description of the way the Holy Spirit brings about "cognitive renewal" in the life of the believer:

> Regeneration heals the ravages of sin—embryonically in this life, and with ever greater fullness in the next. Just what are the *cognitive* benefits of regeneration? First, there is the repair of the *sensus divinitatis*, so that once again one can see God and be put in mind of him in the sorts of situations in which that belief-producing process is designed to work. The work of the Holy Spirit goes further. It gives one a much clearer view of the beauty, splendor, loveliness, attractiveness, glory of God. It enables one to see something of the spectacular depth of love revealed in the incarnation and atonement. Correlatively, it also gives me a much clearer view of the heinousness of sin, and of the degree and extent to which I am myself enmeshed in it. It gives me a better picture of my own place in the universe.[5]

The part of the quotation that I am most interested in is Plantinga's description of having a "clearer view of the beauty, splendor, loveliness, attractiveness, glory of God." What does it mean to have a clearer view of these aspects of God? I might gain a clearer view of someone's goodness by learning certain facts about her. For example, I might learn that my wife was up multiple times last night with the baby. Since this fact makes her current compassionate and cheerful attitude all the more impressive, learning this fact may give me an even clearer view of her loveliness. But I suspect that the "clearer view" Plantinga is referring to is not one that is primarily the product of learning new facts. The unregenerate person may be perfectly familiar with the claims that Christians make about God and yet have very little appreciation of how good it would be were these claims true. The clearer view, I take it, results from looking at the *same* religious claims and having a fuller grasp of their value and significance.

If this is right, then it is hard to hear "clearer view" as meaning anything other than a kind of insight. Merely having *greater confidence* that God is lovely and glorious does not amount to having a clearer view of God's loveliness and glory. The language of "clarity" suggests that some confusion or obscurity has been dispelled. In the wake of such epistemic improvement, one will typically come to see one's earlier plausibility assessments as suffering from some degree of confusion or from inadequate understanding.

---

[5] Plantinga, *Warranted Christian Belief* (New York: Oxford University Press, 2000), 280–281.

If *this* is what the work of the Holy Spirit does in the Christian, then the Christian cannot treat the resultant doxastic changes in an instrumentalist fashion. While the Christian may have a memory of how she thought about matters prior to the cognitive shifts engendered by the Holy Spirit, she will not *presently identify* with that earlier perspective as her *current* preevidential plausibility assessment. She now views that earlier perspective as confused or rationally limited in some way. As such, she has no reason to endorse the credences that would be reached by starting with that earlier confused or limited state and then conditionalizing on facts about her new doxastic inclinations. Such a procedure would suggest that she trusts her earlier plausibility judgments (and is willing to follow what they recommend in response to various evidential inputs), but she does not. Thus, the doxastic evolution that results from her having a "clearer view" of God's glory is not adequately modeled as a process of conditionalization. Rather, it is best modeled as a shift in ur-priors resulting from greater insight into the fundamental plausibility of the Christian outlook.

If many religious experiences are "insightful" experiences that improve one's fundamental plausibility assessments, then rationalist weak conciliationism would not marginalize religious experience as epistemically insignificant. On the contrary, insightful religious experiences could play a crucial role in making it possible for some religious believers to escape the skeptical force of religious disagreement. But is it plausible that many of the religious experiences that play a significant role in the formation and maintenance of religious conviction are insightful? The following sections present an account of religious insight that is supportive of an affirmative answer to this question.

Before I turn to develop this account, it may be helpful to note some important respects in which the focus of my discussion will differ from some other prominent philosophical discussions of religious experience, especially Alston's *Perceiving God*. Because I am interested in ways that religious experience could facilitate religiously important insight, I will not be primarily interested in experiences that are allegedly perceptual, such as experiences of hearing or seeing God or some other supernatural entity. While such experiences *could* be insightful experiences, they will not be insightful in virtue of their perceptual content. As I've emphasized, episodes of perception are not typically episodes of insight that involve a change in one's fundamental plausibility assessments. The experiences I am interested in qualify as *religious* experiences because the putative insight that is produced by the experience has significant bearing on religious outlooks. But such experiences need not be dramatic, unusual, or "supernatural" in any obvious way. Given this encompassing understanding of "religious experience," it is possible that atheists could have "religious" experiences that strengthen their atheism. For example, experiencing a state of suffering (loneliness, say) might give someone a deepened understanding of the ways in which such a state is bad. Such an insight might help to support the judgment that the creation of this world would be unworthy of a good God.

Finally, it is worth noting that the types of claims one could potentially know by rational insight differ significantly from the types of claims one could conceivably come to know by perception. For example, a person could perhaps perceive that God is present and doing such and such a thing. But this kind of contingent fact does not seem to be the sort of thing that someone could know a priori by rational insight. Nonetheless, as I will argue, one may be able to acquire a priori insight into how good or beautiful it would be for God to do such and such a thing (should God exist). Insights into evaluative claims of this sort could have significant bearing on the plausibility of various religious claims.

5.2 Affective Rationalism

I have claimed that justified religious confidence likely requires insight into the greater rational merits of one's own religious outlook. I suspect that many will naturally understand this to mean that the justified religious believer must see why the *evidential and philosophical arguments* that support her outlook are superior to those marshaled on behalf of competing views, and that she must be capable of *defending* this assessment. On this view, justified belief on religious matters is largely reserved for the victors on the playing field of "natural theology." Richard Swinburne is one prominent advocate of this sort of view. While Swinburne allows that apparent awareness of God in religious experience may give some people initial noninferential justification to believe in God, he does not think that such experiential justification has much weight for the person who is aware of significant evidence that counts against theism.[6] In the case of the typical theist who is aware of such counter-evidence, Swinburne maintains that justified theistic belief must be based

---

[6] Richard Swinburne, *Faith and Reason*, 2nd ed. (Oxford: Oxford University Press, 2005), 89–90.

on sufficiently powerful philosophical arguments that start from public evidence and proceed by means of widely shared criteria. He writes:

> In an age of religious scepticism when there are good arguments against theism known to most people, and there are so often authoritative atheists as well as authoritative theists, most theists need arguments for the existence of God which start from rightly basic beliefs held very strongly by theist and atheist alike, and proceed thence by criteria shared between theist and atheist. To produce such arguments is the aim of natural theology. It starts from the most general natural phenomena—the existence of the world, its conformity to natural laws, the laws and initial conditions of the universe being such as to produce human organisms, and so on; and attempts to argue thence to the existence of God either by deductive arguments, or by criteria of inductive reasoning used in other areas of inquiry. And the historical truths of the Christian religion need to be backed up by inductive arguments beginning, in part, from historical data recognized by theist and atheist alike. . . . Detailed historical arguments have not normally been thought as part of 'natural theology', but they clearly belong to the same genre of objective reasoning from public data.[7]

Swinburne's austere rationalism understands genuine religious insight to be a product of analytical sophistication and argumentative virtuosity. The theist and the atheist can reach agreement on all of the relevant data, and the justification of their respective positions can be determined through objective and dispassionate application of shared criteria. Swinburne's description may leave one with the impression that if suitably sophisticated theists and atheists were locked in a room and made to discuss the merits of their respective views, the two sides could be expected to come to an agreement if given sufficient time to work through the relevant arguments.

I grant that insight into the greater rational merits of one's religious outlook could partly consist in argumentative achievements of the sort described by Swinburne. Be that as it may, I want to resist the idea that religious insight must amount to something that is recognizable as a philosophical accomplishment. There are at least two reasons for this. First, one can have insight into the reasons for p without being able to identify those reasons in any clear

---

[7] Swinburne, *Faith and Reason*, 91–92.

and distinct way, much less to articulate them in a clear argument. There are, one might say, "inchoate insights."[8]

Consider the following relatively common phenomenon. Someone rehearses an argument for conclusion C. You sense that the argument has gone wrong in some way, not just because you doubt C but because there is something "fishy" about the reasoning that you have not yet "put your finger on." Then a third person who is present says that the argument trades on equivocation. He points to the term that is being used equivocally, shows that the term is ambiguous between two meanings, and explains that the two premises rely for their plausibility on subtly different meanings of the term. When the third person articulates this diagnosis, you respond (sincerely) by saying: "Yes, that's it! The way that term was being used ambiguously is exactly what was making me uneasy about the argument, though I hadn't yet put my finger on the problem." This sense that someone else has articulated reasons of which one had a dim awareness is not uncommon. And it suggests that some degree of insight into the rational grounds for some view is possible even if one's grasp of those reasons fall far short of what would be needed in order to produce a philosophical argument. At least in some cases, the construction of philosophical arguments is an attempt to articulate reasons that one already appreciates in some inchoate way. If this is right, then a religious believer could be *justified* on account of some religious insight (one that could be given argumentative expression) even though he cannot *justify* his position by expressing his insight in argumentative terms.

There is also some question about whether one should expect reasoning on religious matters to be adequately expressible in argumentative terms, even in principle. The nineteenth-century English philosopher and Christian thinker John Henry Newman writes: "all men have a reason, but not all men can give a reason. We may denote, then, these two exercises of mind as reasoning and arguing, or as conscious and unconscious reasoning, or as Implicit Reason and Explicit Reason. And to the latter belong the words, science, method, development, analysis, criticism, proof, system, principles, rules, laws, and others of a like nature."[9] While argument or "explicit reason" aims to represent in sentence form the reasoning that leads to a particular belief, Newman holds that this representation is nearly always imperfect. Just as any painted portrait inevitably cannot do justice to every aspect of the person

---

[8] Charles Taylor, "Reason, Faith, and Meaning," *Faith and Philosophy* 28, no. 1 (2011): 8.

[9] John Henry Newman, *Fifteen Sermons Preached Before the University of Oxford*, 3rd ed. (London: Longmans, Green and Co., 1872), 259.

it depicts, Newman contends that it would be "hopeless . . . to expect that the most diligent and anxious investigation can end in more than in giving some very rude description of the living mind, and its feelings, thoughts, and reasonings."[10]

Not only is argumentation frequently unable to perfectly represent the streams of reasons that lead one to a particular conclusion but also the attempt to argumentatively represent someone's reasoning will frequently result in a highly distorted representation. Newman thinks that this is an especially salient risk when Christians attempt to give account of their reasons for accepting Christian teaching. He writes:

> This difficulty of analyzing our more recondite feelings happily and convincingly, has a most important influence upon the science of the Evidences [i.e., evidential apologetics]. Defenders of Christianity naturally select as reasons for belief, not the highest, the truest, the most sacred, the most intimately persuasive, but such as best admit of being exhibited in argument; and these are commonly not the real reasons in the case of religious men. Nay, they are led for the same reason, to select such arguments as all will allow; that is, such as depend on principles which are a common measure for all minds. A science certainly is, in its very nature, public property; when, then, the grounds of Faith take the shape of a book of Evidences, nothing properly can be assumed but what men in general will grant as true; that is, nothing but what is on a level with all minds, good and bad, rude and refined. . . . I would maintain that the recondite reasons which lead each person to take or decline them, are just the most important portion of the considerations on which his conviction depends; and I say so, by way of showing that the science of controversy, or again the science of Evidences, has done very little, since it cannot analyze and exhibit these momentous reasons; nay, so far has done worse than little, in that it professes to have done much, and leads the student to mistake what are but secondary points in debate, as if they were the most essential.[11]

According to Newman, philosophical argumentation, which belongs to what he calls "explicit reason," is unable *in principle* to do justice to the reasoning and (putative) insight that is the basis for someone's religious conviction.

---

[10] Newman, *Fifteen Sermons Preached Before the University of Oxford*, 267–68.
[11] Newman, *Fifteen Sermons Preached Before the University of Oxford*, 271–72.

Thus, there is even further reason to resist characterizing insight into the rational merits of one's position as a *philosophical* accomplishment.

Newman's sense that philosophical expression cannot do justice to all of the legitimate reasons and insights that may ground religious conviction has more recently been echoed by the prominent metaphysician Peter van Inwagen. In an essay on his Christian beliefs, van Inwagen raises the question of how he could be justified in holding "that free will is incompatible with determinism or that unrealized possibilities are not physical objects or that human beings are not four-dimensional things extended in time as well as in space" when these views are rejected by David Lewis, whom van Inwagen describes as "a philosopher of truly formidable intelligence and insight and ability" who "understands perfectly" every argument van Inwagen could marshal in defense of these theses.[12] Van Inwagen tentatively suggests that his justification in believing these things, despite his inability to produce arguments that would convince Lewis, is due to an incommunicable philosophical insight lacked by Lewis. With this suggestion, van Inwagen allows that insight may outstrip philosophical articulation (even for someone as gifted in philosophical argumentation as van Inwagen is). The language of *insight* is playing an important role here. Van Inwagen clearly thinks that he has some rational advantage with respect to Lewis, even if he cannot adequately express that advantage in philosophical terms. Imagine that van Inwagen had merely stated that he must have some strong doxastic inclination to believe such and such positions, an inclination Lewis apparently does not have. Exchanging an "insight" for a "strong doxastic inclination" would, I think, result in van Inwagen's steadfast confidence rightly appearing to be objectionably arbitrary. Van Inwagen's account of his own justification presupposes that rational virtuosity and argumentative virtuosity are not equivalent.

One might think that the intellectual capacities that make one good at philosophical argumentation—which for present purposes I am thinking of as the task of representing reasoning in sentential form—are more or less identical with the intellectual capacities that make one a good reasoner on religious matters. Perhaps insight into the rational merits of one's religious views is not a philosophical accomplishment in the sense that it is an accomplishment of explicit reasoning in sentence form. Even so, one might think that the relevant sort of insight can still be thought of as a philosophical

[12] Peter van Inwagen, "Quam Dilecta," in *God and the Philosophers: The Reconciliation of Faith and Reason*, ed. Thomas V. Morris (New York: Oxford University Press, 1994), 42.

accomplishment inasmuch as such insight is a product of the same virtues, skills, and capacities that are required for quality work of explicit philosophical reasoning. One might say that rational insight on religious matters, like good philosophy, is a product of something aptly called "analytical virtue."

I think there is good reason for doubting that religious insight is typically philosophical even in this sense. This brings me to the second reason to resist categorizing religious insight as a species of philosophical accomplishment. Many of the putative insights that are most crucial to some religious or irreligious position are *moral, axiological,* or *aesthetic* insights (or insights in some similar evaluative category). Such insights are very often neither grounded in analytical reasoning nor expressible by such reasoning but are grounded in a certain *affective response* (to an event, an idea, a person, or whatever). This second reason consists of two claims: first, that many of the putative insights driving religious conviction are evaluative insights, and second, that evaluative insights are often grounded in a certain affective response rather than philosophical reasoning (so that the having of such insight cannot properly be thought of as a philosophical accomplishment). I will defend each of these claims in turn.

In the case of traditional theistic religions, it is fairly clear why the plausibility of such religions would depend significantly (though not entirely) on the plausibility of certain evaluative claims. Traditional theism maintains that this world is the creation of a supremely powerful, *perfectly good*, and *loving* God. Thus, theists are committed to maintaining that God's choosing to create a world like the existing one is consonant with moral perfection and love. Given that theism has these rich evaluative implications, an assessment of its plausibility will depend significantly on certain evaluative judgments.

This is especially apparent when one considers the challenge that theism faces in accounting for evil and suffering. According to the "argument from evil" against theism, the suffering that is observed to occur in this world is evidence against theism since it is highly improbable that an omnipotent and perfectly good being would create and sustain a world that contained suffering of such significant scope and intensity. The plausibility of theism arguably depends significantly on whether there is some viable explanation of why God might allow horrific suffering, an explanation that would help to reconcile theistic claims with the evidence of evil that one observes in human history as well as personal experience.[13] Typically, such an explanation proceeds by identifying some good or set of goods that even an omnipotent God

---

[13] Some philosophers contest the common view that the justification of theistic belief (among those who are aware of the problem of evil) depends on whether one possess a plausible explanation

is not able to pursue without making probable the occurrence of a good deal of creaturely suffering. For example, some argue that it is a great good for people to bear significant responsibility for the positive well-being of others and to exercise this responsibility by means of loving and morally courageous actions. Plausibly, for it to be the case that by means of some loving action Person 1 is genuinely responsible for the significant amount of well-being enjoyed by Person 2, it must be the case that Person 1 was free to choose some alternative *non*loving action that would have resulted in Person 2 having less well-being. Thus, it is arguable that in order for God to pursue the good that comes from creatures being responsible for the well-being of others, God must permit suffering to result when creatures fall short and act selfishly.[14] The plausibility of such explanations will depend in significant part (though not entirely) on just how valuable one takes these goods to be—these goods that allegedly cannot be pursued apart from creaturely suffering (or apart from some significant risk of such suffering). So an assessment of theism's plausibility will likely depend to a great extent on one's views about what sorts of goods are most valuable and most worthy of pursuit.

This is not to say that the plausibility of theism depends *exclusively* on one's evaluative sensibilities. Suppose someone has conclusive insight into the soundness of a cosmological argument for God's existence (or some other argument that does not depend on contested evaluative judgments). Or suppose someone has perfectly clear insight into the incoherence of some aspect of traditional theism (for example, the claim that there is a divine being that *necessarily* exists). Such a person could reasonably settle for herself the question of whether God exists without relying on evaluative judgments. But I think it is safe to say that there are very few philosophically informed theists and atheists who take themselves to have such conclusive (and evaluative-free) grounds for their view. For most informed thinkers, evaluative judgments will play a large role in shaping their assessments of theism's plausibility.

The importance of evaluative judgments in shaping one's assessment of theism goes well beyond their significance in an assessment of the challenge

---

for why God allows evil. See, for example, Michael Bergmann, "Skeptical Theism and the Problem of Evil," in *The Oxford Handbook of Philosophical Theology*, ed. Thomas P. Flint and Michael C. Rea (Oxford: Oxford University Press, 2009), 374–399.

[14] This is, of course, just the barest sketch of this approach to explaining suffering within a theistic framework. For a detailed development of this sort of argument, see Richard Swinburne, *Providence and the Problem of Evil* (Oxford: Oxford University Press, 1998).

to theism posed by evil. Consider, for example, that if the world is God's handiwork, then it is (presumably) wondrous and beautiful. Someone who finds immense beauty in the natural environment or in the scientific laws that form the structure of the existing universe is, all else being equal, much more likely to judge theism plausible than someone who is rather unimpressed by the natural world. Moving beyond bare theism to one of its particular manifestations, consider the suggestion that the best explanation for the testimony regarding appearances of Jesus after his crucifixion is that God raised Jesus from the dead to vindicate his teaching and confirm his special status. The plausibility of this explanation depends in significant part on whether Jesus's character, teachings, and works could plausibly be thought to represent the values and intentions of a perfectly good and loving being. So how plausible Christianity seems to be will depend on whether one finds Jesus's life, and the vision of God he conveyed, to be remarkably excellent and beautiful.

Traditional theism and specific theistic outlooks have numerous normative and evaluative implications. Because most people do not have decisive nonevaluative grounds for accepting or rejecting theism, it seems that rational insight into the probability of theism given one's evidence is likely to require having insight into certain evaluative questions that are pertinent to theism. Many of these questions concern whether the world as a whole, or some specific episode in the world's history that is alleged to be the result of special divine action, is *worthy* of being chosen by an almighty and perfectly good being. At the heart of one's evaluation of theism will therefore lie certain judgments of *worthiness*. These "worthiness judgments" are responsive to one's sensibilities pertaining to various dimensions of evaluation, including (but not limited to) moral and aesthetic dimensions.

Good analytical reflection and argumentation may be crucial for the development of an adequate *theory* of what various forms of "worthiness" consist in. It may be, for example, that only someone with the analytical skills resembling those of the best philosophers could articulate an adequate theory of what intrinsic qualities differentiate the most beautiful and praiseworthy works of music from those that are repugnant or jejune. But typically, one's judgments of worthiness are not themselves the result of anything recognizable as analytical reflection or argumentation. Someone who fails to perceive any beauty in the Yosemite Valley does not thereby reveal faulty reasoning or some analytical deficiency. Likewise, someone who spent time with Nelson Mandela and who judged his compassion for his oppressors to

be pathetic rather than commendable would not thereby reveal a lack of analytical sophistication. In this case, such a person would exhibit what may be
called a "defect of the heart" rather than a defect of the head.

If one does not typically achieve insight into the worthiness of something
by means of the analytical virtues that characterize good philosophers, how
does one come by such insight? Here, I agree with those thinkers who emphasize the essential role played by the *affections* in disclosing value. Someone
who was consistently unmoved when listening to some great piece of music
cannot be said to appreciate the beauty of that work. Such a person may *believe* that it is beautiful. For example, someone who has no sense for music
may believe on the basis of others' testimony that it is an excellent piece of
music. But this falls short of *appreciating* the beauty of the work and having
insight into its excellence. Absent the appropriate emotions or affections, the
beauty has not been disclosed to the listener. Arguably, to have insight into
the excellence of a piece of music *just is* to have the right sort of affective response when listening to the work. As Mark Johnston argues, "absence of
the appropriate affect makes us aspect-blind," by which he means blind to
the "ways in which a situation, animal or person is *appealing* or *repellent*."[15]
In speaking of the appealing and repellent, Johnston does not mean to limit
his claim to aesthetic evaluations (though he does think that aesthetic and
ethical judgments are more closely connected than many allow). So, for example, my understanding the badness of some episode of horrific suffering
requires that when I consider the state of affairs involving this suffering,
I have a particular sort of affective response.

Granted, I may confidently and justifiably *believe* that the horrific suffering
is bad without *presently* feeling some sort of negative emotion when I reflect
on the relevant state of affairs. Such a belief without affect might be based
on my memory of past affective responses to relevantly similar situations.
But this belief would lack something epistemically in comparison to a belief
that arises from a present, affectively mediated appreciation of the badness
of the suffering. It may seem appropriate to say that in the case where the belief arises from a present affective response, it arises directly from affectively
mediated *insight* into that suffering's badness. The belief held in the absence
of any present emotional response would at best be indirectly based on such
insight had in the past.

---

[15] Mark Johnston, "The Authority of Affect," *Philosophy and Phenomenological Research* 63, no. 1
(2001): 181.

As an analogy, consider my (very confident) belief that the material conditional $p \rightarrow q$ is logically equivalent to the contrapositive of that conditional, $\sim q \rightarrow \sim p$. However confident I may be about this fact at some time, I may not at that time have *insight* into this truth. My belief may be based on memory, both of having been taught this equivalence and of having "seen" it for myself, after reflecting a bit on what both of these conditionals mean. Now, I can easily enough reacquire the insight into this truth by carefully thinking through the matter. Upon doing so, I've gained insight that can play an important role in overcoming worries raised by disagreement. Similarly, when I believe without any affective response that some episode of reported suffering is an extremely bad state of affairs, I may renew my appreciation of the badness of the suffering by attending to the salient features of the suffering in a focused way that leaves me open to an emotional response. Experiencing the appropriate emotional response would renew my insight into the badness of the suffering.

Suppose it is right that judgments of worthiness (or unworthiness) play a crucial role in shaping one's assessment of the plausibility of theism and that insight into the worthiness of something consists in having the right sort of affective response to that thing. In this case, it seems that having insight into the plausibility or implausibility of theism is likely to depend on one's having appropriate affective responses to various aspects of the world. These aspects may include general features of the world as well as certain episodes of the world's history that are alleged to be the product of special divine action, such as a putative answer to prayer, or the life of Jesus, or the production of the Quran. Since the appropriate affective responses are not the result of analytical virtue, genuine insight concerning the plausibility of theism will not *primarily* be a *philosophical* accomplishment. So, by emphasizing the crucial importance of religious insight to resisting worries raised by disagreement, I do not thereby imply that religious justification (in the face of disagreement) is the special preserve of the philosophically sophisticated.

I grant that all else being equal, good philosophical reasoning should improve one's level of insight concerning the plausibility (or implausibility) of theism. For example, suppose God exists and allows evil partly for the reason that significant creaturely responsibility cannot be pursued without risking suffering. This being the case, it would seem that philosophical reflection that sheds light on the implications of creaturely responsibility should yield greater insight into the plausibility of theism. Nonetheless, seeing that creaturely responsibility necessitates the risk of suffering would not significantly improve one's estimate of theism's plausibility if one greatly undervalued or overvalued genuine creaturely responsibility. The judgment of worthiness plays a crucial and ineliminable role.[16] So even if good philosophical reasoning on balance deepens and improves one's insight into religious questions, it may still be that religious insight is at least as much a product of the properly attuned and responsive affections as it is of careful analytical reasoning.

What I am arguing for here is an *affective rationalism* according to which proper affective responses can play a crucial and ineliminable role in facilitating rational insight into the plausibility or implausibility of some position. It is important to my position that the appropriate affective response may give rise to (or facilitate) not merely justified belief in some proposition but also *insight* into its truth or plausibility. For suppose the appropriate affective response is merely a brute inclination that, while prompting a correct evaluation of some state of affairs S, does *not* result in an outlook that is rationally superior to one that incorrectly evaluates S (on the basis of an inappropriate affective response). In this case, the affective response would not supply a rational symmetry breaker that could justify self-trust in the face of disagreement with an apparent epistemic peer.

Recall once again the dress case. Suppose I know that those with the opposing view on the dress's color are responding to a visual impression that is just as compelling and "normal seeming" as my own, so that there is no internally discernible agent-neutral reason for preferring my own view to theirs. This being so, it would be rationally arbitrary for me to trust my own visual interpretation over the interpretation of those who disagree with me. According to the rationalist account of partisan justification defended in the previous chapter, external facts about the reliability of my belief-forming process are not sufficient to justify self-trust in the face of disagreement with those who (on the basis of p-neutral considerations) appear to be my epistemic peers. I am also not justified in showing agent partiality and trusting my outlook merely because it is mine. Instead, reasonable self-trust demands that I appreciate some rational merit in my position (or rational weakness

---

[16] Moreover, even someone who failed to note how serious responsibility requires the risk of suffering might still be capable of having significant insight into the plausibility of theism if he had a deep appreciation for the choiceworthiness (for God) of certain features of the world. As long as he did not have conclusive reason for thinking that there could *not* be some reason for allowing the sorts of evils he observes, a clear appreciation of the depth of value exhibited in the world might help to justify someone in thinking that the world is probably the product of loving and good intention, however mystifying the existence of evil may be.

in my disputant's position) that gives me good reason for thinking that my position is rationally preferable to the opposing view. This is why it is crucial to affective rationalism that the appropriate affective response may result in an outlook that is *rationally* stronger than one that is occasioned by an inappropriate affective response. Proper emotional engagement with the object of evaluation must be *insightful*, in contrast to the visual impressions in the dress case. Thus, the affective rationalism I wish to defend is a significantly more ambitious thesis than the more limited claim (defended by many) that emotions disclose value. Affective rationalism implies that one's affectively mediated evaluative judgments are rationally deep in a way sense perception normally is not.

5.3 Can Worthiness Judgments Be Insightful?

I've argued that religious convictions often significantly depend on affectively mediated judgments of *worthiness* (or unworthiness). Whether one may justifiably remain confident in a contested worthiness judgment depends in significant measure on whether the affective experiences that give rise to the judgment are genuinely insightful and not merely episodes of brute doxastic inclination. Affective rationalism is the view that such affective experiences can be legitimately insightful. A number of philosophers endorse this claim.[17] Here, for example, is Charles Taylor on the role of emotion in moral judgment and moral motivation:

> Now the view I've been presenting here has some affinities to Hume's. Because like him, I believe that our perception of, say, moral virtues, or morally admirable ends, cannot be dispassionate, that our intuitions here are felt intuitions. But the difference here is crucial. The inclinations that Hume and other "sentimentalists" ascribe to us are brute reactions. They are triggered by certain features of character or action, but not in any sense motivated by insight into the *value* of these features. This in spite of the fact that our emotional reactions are described by Hume as "approbation" or "disapproval," which would seem to carry some implication that the

---

[17] See, for example Mark Wynn, *Emotional Experience and Religious Understanding: Integrating Perception, Conception and Feeling* (Cambridge: Cambridge University Press, 2005); Bas C. van Fraassen, *The Empirical Stance*, rev. ed. (New Haven: Yale University Press, 2004), lectures 3–4.

features are worthy or unworthy of this approval. Whereas what I am saying is that an essential part of our motivation when we act is such an insight into the goodness or badness of the action.[18]

A bit later, Taylor says a bit more that helps illuminate the contrast that he is drawing between sentiments that are "brute reactions" and those that are insightful: "we recognize benevolence as a virtue. Hume's account of this is that we respond to this trait of character, and to the acts it generates with a positive stance of approbation. So much, so agreed. But is this response just a surd, a de facto feature of our emotional makeup, or is it something more, viz., an insight into a (putative) moral good? What's the difference? Well, a favorable reaction is just a reaction, whereas an insight can admit of, maybe even calls for, expansion, development, clarification."[19] These passages suggest that on Taylor's view, the affective experiences of adept moral reasoners are not merely reliable indicators of moral properties in the same way that seeming to smell a skunk is a reliable indicator that a skunk has recently been in the vicinity. Rather, in having the relevant emotional responses one thereby achieves at least some degree of moral insight and understanding that may then be elaborated and clarified through further reflection.

Taylor is, of course, not alone in thinking that worthiness judgments may be insightful and rationally deep in a way that is not characteristic of perceptual beliefs. But is this a well-motivated position? Is there good reason to affirm that affective rationalism is correct?

Before addressing this question, it may be helpful to engage in a bit of expectations management. As I acknowledged in the previous chapter, the nature of rational insight is mysterious, and philosophers do not have an especially illuminating account of how it is that one can come to have immediate awareness of the truth or plausibility of various claims. Philosophers therefore cannot point to an account of how rational insight works in order to conclusively determine whether affectively mediated worthiness judgments are the kind of judgment that can be grounded in rational insight. This being said, one can perhaps adduce some less conclusive considerations in support of affective rationalism.

The first thing to be said in favor of affective rationalism is that the affective experiences giving rise to worthiness judgments are often experienced

---

[18] Charles Taylor, *The Language Animal: The Full Shape of the Human Linguistic Capacity* (Cambridge, MA: Harvard University Press, 2016), 204.

[19] Taylor, *The Language Animal*, 206.

not merely as episodes of belief formation but also as episodes of deepened moral clarity and understanding. Perhaps I can illustrate this with a personal example. Not infrequently, I slip into the habit of interacting with my children in a stern manner. A child leaves a large mess in the living room, despite a recent conversation about cleaning up after an activity; or a child is caught lying (again) about whether or not he has brushed his teeth; or, engaged in conversation that escalates in silliness and volume, the kids completely ignore my wife and me as we attempt to get their attention. When I am in "stern" mode, I am likely to respond to incidents like these with loud, angry lectures, imposition of consequences that quickly escalate in their severity, and a stern attitude that communicates judgment and disappointment; sternness predominates over mercy, affection, and lightheartedness. This stern mode is in part instinctive, especially when I am stressed, but it is also motivated by a certain logic: the kids are being selfish, irresponsible, and so on, and judgment and consequences are entirely appropriate. They need to learn!

Frequently, what disrupts this stern mode and helps me to break out of it (at least for some period of time) is a certain sort of affective experience that renews my commitment to certain values and that reorients how I think about my role as a father and my relationship with my children. More than once, this sort of experience has occurred in the context of musical worship during a church service. Words praising divine mercy and grace that are powerfully set to music elicit in me an appreciation of how beautiful it is when, as one song puts it, "mercy triumphs over judgment." My thoughts turn toward the judgmental tone toward my kids that is so common when I am in stern mode, and the rationale for this sternness now seems insufficient: what is more apparent, something I may always affirm but do not always *feel*, is the value and beauty of a relationship with my kids that prioritizes delight, affection, and warmth over discipline and moral correction.

In light of this renewed appreciation for unconditional love and affection, the reasoning that implicitly motivated my sternness seems not merely mistaken but *confused*. It is not just that I now have contrary doxastic inclinations and now feel drawn to an alternative position. In addition, my former position appears to result from a distorted assessment that gave insufficient weight to a kind of love whose great intrinsic value ought to have been evident. From the new vantage point, I can still endorse the value of moral correction that figured so prominently in the implicit rationale for my sternness, but the relative importance of moral correction is diminished when the value of unconditional love is more fully appreciated. Importantly, the new vantage point possesses a kind of coherence that my stern vantage point lacks. Here is the best way I know how to describe this: sustaining stern mode seems to require a sort of restricted moral vision that focuses on a narrow band of values and keeps the other values in the fuzzy periphery. I know those values are there, but the present sternness would be threatened by bringing them into focus. The attitude that follows my "reconversion," however, does not seem to possess this sort of instability. The prioritization of affection and delight is not threatened by due acknowledgment of values like respect of authority that figured so prominently in the rationale for stern mode.

Moving from the mundane to the momentous, accounts of religious conversions not uncommonly reference some emotionally powerful experience that is described in terms that suggest that the experience played some essential role in facilitating a kind of religious insight. Consider, for example, an account of a transformative religious experience from David Brainerd, a well-known (though short-lived) Christian missionary to the Delaware Indians in New Jersey during the 1740s. Below is one part of Brainerd's account, from a longer selection William James includes in *The Varieties of Religious Experience*. In part of Brainerd's testimony not reproduced below, he recounts how he came to a dispiriting realization about his attempts at religious piety. Brainerd recognized these as self-centered attempts to "procure deliverance and salvation" for himself and recognized that such self-centered "piety" would do nothing to compel God to bestow the salvation Brainerd desired to attain. Then he recounts the following episode whereby his spiritual outlook was transformed:

> Here, in a mournful melancholy state I was attempting to pray; but found no heart to engage in that or any other duty. . . . Then, as I was walking in a thick grove, unspeakable glory seemed to open to the apprehension of my soul. I do not mean any external brightness, nor any imagination of a body of light, but it was a new inward apprehension or view that I had of God, such as I never had before, nor anything which had the least resemblance to it. . . . My soul was so captivated and delighted with the excellency of God that I was even swallowed up in him; at least to that degree that I had no thought about my own salvation, and scarce reflected that there was such a creature as myself. I continued in this state of inward joy, peace, and astonishing, till near dark without any sensible abatement; and then began to think and examine what I had seen; and felt sweetly composed in my mind

all the evening following. I felt myself in a new world, and everything about me appeared with a different aspect from what it was wont to do. At this time, the way of salvation opened to me with such infinite wisdom, suitableness, and excellency, that I wondered I should ever think of any other way of salvation; was amazed that I had not dropped my own contrivances, and complied with this lovely, blessed, and excellent way before. If I could have been saved by my own duties or any other way that I had formerly contrived, my whole soul would now have refused it. I wondered that all the world did not see and comply with this way of salvation, entirely by the righteousness of Christ.[20]

According to Brainerd's understanding of his transformative experience, he was led to a true appreciation of the worthiness of the Christian teaching that salvation is not something that one earns through works of religious piety, but is rather an unmerited gift made possible by the perfectly righteous life of Christ (who shares his righteousness with those who are united with him). Of course, those who do not think that doctrine worthy would want to describe Brainerd's experience differently.

What is most important about this passage for present purposes is the last few lines wherein Brainerd expresses a kind of amazement that he hadn't appreciated the worthiness of this way of salvation before, and indeed amazement that anyone in the world could fail to see the "excellency" of this way. Such amazement would make sense only if it seemed to him that his new perspective more coherently and persuasively accounted for the evidence and considerations that were *already available to him (and indeed, to everyone else)* before the transformative experience. If Brainerd's religious transformation was principally the result of his learning new facts that were conveyed to him in some quasi-perceptual "mystical experience," then there would be no reason to be surprised that his new perspective is not shared by others and his former self: since they lack the critical information conveyed through Brainerd's experience, their erroneous views would need no explanation. The sense of surprise therefore suggests that his delight in the "excellency" of God's ways has the feel of insight; in comparison with this delight, his earlier judgments appear to be *confused* and not merely mistaken.

Of course, the fact that emotional experiences like the ones discussed above are described as insightful does not mean that they *are* insightful. One

---

[20] Quoted in James, *The Varieties of Religious Experience*, 236–237.

can have the *conviction* that greater clarity has been achieved even if one's confusion has only deepened. Nonetheless, the frequent conviction that some worthiness judgment is the product of affectively mediated insight is some evidence that this is in fact correct (and thus that affective rationalism is true).

5.4 Religious Emotions and Religious Concept Possession

One way affective experiences might enable religious insight is by enabling the experiencer to grasp certain concepts that are not available to someone who has not experienced certain "religious" emotions. This idea that religious experience is the occasion for an enriched conceptual repertoire was famously defended by Rudolf Otto in his 1917 book *The Idea of the Holy*. But before discussing Otto, I suggest warming up to his proposal by first turning to a recent discussion by Derek Parfit that pertains to one's possession of the concept of an objective practical reason.

In his magisterial work *On What Matters*, Parfit spends some time considering epistemic worries raised by disagreement about normativity. As an example of an especially worrying sort of dispute, Parfit points to a deep disagreement between himself and Bernard Williams, who Parfit says was "the most brilliant British moral philosopher" he knew.[21] The disagreement concerns the question of whether practical reasons (i.e., reasons that pertain to choices between different actions) should be understood as being subjective or objective. According to "subjectivists," "all practical reasons derive their force from certain facts about our present desires or aims," while "objectivists" hold that "there are no such reasons, since all reasons derive their force from the facts that give us value-based reasons to have particular desires or aims."[22]

Parfit is an objectivist. He thinks that a good reason for one's doing some action is a good reason irrespective of whether one cares about that reason or would be motivated by it. Reasons are objective and external in that their status as reasons has nothing to do with the motivations and aims that are internal to an agent. Williams on the other hand is a subjectivist. For Williams,

---

[21] Derek Parfit, *On What Matters*, vol. 2 (Oxford: Oxford University Press, 2011), 430.

[22] Parfit, *On What Matters*, 2:429.

to say that something is a reason for acting is to make a claim about the motivations internal to any agent who has the reason. What one means when one says that someone has a reason to do some act is "roughly that, after informed and procedurally rational deliberation, this person would be motivated to act in this way."[23] As an example of how these views diverge, Parfit considers this scenario: "unless you take some medicine, you will later die much younger, losing many years of happy life. Though you know this fact, and you have deliberated in a procedurally rational way on this and all of the other relevant facts, you are not motivated to take this medicine." Williams says that in this scenario you have no reason to take the medicine, since you are unmotivated by the attainment of years of happy living. Parfit says that you do have a reason to take the medicine, since a long happy life is intrinsically good and *ought* to be a motivating factor for you.[24]

Parfit holds that he would be unreasonable in maintaining confidence in objectivism about reasons unless he can point to some asymmetry between himself and Williams that would explain why Williams is the party more likely to have made a mistake. Given Parfit's extremely high estimation of Williams as a philosopher, Parfit cannot identify such an asymmetry among the dispute-neutral factors like intelligence or philosophical aptitude. Nonetheless, Parfit thinks that he can point to an asymmetry that justifies him in remaining confident. Parfit identifies this asymmetry as the fact that Williams, unlike himself, does not understand the concept of a reason.[25]

This suggestion may at first sound incredible and insulting: when Williams advances arguments about the nature of reasons, surely he has grasped the bare concept of a reason! But Parfit observes that Williams himself often claims that he can make no sense of the external or objective "sense" of a reason. And if Parfit is right that the primary sense of "reason" (that which is relevant to practical deliberation) is objective, then it would seem to follow that Williams simply has not understood reasons of the sort that Parfit takes to be the proper subject of moral philosophy. Williams may succeed in using the word "reason" competently (except perhaps when he betrays his subjectivism?), he may grasp a subjective sort of "reason" that is in certain respects analogous to the objective reasons that Parfit is concerned with, and he may have some interesting arguments about whether there could be objective

[23] Parfit, *On What Matters*, 2:435.
[24] Parfit, *On What Matters*, 2:432.
[25] Parfit, *On What Matters*, 2:434.

reasons. Nonetheless, he fails to grasp what Parfit and his allies are talking about. This is not insulting since, if Williams is right, the notion of an objective reason is unintelligible and *there is nothing there to grasp*.

Consider this analogy. If I said that some body parts are *objectively ticklish* (so that their status as ticklish does not depend on whether anyone actually feels ticklish sensations at that part), you would probably disagree and deny that there are objectively ticklish parts. You might give arguments for this conclusion. Moreover, you would probably also feel that you cannot even *make sense* of the notion of "objective ticklishness." If I asserted that you don't even understand the property that you are arguing is not instantiated, you would likely concur, since the property is unintelligible. You not only disagree with me, you fail to comprehend me.

As the "objective ticklishness" example helps to bring out, the fact that Williams fails to grasp a concept of an objective reason does not by itself give a reason to suppose that Williams is more likely to be in error than Parfit. The failure to grasp a concept of an objective reason counts against Williams only if there is an intelligible concept there to be grasped. So if Parfit can point to an asymmetry that grounds his confidence in the face of disagreement, the asymmetry must be that there is an intelligible concept of an objective reason that Williams fails to grasp. This is, of course, what Parfit thinks. And presumably, this judgment of Parfit's is partially grounded in his own (putative) grasp of the concept of an objective reason and the resultant appreciation of the intelligibility of such a reason. The (putative) fact that Parfit grasps an intelligible concept of an objective reason is obviously not a nonpartisan consideration. But if Parfit really does grasp such a concept, this is the sort of fact that could account for partisan justification on the rationalist view I endorse.

Inspired by Parfit, I want to explore the possibility that religious disagreement among highly informed and capable thinkers may at least partially be explained by the failure of some to grasp one or more religiously important concepts and that certain affective experiences may be crucial to the acquisition of the concept or concepts in question. Following Otto, I will focus on the concept of the *holy*, though I do not want to maintain that this is the only plausible example of a concept that could play the relevant explanatory role, or even that this concept of the holy is the best example.

Otto suggests that "holy" is a category of value that includes moral content (someone who is genuinely holy is morally upright) but that is not reducible to such moral content. When a religious believer affirms that God is holy, this does not merely affirm certain moral attributes of God (unless she is using "holy" in some attenuated sense). Holiness is not reducible to moral attributes or any other bundle of attributes that one has conceptual access to apart from the experience of the holy itself. Otto invents the term "numinous" to designate that aspect of holiness that goes beyond the moral content of holiness, the "unnamed Something" that according to Otto is the "innermost core" of every religion.[26] He may be overreaching in claiming that *every* religion grows out of the experience of the numinous. But perhaps *some* religious expressions are occasioned by an experience of something as possessing a kind of value that often gets named "holy" and that is "*sui generis* and irreducible to any other" evaluative category.[27]

On Otto's view, when one strips away the moral implications of holiness (which do not exhaust the concept or make up its core), one is left with a "category of interpretation and valuation" that can only be grasped by means of a distinctive sort of religious experience. Just as the category of the beautiful cannot be grasped by someone who has not experienced something as beautiful, grasping the category of the holy requires that one "reach the point at which 'the numinous' in him perforce begins to stir, to start into life and into consciousness."[28] Otto frequently refers to the numinous as "non-rational." However, in using this label he does *not* mean to suggest that one's experience of the numinous is nothing more than a feeling (like an itching sensation) that has no bearing on what may plausibly be said about the fundamental character of the world and one's place in it. The claim that the numinous is nonrational primarily means that the numinous cannot be analyzed in terms of "familiar and definable conceptions."[29] One could say that the category of the numinous is "primitive" in that it cannot be defined in terms of more basic and independently understood ideas.

Otto insists that an appreciation of the category of the numinous does (and should) have rational implications for one's theorizing about reality, though those implications are not immediately apparent. According to Otto, much of religious thought is an attempt to work out the implications of numinous experience, and some theological perspectives can be seen to do more justice to the numinous than others. In one suggestive passage, Otto discusses Jesus Christ's "discovery and revelation" that the God who Jesus's

---

[26] Rudolf Otto, *The Idea of the Holy*, trans. John W. Harvey, 2nd ed. (London: Oxford University Press, 1950), 6.

[27] Otto, *The Idea of the Holy*, 7.

[28] Otto, *The Idea of the Holy*, 7.

[29] Otto, *The Idea of the Holy*, 58.

Jewish contemporaries rightly regarded as *holy* was also a "heavenly Father." Otto writes:

> But though it is necessarily this new message that the parables and discourse and pronouncements of Jesus complete and fill out, it is in such a way that it always remains an overwhelming and daring paradox, claiming our utmost homage, that He who is 'in heaven' is yet 'our Father'. That that 'heavenly' Being of marvel and mystery and awe is Himself the eternal, benignant, gracious will: this is the resolved contrast that first brings out the deep-felt harmony in true Christian experience; and the harmony cannot be heard aright by the man whose ear does not detect always sounding in it this sublimated 'seventh'.[30]

Otto's claim that there is a surprising "harmony" in the teaching that the holy is also a loving "Father" suggests that numinous experience involves grasping a category that is not devoid of rational content and that has ethical significance. This explains why the claim that the holy is loving has a ring of truth that is not possessed (at least to the same extent) by alternative positions (e.g., that the holy is unfeeling or that the holy is self-concerned).

Because numinous experience involves the grasping (or at least partial grasping) of a concept, numinous experience invites theoretical reflection on what may reasonably and plausibly be said of that which is grasped in such experience. As Otto puts it, the "numinous consciousness" is the basis of a "process of rationalization and moralization" in which

> we find the numinous attracting and appropriating meanings derived from social and individual ideals of obligation, justice, and goodness. These become the 'will' of the numen, and the numen their guardian, ordainer, and author. More and more these ideas come to enter into the very essence of the numen and charge the term with ethical content. 'Holy' becomes 'good', and 'good' from that very fact in turn becomes 'holy', 'sacrosanct'; until there results a thenceforth indissoluble synthesis of the two elements, and the final outcome is thus the fuller, more complex sense of 'holy', in which it is at once *good and sacrosanct*.[31]

---

[30] Otto, *The Idea of the Holy*, 84.
[31] Otto, *The Idea of the Holy*, 110.

Following this description, Otto emphasizes that this "moralization" process is not a "suppression of the numinous or its supersession by something else" but a process that "assumes the numinous and is only completed upon this as basis."[32] In other words, the more clearly one grasps the numinous, the more clear it is that it is appropriate to attribute moral significance to "the holy one" (even though moral concepts themselves are insufficient to convey what holiness is). As Otto writes, "the process by which 'the divine' is charged and filled out with ethical meaning . . . is, in fact, *felt* as something axiomatic, something whose inner necessity we feel to be self-evident."[33] He describes this development as a process of acquiring a priori knowledge, which he characterizes this way: "now this is the criterion of all a priori knowledge, namely, that, so soon as an assertion has been clearly expressed and understood, knowledge of its truth comes into the mind with the certitude of first-hand insight."

I myself resist the idea that a priori knowledge must involve certitude. For present purposes, however, the key point is that even if Otto thinks that the "numinous" is "nonrational" in that it cannot be conceptualized by means of antecedently available ideas, it still has the sort of conceptual content that allows one to have rational insight into the character of holiness. Echoing what Taylor says of moral judgment when defending its insightful character, one can say that for Otto the concept of the holy "can admit of, maybe even calls for, expansion, development, clarification."[34]

I want to reiterate that my intention in discussing Otto is not to endorse his discussion of holiness or to appeal to all the specifics of the account. Rather, my aim is to a highlight the possibility, represented by Otto's perspective, that certain religious experiences could be crucial to the acquisition of distinctive religious concepts, and that grasping such a concept could be essential to appreciating the plausibility of a particular religious outlook. Indeed, grasping the concept could be required even to adequately understand what the outlook *is*. For example, the claim that God is holy is centrally important to many monotheistic faiths. The claim is thought to have implications for the significance of human sin, the character of the divine/human relationship, the role played by this relationship in human flourishing, and other matters. Someone who fails to grasp what holiness is clearly could not fully

---

[32] Otto, *The Idea of the Holy*, 111.
[33] Otto, *The Idea of the Holy*, 136.
[34] Taylor, *The Language Animal*, 206.

grasp the content of such a religious outlook. (Of course, if there is no intelligible concept of holiness, then failing to grasp claims that invoke the concept of holiness would not be a fault; rather, religious believers who think they understand the concept would be mistaken.)

Grasping a certain concept may be a necessary precondition for having certain religious insights, and having certain sorts of religious experiences may be required to grasp the concept in question. This possibility could help to explain how religious experiences could contribute to partisan justification *even if one accepts a purely rationalist account of partisan justification*. Someone who has had the right sort of experience may be capable of having insight into the plausibility of a particular religious perspective that is not possible for those who have not had the relevant sort of experience. And having this insight could justify a degree of confidence in a religious outlook that exceeds the confidence that could be justified on the basis of the dispute-neutral fact about someone's *claim* to have insight into some religious matter.

The suggestion that some "nonbelievers" may simply fail to understand a critical religious concept should not, I think, automatically be heard by nonbelievers as insulting, even when the nonbelievers in question are "experts" on religious matters. A failure to grasp such a concept would not be a failure of analytical sophistication or of reasoning or of education if (as in the example of Otto) the relevant concept is acquired only by means of a certain sort of affective experience. Moreover, many nonbelievers would probably be happy to affirm that they fail to grasp the relevant concept since they think there is no perspicuous concept to be grasped. Bernard Williams would presumably not be insulted by Parfit's claim that he (Williams) fails to understand the idea of an objective reason, since Williams himself claims that the idea is unintelligible.

Similarly, I suspect that for many irreligious people, the most reasonable position is to deny that that there is any intelligible sui generis evaluative category designated by the word "holy." Someone who takes this position could still have a good grasp of how the word "holy" gets used (just as Williams understands how Parfit uses the word "reason"). And she could acknowledge familiarity with feelings like awe and bliss that are said to resemble the feelings involved in the "numinous experiences" that awaken the idea of the holy. What such a person denies would merely be that in religious experience a new and important evaluative category is discovered—"holiness"— that could significantly enrich one's understanding of the world's value and meaning.

5.5 Affectively Mediated Insight or Emotional Bias?

Even if there can be affectively mediated insight, as I have been arguing, this does not change the fact that people's reasoning is very often distorted by emotion. Plausibly, emotional bias is at work in most cases where someone is emotionally invested in some belief that is out of step with the view held by most thoughtful and informed people. If this is the case, isn't it most reasonable to abandon belief in such cases, even in those exceptional circumstances where one's minority view is the result of affectively mediated insight?

One referee for this book pushes this conciliatory intuition with the following example. Alma learns that her musical hero, James, has been accused of a crime. In assessing the likelihood of James's guilt, she takes into account the normal sorts of evidence (e.g., the considerations of motive and opportunity), and her opinion is shaped by the same explicit or implicit standards of evidential evaluation she applies in other contexts. Elaborating further, the reader writes:

> Now suppose that Alma's love for her hero affects her thinking as follows: given the same information about someone she did not have feelings for, she'd be much more confident in the person's guilt. Did her emotions affect her fundamental plausibility judgments or ur-priors? Or did her emotions cause her to make a performance error in applying her ur-prior? (I'm not quite sure what, even from a god's-eye perspective, would decide this.) Did her affective response to James enable some rational insight into the situation, or just mess up her thinking? What should Alma think about the source of the disagreement? Is her disagreement with others a deep one, so that weak conciliationism will allow her to remain at least somewhat steadfast? My inclination, for what it's worth, is that she should lose considerable confidence when she finds out that those who don't care about James's music see him as much more likely to be guilty. . . . Of course, it's possible that Alma's feelings enabled rational insight. But given what I know about human psychology, it's more likely that they produced faux insight.

Before responding to the central worry, it is worth emphasizing that even if Alma's idiosyncratic view stems from divergent ur-priors, this does not mean that, by the lights of my theory, she is justified in remaining at least somewhat steadfast in her view. Generic weak conciliationism does deny that there is any demanding impartiality requirement that applies to all (or nearly all) one's ur-priors. But the weak conciliationist can allow that one is sometimes, and perhaps often, required to exhibit impartiality in one's ur-priors. The exclusively rationalist theory of partisan justification defended in chapter 4 implies that partisan ur-priors can justify steadfastness in the face of disagreement only when they are supported by genuine rational insight. So the key question for Alma is not whether her opinion stems from divergent ur-priors (rather than reflecting some performance error in how her ur-priors are applied). The key question is whether her divergent opinion reflects greater rational insight into the plausibility of James's guilt.[35]

On the question of whether Alma has such insight, I agree with the assessment that her minority opinion is much more likely to be the product of distorting emotional bias than of genuine insight. There are good empirical reasons to suspect rational bias, and I also struggle to see a plausible account of why Alma's appreciation of James's music would help to give her more insight into the question of James's guilt. For these reasons, it is unlikely that Alma has the partisan justification that would make it reasonable for her to maintain confidence.

Nonetheless, given my position on disagreement, I cannot say unequivocally that Alma should lose "considerable" confidence when she learns about what others think on the matter. To be sure, conditionalizing on the disagreement evidence should cause her to lose *some* confidence (assuming that she is not rationally certain in the correctness of her assessment). Still, the rationalist weak conciliationist must concede that Alma could reasonably remain quite confident if she presently has genuine insight into the greater plausibility of her position or into the cogency of her reasoning on the matter. For this to be the case, it is not enough that Alma has arrived at her view using appropriate prior probabilities and impeccable reasoning. Even if her priors are epistemically superior to those used by her disputants, this will not help if those priors are brute inclinations. And the cogency of the reasoning that led Alma to her view may be of little help if she cannot presently survey the important steps of that reasoning (or at least the steps in her reasoning where

---

[35] On the idealizing assumption that the disputants reach their credences by correctly conditionalizing on the empirical evidence, then any insight of Alma's that distinguishes her from her disputants would have to be reflected in her ur-priors. If one drops this idealizing assumption, then Alma could also have an insight advantage that was reflected in her updating procedure (though presumably this insight would also be reflected in Alma's ur-priors for various claims about how updating of credences should proceed in various sorts of circumstances).

she and her disputants diverge) in order to discern its cogency. But if Alma presently enjoys genuine insight that supports her perspective, then she will not be required to adopt the credence that could be supported on impartial grounds. And if her insight is sufficiently clear and compelling, then perhaps very little reduction in confidence would be required.

How damaging is this concession? As I argued in chapter 4 (section 4.4.2) one is not well positioned to appreciate the plausibility of rationalist weak conciliationism when focused on examples that describe many of the relevant impartial considerations but do not describe the reasoning and insights that might help to justify continued confidence. Such examples obscure the kinds of first-order reasons that, according to the rationalist, can make it rational to maintain self-trust in the face of disagreement.

Return to the example of Sierra and Arjun from chapter 4 (section 4.4.2). In this example, Sierra correctly and cogently reasons to the right verdict in the Monty Hall problem, though she cannot say exactly how Arjun's reasoning goes wrong. When one focuses on Sierra's reasoning and genuinely appreciates its cogency, it is difficult to maintain that Sierra should give equal weight to Arjun's view. Now I'll modify the example to add that Sierra was emotionally invested in arriving at a certain answer, even before she saw any good reasons for that view. Perhaps her late uncle, whom she deeply admired, used to always say, "Remember, Sierra, if Monty Hall ever gives you the option, switch doors!" Sierra never understood what this meant until she and Arjun encountered the Monty Hall question on their math assignment. Upon reading the problem, she desperately wanted her uncle to be right, and went searching for reasons that would vindicate her uncle. Prescinding from details about the reasoning for her answer, these facts about her emotional state certainly raise worries about her reliability. Taking only impartial considerations into account, one has more reason to trust the dispassionate Arjun. But when one rehearses Sierra's reasoning, grasps its cogency, and understands that she grasps it as well, it is difficult to deny that she is justified in maintaining significant confidence, however emotionally invested she might be in the rightness of her response.

Granted, this insight of Sierra's is not an affectively mediated insight. Emotion may have motivated Sierra in her search for reasons that would support her uncle's position, but the reasoning that is the basis for her position can be appreciated without any particular affective orientation. And one might hold that there is a special problem with affectively mediated insights, since the influence of emotion can so easily be distorting. Perhaps insights that depend on the emotions cannot confer partisan justification, or at least not to any significant extent.

To properly evaluate this suspicion, one would do well to consider examples where one has sympathy for whatever affectively mediated insight the subject in the example is alleged to have. Perhaps the following example will qualify. Arthur is a high-ranking officer in the military. The leadership of this military sanctions torturing of prisoners of war in situations where the expected benefit of the torture is deemed to be sufficient. For example, if torture has a sufficient probability of extracting information that is likely to lead to sufficiently fewer casualties in an upcoming military operation, then torture will be authorized. While the vast majority of leaders think that their standards for determining when to authorize torture are morally appropriate, suppose that those standards are far more permissive than morality allows. One day, Arthur and some soldiers in his command are captured by the enemy. Arthur is tortured and is also forced to watch the other captives being tortured. Eventually, he and the other soldiers are rescued.

Imagine that this ordeal causes Arthur to shift his view of the standards for torture that are supported by the leadership of his military. He has been supportive of these standards, but he now judges that they are too lax. His new perspective is not the result of learning straightforwardly descriptive facts about what happens during torture. As he sees it, in the wake of his experience he more fully appreciates the dignity of an individual human being and the awfulness of torture's dehumanizing effects on victims and perpetrators alike. Suppose that this new perspective does not remain merely an unreflective response to his experience. On the contrary, he systematically and carefully reflects on the issue of torture. In doing so, he attempts to give due consideration to all sorts of factors, and to sympathetically consider the myriad interests of various stakeholders. But his overall assessment remains deeply informed by his emotional response to his experience of torture. In this respect, it is not a *dispassionate* assessment.

Suppose that Arthur becomes an advocate within the military for a policy on torture that is much more restrictive. Other military leaders hear him out, but only a very small number are convinced. Many leaders articulate their defenses of the current standards to Arthur. He is similarly unmoved. As in so many moral debates, neither side has an argument that could conclusively settle the matter. Arthur's passions on this topic run higher than those of nearly everyone he talks to about the issue. And he knows that, in a great many situations, emotional attachment to a position distorts one's reasoning. In light of these considerations, should Arthur abandon his view and give significant credence to the majority view? Should he do this even if he genuinely does have a clearer and more accurate understanding of the morality of torture? Finally, even if he should give more weight to the majority position, should his degree of confidence be limited to what could be justified on purely impartial grounds?

It is far from clear that all of these questions should be answered affirmatively. Considered in the abstract, a policy of deferring to the less emotionally invested majority looks reasonable. But such a policy may appear questionable when considering hypothetical cases where one is inclined to endorse the emotionally informed reasoning of the minority.

As I hope is now clear, I do not want to deny that distorting emotional bias is rampant in people's thinking about religious matters. What I do deny is that the prevalence of such bias vitiates the justification that may be conferred by genuine affectively mediated insight.

5.6 Rationalist Weak Conciliationism Applied

In this penultimate section of the chapter, I consider some scenarios that illustrate more concretely the sort of implications that rationalist weak conciliationism might have for religious belief.

5.6.1 Forgotten Insight

Jill and Flynn are 30-year-olds who both took the same college course in philosophy of religion a decade ago. Jill remembers that when they studied the argument from evil against theism, she was surprised to find herself thinking that theists had really good responses to the argument, and that the atheistic argument was not that compelling when one thought carefully about it. This evolution in her thinking led her to give up atheism and to become a theist. At this point, however, Jill is not able to remember the theistic responses she found to be so powerful, or why she concluded at the time that the atheistic argument was less forceful than she initially supposed. From her current vantage point, where she has lost command of the relevant arguments, it certainly seems highly implausible that a good and omnipotent God would create a world that exhibits the quantity and intensity of suffering that one observes in this world. Nonetheless, since Jill trusts the intellectual process that she went through 10 years earlier, she remains a theist.

Now Jill meets up with Flynn, a friend from college days that Jill believes to be just as smart, thoughtful, and intellectually honest as herself. It comes up in conversation that Flynn remembered having the *opposite* reaction when their class studied the argument from evil. Flynn hoped that theists would have some compelling responses. But Flynn remembers concluding (with dismay) that all of those arguments were inadequate and that after careful examination the argument from evil appeared even *more* formidable than it did on superficial examination. Like Jill, Flynn no longer can recall any significant details of the philosophical considerations but merely remembers his basic conclusions and impressions from that part of the class. Jill and Flynn are confident that they both carefully read everything that was assigned, were equally attentive in lecture, and were equally careful and diligent in thinking through the argument from evil during that portion of the course.

For the sake of discussion, suppose that Jill really *did* have insight into the cogency of theistic responses to the argument from evil and that confused thinking prevented Flynn from properly appreciating the power of those responses. But because they both lack memory of the philosophical details, there is no *present* difference in their level of insight, nor is there any asymmetry in their memories of how hard they thought and how confident they felt that would support putting more trust in one person's assessment. Finally, suppose that Jill and Flynn's disagreement over theism arises entirely from their opposing assessments of the argument from evil in this class a decade ago. More particularly, I'll stipulate that they agree, *bracketing the evidence supplied by their reactions to the unit of the class on evil*, that atheism is slightly more plausible than theism. This is because a superficial examination of the argument from evil (which is all they are presently capable of) leads them both to think that the force of this argument outweighs the force of the considerations favoring theism.

A decade earlier, Jill had insights that shaped her assessment of theism's fundamental plausibility. Suppose that while these insights were present to her, she understood that her previous estimation of the argument from evil had been confused. From the new vantage point that enabled her to appreciate the weaknesses of that argument, it would be appropriate for her to revise upward her assessment of the fundamental plausibility of theism in a world with significant creaturely suffering. In gaining a clearer understanding of the relevant philosophical considerations, her ur-priors would need to be adjusted accordingly. But now, 10 years later, she can no longer "see" that her original estimation of the argument from evil was confused. Having forgotten her earlier insights, the argument from evil looks strong on superficial inspection. Her theism (before encountering Flynn) is therefore not based on an appreciation of cogent responses to the argument of evil. Rather, it is based on the fact that, having carefully and honestly studied the argument from evil 10 years ago, she confidently concluded that the argument was much less compelling than it had originally appeared to be. This fact is evidence that can be treated in an "instrumentalist" fashion.

So one can model Jill's rational position (before meeting Flynn) as one she reaches by starting with a prior credence for theism that is relatively low (on account of the problem of evil) and then updating her credence by conditionalizing on the evidence that someone who is smart and intellectually careful (namely, herself) studied the argument with such and such degree of care in such and such context and concluded that the argument from evil was not compelling after all. Conditionalizing on this evidence leads her to reasonable confidence that the argument from evil is not compelling and that theism is true. (Imagine that Jill thinks that there are strong arguments for theism that would justify a high credence for theism if it turns out that the argument from evil does not have much force.) Then, when Jill encounters Flynn, she learns that someone who is as smart and intellectually careful as herself (namely, Flynn) studied the argument from evil with a similar degree of care in the same sort of context as herself and concluded that the argument supplied very powerful considerations against theism. Since Jill's antecedent estimate of Flynn's reliability is equal to her antecedent estimate of her own reliability, this evidence of Flynn's assessment offsets the evidence provided by the evidence of Jill's own past assessment. Since the evidence supplied by Jill's past assessment is offset by the evidence of Flynn's past assessment, and since the argument from evil presently appears to be quite strong (in light of the superficial assessment that is possible for her), her credence for theism in the wake of the disagreement will be below 0.5.

If Flynn also follows rationalist weak conciliationism, he will become less confident in his atheism, since the evidence supplied by his past assessment of the argument from evil will be offset by the evidence supplied by Jill's assessment. Assuming that Flynn's position is in other respects perfectly symmetrical to Jill's (which means that he also has an equal estimate of his and Jill's reliability during their college days), then when he updates his credence by conditionalizing on the facts about his disagreement with Jill, his position will converge with Jill's and he will also assign theism a credence somewhat lower than 0.5.

The key lesson of this example is that past rational insights do not provide the same epistemic resilience as insights that are *presently available*. When I am confident that p based on a memory of having had insight into p's plausibility, my confidence that p is not directly grounded in the rational considerations I once appreciated. Instead, my confidence is grounded in my confidence in the cognitive reliability of my past self, a confidence that leads me to treat rational judgments of that past self as reliable indicators of what the rational considerations really support. In other words, I am treating my past self as an instrument. When a "cognitive instrument" that I estimate to be equally reliable (i.e., an epistemic peer) is discovered to have reached some conflicting position, the grounds for my confidence that p are undercut, leaving me to rely on whatever rational considerations are *presently and directly available to me*.

Consider the following objection to my suggestion that in the present example, Jill ought to reduce confidence and assign theism some credence below 0.5. One might object to this verdict in the following way. I stipulated in the example that Jill had genuine insight 10 years ago into the cogency of theistic responses to the argument from evil. But this means that Jill's low credence for theism in the wake of the disagreement is in part due to the fact that she's forgotten her past insights and as a consequence is confused about the rational force of the argument from evil. If she were fully reasonable and insightful, then she would not think that the argument from evil is highly compelling, and she would have more confidence in theism. Thus, if Jill was reasoning as she *ought* to reason, then she would come into her conversation with Flynn with a higher credence for theism and, in light of this high credence and the insights that ground it, her post-disagreement credence for theism would exceed 0.5. So the credence for theism that Jill *ought* to have is *greater* than 0.5, not less than 0.5, as I have claimed.

I agree with the imagined objector that in *some* sense Jill "ought" to have a credence for theism higher than 0.5 (on the supposition, assumed for sake of discussion, that genuine insight favors theism). One might say that *ideally*, Jill ought to have a credence for theism that is above 0.5. This is true, since if Jill's first-order reasoning about theism was as it ought to be, *and* her reasoning about the significance of disagreement was as it ought to be, then she would arrive at a final credence for theism higher than 0.5. But I also think that the statement "Jill ought to conditionalize on the disagreement evidence and adopt a credence for theism that is less than 0.5" can express something true in the present context. This statement can mean something like: *given that Jill is less than fully insightful and has a credence for theism that is lower than it ideally ought to be,* she ought to adopt a credence less than 0.5 upon learning of the disagreement. For reasons developed elsewhere, I endorse a "contextualist" semantics for "ought" claims according to which "ought" claims like these can both be true despite the superficial appearance of inconsistency.[36] For the moment, it is sufficient to emphasize that in saying that Jill ought to lower her credence to below 0.5, I am not saying that this is what Jill would do if she did what she rationally ought to do *in every aspect of her reasoning.* Rather, I am saying that this is what Jill would do if she handled the disagreement evidence rationally, holding fixed other aspects of her thinking (which may or may not be mistaken in certain respects).[37]

5.6.2 Fading Insight and the Epistemic Utility of Spiritual Practices

Consider again the example discussed earlier in this chapter of the mystical experience that allegedly brought Brainerd to an appreciation of the "infinite wisdom, suitableness, and excellency" of God's offer of salvation by grace rather than works. Suppose that this episode involved a particular affective experience that resulted in a genuine insight into the worthiness of God's way of salvation as taught in Christianity. One can imagine, for instance, that Brainerd tasted firsthand the bliss of gratitude that results in being saved in this way, as well as the freedom to serve God out of love and without anxiety

---

[36] A "contextualist" semantics for "ought" claims says that the semantic value of "ought" depends on some parameter that can vary with the context of utterance. For example, the semantic value of "ought" may depend on which of the subject's epistemic constraints are taken as given for purposes of the present discussion. For a defense of "metanormative contextualism," see John Pittard and Alex Worsnip, "Metanormative Contextualism and Normative Uncertainty," *Mind* 126, no. 501 (2017): 155–193.

[37] I am here in agreement with an interpretation of conciliationism articulated in David Christensen, "Disagreement, Question-Begging and Epistemic Self-Criticism," *Philosophers' Imprint* 11, no. 6 (2011), 4. According to Christensen, conciliationism concerns "what the proper response is to one particular kind of evidence," namely, disagreement. He writes: "if one starts out by botching things epistemically, and then takes correct account of one bit of evidence, it's unlikely that one will end up with fully rational beliefs. And it would surely be asking too much of a principle describing the correct response to peer disagreement to demand that it include a complete recipe for undoing every epistemic mistake one might be making in one's thinking."

that is made possible by this way of salvation. A firsthand experience of these benefits allowed Brainerd to really appreciate for the first time why salvation by grace is truly the most excellent and worthy way.

It's possible that whatever insights Brainerd gained through this experience would always be accessible to him after the experience. Going forward, perhaps merely thinking about the doctrine of salvation of grace would cause a rush of feelings and thoughts that would allow for a deep appreciation of the excellency (and thus plausibility) of this doctrine. But it is also easy to imagine that Brainerd's experience might not have permanently changed his plausibility assessments in this way and that the rational effects of the experience would fade over time. In this case, his partisan justification (and his ability to withstand disagreement worries) would diminish as the mystical experience receded into the more distant past, unless those epistemic advantages were renewed through other experiences that similarly oriented his affections and attention.

Suppose that the epistemic changes occasioned by an affectively charged religious experience do tend to fade over time. In this case, one could appeal to affective rationalism in order to argue for the *epistemic* importance of the regular engagement in spiritual disciplines that, by eliciting or promoting certain affective states, help to renew (and perhaps deepen) certain religious insights. Regularly practiced disciplines like prayer, service, meditation, musical worship, walks in "nature," fasting, and so on (the list will of course depend on the religious outlook in question), in addition to whatever other benefits they provide, might be necessary for the preservation or recovery of rational religious confidence.

Perhaps, though, religious insights that initially cannot be fully achieved apart from special "religious experiences" may, over time, "sink in" and become available apart from such episodes.[38] Flashes of insight may gradually be transmuted into stable, default ways of thinking. Some interesting comments from Peter van Inwagen might suggest that he experienced this sort of transition. He describes how, sometime during his transition from indifferent agnosticism to Christianity, he could willingly alternate between an atheistic way of seeing the physical universe—one that sees the cosmos as a self-subsistent whole that needs no explanation—and a theistic conception that sees the physical world as something that is *not* self-subsistent and that must be explained by something "radically different" from anything

---

[38] I'm grateful to Adam Eitel for helpful discussion of this idea.

contained in physical reality.[39] As van Inwagen describes it, his ability to shift between these two ways of seeing the world was akin to the way one can, when looking at the well-known duck/rabbit picture, shift between seeing that ambiguous image as a duck and seeing it as a rabbit. Eventually, he says, it was no longer possible for him to induce this kind of gestalt shift: only the conception of the world as dependent now has any plausibility for him. If his Christian convictions are indeed the product of some sort of "incommunicable insight," as he alleges, then this inability to bring about the gestalt shift presumably reflects a deepening and stabilizing of the insight that precipitated his conversion. His former way of seeing things is no longer available as a plausible possibility.

If religious insight occasioned by affectively charged religious experiences tends to fade, or, in the extreme case, if it is only available in the midst of the experience itself, then the rational advantages conferred by such insight will not be persistently available. In those periods where the rational insight is not accessible, a greater degree of deference on religious matters will be required than in periods when one enjoys greater insight into the rational merits of one's position. While an externalist or proponent of agent-centered norms could easily affirm the possibility of *stable* justified religious belief, it seems to me that the rationalist must admit that one's degree of *epistemic* justification on religious matters varies with the degree of insight that is *presently* accessible. No doubt some will see this as an unfortunate consequence of the view. But I don't see this consequence as a reason for thinking that the view is *incorrect*. Disagreement undercuts impartial grounds for epistemic self-trust that are available in domains where there is agreement and thus where it is possible to affirm the reliability of others broadly like oneself. When impartial grounds for trust are unavailable, self-trust must be grounded on rational accomplishments that may be difficult and tenuous. In the absence of normal epistemic supports, instability in one's degree of justification should not be surprising.

It should be noted that even if one's degree of epistemic justification on religious matters is unstable, this need not imply an instability in one's religious *commitment*. As I will discuss in chapter 7, it may be possible to rationally commit to living in accordance with certain religious outlook even if one fails to believe with confidence that the outlook in question is true. Because the degree of one's religious commitment does not correlate in any

---

[39] Van Inwagen, "Quam Dilecta," 35.

straightforward way to one's confidence in any particular religious outlook, instability in one's credences for religious doctrines needn't imply instability in one's devotion to a particular religious path. Nonetheless, religious commitment is certainly easier when one has confidence in the relevant religious outlook. Thus, if insights afforded by religious experiences do fade over time, then in a context of widespread religious disagreement it will be all the more important to engage in those practices that promote the relevant sort of insightful experiences.

5.6.3 Moderate Religious Insight in the Face of Religious Pluralism

How should someone with moderate religious insight (which by itself doesn't seem to justify an especially high degree of certainty) respond to the fact of religious pluralism, when no single party to religious disagreement can claim any clear advantage in p-neutral credentials?

To shed light on this question, consider the following simplified example. Imagine that there are only five religious outlooks, R1–R5, which are mutually exclusive and collectively exhaustive. Each of these views has the backing of a religious group, and all of these groups are of equal size and appear to be equally epistemically qualified, at least when one considers only dispute-neutral qualifications.

Suppose that Mary has thought through the rational and evidential merits of each of these religious positions and has moderately clear insight into considerations that strongly support R1 over its competitors. On the basis of such insight, but prior to taking into account any knowledge about the distribution of opinion concerning R1, Mary's credence would be around 0.8. I'll stipulate that this credence would be justified, given the clarity and degree of insight that Mary has on the matter.

How should Mary's credence for R1 shift when she takes into account information concerning the distribution of opinion and the nonpartisan epistemic credentials of the various groups? In answering this, one should first note that this information might have *first-order* evidential bearing on R1. Suppose R1 gives one reason to expect widespread religious agreement, whereas R2 gives one reason to expect significant disagreement. In this case, the religious disagreement may constitute first-order evidence against R1 and for R2. (I say that it "may" constitute first-order evidence of this sort, since the final evidential import will depend on various details about the distribution of opinion, and on what the other religious positions in play give one reason to expect.) To simplify matters, suppose that facts about the distribution of opinion have no *first-order* evidential bearing. (Perhaps, for example, all of the positions generate the same predictions about the extent of agreement on religious matters.) The facts about religious disagreement may nonetheless have significant *higher-order* evidential significance by challenging the basis for Mary's epistemic self-trust. How should Mary respond to the higher-order worries raised by religious disagreement if she is a rationalist weak conciliationist?

As a rationalist weak conciliationist, Mary knows that she is justified in departing from an impartial evaluation of the disagreement only if she has genuine insight that justifies her in thinking that her position has greater rational merit than its competitors. And the extent of religious disagreement is likely to be recognized by Mary as evidence against the claim that she has genuine insight on the matter. To see why the distribution of opinion should temper Mary's optimism regarding her insight, note first that as I've described the example, Mary's (genuine) insight is not so clear as to effectively rule out the possibility that she actually lacks insight on the matter, or that the insight she has does not support *R1* as decisively as she thinks. (As I'm imagining the case, this uncertainty about her insight is why her prior credence before factoring in the opinion of others is not higher than approximately 0.8.) In light of this uncertainty about the status of her insight into the matter, Mary's assessment of this insight should be open to revision in response to empirical evidence. And the fact that a great many qualified thinkers fail to appreciate Mary's alleged insight should probably be recognized as at least weak evidence that her insight is not genuine. For given some baseline trust in the rational capacities of human beings, the probability that an alleged insight into the truth of *p* is a *genuine* insight is greater, all else being equal, on the condition that most qualified thinkers accept *p* than it is on the condition that most qualified thinkers reject *p*. Thus, when Mary learns about the distribution of opinion on religious matters, she has some evidence for the conclusion that she does not in fact have insight into the greater rational merits of *R1*.

I'll give a concrete illustration of how Mary might update her credences in light of the disagreement evidence and how her final credences will be influenced both by her rationalism *and* by her commitment to agent impartiality. Imagine a hypothetical credence distribution for Mary after she has reflected on the rational merits of the various religious outlooks and after she learns that *either* there is a strong consensus in favor of whatever view she happens to favor *or* opinion is evenly divided across *R1–R5* (and that each group is on a par with respect to its members' *p*-neutral credentials). Of course, there is no actual point of time where Mary has only this information about the distribution of opinion. Nonetheless, Mary could consider what her credences would be in this hypothetical situation, and considering this simplified hypothetical situation is a helpful way of making clear the evidential import of the disagreement over *R1–R5*.

At this hypothetical juncture, there are three salient possibilities Mary must consider: first, that there is consensus in favor of her view (which happens to be *R1*); second, that there is disagreement but one religious group contains members who have genuine insight into the greater rational merits of their perspective; and third, that there is disagreement and none of the five groups contains members who have insight into the greater rational merits of their view. Table 5.1 illustrates one way Mary might distribute her credences across each of these possibilities in conjunction with either *R1* or *~R1*.

The credence distribution in table 5.1 reflects the fact that Mary endorses an exclusively rationalist account of partisan justification rather than either strong conciliationism or some other account of partisan justification, as I will now explain. I'll start by considering the column on the far right, representing the possibility that opinion is evenly divided across *R1–R5* and no group enjoys insight into the greater rational merits of their view. Mary knows that if there is disagreement over the various religious outlooks, the *p*-neutral credentials of each group are equivalent. So in this scenario, she would have no *impartial* reason to think that *R1* is more likely than any of the other perspectives. Moreover, if it is the case that no side enjoys rational insight, then this means that Mary's alleged insights are not genuine and there are no *rationalist* considerations that would justify her

Table 5.1 Mary's credences before knowledge of disagreement

	Consensus	Disagreement but one group has insight	Disagreement and no group has insight
R1	0.63	0.16	0.02
~R1	0.07	0.04	0.08

in favoring *R1* over other perspectives. Now, someone who endorsed a radically permissivist, externalist, agent-centered, or moderately permissivist account of partisan justification might think that even on this supposition, it could be permissible for Mary to assign a higher credence to *R1*. Perhaps this kind of self-favoring assessment can be justified without any symmetry breaker favoring Mary's position; or, if a symmetry breaker is needed, perhaps it can consist of an external factor, an agent-centered consideration, or some partisan reason that Mary acknowledges is not discernibly stronger than partisan reasons offered in support of other positions. But if she is right to reject these views on partisan justification, then she must show perfect impartiality in this column. Since there are five religious options, this means that one-fifth of the credence Mary assigns to this column should be allotted to *R1* and four-fifths to ~*R1* (since ~*R1* encompasses four religious options, *R2–R5*). And that is what table 5.1 shows: the total credence assigned to the column is 0.1, and one-fifth of this (which is 0.02) is assigned to *R1*. In this column, the proportions allotted to *R1* and its negation would match the proportions that would be required of a strong conciliationist. For, conditional on there being no genuine insight, Mary has no basis for partiality toward her perspective.

Next, consider the middle column, which represents the possibility that opinion is evenly divided and one group does benefit from genuine rational insight. If Mary were a strong conciliationist, she would have to show impartiality in this column as well. In this scenario, it is possible that she has genuine insight that supports *R1*. But since such insights would be contested by proponents of other views, someone committed to reasons impartiality could not legitimately appeal to their insight in order to justify greater confidence in their favored perspective. So the strong conciliationist would need to allot one-fifth of the credence for this column to *R1* and four-fifths to ~*R1*. But since Mary rejects any sort of reasons impartiality constraint, and since the scenario of this column does not rule out the possibility that she has genuine insight, her appreciation of the rational considerations for *R1* can give her a reason to show partiality to *R1* in this column. Of course, the scenario of this column is compatible with the possibility that some *other* religious group enjoys religious insight (rather than anyone in the group that endorses *R1*). But the clarity of Mary's insight into considerations favoring *R1* gives her reason to think it more likely that the *R1* group is the group with genuine insight and that *R1* is true. Mary's credences in this column reflect this assessment. Mary has assigned a credence of 0.2 to the entire column, and 80% of this credence (0.16) is allotted to *R1*.

The possibility represented by the first column, where there is consensus favoring Mary's view, is one where Mary would have impartial reasons to believe in *R1*, in addition to whatever rationalist considerations she may have in favor of *R1*. Given some trust in human cognitive faculties, consensus for a particular religious perspective would be evidence in favor of that perspective. Since in this scenario Mary would have rationalist *and* impartial considerations in favor of her view, this column has the highest proportion allotted to *R1*: the total credence for the column is 0.7, with 90% of this (0.63) assigned to *R1*.

I've explained how the proportions *within* each column are sensible given Mary's commitment to rationalist weak conciliationism, but what about the credences assigned to each of the different columns? Here, there is no general principle that will determine these values. Mary's views on human cognitive capacities, both in general and in the religious domain in particular, will inform the probability that she assigns to consensus and to the disagreement possibilities. But it should be emphasized that Mary's appreciation of the cogent rational considerations favoring *R1* will also affect the credences assigned to each column and not just the proportions within each column. The clarity of Mary's insight gives her reason for thinking that one group (namely, her own) does have insight and thus gives her reason for thinking that the possibility of column 3 does *not* pertain. To reflect this, I've assigned a lower credence to this column (0.1) than Mary might assign prior to thinking through religious questions and appreciating the insights that favor *R1*.

At the hypothetical juncture where Mary has the credences indicated in table 5.1, her credence for *R1* would be 0.81 (which one arrives at by adding all the numbers in the top row). Now suppose that Mary learns that there is disagreement, with the opinion evenly divided among the five views. When Mary learns this, she learns that the possibility represented by the first column (consensus) does not pertain and that one of the possibilities of the second and third columns *does* pertain. As a Bayesian and weak conciliationist, Mary will conditionalize on this information. Conditionalization will result in her adjusting her credences in columns 2 and 3 in a manner such that they add up to 1 without any changes in their ratios to one another. Table 5.2 shows the approximate values of Mary's new credences after conditionalizing.

Table 5.2 Mary's credences after conditionalizing

	Disagreement but one group has insight	Disagreement and no group has insight
R1	0.533	0.067
~R1	0.133	0.267

Having added the credences in the first row, one sees that Mary's credence for *R1* has dropped from 0.81 to 0.6. Upon her learning that she lacks any impartial reasons for her view (potential reasons that boosted the *R1* credence in the scenario involving consensus) and upon her learning that the distribution of opinion provides evidence that *no one* enjoys religious insight, Mary's credence has dropped significantly—more significantly than would be required if she endorsed a less demanding account of partisan justification. But her credence is still much higher than the credence of 0.2 that is prescribed by strong conciliationism.

To be sure, I could have chosen values for the initial table that would have yielded a much larger or smaller reduction in Mary's confidence when she updated her credence on the basis of the fact of disagreement. This exercise is not intended to establish any claims about the precise level of credence reduction that will be required of the rationalist weak conciliationist. It is merely meant to illustrate how rationalist weak conciliationism would be applied in this kind of case (which admittedly remains somewhat artificial, even though it is more realistic than the two-person disagreement cases that are so prevalent in the disagreement literature). But it is important to note that even if values were chosen that resulted in a larger reduction of confidence, Mary's final confidence level would still be above the 0.2 level prescribed by strong conciliationism.

5.7 Looking Ahead: Why the Rationalist Should Care about the Implications of Epistemic Impartiality

In this first part of this book, I have argued against a reasons impartiality requirement. In so doing, I have opposed the demanding impartiality requirement that must be presupposed by a plausible higher-order argument for disagreement-motivated religious skepticism. I've also defended rationalist weak conciliationism as an alternative to both the rigorous deference required by strong conciliationism and the highly sanguine approaches endorsed by some externalists, permissivists, and proponents of agent partiality. While I am convinced that rationalist weak conciliationism is the right approach, I do not take myself to have any knockdown argument against strong conciliationism. For the most part, I have simply shown that the arguments offered in favor of strong conciliationism fail to convince, especially when one has at one's disposal a rationalist policy that vindicates many of the commonsense conciliatory verdicts in cases highlighted in arguments for strong conciliationism. For those who think that strong conciliationism remains a plausible possibility despite the inadequacy of extant arguments for that view, I consider in part II what would follow for religious belief (and religious commitment more broadly) if one endorsed strong conciliationism and accepted reasons impartiality as a genuine epistemic ideal.

But suppose that you are fully convinced that rationalist weak conciliationism is correct. Does this mean that you should view the discussion of part II as an intellectual exercise that is irrelevant to how you should go about assessing the evidential implications of religious disagreement? No, it does not. Recall that in the example of Mary just discussed, Mary had to assign some weight to credences that were impartial. Since Mary was not sure that her apparent rational insights were genuine, she had to give some weight to the possibility that no party to the dispute enjoyed rational insight. This required her to ascertain what impartial credences would be appropriate on such a supposition. Generalizing from this example, when a rationalist weak conciliationist is unsure whether the putative insights available to him are genuine, he will have to give some weight to an impartial perspective. In such cases, the rationalist will need to have some view on what credences (or, more broadly, what doxastic attitudes) satisfy the requirement of epistemic impartiality. In the next part of the book, I take up the question of how one should determine which attitudes qualify as impartial. As I will show, when one leaves behind idealized examples of the sort just discussed and attends to the messiness of the real world, it is far from clear what doxastic attitudes on religious matters best accord with the aim of impartial deference.

PART II
WHAT DOES IMPARTIALITY REQUIRE?

6

Elusive Impartiality

The primary aim of part I was to contest the commitment to a highly demanding form of epistemic impartiality that drives the argument for disagreement-motivated religious skepticism. In particular, I opposed the reasons impartiality requirement affirmed by strong conciliationism. While I think the discussion in part I provides good reasons to reject a reasons impartiality requirement, I concede that I have not offered any *decisive* argument against such a requirement. No doubt some who appreciate the arguments of part I will nonetheless retain the view that a demanding reasons impartiality constraint may be correct. Indeed, I myself feel *some* pull toward this conclusion. Though I maintain that it can be reasonable to stand by cogent reasoning even when it is rejected by a majority of those who appear to be epistemic peers, I admit to feeling a degree of suspicion that such steadfastness is objectionably immodest. As long as strong impartiality constraints retain a degree of plausibility, it is worth exploring what the implications would be for religious commitment were one to accept a demanding form of impartiality as an epistemic ideal. This second part of the book is devoted to this exploration. In this chapter, I focus on the question of whether it could be reasonable for the proponent of strong conciliationism to have a confident *belief* or high *credence* for contested religious claims. In the next chapter, I consider forms of religious commitment that may not require doxastic confidence in a contested religious outlook.

A central thesis of this chapter is that in contexts where disagreement is sufficiently deep, as it is in the religious domain, epistemic impartiality is *elusive*. Epistemic impartiality in the religious domain is elusive for two broad reasons. The first reason has to do with complications arising from the fact that many qualified thinkers contest the view that epistemic impartiality is in fact an epistemic ideal. In light of this disagreement over the merits of epistemic impartiality, it would seem that impartiality cannot be consistently pursued. A full commitment to impartial epistemic deference would itself seem to be highly nondeferential, since such a commitment gives no weight to the views of those who reject the aim of impartial deference. In a context where epistemic impartiality is controversial, the commitment to impartiality appears to be self-undermining. After considering the responses to this self-undermining challenge that are available to the conciliationist, I will argue that a viable response to the challenge may be incompatible with the pursuit of full epistemic impartiality in the religious domain.

The second reason why epistemic impartiality proves elusive in the religious domain is that pursuing the ideal of impartiality requires that one take a stand on certain questions that cannot be settled in a religiously neutral way. If I rationally adopt some doxastic stance D in an attempt to be religiously impartial, I must have some reasons R for thinking that D is the stance that best accords with impartiality in the religious domain. I will argue that any plausible reasons I might cite for thinking that D is impartial will themselves be controversial *on religious grounds*, so that in relying on R I fail to be religiously impartial. Or, to put the point another way, any method I might rely on in order to identify the appropriately impartial stance will require that I rely on at least one religiously controversial assumption. The reason why religious impartiality proves to be elusive in this way has to do with the wide-reaching implications of various religious outlooks. Identifying a religiously impartial stance requires that one answer questions about what epistemic qualifications should inspire confidence in someone's assessment of religious questions, about which influences on people's opinions count as illegitimate sources of bias, and about the comparative strength of various sources of bias. In many disagreements about mundane matters, such questions can be answered without taking any stand on the matter under dispute. But in the religious context, the central religious claims that are under dispute bear significantly on the questions that must be resolved in order to pursue epistemic deference. Paradoxically, then, the pursuit of religious deference requires a remarkable degree of cognitive self-trust with respect to contested religious matters.

Given the way that questions about how to pursue impartiality in the religious domain are tied up with matters of religious controversy, a commitment to impartiality does not clearly support any determinate response to religious pluralism. There will be a number of stances that have a plausible claim to being the state that best comports with the goal of impartial deference. I will argue that these stances include some that involve a good deal of religious confidence. Thus, there is reason to doubt that pursuing epistemic impartiality inevitably leads to a skeptical outcome.

6.1 Self-Undermining Worries for Conciliationism

In this and the following section, I describe self-undermining worries for conciliationism and consider some possible responses. Then, in section 6.3, I consider what implications these responses to the self-undermining problem have for situations of religious disagreement.

Epistemologists disagree on questions concerning the rational signif-icance of disagreement. For example, some epistemologists think that it is obvious that disagreements should be assessed from an impartial vantage point, while others entirely reject any such impartiality re-quirement. This poses a difficult conundrum to anyone who endorses a conciliatory approach to disagreement. Suppose, for that sake of argu-ment, that strong conciliationism is correct. This means that one is ra-tionally obliged to respond to disagreements in a way that accords with agent impartiality and reasons impartiality. Given this supposition, how should one respond to the disagreement concerning the merits of strong conciliationism itself?

Initially, it might seem obvious that whatever impartiality requirements apply in other disagreements will also apply to disagreements concerning the merits of such impartiality requirements. If I should significantly re-duce confidence upon discovering that some ethical or metaphysical view of mine is contested by qualified philosophers, why should matters be any different when the view in question happens to be an epistemolog-ical thesis concerning the rational significance of disagreement? A policy that exempted this latter dispute from the requirements that pertain in other cases would appear to be unacceptably arbitrary. Thus, the strong conciliationist should respond to disagreements over strong conciliationism in the same way she responds to other disagreements. Because a great many epistemologists reject strong conciliationism, it would therefore seem that the strong conciliationist must give up confident belief in the merits of strong conciliationism. In the present philosophical climate, strong conciliationism turns out to be *self-undermining*.[1]

The foregoing characterization of the self-undermining problem for conciliationism presumes that a self-undermining problem arises because

---

[1] Several thinkers have pressed self-undermining worries against conciliationism. For one ex-tended discussion, see Jason Decker, "Conciliation and Self-Incrimination," *Erkenntnis* 79, no. 5 (2014): 1099–1134.

there are *actual opponents* of conciliationism. But there is some reason to think that the mere possibility of opponents to conciliationism is sufficient to generate a severe self-undermining problem, at least when one is focused on the most plausible sort of conciliatory policy. I argued in chapter 3 that the conciliationist who wants to both respond impartially to disagreement and respect conditionalization must have *pre*disagreement credences that are already impartial in a certain sense. More specifically, her predisagreement credences must be calibrated with an impartial estimate of her reliability. This is the fundamental calibration requirement, which is one of the central tenets of strong conciliationism. Does fundamental calibration apply to one's initial credences for strong conciliationism and various competitor norms? If it does, then strong conciliationism may fully undermine itself even before information about other people's views are taken into account.

To appreciate the problem, consider the case of Heather, who is trying to decide what her initial credence for strong conciliationism should be. Suppose that after Heather decides on her initial credence, she will talk to Wesley to learn what he thinks about the matter. Heather knows that Wesley endorses either strong conciliationism or a particular version of the so-called right reasons view. The right reasons view says that in disagreements where there is full disclosure (and thus where the disagreement is not explained by one side possessing evidence unknown to the other side), one should ignore higher-order worries raised by disagreement and adopt the credences that are supported by the first-order evidence.[2] As far as I know, proponents of the right reasons view have not explicitly addressed the question of what credence one should have for the right reasons view. But there are multiple reasons for thinking that the most coherent position for a proponent of the right reasons view to hold is that one's credence for the view ought to be 1.[3]

---

[2] For defense of the right reasons view, see Thomas Kelly, "The Epistemic Significance of Disagreement," *Oxford Studies in Epistemology* 1 (2005): 167–196; and Michael G. Titelbaum, "Rationality's Fixed Point (Or: In Defense of Right Reason)," *Oxford Studies in Epistemology* 5 (2015): 253–294. It should be noted that Kelly abandoned the right reasons view in favor of the "Total Evidence View," which is similar in spirit to the weak conciliationism that I endorse. See Thomas Kelly, "Peer Disagreement and Higher Order Evidence," in *Disagreement*, ed. Richard Feldman and Ted A. Warfield (Oxford: Oxford University Press, 2010), 111–174. But Titelbaum remains a defender of the position.

[3] Here, briefly, is one argument for this conclusion. If one is not rationally required to have a credence of 1 for the right reasons view, then it can be rationally permissible to assign some small positive credence to a disagreement norm that is a competitor to the right reasons view. If it can be rationally permissible to assign a positive credence to a competitor norm, then it can be rational to give some weight to the credences prescribed by that norm in situations of disagreement. But competing norms do not always recommend maintaining the credence that is supported by the first-order evidence. So, if it can be rational to give some weight to the credences prescribed by a competitor norm, then it can be rational to adopt a credence value that is not supported by the first-order

In any case, for the purpose of the present example, I'll stipulate that the right reasons view that Heather thinks Wesley might believe is a version of the right reasons view that entails that one should always assign a credence of 1 to the right reasons view. Heather is very confident that strong conciliationism is correct, but she cannot rule out the right reasons view. What credences should Heather adopt for the two policies?

Consider, first, the credences that strong conciliationism recommends at this initial stage. Assume that strong conciliationism issues the normal sorts of conciliatory prescriptions in disagreements over strong conciliationism itself. This means that if Heather learns that Wesley affirms the right reasons view, strong conciliationism will require her to increase her credence for the right reasons view. Strong conciliationism also says that Heather should conditionalize on the information about Wesley's opinion. And conditionalization on the disagreement evidence will lead Heather to increase her credence for the right reasons view only if *before* the disagreement she has a positive credence for the right reasons view. Thus, strong conciliationism requires Heather to have a positive credence for the right reasons view even before she knows what Wesley thinks.

One can also explain this result by appealing to the fundamental calibration requirement. According to the fundamental calibration requirement of strong conciliationism, if Heather is strongly inclined on the basis of first-order considerations to assign some proposition p an ur-prior c (where c is greater than 0.5) then her ur-prior for p should be equal to her *independent* reliability estimate for someone who is relevantly similar and who is inclined to assign an ur-prior c to p or to $\sim p$. This impartiality requirement helps assure that when Heather finds herself in a disagreement over p with someone who is similarly qualified, conditionalizing on the facts about the disagreement will lead her to a credence for p that is properly deferential. If she starts out more confident in p than an independent reliability estimate could support, then conditionalizing on disagreement evidence will not lead her to credences that are appropriately impartial. Does the fundamental calibration requirement of strong conciliationism apply to Heather's initial credence for $\sim RR$, the denial of the right reasons view? Suppose that it does. In this case, strong conciliationism would recommend that Heather's ur-prior for

---

evidence. But if the right reasons view is correct, it *cannot* be rational to adopt a credence value that is not supported by the first-order evidence. Thus, if the right reasons view is correct, one *is* rationally required to have a credence of 1 for the right reasons view.

~RR be equal to her independent reliability estimate of someone relevantly like herself who is inclined to be very confident in his view on ~RR. Suppose Heather has a 0.9 reliability estimate for such a person. In this case, strong conciliationism would recommend that Heather have an initial credence of 0.9 for ~RR and thus a credence of 0.1 for the right reasons view.

Suppose that Heather perfectly conforms to the requirements of strong conciliationism by adopting an initial credence of 0.9 for strong conciliationism and an initial credence of 0.1 for the right reasons view. A problem now comes into view. Plausibly, in order for Heather to be jus-' tified in perfectly conforming to the credence recommendation of strong conciliationism, she needs to be fully confident that this recommendation is correct. If she has a positive credence for a different norm that is- sues a different recommendation for her initial credences, then presumably she will not be justified in perfectly conforming to the dictates of strong conciliationism. This is because rational coherence arguably requires that the weight one gives to the credences prescribed by some norm should be proportioned to one's credence for the proposition that the norm in ques- tion is correct. More precisely, one's credence for p should be a weighted average of the credence values for p that are prescribed by the norms one thinks might be correct, with each prescription weighted by one's cre- dence for the norm in question.[4] Call this view Weighted Averaging of Norms or WAN for short. WAN is extremely plausible, especially when one thinks about Heather's ur-priors for other propositions that have nothing to do with disagreement. If Heather has a credence of 0.1 for the right reasons view, then it seems that she should give a weight of 0.1 to the credence that the right reasons view recommends for, say, some contro- versial moral claim. If WAN is right, and if Heather's initial credences are 0.9 for strong conciliationism and 0.1 for the right reasons view, then her credences for strong conciliationism and the right reasons view should be the credences that result from giving weight 0.9 to the recommendations of strong conciliationism and weight 0.1 to the recommendations of the right

---

[4] This requirement is similar in spirit to a more general "rational reflection" requirement that is discussed in David Christensen, "Rational Reflection," *Philosophical Perspectives* 24, no. 1 (2010): 121–40. This principle, RatRef, says that it should be the case that Cr (A | Pr (A) = n) = n, where Cr is an agent's credences and Pr represents whatever credences would be maximally rational for someone in the agent's epistemic situation. A coherent agent who conforms to RatRef will have credences that are a weighted average of the credence values that the agent thinks might be ideal, with each value weighted by the agent's credence that that value is ideal. Christensen argues that obeying RatRef can lead to violation of other rational requirements in special sorts of circumstances, but that RatRef may still be correct.

reasons view. Applying WAN in this way would lead Heather to a credence for strong conciliationism of 0.81 ($= 0.9 \cdot 0.9 + 0.1 \cdot 0$) and credence for the right reasons view of 0.19 ($= 0.9 \cdot 0.1 + 0.1 \cdot 1$).

Unfortunately, this cannot the end of the story.[5] If Heather adopted credences of 0.81 for strong conciliationism and 0.19 for the right reasons view, then satisfying WAN would require that she give weight 0.81 to the credence recommendations of strong conciliationism and weight 0.19 to the recommendations of the right reasons view. Doing this would yield a credence for strong conciliationism of 0.729 ($= 0.81 \cdot 0.9 + 0.19 \cdot 0$) and a credence for the right reasons view of 0.271 ($= 0.81 \cdot 0.1 + 0.19 \cdot 1$). But upon adopting these lower credences, the new prescriptions of WAN would be lower still; adopting these even lower credences would lead to yet lower prescriptions from WAN, and so on and on. As is easy to see, the only credences that Heather could adopt that would satisfy WAN are a credence of 0 for strong conciliationism and a credence of 1 for the right reasons view.[6]

The problem here does not depend on the simplifying assumption that Heather knows that strong conciliationism and the right reasons view are the only two possibilities in play. Suppose that strong conciliationism recommends that Heather assign strong conciliationism an initial credence of 0.9 and also recommends assigning small but positive credences to a number of other competing norms, including a credence of 0.02 to the right reasons view. If r stands for Heather's credence for the right reasons

---

[5] The idea that a conciliatory adjustment of one's credence for conciliationism should prompt yet another adjustment in one's credence for conciliationism, which should in turn prompt yet another adjustment (and so on), is explored in Matt Weiner, "More on the Self-Undermining Argument," *Opiniatrety* (blog), January 9, 2007, http://mattweiner.net/blog/archives/000781.html; and Brian Weatherson, "Disagreements, Philosophical, and Otherwise," in *Disagreement: New Essays*, ed. David Christensen and Jennifer Lackey (Oxford: Oxford University Press, 2013), 54–73. Weiner and Weatherson both consider a disagreement between a conciliationist and a proponent of a steadfast norm that recommends sticking by one's initial view. Because this steadfast norm recommends that the conciliationist remain confident in conciliationism, the conciliationist's increased confidence in this steadfast norm should, paradoxically, lead him to *increase* his credence for his original conciliatory view. The steadfast norm and the conciliatory norm are both self-undermining in this context. Weiner and Weatherson both show that, in a certain kind of idealized disagreement between the conciliationist and the steadfaster, the equilibrium position for the conciliationist involves a credence of 2/3 for conciliationism and 1/3 for the steadfast norm. This outcome at least has the semblance of reasonability. But the results of the convergence approach explored by Weiner and Weatherson are much more dubious in the case where conciliationism is opposed to a norm like the right reasons view that is *not* self-undermining.

[6] Let's label Heather's credence for the right reasons view r. I am supposing that Heather does not assign a positive credence to any disagreement norms other than the right reasons view and strong conciliationism. So if Heather is probabilistically coherent, her credence for strong conciliationism is $(1 - r)$. The right reasons view says that r should be equal to 1, and strong conciliationism says that it should be equal to 0.9. So, given WAN, it follows that Heather ought to satisfy the following constraint: $r = r \cdot 1 + (1 - r) \cdot 0.9$. Solving, one gets $r = 1$.

view and c stands for her credence for strong conciliationism, then assigning credences that conform to WAN will require that she satisfy the following constraint:

$r = c \times 0.02 + r \times 1 +$ [credence values prescribed for the right reasons view by other norms, weighted by Heather's credences for those norms]

Because no norm can prescribe a *negative* credence for the right reasons view, the only way this constraint can be satisfied is if $c = 0$. More generally, having a positive credence for any "immodest" norm that prescribes a credence of 1 for itself, together with WAN, rules out having a positive credence for any competing "modest" norm that prescribes a positive credence to the immodest norm.[7]

Below, I outline an argument that appeals to this self-undermining result to support the conclusion that one should reject strong conciliationism. In formulating the argument, I use the label *resolute conciliationism* to refer to any version of conciliationism that does not require that one's doxastic attitudes toward conciliationism meet the same impartiality requirements that apply to one's doxastic attitudes toward other propositions. Because resolute conciliationism does not require impartiality toward conciliationism itself, the normal sorts of conciliatory prescriptions will not apply in disagreements over conciliationism. I will use the label *provisional conciliationism* for any version of conciliationism that is *not* resolute. Provisional conciliationism applies the normal impartiality standards to one's doxastic attitude toward conciliationism. Using these labels, the Self-Undermining Argument against strong conciliationism may be formulated as follows:

The Self-Undermining Argument

1. If WAN is correct, then rationality requires one to assign a credence of 0 to provisional strong conciliationism.
2. WAN is correct.
3. Therefore, rationality requires one to assign a credence of 0 to provisional strong conciliationism.
4. It is not rational to accept resolute strong conciliationism.

---

[7] On this point, see David Lewis, "Immodest Inductive Methods," *Philosophy of Science* 38, no. 1 (1971): 54–63.

5. If rationality requires one to assign a credence of 0 to provisional strong conciliationism and it is not rational to accept resolute strong conciliationism, then one should reject strong conciliationism.

6. Therefore, óne should reject strong conciliationism.

It would seem that the defender of strong conciliationism cannot accept the conclusion of the Self-Undermining Argument. So what premise or premises should the strong conciliationist question?

Christensen acknowledges that the epistemic modesty required by conciliationism may conflict with genuine rational ideals, but he challenges the attempt to conclude on this basis conciliationism should be rejected.[8] According to Christensen, there can be *rational dilemmas* where it is impossible to satisfy all genuine rational requirements or ideals. Moreover, dilemmas are likely to result when one attempts to give due weight to worries about one's cognitive fallibility, as conciliatory norms attempt to do. If rational dilemmas are admitted, then one cannot rule out the possibility that it is the case both that some correct norm says that one should have a credence of 0 for strong conciliationism and that some other correct norm says that one should be confident in strong conciliationism. Someone who allows for rational dilemmas, or at least conflicts between rational "ideals," might question (5). Even if having confidence in strong conciliationism violates a requirement (or ideal) of rationality, it might be that rejecting strong conciliationism would also cause one to violate a genuine rational requirement. In this case, one cannot rule out the possibility that accepting strong conciliationism is the least bad option and therefore what one should do. Alternatively, one might accept the conclusion of the argument while contending that the least bad option is to reject strong conciliationism while following it anyway.

Which path should the conciliationist pursue if all choices are acknowledged to be rationally deficient? The answer is by no means clear. Should Heather refuse to apply impartiality requirements to her belief in conciliationism (even though such refusal is irrational)? Or should she apply the impartiality requirements as normal, significantly reduce confidence in conciliationism, yet continue to fully conform to the prescriptions

[8] David Christensen, "Epistemic Modesty Defended," in *The Epistemology of Disagreement: New Essays*, ed. David Christensen and Jennifer Lackey (Oxford: Oxford University Press, 2013), 77–97. See also the discussion of this option in Titelbaum, "Rationality's Fixed Point," 290–292.

of conciliationism? Or should she assign a credence of 0 to strong conciliationism because she respects WAN and then refrain from following strong conciliationism even though it is the only reasonable approach to disagreement? Once it is allowed that *all* such approaches are irrational in some respect, it is difficult to see how to adjudicate between these options in a principled fashion.

Next, consider the option of denying WAN and thus rejecting premise (2) of the Self-Undermining Argument. I concede that WAN is not a fully general requirement. WAN assumes that the competing norms that one thinks may be correct all prescribe some precise credence. But there are imaginable situations where one rationally has a positive credence for some norm that says not to have *any* determinate credence for p. In such cases, WAN would not straightforwardly apply. And perhaps there are other cases where WAN is not the appropriate procedure for dealing with uncertainty between rational norms. But if denying WAN is to help in the present context, one must hold that WAN is sometimes inappropriate even in situations like Heather's, where the subject has determinate credences for competing norms that all prescribe precise credences for p.

Some epistemologists have recently argued that requirements like WAN are entirely misguided, even in a situation like Heather's. These philosophers reject the very natural idea that one's credences for p should reflect one's higher-order beliefs about the value of the ideally rational credence for p.[9] Intuitively, it seems that it is irrational for you to assign p a credence of 0.3 while at the same time confidently believing that this credence is irrational and that the correct epistemic norm implies that your credence for p should be 0.8. This tension between your first-order credence for p and your higher-order views on what first-order credence is rationally ideal exhibits a kind of "epistemic akrasia" whereby one fails to believe what one thinks one ought to believe. And such epistemic akrasia strikes many people as being obviously incoherent.[10] But those who oppose this sort of interlevel coherence requirement claim that it can be rational to exhibit misalignment between first-order credences and higher-order views about the rational status of

---

[9] For example, see Allen Coates, "Rational Epistemic Akrasia," *American Philosophical Quarterly* 49, no. 2 (2012): 113–124; Maria Lasonen-Aarnio, "Higher-Order Evidence and the Limits of Defeat," *Philosophy and Phenomenological Research* 88, no. 2 (2014): 315; and Maria Lasonen-Aarnio, "New Rational Reflection and Internalism about Rationality," *Oxford Studies in Epistemology* 5 (2015): 145–171.

[10] For forceful arguments that such akrasia *is* problematic, see Sophie Horowitz, "Epistemic Akrasia," *Noûs* 48, no. 4 (2014): 718–744.

those first-order credences. According to these philosophers, when one has powerful but *misleading* evidence in favor of an *incorrect* rational norm *N2* and against the *correct* rational norm *N1*, one should follow *N1* (assigning the credences to *p* that *N1* prescribes) while nonetheless believing that *N2* is correct. Such "level splitting" allows one both to properly respond to one's evidence that bears on the question of which norm is correct without being led away from the proper assessment of the evidence that bears directly on *p*.

I will not discuss here the arguments for a level-splitting view that denies WAN and similar level-connecting requirements, or give my reasons for thinking that these arguments are unsuccessful. For present purposes, it suffices to note that however plausible a level-splitting view may or may not be, it is not a view that comports with strong conciliationism.[11] Suppose I am aware of philosophical considerations that strongly support some metaphysical thesis *p*, but I also know that philosophical experts (who are aware of all the evidence and considerations that I am aware of) are evenly divided on whether or not *p* is true. In most cases of this sort, strong conciliationism says that even if first-order considerations justify a high credence for *p*, once I learn about this disagreement my credence for *p* should be approximately 0.5. Why, though, should the disagreement count as such powerful evidence against *p*? And how is it that the disagreement evidence, which one can suppose has no direct bearing on *p*, manages to swamp philosophical considerations that *do* bear on *p* and that clearly support the latter proposition?

The only viable answer is that the disagreement indicates that human beings like me are often unreliable in their reasoning about *p* and thus constitutes (misleading) evidence that my reasoning about *p* is mistaken. And when I have evidence against the cogency of my reasoning, I should reduce confidence in the conclusion of that reasoning, *even if that reasoning was in fact correct*. But this is precisely what level splitters deny: according to the level-splitting view, I should have the credence for *p* that is supported by correct reasoning on the matter even if I am rational in thinking that this reasoning is likely to be mistaken. Strong conciliationism is a well-motivated position only if one rejects the rationality of such level splitting and endorses interlevel coherence requirements. Thus, the strong conciliationist cannot reasonably affirm the arguments that level splitters would direct against WAN.

[11] Weatherson, "Disagreements, Philosophical, and Otherwise," 58–59.

Even if strong conciliationists are committed broadly to level-connecting principles, perhaps there is a principled reason why the weighted averaging procedure recommended by WAN should not be applied to the special case where some norm recommends giving some credence to a competitor norm.[12] Perhaps Heather should set her prior credences equal to a weighted average of the prescriptions of strong conciliationism and the right reasons view *except* when deciding on her credences for these very views. It might be that in deciding on her credences for these competing views about rational import of higher-order evidence, she is "on her own"—forced to rely her first-order reasoning without the guidance of a higher-order norm. This suggestion may turn out to be functionally equivalent to the recommendation that Heather start with high confidence in *resolute* conciliationism and then apply WAN without exception.

This brings me to the option I believe has the most merit, which is to reject (4) and deny that resolute conciliationism is objectionably arbitrary or ad hoc. I defend this response in the next section, arguing that the conciliationist who remains firm in a dispute over conciliationism is being no less deferential to her disputant than one who decreases her confidence in conciliationism. If this is right, then a resolute conciliationism that does not require conciliation in debates over the merits of conciliationism is fully in keeping with the commitment to impartial epistemic deference that motivates conciliationism.[13]

6.2 Why Resolute Conciliationism May Not Be Arbitrary

More basic to conciliationism than any particular policy for adjusting credences is, I suggest, a commitment to impartial epistemic deference. Though one doesn't normally speak of "deferring to oneself," for present

---

[12] As mentioned in note 6, WAN is similar in spirit to a rational reflection principle defended by Christensen and others. Adam Elga argues against this principle and proposes a new rational reflection principle that is said to correct for the defects of the original. ("The Puzzle of the Unmarked Clock and the New Rational Reflection Principle," *Philosophical Studies* 164, no. 1 [2013]: 127–139.) If Elga's proposal is correct, it may provide the basis for a refined version of WAN that would allow Heather to avoid her self-undermining problem. I believe that Heather's following this modified version of WAN would be functionally equivalent to applying the unmodified version of WAN to "resolute" disagreement norms, though I will not try to establish that claim here.

[13] The defense of resolute conciliationism in chapter 6, section 6.2, is adapted from John Pittard, "Resolute Conciliationism," *Philosophical Quarterly* 65, no. 260 (2015): 442–463.

purposes I'll speak of one's own predisagreement perspective as one of the perspectives to which one may show more or less "deference." My contention is that a commitment to impartial epistemic deference does *not* give the conciliationist a basis for reducing her credence in conciliationism when she is in a dispute over conciliationism. To see this, let's imagine that I am a strong conciliationist who is committed to showing equal deference to the different parties to a dispute (including myself). Consider two different disagreements that I am involved in, one concerning some proposition p that I believe and that has nothing to do with the epistemology of disagreement, and the other concerning the merits of my conciliatory view. In the disagreement concerning p, the deferential response that accords with my conciliatory commitment is quite clear: I ought to reduce my credence for p. When I do reduce my credence for p, my new credence for p will be based (in part) on my commitment to conciliationism. One might say that my newly reduced credence for p has a *conciliatory rationale*.

Now consider the case where my disputant contests my belief that conciliationism is correct. Suppose that my initial credence for conciliationism is close to 1, whereas my disputant's well-considered credence for conciliationism is close to 0. To simplify the discussion somewhat, further suppose that I do not know anyone else's view on conciliationism before the disagreement, and that I know my disputant to be my epistemic peer on philosophical matters. This means that my conciliatory policy would normally recommend that I defer equally to myself and to this disputant when we disagree on some philosophical question. My suggestion is that in this dispute over conciliationism, unlike disputes over unrelated matters, decreasing my credence for conciliationism is no more deferential to my disputant than remaining steadfast in my conciliatory views. To see why, suppose that I reduce my credence for conciliationism to 0.5 in an attempt to exhibit the sort of epistemic deference that conciliationism requires. Does this response result in my deferring equally to the views of myself and my disputant? Well, my *credence* accords with equal deference, since it gives equal weight to both of our initial credences for conciliationism; but my *reasoning* that is the basis for this lowered credence is completely *nondeferential* to my disputant, since this is exactly the sort of conciliatory reasoning my disputant maintains is illegitimate. In relying on such reasoning, I seem to simply ignore any worries raised by the disagreement. So at one level (the credence level) I show equal deference, but at another level (the reasoning level) I show my peer no deference at all.

When both the credence and reasoning levels are taken into account, my adopting a credence of 0.5 (on the basis of a conciliatory rationale) does not look like a response that accords well with a commitment to equal deference. Moreover, a response that involves no credence adjustment arguably has at least as good a claim to be a response of equal deference. Suppose that I refuse to treat the disagreement as a reason for lowering my credence for conciliationism, keeping my credence at its initial high value. While this response is completely nondeferential to my disputant at the level of my credence for conciliationism, this response is *fully* deferential to my disputant inasmuch as I give *no weight at all* to contested conciliatory reasoning in setting my credence for conciliationism. Because this response defers fully to myself at one level (the credence level) and defers fully to my disputant at another level (the reasoning level), the response does not clearly privilege either party to the disagreement.

The foregoing reasoning suggests that when I encounter a disagreement over the merits of conciliationism, reducing my credence is not obviously more deferential than remaining steadfast. This is because deference at the credence level trades off with deference at the reasoning level. To the extent that I attempt to defer to my disputant by moving toward a midpoint credence (as equal deference may require in some other domain), I will be nondeferential in my reasoning that grounds the new credence; and to the extent that I attempt to defer to my disputant by minimizing my reliance on any conciliatory rationale, my credence will be nondeferential. And since there is no evident reason for privileging deference at either the credence level or the reasoning level, it seems that the conciliatory commitment to epistemic deference does not supply a reason for favoring any particular response to a disagreement over conciliationism. Conciliatory commitments yield no determinate prescription in this case, leaving me free to base my credence for conciliationism entirely on other evidential and rational factors.

It is important at this point to stave off a potential misunderstanding. I've argued that in a dispute over conciliationism, a steadfast response is deferential to my disputant at the reasoning level. One might protest that steadfastness is deferential only if my dispute is with someone who advocates a steadfast view according to which one ought to "stick to one's guns" in the face of disagreement. Many opponents to conciliationism do not endorse such a view. Recall that advocates of the right reasons view endorse a steadfast response only when one has responded correctly to the first-order, predisagreement evidence. If this view is right, then conciliationism is an irrational position and my remaining steadfast in the face of disagreement over conciliationism is not reasonable. So if my disagreement is with a proponent of the right reasons view, why would my remaining steadfast be deferential at the reasoning level?

The answer is that it is not steadfastness per se but the *nonreliance on a conciliatory rationale* that is deferential. Steadfastness merely results from such nonreliance. So consider a dispute with Elle, who appears to be an epistemic superior to me on epistemological matters and is also an advocate of the right reasons view. Even though Elle thinks that I ought to adopt a credence of 0 for conciliationism, she does not think that I ought to adopt this credence *on the basis of a conciliatory rationale*. She takes such a rationale to be illegitimate. Rather, she thinks that I ought to adopt a credence of 0 for conciliationism because this is what the first-order evidence supports. So my adopting a credence of 0 (or some other low value) on the basis of a conciliatory rationale would involve my relying on reasoning Elle rejects and would on this count be nondeferential. And inasmuch as I avoid relying on such reasoning, I defer to Elle.

At this point, one might retort that there is a more thoroughgoing form of deference to Elle at the reasoning level that is *fully compatible* with deference at the credence level: namely, moving my credence for conciliationism to 0 *not* for conciliatory reasons but because philosophical reflection leads me to think that the right reasons view is correct and conciliationism is wrongheaded. Were I to respond in this way, I would have a deferential credence, and my reasoning would be deferential both because it does not employ any contested conciliatory rationale *and* because I would share Elle's perspective on the merits of the right reasons view. This would be a maximally deferential state, and perhaps conciliationism does give me a reason for preferring this state. Nonetheless, the reason that conciliationism provides for preferring this state cannot be my basis for *adopting* this state. If conciliationism was my basis for the complex action of "adopting a credence of 0 for conciliationism (and 1 for the right reasons view) while refraining from relying on a conciliatory rationale," then I would have to both rely on a conciliatory rationale and refrain from relying on a conciliatory rationale. And this is clearly incoherent. So my main conclusion remains secure: in disputes over conciliationism, my commitment to it does not give me a rational basis for reducing my credence for it.

A practical analogy might help to support the point just made. Suppose that Hugh's principal desire in life is to do what his mother wants him to do. So when deliberating over what career to choose, Hugh asks his mother what she'd prefer. She responds by telling him that she wants him to be a farmer. But she adds that what she wants most is for him to base his career decision on reasons that have *nothing to do* with what she wants. She does not want her desire to play *any* role (however indirect) in influencing Hugh's career choice. His desire to do what his mother wants gives him a reason for preferring a specific outcome, namely, one where he becomes a farmer for reasons that have nothing to do with his mother's wants. This outcome is the one that results in his doing all that his mother wants. But even though his desire to do what his mother wants gives him a reason for preferring this outcome, it is impossible for this desire to be his reason for bringing about this outcome. For suppose it was true that he brought about the outcome of "becoming a farmer for reasons that have nothing to do with Mother's wants" *for the reason that this is what his mother wanted*. In this case, it would have to be true that his mother's wants both did and did not play a role in influencing why he became a farmer, which is obviously incoherent. It seems that in this case, the only course of action that could rationally be based on Hugh's desire to do what his mother wants is to set considerations of her wants aside when deciding what career to pursue. This action satisfies his mother's main wish, and it at least leaves open the possibility that he will ultimately choose to be a farmer for reasons that have nothing to do with her wishes.

The case of disagreement over conciliationism is similar. Conciliationism perhaps gives me reason to prefer the complex action of "decreasing my credence in conciliationism for reasons that are not conciliatory" (since this response seems to be deferential both at the level of credence and the level of reasons). But it is impossible for conciliationism to be my *basis* for this response.

Conciliationism cannot be my basis for reducing confidence in conciliationism on the basis of a nonconciliatory rationale. And reducing my credence for conciliationism on the basis of a conciliatory rationale is not clearly more deferential than refusing to rely on a conciliatory rationale and instead basing my credence for conciliationism on first-order philosophical considerations. If I am right that the aim of epistemic deference does not lead to a determinate prescription in disagreements over conciliationism, then arguably there is nothing arbitrary in setting the concern for deference aside in this situation and basing my credence for conciliationism on other rational factors.

Elsewhere, I give a more extended defense of resolute conciliationism, one that qualifies the view in certain respects and addresses some pressing objections to it.[14] Here, my aim is not to fully develop or defend the position but merely to convince the reader that resolute conciliationism should be on the menu of responses to the self-undermining challenge that deserve to be taken seriously. In the next section, I argue that a viable response to the self-undermining challenge is unlikely to be compatible with full epistemic impartiality on religious matters.

6.3 Implications of the Self-Undermining Challenge for Religious Disagreement

How does the self-undermining challenge bear on religious disagreement specifically? To begin to address this question, consider first the implications of resolute conciliationism for religious disagreement. Initially, it might seem that resolute conciliationism is entirely compatible with impartial deference in the religious domain. While the resolute strong conciliationist does not follow the normal conciliatory prescriptions in disputes over strong conciliationism, doesn't a resolute commitment to strong conciliationism support fully conforming to those prescriptions in other disputes, including those over religious matters? No, it does not. The reason for this stems from the fact that some religious outlooks stand in significant tension with strong conciliationism. And the resolute strong conciliationist cannot show as much deference to religious views that exhibit this sort of tension with strong conciliationism.

While most religious outlooks do not include any explicit stance on the epistemology of disagreement, this does not mean that contested religious views have no bearing on the plausibility of strong conciliationism, or that the truth of strong conciliationism would have no evidential bearing on disputed religious matters. For example, there is arguably a tension between the epistemological commitments of strong conciliationism and Buddhist views on enlightenment. According to a traditional Buddhist picture, in order to achieve the enlightenment that is necessary to escape the cycle of death and rebirth and its attendant suffering, one must overcome

---

[14] Pittard, "Resolute Conciliationism."

the illusion that one has an enduring self.[15] While seeing through the illusion of the self involves much more than merely rejecting the view that there is such a self, confident rejection of this view does seem to be a *necessary* condition for overcoming this illusion. If one is epistemically indifferent between the view that there is an enduring self and the view that there is not such a self, then it seems that one has not achieved full enlightenment. But because many informed people do not accept Buddhist teachings about the self, confident rejection of the view that there is an enduring self is arguably incompatible with the sort of epistemic impartiality required by strong conciliationism. Even withholding judgment on the question of whether there is an enduring self may be incompatible with strong conciliationism, if indeed most people affirm that there is such a self. If some of the doxastic requirements for enlightenment are incompatible with strong conciliationism, and if strong conciliationism is correct, then it follows that someone who is aware of the evidence of religious disagreement and who rationally responds to this evidence cannot achieve (or maintain) enlightenment. But Buddhists typically hold that enlightenment is possible (however difficult it may be to attain) for an informed and rational person. A straightforward reading of Buddhist views would therefore seem to be in conflict with strong conciliationism.

If this is right, then the *resolute* strong conciliationist cannot show significant deference to those who endorse a straightforward Buddhist picture. Oversimplifying, suppose that some Buddhist view B straightforwardly entails that strong conciliationism is false. Now suppose that some strong conciliationist attempts to show deference to her Buddhist disputants by increasing her credence for B. In doing this, she relies on a conciliatory rationale and thus presupposes that strong conciliationism is correct. But in presupposing that strong conciliationism is correct, she also presupposes that B is false. For as I've stipulated, B entails the falsity of strong conciliationism. Thus, her attempt to show deference to her disputants by increasing her credence for B would be entirely *non*deferential at the reasoning level. When deference at the credence level and deference at the reasoning level conflict in this way, resolute conciliationism says that one should set aside the concern of epistemic deference and form one's view on the basis of other

---

[15] For a clear and philosophically rich depiction of early Buddhist views on enlightenment and the sort of ignorance that must be overcome in order to attain it, see Mark Siderits, *Buddhism as Philosophy: An Introduction* (New York: Routledge, 2007), chap. 1.

considerations. Thus, the resolute strong conciliationist should not be moved by her commitment to impartial deference to increase her credence in this particular Buddhist outlook.

It might be pointed out that it is unrealistic to suppose that some Buddhist school of thought could be shown to be unambiguously opposed to strong conciliationism. No complex religious or philosophical tradition admits of exactly one interpretation, and the difficulties of assessing the compatibility between some Buddhist position and strong conciliationism are formidable. Differences in language and cultural lineage should perhaps make one hesitant to conclude that a traditional Buddhist position has clear implications for the states and properties that contemporary Western epistemologists refer to when they talk about "beliefs," "rationality," and so on. Further complications arise when one takes into account the rigorous critiques of the assumption of the sufficiency of linguistic expression that are prominent in many strands of Buddhist thought.

Given these ambiguities, one option that *is* open to the resolute strong conciliationist is to defer to Buddhist thinkers by increasing her credence for an interpretation of Buddhism that is not in tension with strong conciliationism. But even if no one claimed to be able to definitively rule out such an interpretation, it might be the case that many Buddhists would judge this version of Buddhism to be highly implausible. In this case, it might not be deferential for the strong conciliationist to adopt a high credence for an interpretation of Buddhism that is not in tension with strong conciliationism. To see this, imagine that there are just two interpretations of Buddhism, *B1* and *B2*. *B1* rules out strong conciliationism, while *B2* is not in tension with it. Suppose that most Buddhists are confident that either *B1* or *B2* is true, but they have very little credence for *B2*. More strongly, imagine that most Buddhists have a very low conditional credence for *B2* on the supposition that either *B2* is true or Buddhism is false. Now suppose that you are a strong conciliationist who wants to show proper epistemic deference to your Buddhist interlocutors. I've already argued that it would be nondeferential (at the reasoning level) to increase your credence for *B1*. So suppose you increase your credence for *B2* instead, assigning it a credence of, say, 0.5. This too arguably fails to be deferential. Your Buddhist interlocutors think that *B2* is problematic and implausible and that the falsity of Buddhism is much more probable than *B2*. You are hardly giving their thinking significant weight if you hold *B2* to be quite probable and just as likely as the denial of Buddhism. In this hypothetical example, resolute conciliationism arguably prevents you from showing impartial deference by giving significant credence to Buddhism.

Is Buddhism unusual among religions in the degree to which it appears to be in tension with strong conciliationism? I don't think so. Consider one more example. According to the definition of Christian faith of Reformation theologian John Calvin, faith involves "a firm and certain knowledge of God's benevolence toward us."[16] It seems reasonably clear that in the present context of systematic religious disagreement, epistemic impartiality on religious matters is incompatible with a "firm and certain" belief in God's benevolence. So if rationality demands that one exhibit epistemic impartiality, as the strong conciliationist maintains, then a suitably informed person cannot rationally maintain firm and certain belief in God's benevolence. Since irrational conviction cannot be an instance of knowledge (at least according to most philosophers), then it would seem to follow from strong conciliationism that those who are informed about religious disagreement cannot have Christian faith as Calvin has defined it. Yet proponents of a Calvinist conception of Christian faith affirm that such faith is available even to highly informed individuals. It seems, then, that at least a certain brand of Calvinist Christianity is incompatible with strong conciliationism. Given this incompatibility, the resolute strong conciliationist cannot show as much deference to Calvinist Christians as he shows to other similarly qualified thinkers whose religious views are not in tension with strong conciliationism.

Ironically, the resolute *weak* conciliationist who *rejects* any sort of radical impartiality requirement may be able to show greater deference in the religious domain than the resolute *strong* conciliationist who *accepts* a radical impartiality requirement. The weak conciliationist acknowledges the possibility of partisan justification (i.e., justification that does not depend on the availability of dispute-neutral support). Thus, the weak conciliationist can acknowledge the possibility that an informed person could rationally maintain confident religious belief in the face of disagreement. For example, a rationalist weak conciliationist like myself could allow for the possibility of Buddhist enlightenment or knowledge of God that is grounded in genuine insight and is therefore not defeated in the face of disagreement worries. Thus, weak conciliationism does not stand in tension with such religious perspectives on knowledge in the same way that strong conciliationism does.

---

[16] John Calvin, *Institutes of the Christian Religion*, ed. John T. McNeill, trans. Ford Lewis Battles, vol. 1 (Louisville: Westminster John Knox Press, 1960), 551.

For this reason, a resolute commitment to weak conciliationism will not limit the degree of deference that can be shown to these religious views.[17]

I'll now briefly consider the implications for religious disagreement of other responses to the self-undermining challenge. As I argued in section 6.1, the conciliationist cannot plausibly hold that principles like WAN are totally misguided, since conciliationism would be unmotivated if one rejected interlevel coherence requirements. But perhaps WAN does stand in need of a minor correction that will resolve the self-undermining problem. In particular, a corrected version might say that one should not give any weight to the prescriptions of norm N in situations where N modestly recommends positive credence for some view that entails that N is false. As already suggested, I think it is likely that applying such a corrected form of WAN would be functionally equivalent to a procedure that assigns positive credences only to *resolute* disagreement norms (which do not issue modest prescriptions in the first place) and then applies an *unmodified* version of WAN. If this is right, then the option of revising WAN to prevent self-undermining would limit religious deference in exactly the same ways as following resolute strong conciliationism.

Finally, what about strong conciliationists who hold that one faces a rational dilemma in deciding what credence to assign to strong conciliationism? Can these strong conciliationists reasonably pursue full epistemic impartiality in the religious arena? Perhaps. If violating WAN is the best option in this rational dilemma, then the strong conciliationist's best approach might be to decrease confidence in provisional strong conciliationism while continuing to fully conform to provisional strong conciliationism in religious disputes. The conciliationist who took this approach could show significant deference even to religious views that are straightforwardly inconsistent with strong conciliationism. But it is not clear that this would in fact be the best option. Perhaps the option that would be least problematic would be to allow one's conciliatory position to self-undermine and to refrain from applying a conciliatory policy. In this case, the best approach would involve little to no deference on religious matters. Alternatively, the best of the rationally deficient options might be to believe and follow resolute strong conciliationism

---

[17] Of course, there may be *other* factors that limit how much the resolute rationalist weak conciliationist should defer to these other views. For example, insight into the greater rational merits of one's own perspective might make significant deference inappropriate. But when such insight is lacking, resolute commitment to weak conciliationism will not itself significantly constrain religious deference.

(despite the alleged arbitrariness of that view). Again, I see no clear way of adjudicating between these possibilities on the supposition that the strong conciliationist faces a genuine rational dilemma.

6.4 The Plurality Approach to Religious Impartiality

Thus far, I've argued that a viable response to the self-undermining challenge facing strong conciliationism may not be rationally compatible with a commitment to full impartiality in the religious domain. I now set aside worries posed by the self-undermining challenge in order to discuss another reason why religious impartiality proves to be elusive. I will argue that in attempting to identify the doxastic stance on religious matters that best accords with the goal of impartiality, the strong conciliationist must take a stand on a range of questions that cannot be settled in a religiously impartial manner. Even if all sides were in agreement that epistemic impartiality is a legitimate ideal, it seems that there is no clearly impartial way to go about pursuing that ideal.

How should one go about determining the stance on some contested matter that best accords with the aim of epistemic impartiality? I'll begin by considering a simplistic approach to epistemic impartiality that, while obviously naïve, is a useful starting point for my discussion. To illustrate the approach, imagine that Charlotte has reasoned through a tricky multiple-choice math problem on her homework assignment. There are three choices, A, B, and C. Charlotte thinks that C is correct, though she can see a certain line of reasoning that would support A and a certain line of reasoning that would support B. These alternative ways of thinking about the problem look faulty to her, but she is not fully certain in this judgment. So she decides to form her opinion in an impartial manner, without giving any special weight to her way of reasoning about the question. To do this, she polls 99 friends, so that she knows how 100 different people (including herself) answer the multiple choice question. After the poll, she learns that 30% get answer A, 30% get answer B, and 40% get answer C.

Suppose Charlotte thinks that, on average, she and her friends are more reliable than they would be if they just guessed at random. Conditional on this assumption being correct, the distribution of opinion among Charlotte's friends would seem to provide evidential support to the hypothesis that C is the correct answer. Suppose, for example, that Charlotte and her friends are 40% reliable in this situation (which is just slightly better than the 33% that would result from random guessing) and that they all formed their views independently of one another. Given these assumptions, this 30/30/40 distribution of opinion is *much* more likely conditional on C being correct than on A or B being correct. In fact, if Charlotte starts with an indifferent credence of 1/3 for each answer and then conditionalizes on the information about the distribution of opinion, her updated credence that C is correct will be approximately 0.90.[18] As this example illustrates, given a large enough polling sample, modest pluralities can provide very strong confirmation of a particular view.[19]

I'll call Charlotte's method of arriving at an impartial credence the "plurality approach."[20] It says that one should start from some sort of neutral prior credences that are indifferent across a menu of options and then, using a reliability estimate for an average thinker in the population, conditionalize on information about the distribution of opinion among the sample of those polled.

Discovering that some view enjoys a plurality among those sampled from class or group G provides evidential confirmation for the view only to the extent that one is confident that a plurality of G favors the correct view. Say that G is "collectively correct" when this is the case. If G is collectively correct, then the probability that a plurality of a randomly sampled subset of G favors the correct view converges on 1 as the size of the sample increases. If some false view enjoys a plurality among the members of G, then one could say that G is collectively incorrect. If one knows G to be collectively incorrect, then learning that some view enjoys a plurality among some arbitrary sample of G will serve to *disconfirm* that view. It is, of course, not uncommon for there to be situations where a group of thinkers is collectively incorrect in this way.

---

[18] The probability of any particular realization of the 30/30/40 distribution conditional on A or B being correct is $0.4^{30} \cdot 0.3^{70}$, whereas the probability of any particular realization of this distribution conditional on C being correct is $0.4^{40} \cdot 0.3^{60}$. Using Bayes's theorem, the probability that C is correct given the information about everyone's opinion (which results in a 30/30/40 distribution) is $(0.4^{40} \cdot 0.3^{60}) \cdot 1/3 \, / \, (1/3 \cdot (0.4^{40} \cdot 0.3^{60}) + (1 - 1/3) \cdot (0.4^{30} \cdot 0.3^{70})) \approx 0.899$.

[19] Condorcet's jury theorem shows that, when there are just two options, the probability that the majority view is correct rapidly approaches 1 as the number of voters increases, assuming that each voter has a reliability that is better than random chance. This theorem has been generalized to support trusting the plurality in cases where there are more than two options. See Christian List and Robert E. Goodin, "Epistemic Democracy: Generalizing the Condorcet Jury Theorem," *Journal of Political Philosophy* 9, no. 3 (2001): 277–306.

[20] Thomas Kelly discusses the implications that this sort of plurality approach would have for *philosophical* disagreements in "Disagreement in Philosophy: Its Epistemic Significance," in *The Oxford Handbook of Philosophical Methodology*, ed. Herman Cappelen, Tamar Szabó Gendler, and John Hawthorne (Oxford: Oxford University Press, 2016), 374–393.

Suppose, for example, that Charlotte's math question was selected from a book entitled *Trick Questions: Math Problems Even Your Smart Friends Will Probably Get Wrong.* In this case, it might be reasonable to assume that her typical friend will do worse than a random guesser, and that the 40% plurality of people who chose answer C is the group of people who fell for the "trick." One situation where even a group of ideally rational thinkers will be collectively incorrect is one where the evidence supports a false conclusion and is therefore misleading. When the evidence supports a false conclusion about p, then someone who forms a belief about p that perfectly accords with the evidence is guaranteed to have a false belief about p.

In contexts where the evidence could be misleading, one cannot dismiss the possibility that even rational agents are collectively incorrect. In such contexts, there will typically be a ceiling on the degree to which a view can be confirmed by a plurality. For example, suppose that everyone agrees that there is a 10% probability that the evidence bearing on whether or not there is an afterlife is misleading (and that this probability is independent of whether or not there actually is an afterlife). In this case, even if the most trustworthy thinkers judge that the evidence points to an afterlife, your credence that there is an afterlife should not exceed 90%. For you should reserve at least 10% credence for the possibility that these thinkers are collectively incorrect on this question (in virtue of misleading evidence). And on the supposition that they *are* collectively incorrect, the fact that they believe in the afterlife would serve to disconfirm that hypothesis.

One way of bypassing complications raised by the possibility of misleading evidence for p is to apply the plurality approach not to p itself but to the higher-order question of whether the evidence supports p, or to the question of whether the belief that p is rational. (Many, of course, would say that these questions amount to the same thing.) Even if ideally rational thinkers are collectively incorrect concerning p in situations where the evidence is misleading, it seems that such thinkers will still be collectively correct with respect to the question of whether believing that p is rational (or supported by the evidence). With respect to this higher-order proposition, there need not be a ceiling on the degree of confirmation that can result from the distribution of opinion.

So when one considers how to apply the plurality approach in the religious domain, it will be useful to apply the approach to higher-order propositions about the evidential support of religious outlooks, rather than to the outlooks themselves. Doing so allows one to bypass complications raised by the possibility that the evidence bearing on first-order religious questions is misleading.

With this clarification in place, consider what doxastic stance would be supported if one attempted to use a crude plurality approach to arrive at impartial credences on religious matters. A 2010 Ipsos poll of over 18,000 adults found that 45% of "global citizens" believed in a "God or a Supreme Being," 6% believed in "many Gods or Supreme Beings," 18% didn't believe in any sort of God or Supreme Being, and 30% answered that they either didn't know what they believed, or sometimes believed and sometimes did not believe.[21] Suppose one assumes that global citizens are collectively correct in their assessment of whether it is reasonable to believe in God or gods and that individuals who believe in God also believe that it is reasonable to do so. In light of this assumption, the crude partiality method would seem to provide significant support to the reasonability of believing in a single God or Supreme Being. For given such a large sample size, even a modest plurality could provide overwhelming support to the position endorsed by that plurality.

The same survey also found that 51% of respondents believed in some sort of afterlife. Multiple conceptions of the afterlife received significant support, with 19% believing in heaven and hell; 2% believing in heaven alone; 23% believing in an afterlife but "not specifically heaven or hell"; and 7% believing in reincarnation. The portion that denied the existence of an afterlife was 23%, and 26% reported that they "don't know what happens."[22] Again assume that the respondents to the poll were better than a random guesser in answering the question of what view the evidence adequately supports (making it overwhelmingly likely that they are collectively correct). What doxastic stance would result from applying the plurality approach?

Here, one confronts a difficulty facing the plurality approach. When considering the fine-grained choices, the option that has the plurality (by a slim margin) is agnosticism, the choice of 26% of respondents. But if one partitions the options more broadly and focuses on the choices of afterlife, no afterlife, and agnosticism, the first option enjoys a much more significant plurality. Thus, the recommendations of the crude plurality approach are sensitive to

---

[21] Ipsos, "Belief in Supreme Being(s) and Afterlife Accepted by Half (51%) of Citizens in 23 Country Survey, But Only 28% Are 'Creationists,'" news release April 25, 2011, https://www.ipsos.com/en-us/news-polls/ipsos-global-dvisory-supreme-beings-afterlife-and-evolution.

[22] The choices here make a philosopher squirm. It is, of course, entirely compatible to *believe* in an afterlife *and* maintain that one doesn't *know* what happens.

how one partitions the space of possible views. I will not here consider possible solutions to this partition-sensitivity problem. Still, it is plausible that someone attempting to follow the plurality approach should take the large plurality of those who believe in some sort of afterlife as providing significant confirmation of the view that the evidence supports believing in some sort of afterlife (even if not a specific vision of what the afterlife involves). So suppose one looked to the plurality approach as one's starting point for thinking about how to form impartial credences in the religious domain. One would then have some reason to think that a belief in theism and the afterlife would be included in the religiously impartial stance.[23]

A key premise in the argument for disagreement-motivated religious skepticism developed in chapter 1 was the following:

NO INDEPENDENT REASON: S does not have a good dispute-independent agent-neutral internal reason for believing that S's process of religious belief formation is significantly more reliable than the collective reliability of the processes that (otherwise) epistemically qualified people use to form religious beliefs.

Consideration of the plurality approach has given an initial reason to question NO INDEPENDENT REASON. Go back to the example of Charlotte and the math problem. The fact that more people agree with her initial answer C than with either of the other two options gives Charlotte a reason for thinking that her way of reasoning about the question is superior to alternative ways of reasoning that led to different results. And this reason for being confident in answer C is independent of any contested details of the reasoning she used to arrive at the problem. Likewise, suppose that subject S is someone who is inclined to affirm theism and an afterlife on the basis of first-order evidence. S can then point to facts about the distribution of opinion as *dispute-neutral* support for the claim that S has reasoned about religious matters in a way that is more likely to be reliable than alternative ways of thinking that support contrary conclusions. Or, if S is *not* inclined toward theism and a belief in the afterlife on the basis of the first-order evidence, S might point to facts

---

[23] For an in-depth consideration of whether widespread theistic belief provides significant evidential support to theism, see Thomas Kelly, "Consensus Gentium: Reflections on the 'Common Consent' Argument for the Existence of God," in *Evidence and Religious Belief*, ed. Kelly James Clark and Raymond J. VanArragon (Oxford: Oxford University Press, 2011), 135–156. Kelly considers many of the issues explored in this chapter, including bias and independence in the formation of people's religious views.

about the distribution of opinion as reason to change her view and adopt high credences for theism and the reality of an afterlife.

Of course, the simplistic plurality approach is objectionably crude. Objections to the approach will be discussed shortly, and more sophisticated ways of pursuing religious impartiality will be considered. But however crude the partiality approach may be, applying it to the religious domain is instructive since it powerfully illustrates a crucial point: even when there is nothing approaching consensus in a given domain, confidence in one of the views on offer may nonetheless be justified on impartial grounds. For this reason, it cannot simply be taken for granted that religious skepticism is the stance that best accords with epistemic impartiality. The disagreement skeptic must argue for this position, and in doing so, she should (presumably) identify the flaws in the plurality approach and point to a superior method for identifying the impartial epistemic stance.

6.5 Religious Upbringing, Bias, and Group Reliability

The most glaring problem with applying the plurality approach in the religious domain is that it does not take seriously enough the possibility that human beings are collectively incorrect in their assessment of central religious questions. Even when one focuses on the second-order question of what religious outlook is best supported by the evidence (thereby bypassing worries raised by misleading first-order evidence), there are multiple reasons why the correct view may not receive a plurality of support. First, questions about the rational merits of religious outlooks could be tricky in a way that leads many thinkers to converge on a mistaken answer. For example, perhaps a tendency to remember the remarkable and unexpected (and to forget the mundane and unsurprising) biases one's attempts to assess the plausibility of different views about divine providence and intervention.

Second, if individuals do not form their beliefs independently of one another, then this can greatly add to the probability that a group is collectively incorrect. Returning to the example of Charlotte, imagine that of the 99 friends polled, only three made up their own minds about the math question. The other 96 were lazy and arrived at their view this way: they began calling Charlotte's other friends until they found someone who already had a view on the problem and then they adopted that view as their own.

Eventually, all 99 friends would have opinions, but each of these opinions would be traceable to one of only three independently formed opinions. It's intuitively clear (and mathematically demonstrable) that a plurality of support is less evidentially significant when the beliefs in the sample exhibit this sort of interdependence.[24] Forming a belief by free-riding on someone else's opinion may on average be just as reliable a method as arriving at a belief by thinking through the problem for oneself. But the frequent employment of this method would make the overall distribution of opinion less informative, since a plurality of support would not indicate significant independent corroboration.

It is obvious from experience and observation that the religious beliefs of most people are heavily influenced by the beliefs of their family and wider community. Typically, ties to a religious community influence a person toward a favorable assessment of that religion. Of course, the influence needn't always work in that direction. A child with contrarian tendencies or whose relations with his parents are severely strained may be disposed to *reject* the religion of her upbringing. But in general, someone is much more likely to subscribe to a particular religious view if his parents affirmed the view than if they did not. Given this influence of religious upbringing on future religious opinion, it's easy to imagine that religious outlooks with the right sort of cultural momentum could gain far more adherents than would be expected among some idealized group of "independently minded" people. Thus, the possibility that human beings as a whole are collectively incorrect with respect to central religious questions does not seem all that far-fetched.

Granted, from the fact that *individuals'* convictions are highly influenced by family and their particular community, it does not automatically follow that a plurality of support is of little evidential significance. If no religious community enjoyed a population advantage for reasons that are epistemically irrelevant, then the fact that individuals are influenced toward the religion of their own community would perhaps not significantly detract from the probability of collective correctness. If this influence was equally strong in all religious communities, then the various influences would offset one another. The religion that enjoyed a plurality would arguably have it on account

---

[24] Krishna K. Ladha, "The Condorcet Jury Theorem, Free Speech, and Correlated Votes," *American Journal of Political Science* 36, no. 3 (1992): 617–634.

of being the most likely option among those who were moved by evidence to give up the view espoused by their families and communities.

But of course religious views have *not* at any point enjoyed this sort of equal footing, and distorting cultural influences do *not* nicely cancel one another out. The sizes of religious communities have been influenced by historical contingencies that appear to be epistemically irrelevant. Some religions have enjoyed greater political support than others. Some religious views were represented among early industrial societies; others were not. Some religious views encouraged procreation; others did not. Some religious views have been highly represented among nations with colonial ambitions; others have not. These factors have greatly shaped the populations of various religious communities, which means that the distribution of religious opinion may be significantly distorted by factors that are epistemically irrelevant. If a false religious view has significantly benefited from such epistemically irrelevant factors, *and* if the influence exerted by a person's religious upbringing is especially strong (as it seems to be), then there is very good reason to doubt the collective correctness of humanity on religious matters.

In the preceding paragraphs, I have intentionally avoided saying that religious believers are *biased* by their religious upbringing. The influence of religious upbringing that confounds the plurality approach need not be the result of rational "bias," at least not in any of the normal pejorative senses of that word. For example, religious upbringing could heavily influence even unbiased thinkers by shaping the testimonial evidence that they receive. People in a religious community will tend to be exposed to testimonial evidence that is weighted in favor of their community's beliefs. Granted, this does not explain why so many maintain their childhood beliefs even after they are informed about rich testimonial traditions in competing religious communities. If the arguments of chapter 4 are correct, it is not rational to give more weight to some particular strand of testimony merely because it is the strand of one's own community. If one wants to give a charitable explanation of why even people who are informed about religious pluralism often stand by the views of their upbringing, it is not clear that one can appeal to differences in testimonial evidence.

A more promising way of explaining the influence of religious upbringing without positing rational bias might be to appeal to differences in the kinds of insights that are fostered by differing religious and irreligious ways of life. Consider the following hypothetical example. Imagine that those who are raised in atheist homes as well as those who are raised in theist homes

typically have experiences of insight into the moral significance of horrendous suffering and that this insight provides strong prima facie support for atheism. But those who are raised by theists and who participate in
worshiping communities frequently experience a second sort of apparent insight. This apparent insight concerns the tremendous value and beauty that
results when God finds ways of bringing significant good out of otherwise
horrible situations. And imagine that this alleged insight is an important
reason why more theists aren't moved by the evidence of horrendous evil to
give up their theism.

Even if this latter theistic insight were genuine, atheists might be fully
reasonable in suspecting that theists do not enjoy any sort of actual insight that significantly lessens the force of the atheistic argument from evil.
Atheists' appreciation of the weighty reason for preventing horrendous
suffering might lead them to think it more likely that theists are severely
biased on religious matters than that there is in fact a reason that would
justify God in creating a world with so much horrendous suffering. In a
scenario like this, both sides could be responding reasonably to the insights
available to them, in which case neither side would in fact be rationally biased. Nonetheless, the influence of upbringing on belief would allow for an
epistemically unfortunate sort of upbringing to be perpetuated from generation to generation.

The strong influence of religious upbringing on future religious conviction does not *entail* that many human beings are biased on religious
matters. That being said, I have little doubt that most of us *do* exhibit biases
in our religious thinking that are the result of our religious (or irreligious
or nonreligious) upbringing. Many of us, no doubt, are liable to overlook
or underestimate certain problems in the perspectives passed on to us by
family and loved ones. Does this mean that it would have been epistemically better to have been raised in a household with parents who, with the
aim of minimizing religious bias in their children, refrained from encouraging them toward any religious (or explicitly irreligious) way of life? This
question is not completely tangential to my present concerns: if religious
bias could be minimized by an upbringing that aims at religious neutrality,
then perhaps the problem that bias poses to the plurality approach could be
corrected for by focusing on those who have the most epistemically desirable sort of upbringing.

I am skeptical of the suggestion that there are impartial epistemic reasons
to prefer an upbringing that aims at religious neutrality for the purpose

of minimizing religious bias.[25] There is no reason to think that simply ignoring religious questions in the education of children is an effective way of preventing religious bias. Parents who ignore questions about God, cosmic purpose, life after death, and so on implicitly communicate that such questions are not very important—less important than other topics that might receive significant attention in the home, for example math, politics, and environmental stewardship. This appearance of a lack of concern is likely to have significant effects on a child's affective orientation toward religious commitment and religious exploration. The resulting bias could be significant.

Of course, silence is not the only available strategy to those who want to minimize religious bias in their children. Parents who are religious but who want to mitigate bias could communicate to their children the importance they attach to religious matters while nonetheless refusing to commend their own religious outlook or involve their children in worshiping communities. To encourage religious investigation without endorsing particular viewpoints, such parents could provide resources that describe religious and irreligious outlooks, as well as the justifications offered for such outlooks. They could also ask questions that would help spur their children to arrive at their own well-considered answers using these resources. Might this sort of "nondirective encouragement and capacity building" be the epistemically optimal approach? One obvious worry about this approach is that any attempt to promote and facilitate religious exploration will inevitably reflect certain religious biases (since equal attention cannot be given to every specific religious outlook, to every question of potential religious significance, and so on). While this is no doubt true, a proponent of nondirective encouragement and capacity building could maintain that these biases are much less pronounced than the biases that are likely to be the result of a more traditional religious upbringing where the parents inculcate children into their views and religious way of life (if any).

---

[25] For a helpful overview of epistemic considerations *in favor* of religious "indoctrination," see Charlene Tan, "Michael Hand, Indoctrination and the Inculcation of Belief," *Journal of Philosophy of Education* 38, no. 2 (2004): 257–267. Tan defends religious "indoctrination" by arguing that noncritical acceptance of orienting worldview beliefs is crucial to the healthy rational development of children. This being said, Tan opposes religious indoctrination that stifles a spirit of open-minded religious questioning. Tan rightly sees that a handing down of religious beliefs does not need to involve protective efforts at squashing questions and intellectual exploration, and that a religious upbringing can nurture those very intellectual virtues that are needed for religious investigation that is appropriately empathetic, critical, and imaginative.

But beyond worries about different levels of attention given to various outlooks and questions, there are other subtle and more significant worries about the religious assumptions underlying this entire approach to religious education. For example, suppose that parents with confident theistic beliefs adopt the approach of nondirective encouragement and capacity building. Would this not communicate that promoting the autonomy and authenticity of their children's religious thinking is more important than helping them to have the kind of vital relationship with God that is made possible by faith and by participation in a worshiping community? After all, the nondirective approach promotes autonomous religious thinking at the cost of delaying theistic commitment and making such commitment less likely. Furthermore, wouldn't this nondirective approach suggest that the parents believe that they can have an appropriately intimate and honest parent-child relationship even if a parent does not often express those of her hopes and desires that are theologically grounded—for example, the desire to experience an increasingly intimate relationship with God in this life and beyond, the hope that her children will love God above all else, and so on? And wouldn't this in turn suggest that these hopes and desires are not all that significant or central to the parent's identity? It seems to me that these highly contestable perspectives are implicitly communicated by the nondirective approach. As a result, such an approach might produce very significant religious bias.

Even if formation in a religious community tends to produce rational bias favoring the outlook of that community, such formation may also help to counter other biases that people are prone to suffer from and that may cripple one's thinking on moral and religious matters. Which biases? The answer, of course, will depend on one's religious perspective. But possible answers include: a natural inclination to believe in an enduring self despite a failure to observe some substance that persists throughout one's development; a tendency toward self-justifying rationalization that makes it difficult to acknowledge the seriousness of one's moral failings; a related tendency to understate the rigors of moral requirements; a myopia that causes one to discount the importance of the afterlife (should it exist) and to overweight the significance of one's earthly existence; an inflated sense of how well one understands reality (which causes one to be overly dismissive of the idea of ineffable reality and of entities that are not directly perceived); a bias against worldviews that are "nonscientific" in virtue of their narrative form; and so on and on. The individual and corporate practices commended by a particular religious tradition are offered as therapies that can help to counter putative biases such as these, biases that may severely distort one's evaluation of religious questions.

Finally, participation in the practices of a religious community may also make possible forms of insight that are not easily available to those who are not engaged in the same sort of practices. And the epistemic advantages of such insight could be greater than the epistemic disadvantages stemming from religious bias. Recall Otto's suggestion, briefly discussed in chapter 5, that religious worship helps to elicit the affective experiences that help one to more fully grasp the concept of holiness. If this is right, then sustained engagement in worship may help someone to develop the conceptual repertoire that is essential if one is to adequately understand and evaluate certain core religious claims. In light of this sort of possibility, it might be that the epistemically ideal approach would be for parents to raise children in the right sort of religious community while also emphasizing intellectual humility, showing openness to doubt and challenging questions, and encouraging empathetic attempts to understand the merits of other positions.

To be clear, I am not claiming that the practices of any religious community *do* counter various forms of rational bias or facilitate insight that improves one's assessment of religious questions. My point is that it would be question-begging to expect those raised outside any particular religious tradition to be less affected by religious bias and therefore better positioned to fairly evaluate religious questions.

6.6 The Defector Approach

The distribution of religious opinion within a group is less informative to the extent that the distribution is distorted by belief interdependence and bias. If there is some impartial way of identifying a population less affected by these distorting factors, then perhaps one can make headway in identifying an impartial doxastic stance by applying the plurality approach to this particular population. In the previous section, I expressed pessimism about an approach that focuses on those with the ideal sort of upbringing. A different approach would be to focus on the subset of individuals who have broken with the views of their religious communities. The rationale for this approach is that when one has chosen to adopt some religious belief or doxastic stance other than the view of one's community, one's choice between the *other* religious/irreligious options is likely to be more sensitive to the evidence and less biased by emotional attachments to a particular community.

Call this basic strategy the "defector approach." What verdict would the defector approach support? The answer is not entirely clear. A Pew Research Center survey of more than 35,000 Americans conducted in 2007 and then again in 2014 found that belief in God declined from 92% to 89% from 2007 to 2014.[26] If one assumes that this change reflects the numerical growth of atheism in the United States (and not just young atheists being counted as adults in 2014 who didn't count as adults in 2007), and if one assumes a steady adult population during those 7 years, then this would amount to an astounding 4.7% annual growth rate of atheism in the United States. This proportional shift toward atheism may suggest that individuals who *do* overcome the bias stemming from their upbringing are more likely to accept atheism than some alternative theistic perspective. So when one limits one's attention to the US population, one has reason to suspect that the defector approach provides a dispute-independent reason for assigning a higher credence to atheism than to theism.

Unfortunately, however, the defector approach does not always point in the same direction when one looks at other populations. Consider the case of the growth of Christianity in China. It is difficult to acquire data on religious belief in China, and estimates of the size and growth of the Christian population can differ greatly. But one moderate view from Purdue sociologist Fenggang Yang estimates that there were 66 million Christians in China in 2010 and that this number is growing at a rate of 7% annually.[27] As China was recently the most secular country in the world (according to Yang), this growth is coming almost entirely at the expense of secular atheism.

It might be argued that one should simply apply the defector approach to the combined populations of religious switchers or converts in China, the United States, and any other place for which the relevant data is available. But in reality, the opposed results when one looks at China and the United States point to a shortcoming in the defector approach that is almost as severe as the

---

[26] Pew Research Center, "U.S. Public Becoming Less Religious," November 3, 2015, https://www.pewforum.org/2015/11/03/u-s-public-becoming-less-religious/.

[27] Fenggang Yang, "When Will China Become the World's Largest Christian Country?," *Slate*, December 1, 2014, http://www.slate.com/bigideas/what-is-the-future-of-religion/essays-and-opinions/fenggang-yang-opinion, accessed November 14, 2016.

problem with the plurality approach applied to the entire population. Just as there can be biases that distort one's *initial* religious stance, there can also be biases that distort one's choice of a *new* religious stance. In particular, there can be cultural pressures that influence one's religious views in a particular direction for what are arguably epistemically irrelevant reasons.

In the case of China, some have argued that the growth of Christianity there is at least in part due to the perception that the cultural, scientific, and economic success of the West must stem at least in part from its Christian heritage.[28] Looked at cynically, one might take this to imply that the strength of Christianity in China is not primarily a reflection of its rational merits but instead is largely a product of a highly contingent connection between Christianity and nation-states with strong cultural and political institutions and advanced economies.

This sort of genealogical skepticism may also be used to question the evidential significance of the growth of atheism in the West. Consider, for example, Charles Taylor's attempt to explain why atheism presents itself as the only live option for many Western intellectuals. Taylor argues that post-Enlightenment Western intellectual culture has increasingly valorized the "courageous acknowledger of unpalatable truths."[29] Breaking from the comforting narratives one received in childhood has been seen as a sign of maturity, glorious autonomy, and intellectual mastery, while persisting in the hopeful convictions of one's youth has been seen as pitiably childish. In light of these evaluations of skepticism and faith, Taylor suggests that it is hardly surprising that many intellectuals would break from faith for reasons that were objectively far less compelling than they thought them to be. Of course, many who have made the break have given expression to a kind of mourning for the loss of their childhood faith and a nostalgia for the "magical" world-view they once inhabited. But this mourning and nostalgia is are not evidence that the unbelievers have been in fact biased *toward* religious faith. Rather, the feeling of loss associated with giving up their faith has been, somewhat paradoxically, part of what has made giving up that faith so appealing. Precisely because faith has been characterized as soothing and comfortable, leaving the faith can be understood as exhibiting the sort of intellectual

---

[28] "Cracks in the Atheist Edifice," *Economist*, November 1, 2014, https://www.economist.com/briefing/2014/11/01/cracks-in-the-atheist-edifice.

[29] Charles Taylor, *A Secular Age* (Cambridge, MA: Harvard University Press, 2007), 562.

courage that is so highly esteemed in the cultural contexts that have absorbed Enlightenment values. The recent growth in atheism can perhaps be understood as an intensification of this trend as trust in traditional institutions has eroded and as more and more young people find themselves in cultural contexts where Enlightenment values are taken for granted.

I do not wish to defend either of these broadly sociological accounts of on the one hand the ascendancy of Christianity in China or on the other the rise of atheism in the West. The point is that such accounts have been taken seriously by thoughtful scholars and that the defector approach is hopelessly naïve unless one attempts to correct in some way for biasing influences on the direction of conversion. Now, one might simply argue that some of these genealogical accounts are more plausible than others. If one could differentiate between the social contexts where the direction of conversion is heavily biased and those where it isn't, then maybe one could apply the defector approach to the limited contexts where the biasing influences are not especially significant. But while it is no doubt true that some of these genealogical accounts are better than others, can one go very far in distinguishing between the plausible and implausible accounts while maintaining one's religious impartiality? Is there, for example, a religiously neutral way of comparing the strength of proatheism bias in certain Western contexts and pro-Christian bias in certain segments of Chinese society?

I doubt it. Taylor, a Catholic, sees the valorization of unbelief and the scorn directed toward traditional faith as a source of bias, one that makes it easy to overlook significant weaknesses in the arguments for unbelief and that therefore biases people's judgment. Those who do not think that the arguments for unbelief *have* significant weaknesses feel no pressure to give a nonevidential explanation of why unbelief thrives in the educated West. Even if they acknowledge that cultural biases tilt toward atheism in the academy, for instance, they may doubt that these biases exert much in the way of epistemically illegitimate pressure. Whatever dismissive attitude there may be toward traditional religious faith may be thought to be primarily a *result* of people's evidential assessment rather than an *influence* on that assessment. It seems that one's views on the strength of these biasing factors cannot be cleanly separated from one's views of the evidential merits of atheism and competing religious views. If that is right, then different religious and irreligious groups are unlikely to reach agreement about which group of defectors can be assumed to be sufficiently untainted by rational bias.

6.7 The Expert Approach

A more promising way of modifying the plurality approach in order to correct for the possibility of collective incorrectness is to look to the views not of humanity as a whole but of *experts*—those best positioned to assess the rational standing of various religious outlooks. As a general rule, experts in a given domain are less likely to arrive at a false conclusion because of the trickiness of a question. And since they are more informed and perhaps in possession of superior intellectual virtue and skill, they are more likely to overcome the distorting influence of various biases. When confining one's attention to experts, it is more reasonable to think that collective correctness is a likely possibility. What I will call the "expert approach" says to focus on the group of those who are most expert in assessing the central claims of competing religious perspectives and to follow the recommendations of the plurality approach as applied to this narrow group. As long as the number of experts in one's sample is not too small, then a plurality in favor of a particular view should provide substantial dispute-independent confirmation of that view.

Which experts should one turn to? One initially plausible proposal (at least to a philosopher of religion like myself!) is that one should turn to professional philosophers of religion. Philosophers are practiced in the sort of slow, tentative, and careful reasoning that has the best chance of being resistant to bias. And philosophers of *religion* are of course well versed in the many arguments and counterarguments that are brought to bear on religious matters.

So, what do philosophers of religion typically believe with respect to religious questions? One source of data bearing on this question is a large 2009 survey of the views of professional philosophers conducted by Bourget and Chalmers at 99 leading departments.[30] The data collected by Bourget and Chalmers allow one to view the distribution of opinion among philosophers as a whole as well as the distributions within particular specialties. Among the philosophers of religion who responded to the survey, 72% accepted or leaned toward theism while only 19% accepted or leaned toward atheism. Taken by itself, this fact would arguably provide very strong impartial

---

[30] David Bourget and David Chalmers, "The PhilPapers Surveys: Results, Analysis, and Discussion," http://philpapers.org/surveys/. See their discussion at David Bourget and David J. Chalmers, "What Do Philosophers Believe?," *Philosophical Studies* 170, no. 3 (2013): 465–500.

evidence for theism. But matters appear more complicated when one looks not only at the views of philosophers of religion but also at the distribution of opinion among all professional philosophers. Among all of the professional philosophers who responded to the survey, 73% accepted or leaned toward atheism, while only 15% accepted or leaned toward theism. If the sample who responded to this survey is representative, then the distribution of opinion among philosophers as a whole is essentially a reverse image of the distribution among specialists in philosophy of religion.

Normally, one would expect a straightforwardly positive correlation between the expertise level of a particular group and the group's collective reliability (at least when focusing on the higher-order question of evidential support, so as to correct for worries about misleading evidence). But the expected positive correlation between expertise and reliability does not hold in this case. Suppose atheism is true. In this case, group reliability increases when one narrows one's focus from the general population to professional philosophers (a more expert group). But then group reliability *decreases* when one narrows one's focus even further and looks to the group of philosophers who, based on their area of specialization, are most expert of all. Or, if theism is true, then group reliability initially decreases when one looks to the more expert group of professional philosophers; reliability increases only when one looks to the smaller group of those specializing in philosophy of religion.

This unusual nonlinear relationship between expertise and collective reliability raises doubts about the appropriateness of the expert approach in this context. The rationale for the expert approach is that expertise tends to mitigate the influence of bias. But it seems plausible that in this particular case, narrowing one's focus to those with a particular level of expertise may cause one to focus on a group where the influence of bias is stronger rather than weaker.[31]

In considering how best to explain the odd mismatch between the religious opinions of philosophers of religion and philosophers as a whole, it will be helpful to distinguish between two ways the distribution of opinion in a

---

[31] To be sure, a perverse association between a certain level of expertise and bias isn't the *only* possible explanation. It could be that the philosophical case for atheism initially looks strong but ultimately proves to be quite weak when subjected to careful scrutiny. In this case, philosophers as a whole might tend to be atheists because, unlike many in the general population, they have at least engaged in the initial philosophical assessment of theism (which is enough to overcome prejudices favoring theistic belief), while a plurality of those same philosophers would have ultimately endorsed theism if they had explored the scholarship pertaining to the theism/atheism debate more fully.

group could be biased. First, the individual opinions of many members of the group could be rationally biased in a common direction due to the influence of epistemically irrelevant factors (like the cultural prestige of some religious outlook). Call this "influence bias." It has been the focus of the discussion so far. Second, the distribution of opinion in a group might be subject to what is often called "selection bias." It distorts the distribution of opinion regarding p in group G when an individual's opinion regarding p makes it more or less likely that the individual becomes a member of G, even if one holds fixed the individual's epistemic credentials.

To illustrate selection bias, imagine that among those who are well suited for philosophical work, professional philosophy is a more attractive option to atheists than to theists. There are many imaginable reasons why this might be the case, some more realistic than others. There might be certain career possibilities outside philosophy that are a good fit for philosophically inclined theists but not philosophically inclined atheists—for example, theology, biblical scholarship, or ministry in a synagogue or church. Or perhaps theists think (rightly or wrongly) that the climate of academic philosophy is hostile or dismissive toward theism (and theists) and are for this reason less likely to pursue careers in philosophy (however talented they may be). More positively, atheists might be especially drawn to philosophy if they perceive that philosophical circles are unusually hospitable to their views and concerns. In addition, theists might feel less need to pursue philosophy in order to satisfy their desire for philosophical discussion of ethically and existentially significant topics, if such discussion is a regular feature of religious communities. Or perhaps satisfied theists are less likely than their atheist counterparts to feel the urgency of certain worries and questions that lie at the heart of academic philosophy and for this reason theists are less likely to pursue careers in philosophy. If some such possibilities hold, then the distribution of opinion among professional philosophers would be at least somewhat distorted by selection bias.

Even if selection bias tilts the distribution of opinion among philosophers as a whole toward atheism, it is easy to see how selection bias could have the opposite effect in the specialization of philosophy of religion. It would not at all be surprising if those who believe in God are, on average, more interested in working on philosophical questions concerning the existence and nature of God. It is perhaps more exciting and gratifying to defend a positive view of the world, especially one that is of existential significance, than to attack such a view. And those who think that theism is not only false but *obviously* so are not likely to feel that work in philosophy of religion is "cutting edge" work with a vital future.

I suspect that selection bias does help to explain the prevalence and distribution of theistic belief among philosophers. But one might think that it cannot be the whole story and that influence bias must also play a significant role. After all, even if atheists are more likely to self-select into philosophy than theists, and even if theists are more likely to self-select into philosophy of religion than atheists, it *is* possible for philosophers to change their views. One would expect that over time philosophers who are free of influence bias would converge toward the correct view, however different their initial stances may have been. Doesn't the lack of convergence suggest that at least one group is afflicted by influence bias that prevents them from properly assessing the rational and evidential merits of theism?

Many do think that influence bias plays a significant role in explaining the discrepancy between the distribution of opinion among philosophers as a whole and the distribution of opinion among philosophers of religion. In their article "Diagnosing Bias in the Philosophy of Religion," Paul Draper and Ryan Nichols argue that there is a strongly distorting protheism bias in philosophy of religion. As evidence of this, they point to polemical language, narrowness of focus (with much work devoted to traditional theism, and very little devoted to nontheistic religious options such as pantheism, deism, Buddhism, etc.), and frequent invocation of theological considerations in the assessment of philosophical views (e.g., concerning the nature of God).[32] Draper and Nichols do not think that most philosophers of religion consciously understand themselves to be engaging in an "apologetic" enterprise, one that aims to strengthen believers and win converts through philosophical arguments. The charge is rather that the identity of these philosophers as believers (most typically *Christian* believers) results in affective attachments that lead to unconscious bias. Draper and Nichols cite research by Edwards and Smith that shows that emotional investment in a view intensifies the cognitive biases that lead one to denigrate opposing evidence and to seek out confirming evidence (and to treat it uncritically).[33] The tendency of emotional investment to exacerbate cognitive bias poses a special challenge to philosophers of religion, according to Draper and Nichols,

---

[32] Paul Draper and Ryan Nichols, "Diagnosing Bias in Philosophy of Religion," *Monist* 96, no. 3 (2013): 420–446.

[33] Kari Edwards and Edward E. Smith, "A Disconfirmation Bias in the Evaluation of Arguments," *Journal of Personality and Social Psychology* 71, no. 1 (1996): 5–24.

since "philosophers of religion, having committed their whole lives to a body of religious doctrine, have strong emotions about their religious beliefs."[34] Draper and Nichols note:

> Philosophers of religion occupy a unique place in philosophy. When a four-dimensionalist [about the nature of persistence through time] comes to give up that theory [four dimensionalism], she does not get fired from her job (as would most religious philosophers of religion at religious institutions were they to change their minds about theism). When a four-dimensionalist gives up her theory, she does not put her marriage in serious jeopardy (as would religious philosophers whose spouses believe that the truth of Christianity is the foundation of their marriage). Finally, the sort of emotional convictions that religious philosophers of religion have about things like God's existence or Jesus's forgiveness of sins obviously has no parallel in the case of four-dimensionalists.[35]

These observations are apt, and I do not doubt that the influence of cognitive bias is intensified in the assessment of questions in philosophy of religion for precisely the reason Draper and Nichols have identified.

Nonetheless, it is far from clear how this legitimate concern should be taken into account when attempting to pursue epistemic impartiality in religious matters. For starters, there are accounts of emotion-driven bias that cut in the other direction, with Charles Taylor's account described in the previous section being one example. Given certain default secular assumptions in the academy, adopting a religious identity is *unimaginable* for many secular academics. The idea, for example, that discussions of human welfare should properly include as a matter of central importance a concern for one's relationship with God (and not one's health, happiness, and prosperity as conventionally understood) is, for many secular academics, so foreign as to be incredible. Many conventionally religious academics on the other hand have already internalized certain apparently secular concerns and ways of thinking, so that it is easy for them to imagine adopting a secular way of living, speaking, and thinking. For example, for many Christian academics, it is all too natural to think about human welfare in secular terms. The challenge for these Christian academics is to consistently think of welfare in a

---

[34] Draper and Nichols, "Diagnosing Bias in Philosophy of Religion," 428.
[35] Draper and Nichols, "Diagnosing Bias in Philosophy of Religion," 428.

way that comports with their Christian convictions, however out of step this may be with the default assumptions of their professional context. Given the dominance of secular ways of thinking and speaking in the academy, I think there is an asymmetry in the *imaginability* of inhabiting the "other" perspective. Plausibly, this asymmetry is a biasing factor that illegitimately disposes many academics toward ways of thinking that align with secular atheism. How should the strength of this biasing factor be compared to the strength of the biasing factors cited by Draper and Nichols? At present, I see no way of answering this question in an impartial manner.

Suppose it is conceded that the biasing factors that tend to reinforce theistic belief have a greater potential to distort rational thinking than the biasing factors that tend to encourage atheistic belief. This still does not settle the question of how much weight should be given to the views of philosophers of religion in comparison to the views of philosophers as a whole. How should a greater risk of bias among philosophers of religion be compared to the epistemic benefits that come with their greater degree of specialization? Many, no doubt, will think that the risk of bias more than offsets the specialization advantage. The greater degree of specialization, on this view, simply affords one more time and energy to devote to rationalizing a bankrupt religious outlook. When the very accomplished philosopher Peter Unger, who has not worked significantly in philosophy of religion, takes up the question of the existence of an "almighty benevolent creator," he writes: "well, really, now, how credible do you find [the hypothesis of a benevolent almighty creator]? Or, for that matter, how credible do you find any proposition even just remotely like that traditional, or traditional-sounding, doctrine? Well, you can put me down for a big loud, 'Not Very!' And, boy, it's a veritable landslide here, as the case for a negative answer is almost absurdly overwhelming."[36] Unger then spends two pages cataloguing the quantity and intensity of human and animal suffering, both present and throughout evolutionary history, before pausing to ask the reader: "How horrible is *that*, I ask you, all you who dare to uphold, quite as heartlessly propounded as it's brainlessly affirmed, any claim that's even the least bit like the utterly incredible BENEVOLENT AL-MIGHTY CREATOR [Unger's label for the theistic hypothesis]? It's certainly too horrible, I tell you, to have anyone believing, even the least bit reasonably, or the least bit intelligently, anything remotely like that extremely dubious doctrine."[37] Contrast this candid assessment with the judgment of Peter van

---

[36] Peter Unger, *All the Power in the World* (New York: Oxford University Press, 2006), 506.
[37] Unger, *All the Power in the World*, 507.

Inwagen (a metaphysician who also specializes in philosophy of religion), who argues that the atheistic argument from evil is a "philosophical failure." In saying that the argument is a failure, he means that an audience of suitably neutral and reasonable agnostics who heard the most compelling version of the argument and the most compelling rebuttal would not find any decisive reason to accept the argument's conclusion.[38] (It should be noted that, according to van Inwagen, nearly all philosophical arguments for substantive conclusions are failures in this sense.)[39]

Unger and van Inwagen are both accomplished and respected metaphysicians. No doubt Unger has respect for much of van Inwagen's philosophical work. But since van Inwagen is a theist, Unger appears to be committed to thinking that van Inwagen is not being the least bit reasonable in holding his religious views. More strongly, on Unger's view, van Inwagen holds them heartlessly and brainlessly. Quite clearly, Unger would heartily endorse Draper's and Nichols's suggestion that the theistic beliefs of a great many philosophers of religion are deeply infected by bias. For this reason, Unger would deny that the greater degree of specialization of philosophers of religion is a good reason to trust their judgment on the merits of theism. Obviously, though, this assessment of Unger's is based on his assessment of the arguments for and against theism—it is not a conclusion he pretends to support on the basis of impartial considerations alone.

Is there a way to apply the expert approach while correcting for bias in a way that all parties can recognize as religiously neutral? Again, while I have no decisive argument that this cannot be done, the prospects for it appear to be quite bleak.

6.8 The Challenge of Deep Disagreement

The challenge I am hitting upon here is less obvious in the sort of two-person disagreements that are typically the focus of the disagreement literature. In two-person disagreements, even if both parties disagree on how to measure their epistemic credentials impartially, there is still the uncontroversial fact that one person believes that p and one person denies that p. Given this symmetry, it is plausible to maintain that there is one uniquely impartial

---

[38] Peter van Inwagen, *The Problem of Evil* (Oxford: Oxford University Press, 2006), 47.
[39] Van Inwagen, *The Problem of Evil*, 53–54.

credence—0.5—that best comports with impartiality even if nothing else can be agreed on. But now consider a multiperson case where the noncontroversial facts are these: two people endorse view A, three people endorse view B, four people endorse view C, and A and B are similar views and thus arguably different versions of some broader perspective that is opposed to C. At this level of abstraction, there is no single credence that obviously best comports with the aim of impartiality. Should one give greater credence to C because it enjoys a plurality? Should one give greater credence to the disjunction A or B because these views are similar and the disjunction of A and B wins a majority? And how extreme should one's credence for the winner be?

There is no plausible way of determining the impartial credence on the basis of this bare information alone. Because the situation does not exhibit symmetry, even in the most stripped-down description of the case, determining the impartial credence requires that one know more information about the likely reliability of the thinkers involved and about the relative significance of any potentially biasing factors at play. If views A, B, and C support incompatible views on how to assess the influence of these potentially biasing factors, then one arguably cannot take a stand on the likely influence of various biasing factors without in some way presupposing some stance on A, B, and C, the very outlooks under dispute. So in attempting to specify the information one needs in order to identify impartial credences, one violates impartiality.

I've focused on second-order disagreements concerning the strength and significance of certain biasing factors. But this is only one area of disagreement that contributes to the elusiveness of impartiality. For example, religious views may also have different implications for what factors are epistemically irrelevant and therefore a source of bias. And competing religious views may also have different implications for questions about what skills, virtues, and experiences most contribute to the sort of expertise that positions one to reliably assess religious questions.[40] In this respect, religious disagreement is quite different from controversies in many other domains. Consider two civil engineers with opposing views on the merits of some bridge proposal. They will most likely agree on what sort of training and cognitive capacities are required to be a good judge of engineering questions and on what institutional signals (for example, academic degrees, professional experience,

---

[40] John Pittard, "Conciliationism and Religious Disagreement," in *Challenges to Moral and Religious Belief: Disagreement and Evolution*, ed. Michael Bergmann and Patrick Kain (Oxford: Oxford University Press, 2014), 80–97.

publications) serve as reliable evidence that someone possesses these capacities. In many religious disputes, however, whether the disputed proposition is true or false has significant implications for the question of which qualifications best position one to assess the disputed proposition. To mention just one example, some Buddhists maintain that meditative disciplines are required in order to loosen the grip of certain illusions and to enable an adequate appreciation of the truth of Buddhist teachings concerning the nonexistence of a personal self. Those who have considered Buddhism and who are not convinced are unlikely to accept that engagement in these meditative disciplines is an important qualification for an assessment of Buddhist claims.   ·

Religious disagreements are "deep" precisely because the primary questions under dispute have implications for second-order questions that must be resolved in order to make headway in identifying impartial credences. In many mundane disagreements, something like the expert approach can be unproblematically applied. But these approaches do not yield determinate prescriptions in deep disagreements.

6.9 The Imprecision Approach

While the approaches to epistemic impartiality considered thus far fail to identify an impartial stance in the religious domain, perhaps the reason for this is that each approach aims to identify *precise* credences that best comport with the aim of epistemic impartiality. In contexts of deep disagreement, perhaps the aim of epistemic impartiality is best served by refraining from assigning precise credences and instead adopting a more thoroughly agnostic stance. I explore this possibility in this section.

A traditional Bayesian framework assumes that a rational agent's doxastic state can be represented by a single probability function that assigns a precise credence to every proposition toward which the agent has a doxastic attitude. This framework supplies a useful model for theorizing about rational norms and for measuring the significance of various pieces of evidence. However, it is plausible that one's doxastic attitudes are often not so precise as to be accurately represented by a single number. Consider your doxastic attitude toward the proposition that there are, at the exact moment you read this, more than two people in the world who are typing the word "Cantabrigian." Call this proposition CANTAB. After a moment's reflection on CANTAB, you most likely have some doxastic attitude (or multiple doxastic attitudes) on the matter. For example, you might think that the probability of CANTAB is not especially close to 1. You might also think that the probability is not extremely close to 0. But whatever your initial take on the matter may be, it is perhaps doubtful that there is a single number between 0 and 1 that most accurately represents your doxastic attitude toward CANTAB.

Given this apparent imprecision of many of one's doxastic attitudes, many philosophers have argued that a single probability function cannot adequately represent the doxastic state of a normal human being. Many have endorsed instead an "imprecise credence" framework that models an agent's doxastic state not with one probability function but with a *set* of probability functions. The set of probability functions that represents the agent's doxastic state is called the "representor." If all the functions in the representor assign proposition p credence c, then the agent's credence for p is c. If the functions in the representor are not unanimous in their assignments for p, then the agent does not have a determinate credence for p (though she may have a determinate credence range for p). Agents who do not have a determinate credence for p are sometimes said (somewhat misleadingly) to have an "imprecise credence" for p, one that ranges over the probability values for p that are assigned by the many probability functions in the agent's representor.

Proponents of the imprecise credence framework do not only claim that their framework is superior to the standard framework in representing the doxastic states that people *in fact* exhibit; they typically claim that the imprecise credence framework is also superior as a model of the doxastic states that people rationally *ought* to exhibit. As James Joyce urges, "since the data we receive is often incomplete, imprecise or equivocal, the epistemically *right* response is often to have opinions that are similarly incomplete, imprecise or equivocal."[41]

Since the imprecise credence framework is offered as a model of a *rational* agent's doxastic state, it is legitimate to ask about the rational significance of various elements of the model. How should one characterize the rational significance of the individual probability functions in a rational agent's representor? What are these functions, exactly? Here is one way to think about these functions, a way that comports well with the epistemological motivations for the imprecise credence framework. While one often asks

---

[41] James M. Joyce, "A Defense of Imprecise Credences in Inference and Decision Making," *Philosophical Perspectives* 24, no. 1 (2010): 283.

what subjective probability or credence for some proposition is supported by one's evidence, perhaps this question is based on a faulty premise. Perhaps one should think of evidence's role not primarily as one of *supporting credences* but as one of *ruling out various probability functions*. If this is right, then cases where the evidence is rightly said to "support" some precise credence *c* for *p* are simply a special sort of case where the evidence has ruled out as inadmissible all probability functions that do not assign credence *c* to *p*. If one thinks of evidence as playing this "ruling out" role, then the probability functions in a rational agent's representor are simply those probability functions that are rationally compatible with her evidence. If it is rational for you to have a precise credence of 0.5 that a coin about to be tossed will land heads, then this means that your evidence has ruled out all probability functions that assign this proposition a probability other than 0.5. If you rationally ought to have an imprecise credence for CANTAB, then the probability functions not ruled out by your evidence will not be unanimous in the probability assigned to CANTAB.

Having introduced the imprecise credence framework, I am now in a position to describe the "imprecision approach" to identifying an impartial doxastic stance on religious questions. For the sake of argument, suppose that the expert approach is the best way to identify impartial credences in contexts where disagreement is not deep and where that approach can be applied in a genuinely impartial way. I've argued that the expert approach can lead to divergent outcomes when it is applied to religious disagreements. This is because applying the expert approach requires answering certain questions about the relevant epistemic credentials and biases, and one's answer to these questions cannot be cleanly disentangled from one's stance on the primary religious questions under dispute. This problem might lead one to conclude that the approach is of no help to the strong conciliationist who is assessing the significance of religious disagreement. But if one is supportive of the imprecise credence framework, then the expert approach may be of use in the religious context after all. If a rational agent does not need to exhibit precise credal attitudes, then she is not forced to choose between the inevitably partisan applications of the expert approach. The imprecision approach to impartiality says that she should allow *all* of these partisan applications to define her doxastic state. More precisely, the imprecision approach says that her representor should consist of the probability functions that result from the various partisan ways of applying the expert approach (or whatever approach is correct in contexts where the disagreement is not deep). Such an agent rejects all probability functions that do not result from an attempted application of the expert approach, and beyond this she has no further opinions.[42]

It is important to note that the probability functions in an agent's representor are not weighted in any way. If they were, then it would be possible to identify a single credence for some religious hypothesis that is the weighted average of the credence values assigned to that hypothesis by the functions in the agent's representor. And this credence would fail to be impartial since the question of how to impartially weight the various probability functions in the representor would succumb to the same difficulties that proved to be the downfall of the approaches considered earlier. Presumably, any weighting should assign more weight to those probability functions that are endorsed by a significant number of experts. But then one is again required to settle questions about the nature of expertise in the religious domain, and one will also need to correct for belief interdependence and religious bias. I've argued that there is no impartial way to do this. The promise of the imprecision approach is that it sidesteps questions about how much weight should be assigned to the views of any particular person or group. To invoke Yogi Berra, when one comes to a fork in a road, one takes it. In this context, this doesn't mean arbitrarily choosing among the many *partial* ways of calculating impartiality; rather, all such ways are incorporated into an imprecise and deeply agnostic attitude.

Epistemologists do not agree on whether imprecise credences are rationally permissible (much less rationally required).[43] Objections to imprecise credences *in general* will also constitute objections to the imprecision approach to impartiality. I do not myself think that one *ought* to respond to

---

[42] While I am considering credal imprecision as an option in deep disagreements when standard conciliatory approaches fail to deliver a determinate credence, some philosophers have argued that the proper response to peer disagreement should always involve imprecise credences. For example, see Lee Elkin and Gregory Wheeler, "Resolving Peer Disagreements through Imprecise Probabilities," *Noûs* 52, no. 2 (2018): 260–278.

[43] There is a lively debate among epistemologists and decision theorists concerning the rationality of imprecise credences. Adam Elga offers a decision theoretic objection which says that imprecise credences license irrational betting behavior; "Subjective Probabilities Should Be Sharp," *Philosophers' Imprint* 10, no. 5 (2010): 1–11. Two forceful responses to Elga's worries include Sarah Moss, "Credal Dilemmas," *Noûs* 49, no. 4 (2015): 665–683; and Susanna Rinard, "A Decision Theory for Imprecise Credences," *Philosophers Imprint* 15, no. 7 (2015): 1–16. Objections to imprecise credences that are more persuasive (to my mind) are developed in Roger White, "Evidential Symmetry and Mushy Credence," *Oxford Studies in Epistemology* 3 (2010): 161–186. James Joyce responds to White in "A Defense of Imprecise Credences in Inference and Decision Making." For a good rebuttal of Joyce's treatment of White's worries, see Brett Topey, "Coin Flips, Credences and the Reflection Principle," *Analysis* 72, no. 3 (2012): 478–488.

ambiguous evidence with imprecise credences, since on my view a thinker who has a precise but tentative credence for *p* does not thereby commit herself to thinking that her evidence unambiguously supports that credence and no other. I am also skeptical of the claim that the imprecise credence framework is a better *descriptive* model than the precise credence framework. The imprecise credence framework does not avoid artificial imprecision, since there are still precise endpoints of the range of credences that are assigned to *p* by functions in the representor. It may be artificial to depict some agent as having a precise credence value for CANTAB at any given time, but it is equally artificial to depict that agent as having some precise credence *range* for CANTAB at any given time. One could avoid apparently arbitrary endpoints by having *all* credal values from 0 to 1 assigned by some function in one's representor (perhaps including the endpoints 0 and 1, or perhaps not). But this proposal faces severe objections, as Susanna Rinard persuasively argues.[44] As I have little to add to the debate concerning the imprecise credence framework, I will not attempt to assess the objections to it here.[45] At present, I will simply explain my reason for doubting that the imprecision approach succeeds in delivering the kind of impartiality sought by strong conciliationists.

Suppose that as a result of my applying the imprecision approach, my representor includes some probability functions that assign high probability values to religious view *R1* as well as other probability functions that assign equally high probability values to some opposing religious view *R2*. Since the probability functions in a representor are not weighted in any way, my doxastic state is more deeply agnostic than the state of someone with precise credences who assigned approximately equal credence values to *R1* and to *R2*. In adopting the deeply agnostic and noncommittal state commended by the imprecision approach, do I thereby show impartiality in the degree to which I defer to the adherents of *R1* and to the adherents of *R2*? Arguably not. The influence of the *R1* group on my doxastic state is equal to the influence of the *R2* group, and this equality of influence can amount to a kind of partiality. For example, suppose that the number of *R1* adherents is much smaller than the number of *R2* adherents. Since my noncommittal stance does not give any more weight to *R2* despite *R2*'s greater share of adherents, my doxastic

[44] Susanna Rinard, "Against Radical Credal Imprecision," *Thought: A Journal of Philosophy* 2, no. 2 (2013): 157–165.
[45] Interested readers may begin by exploring the references in notes 43 and 44.

stance arguably shows partiality to the *R1* group by giving it an influence that far outstrips its size. Alternatively, suppose that the two groups are approximately equal in size but that the epistemic credentials of the *R2* group are superior to the credentials of the *R1* group (though there is no dispute-neutral way to determine this). In this case, my noncommittal doxastic stance would be unduly influenced by the less qualified group, and I would show significant partiality to the members of that group by giving them influence that is out of proportion to their qualifications. Because the imprecision approach avoids controversial attempts to weight groups according to their size or epistemic qualifications, the approach will often support a stance that gives undue influence to some group. Granted, there is no impartial way to determine *which* group is being given undue influence over one's doxastic state. But throwing up one's hands and refusing to make tough choices does not amount to showing impartiality. Rather, it shows partiality to groups who, while perhaps lacking in either size or genuine epistemic credentials, have self-favoring outlooks that support inflated estimates of their own epistemic significance.

6.10 Conclusion

Even if I am right that the imprecision approach fails to deliver full epistemic impartiality, this is not by itself a sufficient reason for rejecting the approach. After all, none of the approaches examined in this chapter can be used to identify a fully impartial doxastic stance. And perhaps the case could be made that the imprecision approach best realizes the aim of epistemic impartiality, however imperfectly. But if a strong conciliationist rejects the imprecision approach, then the strong conciliationist must seek to identify some relatively precise doxastic attitude that seems to comport well with the aim of epistemic impartiality in the religious domain. This task will require the strong conciliationist to assess the epistemic credentials of various groups, and to make judgments about sources of bias and their significance. Because religious outlooks bear on questions about the relevant epistemic credentials and sources of bias, the strong conciliationist's attempt to take credentials and bias into account will inevitably fail to be religiously impartial. For this reason, impartiality proves elusive.

This does not mean that there is no point in attempting to pursue the ideal of epistemic impartiality (albeit while relying on assumptions infected with partiality). Applying something like the expert approach and adjusting one's credences accordingly results in one showing *more* impartiality than if there had been no attempt to defer to other thinkers. But there is no guarantee that a sincere pursuit of impartiality will eventuate in a religious skepticism that lacks confidence with respect to any contested religious matter. The pursuit of epistemic impartiality could lead some thinkers to adopt a healthy degree of confidence in a controversial religious or irreligious outlook.

7

Unpalatable Conclusions
and Deliberative Vertigo

The discussion up to this point has been focused on whether someone who is aware of facts about religious disagreement can rationally believe, or assign a high credence to, some controversial religious outlook. But answering this may not settle the question of whether such a person can rationally maintain robust religious commitment. While a religiously committed life often involves doxastic confidence in the core tenets of some religious outlook, it's clear that a religiously committed life does not *require* such confidence. For example, someone who does not believe that God exists could nonetheless seek God's guidance in prayer, worship in a community of believers, evaluate his life according to the standards of a religious tradition, and hope for the fulfillment of God's (alleged) promises. As Jewish theologian Norman Lamm puts the point, one can maintain *functional* faith—a commitment to obeying God and seeking right relationship with God—even as one's *cognitive* faith is significantly weakened by doubt.[1] Lamm acknowledges that functional faith may require for its rationality that one assign some nontrivial degree of probability to religious teaching. But this doxastic threshold might be modest, and once it has been reached, the functional commitment could be uncompromising. Lamm supports this point with a dramatic analogy:

> Even if the probability is quite low it can, if the issue is momentous enough and means enough to me, lead to a commitment that is absolute and in which probability thereafter plays no role. Thus, I see a child drowning, and I discern that there is a chance of saving him. Now I may estimate my swimming ability, the child's chance of survival until I reach him, and my chance of saving him, as very low, and the risk to myself as high. Yet, the fact that I believe there is some chance of saving him and that I consider it eminently

[1] Norman Lamm, "Faith and Doubt," *Tradition: A Journal of Orthodox Jewish Thought* 9, no. 1/2 (1967): 30.

worthwhile to do so, leads me to a commitment: I jump in and swim to the child. My discernment was plagued with serious doubts and grave misgivings. My commitment, however, is not one whit less total than if I had been a champion life-saver; I will spare no effort in achieving success.[2]

Someone who stakes her life on the truth of some religious outlook clearly counts as having a robust religious commitment, even if that commitment is *nondoxastic* in that it does not involve high doxastic confidence in the outlook to which she is committed.[3]

Might nondoxastic religious commitment be rational even if controversial religious beliefs are defeated on account of disagreement? Some thinkers heartily commend nondoxastic religious commitment as a fully satisfactory option that is unthreatened by disagreement-motivated religious skepticism.[4] But for reasons I develop in this chapter, I do not share this enthusiasm. While nondoxastic religious commitment does not involve believing all of the core tenets of the religion to which one is committed, rational nondoxastic religious commitment arguably *does* require having justification to believe certain propositions concerning the practical value of the particular kind of commitment in question. Because these latter propositions are also contested, it is by no means obvious that a believer's favored form of nondoxastic religious commitment will evade disagreement skepticism. I present two worrying arguments on this front. According to the first

---

[2] Lamm, "Faith and Doubt," 31.

[3] Some are prepared to say of such a person that she has *faith* that the outlook in question is true, since having faith that *p* does not require believing that *p*. For an example of a nondoxastic account of "propositional" faith (i.e., faith *that* something is the case), see Daniel Howard-Snyder, "The Skeptical Christian," *Oxford Studies in Philosophy of Religion* 8 (2017): 142–167. For my purposes, it does not matter whether one endorse this particular terminology of faith. What is crucial here is that religiously committed persons need not believe the religious outlook that provides the framework they use for evaluating their lives, structuring ritual practices, making decisions, and so on.

[4] For example, Schellenberg, who characterizes "faith" as a kind of nondoxastic commitment, points to faith as the ideal option for religious people faced with skeptical worries raised by disagreement. He writes: "religious belief is justified only if there is no *better* response, and . . . even a religious person should say that there *is* a better response to the deliverances of religious experience than belief—namely, the faith response. The faith response is quite capable of embodying religious commitment; it too provides incentive for 'staying in the game'; it is more accommodating of the investigative imperative than belief since not as likely to be 'blinkered' by a psychological sense of sureness and conviction; and, indeed, it is quite compatible with religious skepticism. The complex consisting of propositional and operational faith can draw on a wider range of good-related considerations to defend itself, and obviously circumvents altogether the objection to continued belief represented by diversity since not itself a species of the belief response. Thus such faith seems tailor-made for someone who wishes to persist in a religious commitment while recognizing the force of skepticism." *The Wisdom to Doubt: A Justification of Religious Skepticism* (Ithaca: Cornell University Press, 2007), 179.

argument, those who adopt a cost-benefit approach to religious decision-making (like expected utility theory) and who adopt impartial credences are likely to find that their approach to decision-making requires adopting a highly unpalatable form of religious commitment. The second and more troubling argument concludes that no religious or irreligious commitment is rational if strong conciliationism is correct. According to this argument, the normative uncertainty that results from the pursuit of epistemic impartiality brings about a "deliberative vertigo" that prevents rationally grounded engagement in any religious or irreligious way of life.

7.1 Cost-Benefit Reasoning and Unpalatable Conclusions

For sake of discussion, I assume in this chapter that strong conciliationism is correct and that, for anyone familiar with the basic facts about religious disagreement, doxastic confidence in any controversial religious position is unjustified. More specifically, for any specific religious outlook R (excluding unnatural disjunctive outlooks like "Islam *or* atheism"), the impartial reasoning that accords with strong conciliationism requires assigning R a credence value less than 0.5. I'll label this latter condition *doxastic defeat*.

Could it be rational to commit to one's preferred religious (or explicitly irreligious) way of life even given doxastic defeat? It might initially seem obvious that the rationality of nondoxastic religious commitment is not threatened by doxastic defeat. Schellenberg, for example, maintains that nondoxastic faith "obviously circumvents altogether the objection to continued belief represented by diversity" for the reason that such commitment is "not itself a species of the belief response."[5] On further reflection, however, it is by no means clear that one's favored form of nondoxastic religious commitment will avoid the skeptical threat posed by disagreement.

To illustrate how doxastic defeat may have unpalatable implications for religious decision-making, I assume in this section that rational choices accord with a "cost-benefit" approach to decision-making like that of expected utility theory. I do not think that expected utility theory or any similar cost-benefit approach is a fully adequate framework for religious decision-making. Nonetheless, it is plausible that cost-benefit considerations ought to

---

[5] Schellenberg, *The Wisdom to Doubt*, 179.

have significant bearing on one's religious commitments, even if they are not the whole story. So the problem explored in this section cannot be ignored on the grounds that expected utility theory is not a fully adequate decision theory in the religious domain.

The starting point for the discussion in this section is Pascal's famous "wager argument" for belief in God, an argument that is the target of some well-known and formidable objections.[6] Pascal's original argument may be a failure, but if one weakens some of the assumptions that drive his argument, the cost-benefit framework he employs may very well be useful in assessing the rationality of religious commitment. Moreover, that framework might give significant support to the conclusion that a great many religious people are rational in their religious commitments. But I will argue that this conclusion is threatened by the supposition of doxastic defeat. In light of doxastic defeat, there is reason to worry that cost-benefit considerations strongly support forms of religious commitment that many would find repugnant.

I will focus on the wager argument as it has typically been presented by philosophers. The wager argument presupposes that *if there is a God*, then all and only those who put their faith in God will receive eternal salvation, and that eternal salvation is infinitely valuable to the recipient. (I will consider the implications of questioning this presupposition shortly.) According to the argument, one has two choices: wagering on God (by putting one's faith in God), or refraining from wagering on God. If an agent wagers on God and God exists, then she will enjoy infinite "utility" (where utility is a measurement of the agent's well-being). If she wagers on God and God does not exist, then she will enjoy some finite amount of utility $f1$ (the utility resulting from the goods enjoyed, and evils suffered, over the course of a life of finite duration). If she does *not* wager on God, then she will enjoy some finite utility $f2$ if God exists or some finite utility $f3$ if God does not exist. These claims are reflected in the decision matrix presented in table 7.1.

If one accepts this matrix as an adequate characterization of one's choices and possible outcomes, and if one grants that one should maximize expected utility, then it would appear to follow that anyone who has a positive credence for God's existence should wager on God's existence (even if her credence for theism is very small).[7] For as long as there is some small probability

---

[6] Blaise Pascal, *Pensées* (London: Penguin Books, 1995), 121–125. For a good overview of arguments against various versions of Pascal's wager, and a vigorous defense of one version of the wager, see Jeff Jordan, *Pascal's Wager: Pragmatic Arguments and Belief in God* (Oxford: Oxford University Press, 2006).

[7] This result assumes that infinitesimal credence values are excluded.

Table 7.1 Decision matrix for Pascal's wager argument

	God exists	God does not exist
Wager	∞	$f1$
Do not wager	$f2$	$f3$

assigned to God's existence, the expected utility of wagering will be infinite, while the expected utility of not wagering is guaranteed to be finite.

One criticism of the wager argument, advanced by Alan Hájek, notes that wagering on God is not the only action with an infinite expected utility, even if one takes for granted Pascal's claims about the utilities associated with the various outcomes. A "mixed strategy" that assigns a positive probability to wagering and a positive probability to not wagering also has an infinite expected utility.[8] For example, the strategy "wager if (and only if) the coin I am about to flip lands heads" has an infinite expected utility and therefore cannot be ruled out by appealing to expected utility. In fact, *any* action that has some finite probability (however small) of leading to wagering will have an infinite expected utility. If there is some tiny but positive probability that my cursing God would set in motion a chain of events that would ultimately result in my wagering on God, then the expected utility of my cursing God will also be infinite.

As interesting as this objection is, the (very difficult) problems that infinite utilities pose for expected utility theory are orthogonal to the challenges to rational deliberation raised by disagreement. So I will set Hájek's objection aside. Going forward, I'll make the simplifying assumption that all utilities are finite. As long as the utility benefit from salvation is *extremely* large, a wager argument using finite utilities may still carry significant force. Given a suitably large utility benefit from salvation, wagering on God can have the greatest expected utility even if one's credence for God's existence is extremely small.

A second prominent criticism of the wager argument, the "many gods objection," raises worries that are *not* orthogonal to concerns raised by religious disagreement, since these worries are arguably intensified in light of the assumption of doxastic defeat. Pascal's wager argument assumes that there are only two possible states of the world that one needs to consider when

[8] Alan Hájek, "Waging War on Pascal's Wager," *Philosophical Review* 112, no. 1 (2003): 31.

reflecting on one's religious options: the state where the God of traditional Christianity exists and the state where there is no god at all. According to the many gods objection, an adequate decision matrix must take other possibilities into account. For example, perhaps some version of Islam is true according to which many of those who affirm the divinity of Christ will experience divine judgment, or at least will miss out on the full riches that are available to faithful Muslims. Or perhaps Buddhism is true and enlightenment of unsurpassable worth is attainable only to those who follow a particular Buddhist path.

Different theological perspectives within a given religion may also be relevant to the question of how to wager. Focusing on the example of Christianity, the value of eternal salvation would be less significant to one's present decision-making if Christian universalism was seen as probable, where Christian universalism holds that ultimately everyone is saved through Christ and is welcomed into eternal communion with God (though for some, perhaps only after experiencing some degree of punishment). Less weighty theological debates may also bear on the question of what religious wager should be taken. For example, Christians who think that God does not intervene in the course of nature may think that someone who prays for healings and other sorts of interventions acts in a way that is immature and that trivializes his relationship with God. On this view, to pray for health and practical blessings is to cheapen God's love and miss out on the aspects of the divine/human relationship that are most important. Against this, some Christians contend that God frequently does intervene in miraculous ways, and that in bringing even trivial concerns before God in prayer, one displays confidence in the expansiveness of a divine love that does not disdain even the smallest matters of concern. Because these alternative Christian perspectives rationalize different sorts of wagering (one that prays for "small" matters and one that does not), an adequate decision matrix would arguably need to include additional columns to distinguish between these Christian outlooks as well as additional rows for each form of Christian wagering.

Suppose that one greatly expands the decision matrix, adding columns to represent relevant religious hypotheses and rows to represent many different forms of religious and nonreligious "wagering." While this greatly complicates the practical reasoning that informs one's religious choices, the mere expansion of the decision matrix does not undermine one critical lesson of the wager argument: that the possibility of supremely valuable spiritual rewards can make it rational to commit to a particular religious outlook even if one does not have an especially high credence for that outlook. Given the immensely valuable goods promised by various religions, it is plausible that the action with the highest expected utility will be some sort of religious wager, even if the state of affairs thought to be most likely is one where there are no gods or transcendent religious goods. Moreover, it is likely that for many of Pascal's readers, both during his time and ours, there are only a handful of "live" religious options that receive a significant credence. Thus, the many gods objection does not doom the basic strategy exemplified by Pascal's wager argument.

Much more would need to be said to give a thorough defense of the claim that expected utility considerations can provide support to many religiously committed people, even when a wide array of religious possibilities is acknowledged. But the point I wish to develop here is that on the assumption of doxastic defeat, religious people are much less likely to find support from expected utility theory for their favored form of religious commitment.

Doxastic defeat may undercut an attempt to deploy wager arguments to justify one's favored form of religious commitment for the following reason. Strong conciliationism is likely to require that one assign nontrivial credences to "severe" religious outlooks that one otherwise might not have found plausible, and expected utility calculations will tend to support wagering on a severe outlook when there is a severe outlook that is not assigned a trivial credence. A *severe* religious outlook, as I am using the term, is severe with respect to its views on eternal reward and punishment in that it says that there is a vast gap in the benefit enjoyed by those who have the right religious commitment and those who have the wrong sort of commitment. A *gentle* outlook, in contrast, does not posit extreme differences in the eternal rewards enjoyed by those who wagered differently.

Severity and gentleness come in degrees, and a religious outlook may be gentle with respect to many sorts of religious wagering but severe with respect to others. Despite these complications, the problem posed by severe outlooks in the context of doxastic defeat can be illustrated simply enough. Suppose that there are only three possible states that Rima needs to consider—Gentle God, Severe God, and No God—and she must make a wager that corresponds to one (and only one) of these options. And suppose that the decision matrix shown in table 7.2 accurately represents the utilities that each outlook promises will result from the various possible wagers.

Suppose that, prior to taking into account the evidence supplied by disagreement, Rima assigns the following credences: 0.49 to Gentle God, 0.01

Table 7.2 Rima's decision matrix

	Gentle God	Severe God	No God
Wager on Gentle God	100	1	1
Wager on Severe God	90	100	1
Wager on No God	90	1	2

to Severe God, and 0.5 to No God. Given these credence assignments, the expected utility of wagering on Gentle God is 49.51, the expected utility of wagering on Severe God is 45.6, and the expected utility of wagering on No God is 45.11. In this example, expected utility theory says that Rima should wager on Gentle God, the only theistic perspective that she finds credible. Even though Severe God says that substantial eternal reward is reserved only for those who wager on the correct God, the fact that Rima assigns such a small credence to Severe God accounts for the rationality of committing to the gentler perspective that she finds significantly more plausible.

But if a nontrivial number of apparently qualified thinkers find Severe God to be the most plausible view, it is unlikely that assigning such a low credence to Severe God will be compatible with the impartiality requirements imposed by strong conciliationism. So in a context of doxastic defeat, Rima will likely need to assign a higher credence to Severe God. In this particular example, the expected utility of wagering on Severe God will outweigh the expected utility of wagering on Gentle God when the ratio of Rima's credence for Severe God to her credence for Gentle God is greater than 10/99. So even if she was required to push her credence in Severe God only to 0.05 (while keeping her credence for Gentle God at or below 0.49), this would be enough to make it irrational to wager on Gentle God (assuming that she should maximize expected utility). Because extremely small credences for severe views are less likely to be permissible on the supposition that strong conciliationism is correct, it is quite likely that utility maximizers who accept strong conciliationism will be pushed to wager on some severe religious view even if such a view is assigned a much smaller credence than a gentler option that is thought to be more believable. Even if wager-style argumentation supports religious commitment, in many cases such argumentation will not vindicate commitment to a view that is seen as both plausible and palatable.

A strong conciliationist who does not endorse a cost-benefit approach to religious decision-making might be tempted to dismiss the discussion of this section as irrelevant. But such a reaction would, I think, be overly hasty. The strong conciliationist's commitment to epistemic impartiality will require her to show some deference toward a number of different views about the content of the norms that should guide religious decision-making. Some deference will need to be shown to views that commend a cost-benefit approach. And it is at least plausible that normative views that are assigned a positive credence should have at least some weight in one's decision-making. For this reason, the strong conciliationist cannot dismiss as irrelevant the prescriptions of a cost-benefit approach, or any other approach that has support, before carefully considering how decision-making should proceed in light of disagreement-induced uncertainty about the relevant practical norms. To this question I now turn.

7.2 Normative Uncertainty and Deliberative Vertigo

The strong conciliationist's commitment to impartiality arguably requires uncertainty with respect to the practical norms that bear on religious decision-making. In this section, I begin to explore what implications this kind of normative uncertainty may have for the rationality of religious or irreligious commitment. I argue that the normative uncertainty induced by doxastic defeat may lead to a kind of deliberative vertigo that makes it impossible to rationally pursue any religious or irreligious way of life. As I will explain, it is not the mere fact that one must act in the face of normative uncertainty that undermines the possibility of rational action. The problem is that the doxastic defeat resulting from religious disagreement produces uncertainty not only with respect to the *first-order* norms governing religious decision-making but also with respect to *higher-order* norms that say how one should act in situations where one faces first-order uncertainty (or, more generally, uncertainty at some lower order). This iteration of uncertainty is what threatens to undermine the possibility of rational decision-making.[9]

---

[9] The argument I advance in the following paragraphs is somewhat similar to Peter Unger's argument that radical skepticism about knowledge leads to irrationality. (See *Ignorance: A Case for Scepticism* [Oxford: Oxford University Press, 1978], chap. 5.) Unger argues that rational action requires having a (propositional) reason or reasons for what one does, that having some proposition *p* as a reason requires that one know *p*, and that knowing *p* entails having justification to be absolutely certain that *p*.

A theory about the practical norms that pertain to religious decision-making is likely to be controversial at a number of levels. Even those who agree that some sort of cost-benefit approach is correct will likely be divided by their answers to a number of significant questions, including the following. Should religious decision-making be determined primarily by the costs and benefits that accrue to oneself, or to some select group of people, or are the *total* costs and benefits all that matter? Is well-being the only thing that matters when measuring the goodness of outcomes? Can risk aversion (or risk loving) be rational, or is risk neutrality the only rational position? What moral constraints should be satisfied (if any) that are not already captured by the cost-benefit framework? Among those who reject a cost-benefit approach, a number of competing normative views are likely to be represented. Some views will hold that one has significant relational obligations to God (should God exist). Such views might enjoin one to worship and obey God as characterized by the most plausible version of theism, even if it's fairly likely that God does not exist, and even if other forms of religious commitment (e.g., following a more "severe" God) might have a higher expected utility. Another view might privilege accuracy and hold that one should adopt a religious and/or irreligious commitment that is in keeping with the outlook on religious questions that one takes to be most probable. An alternative position maintains that one should commit to an outlook that one deeply desires to be true, and that can be the object of passionate commitment. It is easy to imagine realistic situations where these and other plausible normative views support a number of incompatible prescriptions.

Supposing that strong conciliationism rightly requires that one assign a positive credence to several of these competing normative positions, how does the resulting normative uncertainty bear on what decisions may be rational? To begin to answer this question, note first that the fact that some subject S is rational in having a very high credence for some correct practical norm is not by itself sufficient to make it rational for S to do some action that she knows conforms to that norm. In other terminology, a rational high credence for some correct norm is not sufficient to *rationalize* S's conformity to that norm.

To see this, consider a situation where (1) S rationally has a credence of 0.9 for some correct practical norm NA (which S knows prescribes action A in her situation) and a credence of 0.1 for norm NB (which S knows prescribes action B in her situation, an action that S knows to be incompatible with A); (2) S knows that her choosing A would be a "moral disaster" conditional on

NB being correct; and (3) *S* knows that her choosing *B* would be wrong but not a "big deal" conditional on *NA* being correct. There are various *second-order* rational norms that offer competing perspectives on how *S* should proceed in this situation involving uncertainty between the competing *first-order* norms *NA* and *NB*. Some thinkers, for example, have endorsed a "hedging" norm that would require *S* to choose *B* in order to avoid moral disaster; others have endorsed a "winner-take-all" norm that would require *S* to choose *A* since this choice is supported by the first-order norm that is assigned the highest credence; and some, to mention just one more example, say that what one should do *given uncertainty concerning the correct first-order norm* is always identical to what one should do simpliciter.[10] On this last view, uncertain or mistaken normative views can never license behavior that fails to accord with the correct first-order norm. It is plausible that if *S* has views on this second-order question of how to act in light of first-order uncertainty, then these views could have a bearing on whether *S* is rational in performing some action. For example, *S* arguably does not act rationally if she chooses action *A* despite being *certain* that the aforementioned moral hedging norm is correct, a norm that recommends choosing *B* in *S*'s present situation.

Thus far, I've suggested that *S*'s rational high credence for the correct norm *NA* is not enough to make conforming to that norm rational. For example, choosing *A* would seem to be irrational if *S* believes with certainty that, given her uncertainty between *NA* and *NB*, she ought to choose action *B*. Arguably, then, there is at least a *negative* requirement on rational action that it not conflict with one's higher-order views (that are held with certainty) on how to act in the face of normative uncertainty. But is there also a *positive* requirement

---

[10] For an example of a defense of the hedging strategy, see Andrew Sepielli, "What to Do When You Don't Know What to Do," *Oxford Studies in Metaethics* 4 (2009): 5–28. A winner-take-all approach is defended in Johan E. Gustafsson and Olle Torpman, "In Defence of My Favourite Theory," *Pacific Philosophical Quarterly* 95, no. 2 (2014): 159–174. The last view mentioned, which denies the moral significance of moral uncertainty, is defended in Brian Weatherson, "Running Risks Morally," *Philosophical Studies* 167, no. 1 (2014): 141–163; and Elizabeth Harmon, "The Irrelevance of Moral Uncertainty," *Oxford Studies in Metaethics* 10 (2015): 53–79. Alternatively, one might hold that second-order claims about what *S* should do *given her uncertainty concerning the first-order norm* are in some way defective or meaningless claims, at least if such claims in some way presuppose that the norms that apply in conditions of uncertainty might differ from the first-order norms. (Thanks to Emad Atiq for this suggestion.) It seems to me that someone who accepted this latter view would, in practice, be in the same deliberative position as someone who acknowledged the meaningfulness of second-order normative claims but who thought that what one ought to do given first-order uncertainty must be identical to what one ought to do simpliciter. For it follows from both of these positions that there is no second-order normative claim that one could rationally know to be true while remaining uncertain about what one ought to do simpliciter.

for rational action in the face of normative uncertainty according to which one must have justification for higher-order views that rationalize one's choice?

I suggest that there is such a positive requirement. Suppose that S sees that there is a second-order question about what she ought to do in light of her first-order uncertainty but that she does not settle this question and forms no belief or other doxastic attitude on the matter. She then goes ahead and does action A. In this case, her action does not conflict with her higher-order views about how to act in light of her normative uncertainty, since she has no views on this matter. So, can one affirm that S acts rationally, given that NA is correct and that S rationally has a high credence for NA? I think not.[11] Suppose that S does not have justification for believing the second-order claim that choice A is appropriate in light of S's uncertainty regarding NA and NB. And suppose further that S does not have justification for assigning anything more than a very small credence to this second-order claim. Even if the correct second-order norm *does* in fact license choosing A in this particular case of normative uncertainty, the fact that S cannot justifiably affirm the appropriateness of this choice gives one reason to doubt its rationality.

Clearly, if S was rationally *certain* in a correct second-order norm that required her to choose A in her present situation, then she would be rational in choosing A. But would confidence in such a second-order norm that falls short of certainty be sufficient to rationalize choosing A? Again, it seems not. Given that less-than-certain confidence in a *first-order* norm like NA is not sufficient to rationalize choosing in accordance with NA, why would less-than-certain confidence in some *second-order* norm be sufficient to rationalize choosing in accordance with that second-order norm? After all, the same sorts of considerations used to question the rational sufficiency of high but nonmaximal confidence in a first-order norm also apply at the second-order level.

Suppose, for example, that S rationally has a credence of 0.8 for a "moral hedging" second-order norm that says that she ought to choose B, given her first-order uncertainty and the risk that attends action A; and she also has a credence of 0.2 for the "winner-take-all" second-order norm that would prescribe action A in her present situation. And suppose further that S knows that moral hedging with respect to the choice between A and B has a significant downside if moral hedging is an incorrect second-order norm.

---

[11] A contrary view will be considered in the next section.

For example, suppose S knows that if she chooses B, many of her admirers will notice this act, will recognize that it reflects her commitment to moral hedging, and as a result will be influenced to endorse moral hedging as a correct approach to moral uncertainty. If on the other hand S chooses A, no one will notice what S does and she will have no influence on her admirers' views about how to act in conditions of moral uncertainty. In this case, S expects that her admirers' views on how to navigate moral uncertainty will be influenced by moral experts that she thinks are highly trustworthy. Given this setup, the cost of moral hedging on the condition that moral hedging is incorrect may greatly outweigh the cost of following a winner-take-all norm on the condition that the winner-take-all norm is incorrect. It seems that in such a situation, the mere fact that S has a rational credence of 0.8 in the second-order hedging norm is not sufficient to rationalize following this norm, even if in fact the moral hedging second-order norm is correct. Whether S is rational in following a given second-order norm is sensitive to what she has justification to believe regarding the *third-order* question of how she ought to proceed given her uncertainty both about whether NA or NB is the correct first-order norm *and* about whether the correct second-order norm prescribes moral hedging or a winner-take-all approach.

Just as a high but less than maximal credence in some second-order norm is not sufficient to rationalize conforming to that norm (even if that credence is rational, and even if that second-order norm is correct), a high but less than maximal credence in some third-order norm will not be sufficient to rationalize conforming to that third-order norm. And this reasoning iterates indefinitely: at any order of normative reflection, a high but nonmaximal confidence in some norm is not sufficient to make conformity to that norm rational.[12]

What condition or conditions *are* sufficient to account for the rationality of S's choice in the face of first-order normative uncertainty? Well, if at some level of normative reflection, S is rationally *certain* about how to proceed in light of her uncertainty at lower levels, then it seems clear that S can act rationally. And perhaps it suffices for rationality if S has propositional justification to be certain in one of the relevant higher-order norms that guides her action, even if S does not actually adopt the doxastic attitude of certainty toward this norm. But could S act rationally if she is not certain, and has no

---

[12] For a view according to which the rational action in face of nth-order normative uncertainty depends on one's views concerning $(n + 1)$-order norms, see Andrew Sepielli, "What to Do When You Don't Know What to Do When You Don't Know What to Do . . . ," *Noûs* 48, no. 3 (2014): 521–544.

justification to be certain, in any first-order or higher-order norm that issues a prescription in her case?

Nothing I've said so far rules this out. I've argued that rationally high confidence in a norm is not sufficient to rationalize conformity to that norm, and that rational certainty in some norm *is* sufficient to rationalize conformity to the norm. But perhaps there is some other condition besides certainty that, when added to high confidence in a relevant norm, can make it rational to conform to that norm. Later, in subsection 7.3.2, I will consider the most plausible candidates I can think of for a condition that is sufficient for rational action and does not involve normative certainty (or justification for normative certainty). For the moment, however, I will assume that for S to act rationally, there must be some level of normative reflection at which S is certain (or has justification to be certain) about what she ought to do in her present situation. There is no requirement that there be justification for certainty at any *particular* level of normative reflection. For example, justification for certainty with respect to the first-order norm NA is not required for rational action, nor is justification for certainty required at the second order of reflection. All that is required is that at *some* level of reflection, S has justification to be certain about how she should proceed in light of her normative uncertainty at the lower levels.

The *certainty requirement*, as I will call it, is the thesis that certainty (or justification for certainty) is needed at one of these levels in order to act rationally. If the certainty requirement is correct, then the doxastic defeat resulting from disagreement threatens to undermine the rationality of any religious (or irreligious) decision. This is because at *any* level of normative reflection, there is likely to be controversy about what norms rightly obtain at that level. A commitment to impartiality will forbid certainty at any level, thereby preventing one from arriving at religious decisions in a rational manner.

Call this argument the "Nowhere to Stand Argument." It says that rational religious decision-making must proceed from a standpoint of normative certainty (even if only at some higher order), and that such certainty cannot itself be rational for the strong conciliationist who is aware of the extent of disagreement concerning the norms that bear on religious decision-making.

One might question whether it really is the case that practical norms at every level are likely to be contested by apparently qualified thinkers, so that certainty at any level is incompatible with strong conciliationism. There is, of course, substantive disagreement about the first-order practical norms that bear on religious decision-making. For example, there is disagreement concerning the appropriateness of cost-benefit type reasoning. But are second-order norms also controversial? Will disagreement really iterate at each level of normative reflection?

In short, yes. One very natural approach to normative uncertainty that has been endorsed by some philosophers is to maximize "choice worthiness," where choice worthiness is some generic measure of the goodness or badness of a choice that is neutral between various competing first-order norms (including both consequentialist and nonconsequentialist norms).[13] But as several critics of this approach have emphasized, this approach faces at least two serious challenges.[14] First, some first-order normative theories merely rank choices without providing any basis for measuring how much better one option is than another. Second, even if competing normative theories *do* provide a basis for measuring choice worthiness (rather than merely ranking options), there may be no principled way of comparing choice worthiness measurements across theories that have disparate views on what choice worthiness ultimately amounts to. The gravity of these problems has led some to endorse versions of the winner-take-all approach.[15] William MacAskill proposes a different sort of approach that is analogous to certain voting procedures in social choice theory and that can be applied in contexts where choice worthiness maximization is not possible.[16] No doubt other theories will be developed as more attention is given to the topic of normative uncertainty, a topic that has been largely neglected until recently. What's clear is that second-order norms are controversial. And there is no reason to think that there will be greater consensus when one considers the norms that apply at even higher orders of normative reflection.

Someone might acknowledge the controversial character of higher-order norms while nonetheless remaining optimistic about the attainability of higher-order normative certainty, even on the condition of doxastic defeat. After all, even if thinkers endorse different general normative *theories* about how one ought to proceed in light of *nth*-order uncertainty, perhaps at some

---

[13] Choice-worthiness maximization is defended in William MacAskill and Toby Ord, "Why Maximize Expected Choice-Worthiness?," *Noûs*, 2018, doi.org/10.1111/nous.12264. Also see Sepielli, "What to Do When You Don't Know What to Do."

[14] These challenges are discussed in Gustafsson and Torpman, "In Defence of My Favourite Theory"; and William MacAskill, "Normative Uncertainty as a Voting Problem," *Mind* 125, no. 500 (2016): 967–1004.

[15] For example, Gustafsson and Torpman, "In Defence of My Favourite Theory."

[16] MacAskill, "Normative Uncertainty as a Voting Problem."

level the competing theories will converge on a common prescription (even if for different reasons). Or perhaps thinkers who disagree about every *nth*-order prescription will nonetheless agree on a "meta norm" that says how one ought to proceed if, for every natural number *n*, there is uncertainty at the *nth* order of normative reflection.

While I cannot entirely rule out the possibility of such convergence, I have strong reason for thinking that this is unlikely. Recall that, according to some, normative uncertainty is of no normative significance, so that the *nth*-order question of what S ought to do given her uncertainty concerning norms at levels lower than *n* always has the same answer as the question of what S ought to do simpliciter. In other words, the answer to the first-order question also answers all of the higher-order questions. If proponents of this view disagree on the correct first-order norm, then this disagreement *automatically* translates into disagreement concerning *all* of the relevant higher-order questions. For this reason alone, it is likely that there will be disagreement concerning *every* higher-order question about what a given person ought to do in the religious domain. Thus, if one conforms with the requirements of strong conciliationism, it is probable that one should be uncertain about *any* higher-order questions that one might ask, including the question of what one ought to do given this iterated uncertainty.

If the Nowhere to Stand Argument is correct, then when a rational subject S who is suitably informed about religious disagreement faces a religiously significant choice, this choice cannot be settled in a rational way. The problem just sketched arises in all choice situations where the relevant first-order and higher-order norms are controversial. Such choices could be momentous, like the choice of whether or not to take on some lifelong religious commitment, or relatively mundane, like the choice of whether or not to participate in the singing of some song of worship. Of course, one must live one's life, and in doing so one must make choices that will determine what sort of religiosity or irreligiosity characterizes one's life. On any given occasion, S will either pray or not. She will either worship or not. If she does pray or worship, she will, of course, pray or worship in some determinate way that may conform to the prescriptions of some religious outlooks and not others. So S must engage in religious decision-making, but the *content* of her religious decisions cannot be settled rationally since (1) she is uncertain about what she ideally ought to do, (2) she is uncertain about what she ought to do given that (1) is the case, (3) she is uncertain about what she ought to do given that (2) is the case, and so on.

Importantly, the Nowhere to Stand Argument implies that S is doomed to act without rational basis whether or not she chooses to act in a "religious" manner. The nonreligious life does not enjoy some sort of privileged status that is rational by default. Just as S lacks the standpoint of certainty that would make praying rational, she also lacks the standpoint of certainty that would make *refraining* from prayer rational. *All* humans are condemned to nonrational decisions (assuming that strong conciliationism is correct, and that one is suitably informed about the facts of disagreement), whether one pursues a religious or secular way of life.

Does the Nowhere to Stand Argument imply that S's living in some religious way would be *irrational*, rather than merely *non*rational? I think not.[17] Suppose I am driving down the highway and my lane splits into two lanes, one to the left and one to the right. I lack any reason to prefer moving to the left over moving to the right, and I also lack any reason to prefer moving to the right over moving to the left. Knowing that I lack any reason to prefer one lane or the other, I choose the right lane. My choice is rationally arbitrary, but it is not thereby irrational. Similarly, in showing that S has no rational basis for religious decision-making, the Nowhere to Stand Argument does not show that S's religious decisions are irrational. Rather, the argument merely shows that they are rationally arbitrary, inasmuch as S does not have justification for a doxastic state that rationalizes any particular religious or irreligious stance.

Of course, if S commits to some religion *on the basis of some rationale*, then this *would* be irrational. For it is irrational to act on the basis of a rationale that is not rationally justified or that does not sufficiently support the action in question. S would act irrationally even if she reasoned as follows: "well, given the facts of disagreement and the logic of the Nowhere to Stand Argument, I cannot avoid rational arbitrariness in choosing between various religious and nonreligious ways of life. But among the religious options that are not ruled out as *irrational* (on account of unanimous rejection, for example), R is the most attractive to me. So I choose to commit to R." This line of reasoning would seem to presuppose the correctness of some principle like the following: when all other first-order and higher-order normative considerations are undermined by disagreement, it is reasonable to choose a particular religious way of life on the basis of the reason that one prefers this way of life. But surely some thinkers will contest this idea that it is reasonable

---

[17] A similar point is made in Unger, *Ignorance*, 204.

to give tie-breaking force to personal preference when all other normative considerations are undercut. If there must be some privileged consideration that can continue to ground rational choice when systematic disagreement has induced "deliberative vertigo," why think that personal preference should enjoy this status? Perhaps this special status should be granted to majority preference, or to some normative consideration that has nothing to do with preference. In short, the higher-order norm that says to choose in accordance with one's preferences when all other first-order and higher-order norms are undercut is threatened by disagreement just like any other higher-order norm.

7.3 Grappling with the Nowhere to Stand Argument

If the Nowhere to Stand Argument is sound, then it follows that decisions to live in some determinate religious or nonreligious way cannot be fully rational if strong conciliationism is correct. At least two groups of people will find this conclusion unwelcome. First, the Nowhere to Stand Argument presents a challenge to those who think that the rational viability of religious commitment does not turn on the merits of strong conciliationism, since nondoxastic religious commitment can be rational even if doxastic confidence is defeated in the face of religious disagreement. If the Nowhere to Stand Argument is correct, then following strong conciliationism undermines the rationality of nondoxastic as well as doxastic religious commitment. In this case, defending the rationality of a particular religious or irreligious way of life *would* require one to argue that it can sometimes be reasonable to violate the requirements of strong conciliationism.

Advocates of strong conciliationism constitute the second group that should be troubled by the Nowhere to Stand Argument. Normative disagreement obviously extends well beyond the religious domain. Most conciliationists will not be comfortable embracing a strong conciliatory position if this implies that, at least in a great many contexts, people are incapable of acting rationally. Conciliationists typically seek to distance conciliatory views from radically skeptical positions that are judged by most philosophers to be implausible. But if the Nowhere to Stand Argument is correct, then strong conciliationism imposes a form of skepticism that is particularly pernicious in its practical implications. Perhaps conciliationists could accept the conclusion that their conciliatory view requires significant revision of credences across a large number of questions. While such a conclusion may be difficult to swallow, the rigorous pursuit of epistemic deference could potentially promote individual and collective flourishing. But there is nothing to like about the news that rational decision-making is *impossible* in the religious arena (and perhaps in other domains characterized by systematic disagreement). In its very bleakness, this conclusion is implausible. If it were accepted that strong conciliationism leads to such a bleak outcome, then no doubt many conciliationists would give up their conciliatory position. Arguably, a viable defense of strong conciliationism must show that strong conciliationism does not undermine rational action in the religious domain as the Nowhere to Stand Argument charges.

How, then, should the strong conciliationist respond to the Nowhere to Stand Argument, assuming that she is not willing to bite the bullet and allow that people have no capacity for rational decision-making in the religious domain? I'll consider three possible lines of response.

7.3.1 Questioning the Endorsement Requirement

The Nowhere to Stand Argument presupposes that rational actions must cohere in some way with the attitudes that one has justification to hold on normative matters. A rational agent must endorse, or at least have justification to endorse, his actions. One might respond to the Nowhere to Stand Argument by contesting this sort of "endorsement requirement." In particular, one could maintain that it is possible to act rationally even when one's action is not rationalized by what one has justification to believe about normative matters. There is a radical version of this proposal and a less radical version. On the radical version of the proposal, one can sometimes rationally perform action *A* while confidently and rationally believing that one should instead do some alternative action *B* (and without endorsing *A* at some higher level of normative reflection). I will call this the "rational self-indictment" view, since it allows that an act could be rational even though one rationally believes that the act is not appropriate. The less radical version of the proposal acknowledges that there is some sort of negative requirement that rational action not conflict with one's actual views about what one ought to do but denies that there is a positive requirement according to which one must have propositional justification to affirm the appropriateness of one's actions.

I will call this the "rational nonendorsement" view, since it allows that an act could be rational even though one neither endorses it nor has justification to endorse it.

The rational self-indictment view is analogous to the "level-splitting" view briefly discussed in chapter 6. According to that view, when you find yourself with sufficiently powerful but misleading evidence in favor of an incorrect epistemic norm N2 and against the correct epistemic norm N1, you should follow N1 while nonetheless believing that N2 is correct. This may result in cases of rational epistemic akrasia—cases where you both rationally believe that p and rationally believe that it is irrational to believe that p. Similarly, an advocate of the rational self-indictment view maintains that when you have powerful but misleading evidence against the correct *practical* norm, it can be rational to act in accordance with that norm while believing that you should not do so.

Because the rational self-indictment view is the practical analog of the level-splitting view, there is good reason to think that the two views stand or fall together. If that is right, then strong conciliationism cannot plausibly be combined with the rational self-indictment view. As discussed in the previous chapter, the level-splitting view does not comport with strong conciliationism. The strong conciliationist thinks that one's credence for p must cohere with a p-neutral assessment of the higher-order claim that one has formed this credence in a rational and reliable way. This conflicts with the level-splitting view, which does not require that one's credence for p cohere with one's credences for higher-order claims about what credence value for p is rational. Because strong conciliationism is opposed to the level-splitting view, and because the rational self-indictment view and the level-splitting view probably stand or fall together, it is not plausible to affirm both strong conciliationism and the rational self-indictment view. And this means that the rational self-indictment view can be set aside for present purposes. The aim of this chapter is to consider what it would mean for religious commitment if strong conciliationism was true. There is therefore no need to consider theories of rationality that are almost certainly false on the supposition that strong conciliationism is correct.

Even if the rational self-indictment view is not available to the strong conciliationist, could the strong conciliationist successfully resist the Nowhere to Stand Argument by appealing to the rational nonendorsement view? On the rational nonendorsement view, what is important is avoiding incoherence between one's actions and one's normative views. And this *lack* of incoherence might be achieved merely by failing to form any views what-soever on the relevant normative questions, thereby avoiding any explicit or implicit view on the rational status of some action. For example, S might have positive credences for two competing first-order norms and also for two competing second-order norms while lacking *any* doxastic attitudes (even implicit ones) toward the relevant third-order normative question. In this scenario, S might act rationally even if she does not have justification to af-firm a third-order norm (or a norm at an even higher level) that would ra-tionalize her action.

I find this way of resisting the Nowhere to Stand Argument implausible. It is perhaps true that rational action need not be accompanied by an explicit belief that the action is appropriate. But it does seem that to act rationally, one must at least be in a position to rationally endorse the appropriateness of one's action.[18] Even when someone acts in response to objectively good reasons, the action may still fail to be rational if the subject lacks any jus-tification to believe that the action is appropriate (perhaps because of mis-leading evidence that undermines a positive appraisal of the subject's reasons for acting).

Even if I am wrong and the rational nonendorsement view is correct, ap-pealing to this view does not provide a very satisfactory way of responding to the worries raised by the Nowhere to Stand Argument. This is because the ra-tional nonendorsement view can at best exonerate the strong conciliationist who is unreflective or who has not appreciated the logic of the Nowhere to Stand Argument. To see why, consider first the situation of an ideally re-flective strong conciliationist who, *at every level of normative reflection*, has justified credences for answers to the normative questions that bear on her religious decisions. Because this idealized conciliationist will have explicit attitudes toward all of the relevant higher-order questions, she cannot avoid incoherence by virtue of *lacking* attitudes toward some higher-order ques-tion. Achieving coherence will require that her action be rationalized by the positive doxastic attitudes she adopts toward the higher-order questions. If I am right that her doxastic attitudes cannot rationalize any action if there is uncertainty at every level of reflection and that strong conciliationism requires her to be uncertain at every level of reflection, then this idealized conciliationist will not be able to act rationally. But once one realizes that

---

[18] In support of this point, see Valerie Tiberius, "Practical Reason and the Stability Standard," *Ethical Theory and Moral Practice* 5, no. 3 (2002): 339–354.

this idealized conciliationist could not rationally commit to any religious or irreligious way of life, the rationality of one's own religious or irreligious commitment is surely undermined. For it is not rational to persist in some religious commitment when one knows that neither this commitment nor any similar commitment could be rationally maintained in the face of suitably thorough reflection.

7.3.2 Challenging the Certainty Requirement

Going forward, I'll grant that in order to act rationally, one must have justification to adopt a doxastic state that includes attitudes toward all of the relevant first-order and higher-order normative questions and that rationalizes one's action. I suggested that in order for such a doxastic state to rationalize one's action, that doxastic state must involve normative certainty, either with respect to the first-order normative question or with respect to some higher-order question about how to proceed in light of one's uncertainty at lower levels of reflection.

The second response to the Nowhere to Stand Argument challenges this certainty requirement by identifying some doxastic state that rationalizes action despite the lack of normative certainty at any level of reflection. The most obvious suggestions to consider are that rationally *believing* or *knowing* that some first-order or higher-order norm is correct could rationalize acting in accordance with the norm even if one is not certain about the correctness of the norm in question. I will argue that these proposals either are implausible or fail to be genuine alternatives to the certainty requirement. I will then consider a different and more plausible competitor to the certainty requirement.

I'll begin with the proposal that rational belief in the correctness of some norm can be sufficient to rationalize acting in accordance with that norm, even if rational belief does not require certainty. If belief is compatible with uncertainty, then the following situation would, on initial inspection, seem to be possible: S has a credence of 0.9 for NA (which prescribes action A); S has a credence of 0.1 for NB (which prescribes action B); S thinks that choosing A would be a moral disaster conditional on NB being correct; S thinks that choosing B would be wrong but not a "big deal" conditional on NA being correct; S *believes* that NA is correct; and S is rational in having all of these attitudes. I suspect that many will agree with me in thinking that in such a situation, action B may be rationally preferable to action A. Those who

304   WHAT DOES IMPARTIALITY REQUIRE?

do agree will naturally have to deny that S's belief in NA is sufficient to rationalize choosing A.

Even if one rejects any sort of hedging approach to normative uncertainty, there are still problems for the proposal that rational belief in a norm is sufficient to rationalize conformity to the norm. If most philosophers affirm that hedging in this sort of situation is rationally preferable, then on the assumption that S is aware of this fact and is a good conciliationist, S may be required to have a high credence for the second-order normative claim that in S's present situation of normative uncertainty, the rationally appropriate action is to hedge and choose B. And if one supposes that S *does* have a high credence for this second-order claim, it becomes even harder to believe that the mere fact that S rationally believes NA is sufficient to make it rational for S to choose action A. The fact that S believes NA does not explain how it could be rational for S to do A while thinking it highly probable that B is the only rationally appropriate action.

One way to overcome these worries and to advance the idea that belief is a rationalizing attitude is to deny the possibility of the situation described above, where S rationally believes NA despite the fact that, by her lights, following NA has a 0.1 probability of leading to moral disaster (while following NB does not pose a similar risk). According to many who theorize about the relationship between belief and credence, whether S's credence of 0.9 for NA is sufficient for rational belief depends on how much is practically at stake—in particular, how much would be gained by believing NA (in comparison to withholding judgment on the matter) in the event that it is true and how much would be lost by believing NA in the event that NA is false.[19] On this sort of view, believing some proposition involves taking it for granted in theoretical and practical reasoning. To the extent that the cost of erroneous belief is high, the level of confidence that is required for rational belief will tend to be pushed higher. And to the extent that the benefit of true belief is significant, the confidence threshold for rational belief will tend to be pushed lower. If rational belief is *stakes sensitive* in this way, then the situation described above is simply incoherent. Since it would be disastrous for S to take NA for granted (and thus to choose A) were NA false, yet not especially valuable for

---

[19] See, for example, Brian Weatherson, "Can One Do Without Pragmatic Encroachment?," *Philosophical Perspectives* 19, no. 1 (2005): 417–443; Dorit Ganson, "Evidentialism and Pragmatic Constraints on Outright Belief," *Philosophical Studies* 139, no. 3 (2008): 441–458; and Michael Pace, "The Epistemic Value of Moral Considerations: Justification, Moral Encroachment, and James' 'Will to Believe,'" *Noûs* 45, no. 2 (2011): 239–268.

S to believe NA were it true, the confidence level that is required for rational belief will be extremely high—*much* higher than 0.9. So the envisioned situation is not possible and therefore does not provide a counterexample to the claim that belief is a rationalizing attitude.

I'm happy to grant, for the sake of argument, that this stakes-sensitive view of rational belief is correct, and that on this view, every situation where S rationally believes NA is also a situation where S can rationally do what NA requires. But these concessions do not help one to evade the certainty requirement. On the stakes-sensitivity account of rational belief, the fact that S rationally believes NA does not *make it* rational for S to take NA for granted; rather, the fact that it is rational for S to take NA for granted is what makes it rational for S to believe NA. On this view, belief does not supply the rationalizing ground for conforming to NA but is the outcome of there being such a ground. Thus, the claim that S could rationally believe NA simply *presupposes* that S can rationally take the truth of NA for granted despite her uncertainty about NA. To explain why it would be rational for S to take the truth of NA for granted, one would presumably have to appeal to other features of S's epistemic position. This leaves open the possibility that, in order for S to rationally believe that NA is correct (despite her lack of certainty on the matter), she must have justification to be certain about some higher-order norm that prescribes acting in accordance with NA. Once one has acknowledged the stakes-sensitivity of rational belief, the claim that rational belief is sufficient for rational action turns out not to be a competitor with the certainty requirement.

Everything I've said about the proposal that rational belief in some norm is sufficient for acting in accordance with the norm may also be said about the proposal that *knowing* some norm to be correct is sufficient for acting in accordance with it. If knowledge is compatible with uncertainty and is not stakes-sensitive, then one can describe an apparently coherent scenario where, despite the fact that some subject S knows that NA is correct, it seems foolhardy and irrational to do what NA prescribes (because of the lopsided cost associated with following NA in the event that it turns out to be incorrect). But many will say that such scenarios are impossible for the reason that knowledge is stakes-sensitive.[20] If that is right, then the fact that S knows NA to be correct does not explain why it is rational for S to act in accordance

---

[20] For one extended defense of the claim that whether one knows is sensitive to one's practical interests, see Jason Stanley, *Knowledge and Practical Interests* (Oxford: Oxford University Press, 2005).

with *NA*; rather, the fact that it is rational for *S* to act in accordance with *NA* will be part of the explanation of why *S* succeeds in knowing that *NA* is correct (despite being less than certain about the matter). To explain why it is rational for *S* to act in accordance with *NA*, presumably one would need to appeal to other features of *S*'s epistemic position. And it is possible that such an explanation would have to appeal to the fact that *S* has justification to be certain about the correctness of some relevant higher-order normative claim. So again, on the assumption that knowledge is stakes-sensitive, the claim that knowledge is sufficient for action turns out to be compatible with the certainty requirement.

I'll now turn to what I think is the most plausible alternative to the certainty requirement. Consider the situation of some rational subject *S* who is rationally confident, but not certain, that in his present situation he ought to do action *A*. For ease of exposition, imagine that *S* does not share most people's cognitive limitations and that he has rationally justified views on every relevant higher-order question about what he ought to do given his uncertainty with respect to lower-order normative questions. (Focusing on such a subject allows one to simply speak of *S*'s views rather than always speaking of the views that *S* has rational justification to adopt.) Suppose that *S*'s situation is as follows. In answering the first-order question of what *S* ideally ought to do, he assigns a credence of 0.9 to the proposition that he ideally ought to do action *A*. In answering the second-order question of what *S* ought to do given his uncertainty about (1), *S* also assigns a credence of 0.9 to the proposition that *even given his uncertainty with respect to (1)*, he ought to do *A*. More generally, *S* answers *every* relevant higher-order question by assigning a credence of 0.9 to the claim that even given his less than perfect certainty at lower orders, he ought to do *A*. I'll use the label *higher-order concurrence* to refer to this sort of state, one where there is an infinitely iterated structure of confident, though perhaps uncertain, higher-order opinions that concur in the action they prescribe. Does the fact that *S* rationally exhibits higher-order concurrence favoring action *A* make it rational for him to do *A*?

The suggestion that higher-order concurrence is sufficient to rationalize action has much more plausibility than the suggestion that an action can be rationalized merely by a high (but nonmaximal) rational credence for some norm prescribing the action. As I've emphasized, having a high credence that one ideally ought to do *A* is compatible with the possibility that, when taking into account the risks posed by one's normative uncertainty, one has most reason to perform some other action instead. For example, one might have good reason to deliberate further while knowing that A, which one thinks is probably the ideal response, would require that one cease deliberating in order to take more definitive steps *now*. But in the present case, where S exhibits higher-order concurrence favoring action A, one can rule out the possibility that a lower-order view favoring A is overturned by some confident higher-order attitude that favors a different action.

Despite the initial plausibility of the suggestion that higher-order concurrence can rationalize action in the absence of normative certainty, I do not think that this proposal is correct. I will argue that someone who acts while being uncertain at every level of normative reflection (and while lacking justification for certainty at each level) fails to act rationally because he knowingly takes on a risk without any rational basis for thinking that bearing the risk is acceptable. This deficiency applies even to someone like S, who exhibits higher-order concurrence. As I will argue, when one is engaged in higher-order reasoning about how to proceed in light of one's uncertainty concerning competing lower-order norms, one should reason in a way that is suitably independent of the "dispute" between these lower-order norms. Higher-order deliberation that involves the same form of questionable reasoning that lies behind some lower-order norm N cannot properly assess the significance of the risk posed by the possibility that N is incorrect. But there is surely not an infinite supply of independent (and plausible) approaches to higher-order reasoning. For this reason, someone who continues to be uncertain at every level of normative reflection will eventually be unable to engage in higher-order deliberation that is suitably independent of the norms employed at lower orders of reflection. Lacking a suitably independent way of deliberating, such a person will be unable to rationally assess which of the risks posed by normative uncertainty are acceptable to bear.

The argument just sketched is most easily grasped in the context of a concrete example. So consider the case of Zeynep, who is uncertain whether she should adopt the religious stance recommended by an expected utility norm or instead follow some "authenticity norm" that recommends adopting the religious stance that most fully expresses her passions. By the lights of the authenticity norm, religious faith would be sapped of much of its value if it was seen to be justified on the basis of utility maximization. This is because faith is most valuable when it involves movements of passion that cannot be justified by the risk-neutral calculations of expected utility theory.[21] Zeynep has a 0.9 credence that the expected utility norm is correct and a credence of 0.1

---

[21] My inspiration here is the depiction of faith in Søren Kierkegaard's *Concluding Unscientific Postscript to Philosophical Fragments*, which Kierkegaard presents as the work of the pseudonymous

that the authenticity norm is correct. She also knows that the expected utility norm supports committing to Severe God (as discussed in section 7.1) and that the authenticity norm supports committing to Gentle God. Finally, I'll stipulate that Zeynep is ideally reflective in that, prior to deciding on a religious stance, she can and does form attitudes pertaining to all of the relevant higher-order normative questions.

Zeynep's normative uncertainty raises the prospect of certain risks that she would not need to consider were she certain about the correct approach to religious decision-making. One such risk is that she might sacrifice authenticity for the sake of maximizing expected utility even though a cost-benefit way of thinking about religious decisions is wrongheaded and the authenticity norm is correct. In deliberating over whether she should adjust her action in light of this risk, to what sorts of reasons and principles can Zeynep reasonably appeal? Would it be reasonable for her to employ expected utility reasoning at this second order of normative reflection? Suppose Zeynep does engage in expected utility reasoning at this second-order level of reflection and beyond. She calculates the expected utility of various religious stances while explicitly considering possibilities where the expected utility first-order norm is correct as well as possibilities where the authenticity first-order norm is correct. And suppose that this second-order expected utility reasoning also supports a commitment to Severe God.[22] Since Zeynep is not fully certain that expected utility reasoning is the appropriate approach to *second*-order reasoning, she engages in third-order reflection on how to act in light of her second-order uncertainty, making use of expected utility reasoning once again. Suppose that this reasoning also supports a commitment to Severe God, and this pattern iterates infinitely: at every level of reflection, Zeynep has a high but nonmaximal credence for some bit of expected utility

---

author "Johannes Climacus." As Climacus writes, "without risk, no faith. Faith is the contradiction between the infinite passion of inwardness and the objective uncertainty. If I am able to apprehend God objectively, I do not have faith; but because I cannot do this, I must have faith." *Concluding Unscientific Postscript to Philosophical Fragments*, ed. Howard Vincent Hong and Edna Hatlestad Hong (Princeton: Princeton University Press, 1992), 204. Climacus is arguing here that the security provided by the evidential probability of one's religious outlook would undermine the passion that is essential to valuable faith. But his position also gives one reason to spurn any support provided by expected utility theory. Having noted my inspiration, I should emphasize that I do not pretend that the authenticity norm as I've described it succeeds as a distillation of the Kierkegaardian position.

[22] Perhaps the risk of missing out on authentic commitment to Genuine God does not have much weight in expected utility terms since the loss is likely to be temporary. It would be temporary if Gentle God would ensure that the formation of a properly authentic commitment would remain a possibility in the afterlife, one that eventually would be chosen by all.

reasoning that supports the conclusion that she should commit to Severe God even given her uncertainty at lower orders of reflection. By engaging in this infinitely iterated train of expected utility reasoning, has Zeynep adequately accounted for the risk that expected utility reasoning is entirely wrongheaded?

It seems fairly clear that this infinitely iterated expected utility reasoning is *not* a satisfactory way of assessing the risk posed by the possibility that such reasoning is inappropriate in the religious domain.[23] If expected utility reasoning is wrongheaded in the religious domain, then there is no reason to think that one can use expected utility reasoning to adequately articulate what one stands to lose by relying on expected utility reasoning, or to capture the significance of this loss. It seems that to properly assess the risk posed by the possible incorrectness of expected utility norms, one would need to occupy a deliberative standpoint that does not presuppose the correctness of expected utility reasoning. Of course, "authenticity reasoning" may be able to capture what is allegedly lost by relying on expected utility reasoning. But again, there is no reason to think that the values and principles presupposed by authenticity reasoning are capable of adequately capturing the significance of what would be lost by pursuing authenticity when in fact the expected utility norm is correct.

For Zeynep to rationally and nonarbitrarily decide how to act in light of the risks posed by her uncertainty concerning expected utility reasoning and authenticity reasoning, she must deliberate in a way that does not presuppose the correctness of either of these forms of reasoning. It is not clear what approach to second-order deliberation Zeynep could employ that is both plausible and neutral with respect to the dispute between the first-order norms she thinks might be correct. But suppose that Zeynep does identify some such approach to second-order reasoning that she is fairly confident

---

[23] It is possible to imagine in the abstract a situation where a rational person has doubts about the appropriateness of expected utility reasoning at the first order *in particular* without having any doubts about the appropriateness of expected utility reasoning at the second order. In this sort of case, expected utility reasoning at the second order might provide a suitably independent way of rationally deciding how to act in light of one's first-order uncertainty. But this is not Zeynep's situation. Zeynep has doubts about the appropriateness of expected utility reasoning at both the first order and at all higher orders. Perhaps her doubts about first-order expected utility reasoning are independent of her doubts about second-order expected utility reasoning. But if Zeynep continues to doubt expected utility reasoning at higher-order levels of reflection, then she will surely reach a point where her doubts about expected utility reasoning at the nth-order would equally apply to expected utility reasoning at level $n + 1$. When this point is reached, expected utility reasoning at level $n + 1$ would not provide a suitably independent way for her to assess the risks posed by the possibility that expected utility reasoning at level n is misguided.

is correct, though she also has some credence for an alternative approach to second-order deliberation that supports a different prescription. Because she is uncertain about the correctness of the second-order norm that she favors, she will recognize that there is a risk that she will follow this norm even though its prescription is incorrect. To genuinely take this risk into account in her deliberation, Zeynep will need to engage in third-order reasoning that is suitably independent of the dispute between the second-order norms that she thinks might be correct. If this ascent through higher orders of reflection does not eventually terminate in certainty, then Zeynep will eventually reach a point where she cannot identify any plausible way of deliberating about how to act in light of her lower-order uncertainty that is independent of all the "disputes" between the lower-order norms that she thinks might be correct.[24]

When this happens, any attempt to deliberate about how to act in light of her lower-order uncertainty would simply reapply some form of reasoning that Zeynep employs at a lower level and that she thinks may be incorrect. And one cannot rationally rely on reasoning of type R to assess the risk posed by the possibility that reasoning of type R is misguided. So when Zeynep acts in the face of indefinitely iterated normative uncertainty, she knowingly takes on risks whose significance she has no way of rationally assessing. Since she is choosing between religious stances that each involve some risk whose significance she cannot rationally assess, any choice she might make will involve taking on a risk without rational grounds for thinking that bearing this risk is acceptable. And someone who knowingly takes on a risk without grounds for thinking that doing so is acceptable does not act in a way that is guided by reason. In light of Zeynep's indefinitely iterated normative uncertainty, she has no choice but to act in a manner that is rationally arbitrary.

This argument for the certainty requirement that I've just sketched may not be decisive. It no doubt merits more scrutiny than I'm able to give it here. But the argument does, I think, pose a serious challenge to those who

---

[24] In claiming that indefinitely iterated normative uncertainty prevents Zeynep from rationally assessing the risks posed by that uncertainty, I do *not* thereby claim that mere certainty at some level of normative reflection is sufficient for Zeynep to rationally assess those risks. *Rational* certainty is sufficient, but mere certainty is not. Suppose, for example, that Zeynep was irrationally certain in the correctness of expected utility reasoning at the third-order, even though this reasoning was equally threatened by the worries that rightly cause Zeynep to doubt her second-order expected utility reasoning. While Zeynep would be entirely confident in this third-order expected utility reasoning, such reasoning would not provide a suitably independent way of evaluating the risks posed by her normative uncertainty, since the factors that lead to her uncertainty about the second-order expected utility reasoning *should* lead her to doubt this third-order reasoning as well.

optimistically assume that a commitment to rigorous epistemic impartiality is compatible with the rational pursuit of some religious or irreligious way of life. The deep normative uncertainty required by epistemic impartiality may close one off from the sort of rational endorsement of one's actions that must be available to a rational actor.

7.3.3 Questioning Whether Certainty Is Available to Nonconciliationists

The third response to the Nowhere to Stand Argument I will consider is to argue that the challenge raised by the argument is in no way unique to those who endorse conciliatory positions. Arguably, few if any of one's beliefs are so secure as to merit a credence of 1. And one's normative beliefs are no exception to this: for the overwhelming majority of one's normative beliefs, one can entertain the possibility of error, and therefore it seems that one's degrees of confidence should fall short of maximal certainty. There is no need to appeal to facts about disagreement in order to support this conclusion. And when one shifts focus from first-order normative questions to higher-order questions about how to proceed in light of normative uncertainty, concerns raised by cognitive fallibility and imperfect clarity remain. Thus, one should be uncertain in one's higher-order normative beliefs as well as in one's first-order normative beliefs.

If this is right, then the premises of the Nowhere to Stand Argument may be used to show that there are many contexts where fully rational action is not possible *even if one does not have conciliatory commitments.* So someone who thinks that the Nowhere to Stand Argument is sound should acknowledge that conciliationists and nonconciliationists alike are afflicted with rationality-destroying deliberative vertigo. And if deliberative vertigo is a problem for conciliationists and nonconciliationists alike, then the fact that strong conciliationists suffer from this vertigo does not give us a reason to reject strong conciliationism. Alternatively, if one insists that nonconciliationists *are* capable of rational action, then one should conclude that there must be some flaw in the Nowhere to Stand Argument. And if the argument is thought to be flawed, then it does not give one a good reason to worry about strong conciliationism.

This *tu quoque* rejoinder is, I think, the most promising response to the Nowhere to Stand Argument available to the strong conciliationist (and to those who think that the strong conciliationist is capable of rational nondoxastic religious commitment). Unless one can show why normative uncertainty is a problem for the strong conciliationist *in particular*, then the Nowhere to Stand Argument, while interesting, should not have a bearing on one's conciliatory commitments.

In response, I suggest that those who are not committed to rigorous epistemic impartiality may sometimes have justification to be certain in some contested normative claims. A standard way of objecting to such a suggestion is to point to evidence that rational individuals are unwilling to treat even the most obvious of propositions as being absolutely certain. Consider my belief that it is morally permissible for me to refrain from torturing some kitten for fun. If I am certain in any of my normative beliefs, this seems like a good candidate. Would I take a bet where I gain $1 if this belief is true and lose my life's income if it is not? No. And this refusal at least initially seems to me to be rational. But it is arguably irrational to refuse a bet that is certain to return $1 and to cost nothing. Thus, there is reason to think that I am *not* certain in this belief.

How compelling is this line of reasoning? In my view, it is far from conclusive. Perhaps my refusing to take the bet would not in fact be rational. A person's tendency to refuse high stakes/low gain bets on propositions in which he is certain may evince an irrational nervousness about "gambling," nervousness that may lead him to reject bets even when he rightly assigns zero credence to the possibility that he will lose.

Alternatively, perhaps it can be rational to refuse zero-risk bets when the gains are trivial and the costs of losing high enough. Suppose that Bob is reviewing the designs for a proposed nuclear waste storage facility. He realizes that due to a quirk in the design of the facility, if any two plutonium atoms stored there begin to undergo radioactive decay at *exactly* the same time, there will be a massive nuclear explosion that will destroy the local community; but as long as no two atoms commence decay at the exact same time, everything will be just fine. Suppose that Bob knows with certainty the following facts: for any atom, the initial moment of decay could occur at any time on a continuum; for any particular time t, the probability that some particular atom commences decay precisely at t is at most infinitesimal; and the decay times for various atoms are causally independent.[25] In this case, given

---

[25] An "infinitesimal" probability is greater than 0 but less than every real number $x > 0$. Infinitesimals have been invoked as a way of preserving an intuitive "Regularity" constraint on probability distributions. (See A. R. Bernstein and F. Wattenberg, "Non-standard Measure Theory,"

a finite number of atoms at the facility, the objective probability that any two atoms will commence decay at the same moment is zero or infinitesimal. This means that expected utility theory cannot support fixing this design "flaw" even if the cost of fixing the problem was only a nickel. Nonetheless, I suspect that many will judge that Bob should order that the problem be fixed, if doing so costs a trivial amount of money, and that such a decision is compatible with prudential rationality.

Examples like the nuclear facility case provide reason to doubt that expected utility theory is the right theory for assessing the rationality of low upside/high downside bets on propositions that are certain (or an infinitesimal amount shy of certainty). Perhaps expected utility theory needs to be situated within a larger theory of practical norms that can explain why one should sometimes refrain from betting on propositions that one rationally assigns a credence of 1 (or a value infinitesimally smaller than 1).[26] Arguably, certain forms of "rule consequentialism" could explain why it may be rational to refrain from many such bets. According to rule consequentialism, morality requires following rules that are "optimific" (or at least sufficiently good) according to certain standards of evaluation. On some rule consequentialist accounts, the goodness of a set of rules is determined by the consequences that would result if everyone internalized the rules and tried to follow them. (That's a rough statement of the view but adequate for my purposes.) Now, consider the following rule: when you are rationally certain that p, accept any bet on p that results in a good outcome in the event that p is true, no matter how bad the consequences of losing the bet may be. This rule is unlikely to be a good rule according to the version of rule consequentialism just described. Some people may irrationally assign a credence of 1 to a proposition p even when certainty is not epistemically warranted; when this happens, the attempt to conform to the aforementioned rule could easily lead to disaster. The best rule would likely require that one always reject large downside/ trivial upside bets even when one is epistemically justified in assigning a credence of 1 to the proposition one is betting on. So if it is rational to meet one's

---

in *Applications of Model Theory of Algebra, Analysis, and Probability*, ed. W. A. J. Luxemberg [New York: Holt, Rinehart and Winston, 1969], 171–185.) Regularity says that every contingent possibility has a positive probability less than 1. If probabilities must be real numbers, Regularity cannot be coherently satisfied in cases (like the atomic decay case under discussion) where there are uncountably many contingent possibilities that are mutually exclusive.

[26] My suggestion in this paragraph is similar in spirit to a proposal discussed in John Hawthorne and Jason Stanley, "Knowledge and Action," *Journal of Philosophy* 105, no. 10 (2008): 588–589.

moral obligations, then there is at least one type of moral theory that can explain why it could be rational to refuse to bet on p even when one is justifiably certain that p.

The foregoing reflections suggest that one cannot easily reason from claims about rational betting behavior to the conclusion that people are never justified in assigning a credence of 1 to some normative claim. But even if facts about rational betting behavior do not rule out the possibility of rational normative certainty, aren't there more straightforward epistemic considerations that do rule this out? Even intelligent and careful thinkers make mistakes in their reasoning with regularity, and normative thinking is not somehow immune from error. In light of human cognitive fallibility on normative matters, it seems that one can never rule out the possibility of error, and that one is therefore never justified in being certain with respect to any normative claim, even the claim that it is permissible for me to refrain from torturing a kitten for fun.

In response, I readily grant that a person's normative judgments are the product of broad process types that are fallible, for example the process of "forming a conclusion on some normative question after thinking hard about the matter." *That* process often produces false beliefs! But when I form a judgment about some specific normative question, I not only employ the broad process of "forming a conclusion on some normative question after thinking hard about the matter," a process that is very imperfect indeed; I also employ some narrow process of "believing that p on the basis of such and such reasons, reasons that have such and such character." And this narrow process, which is defined in terms of the specific reasoning I use to arrive at my belief, may very well be infallible, and infallible for reasons I am in a position to appreciate. As emphasized in earlier chapters, the requirement that one's credences be "calibrated" with the reliability of one's cognitive processes does not provide a determinate constraint on credences until one specifies the relevant level of "generality" that someone should use in characterizing these processes. The strong conciliationist has something to say about this: processes must be characterized in a dispute-neutral, non-question-begging way. This view would rule out certainty in normative claims even before disagreeing parties are on the scene, since apart from the *obvious correctness* of the judgment that one is not obligated to torture kittens for fun (a consideration that can bear no weight in a *neutral* evaluation of my reliability), I have no reason for thinking that my reasoning on this matter is infallible. But if strong conciliationism is rejected, then it is not clear that *general* fallibility worries should always threaten a person's certainty in judgments that are the product of narrow process types that are in fact infallible.

Suppose it is granted that I have justification to be certain that it is permissible for me to refrain from torturing a kitten for fun. One might understandably wonder whether this conclusion really does much to support the contention that, in everyday decisions, the certainty required for rational action is attainable.[27] People frequently face choices between options that are not easily ranked, such as giving to Charity 1 or to Charity 2, or grounding a child for x days rather than y days. It seems that justified moral certainty is not attainable in such situations. And if certainty is not available in these difficult though quotidian choice situations, then why think that nonconciliationists can escape the deliberative vertigo that allegedly afflicts strong conciliationism?

Crucially, the certainty requirement does *not* say that rational action requires justified certainty with respect to *first-order* normative questions pertaining to one's action. For example, in order to be rational in grounding my child x rather than y days, it is not required that I be rationally certain that punishment for x days is better than punishment for y days, or even that punishment of any sort is merited. On the view I've defended, rational action is fully compatible with uncertainty concerning such first-order matters. Normative certainty is required, but the certainty could attach to some *higher-order* claim about what action is appropriate *given my first-order uncertainty*. For example, while being highly uncertain about how long I should ground my child, or whether I should ground him at all, I could still be certain in some higher-order normative claim like the following: "given that (1) it seems unlikely that further deliberation will resolve my uncertainty about whether and how long to ground my son, (2) grounding him for x days currently seems like the best action and is unlikely to result in disaster, and (3) I've deliberated about this for a while and need to get onto other things, I should go ahead and ground him for x days." It's plausible that one has justification to be certain with respect to this sort of higher-order claim even if certainty regarding the first-order moral question is out of reach.

I do not claim to have shown that absolute certainty in normative claims can be justified. But it is by no means clear that such certainty is irrational. Thus, the *tu quoque* rejoinder to the Nowhere to Stand Argument is at best inconclusive. The sort of normative certainty that is required

---

[27] Thanks to a referee of this book for raising this challenge, and for the examples that follow.

to avoid deliberative vertigo may very well be rationally attainable for the nonconciliationist. If it is, then the premises of the Nowhere to Stand Argument do not support the conclusion that all people are incapable of rational decision-making (whether or not strong conciliationism is correct). And if these premises do not support this radical conclusion, then one has greater reason to be confident in the premises, as well as in the conclusion that the strong conciliationist cannot rationally and nonarbitrarily decide on a specific religious or irreligious way of life.

7.4 Refusing Doubt

The argument of this chapter casts the discussion of the previous chapter in a new and less optimistic light. I argued in chapter 6 that a high credence for a religious (or irreligious) outlook may be compatible with a commitment to reasons impartiality, since it is far from clear which doxastic attitudes on religious matters have the best claim to being nonpartisan. But even if a high credence for one's favored religious outlook is compatible with strong conciliationism, strong conciliationism may rule out the possibility of rationally committing to a way of life that is consonant with that religious perspective.

In an effort to resist this bleak conclusion, the proponent of epistemic impartiality may object that my arguments have force only if the impartiality requirement is treated as being absolute and exceptionless. And perhaps the reasonable strong conciliationist should not undeviatingly pursue epistemic impartiality, even if some sort of epistemic impartiality requirement is correct. Perhaps the reasonable strong conciliationist will, at various points, take a stand and refuse the doubt that impartiality seems to require. For example, in determining what credence to adopt for theism, he might decide on a determinate way to weight the opinions of various groups (e.g., the general population, academic philosophers in general, and academic philosophers specializing in philosophy of religion), and he might confidently trust in this weighting even though he recognizes that many would judge it to be unduly biased. Or the strong conciliationist might maintain perfect certainty in some contested practical norm. For example, she might remain certain that moral "hedging" is appropriate in contexts of moral uncertainty, giving no weight to the opinion of those who argue that moral uncertainty is of no normative significance. Refusing to follow impartiality requirements at select junctures would allow the strong conciliationist to apply the impartiality requirements quite broadly without undermining her ability to reason toward a determinate doxastic state and toward determinate decisions.

In response to the strong conciliationist who refuses doubt in this way, I would want to ask the following questions. Consider some belief that you hold with a degree of confidence that outstrips what can be justified on impartial grounds; what accounts for the justification of this degree of confidence? Perhaps you know that the commitment to impartiality must be constrained to limit its corrosive effects on epistemic and practical rationality, and that this belief seems to you to be an appropriate juncture at which to take a stand (even though others would contest this). If this accounts for your justification, might it be reasonable for someone to take a stand and remain confident in his answer to some controversial religious question, if this question seems to him to be an appropriate point to draw the line that limits the reach of impartiality requirements? Or, perhaps your confidence in the present case is justified because it is so clear to you that those who reject your view do not have good reasons for their contrary positions. If this clarity serves to justify your confidence, despite your lack of impartial grounds, might clarity of this sort justify someone in confidently affirming some religious or irreligious outlook, even if this confidence is not sanctioned by impartial considerations? Or if there is some other account of your partisan justification in this case, what is it? And might it apply to some cases of religious belief?

The intended force of these questions is clear. The strong conciliationist may very well be reasonable in maintaining confidence in some contexts where such confidence does not accord with epistemic impartiality. But until there is a principled and plausible account of when it is reasonable to refuse doubt in this way, it will be difficult to convincingly argue that religious skepticism is the rationally required response to religious disagreement.

Conclusion

Some might hope that a book on religious disagreement would show that in today's pluralistic context, significant religious confidence is unreasonable. It might be hoped that a theory on the rational significance of disagreement could be used to undercut problematic forms of religious extremism in one fell swoop, without having to directly engage in first-order metaphysical, theological, and ethical argumentation. Those who harbor such hopes may have mixed feelings about the position I have defended here.

On the one hand I have argued that it is irrational to remain confident in one's religious outlook while acknowledging the internal rational parity of competing outlooks. Even if one's own religious group had the distinction of being the only group whose religious beliefs were produced by reliable and properly functioning faculties, this would not make it reasonable to sustain confidence in situations where there is acknowledged rational parity with respect to internally discernible factors.

On the other hand I have argued that genuine rational insight into the truth or plausibility of one's religious outlook can help to justify a degree of confidence that could not be supported on purely impartial grounds. Facts about disagreement should temper one's confidence, and perhaps significantly so. But rationalist weak conciliationism does not rule out the possibility that some are reasonable in maintaining a significant degree of confidence on religious matters, even in the face of pervasive and seemingly intractable disagreement.

Granted, only *genuine* insight can make it reasonable to maintain a level of confidence that could not be justified impartially. My view does not vindicate religious confidence that is sustained by confused and distorted thinking. But many who do not believe on the basis of genuine insight nonetheless take themselves (ourselves?) to have such insight. Those who are mistaken in this way might appeal to rationalist weak conciliationism in giving an account of their sustained religious or irreligious confidence. My arguments for widening the notion of rational insight to include affectively mediated insights might provide false comfort to those whose emotions affect their thinking in ways that are distorting rather than illuminating. In short, an attempt to apply my view may fail to mitigate error, unlike more demanding conciliatory views. While more demanding conciliatory policies may have the unfortunate effect of undermining (ir)religious belief that is both true and well-supported by the first-order evidence, adoption of such policies would at least temper the unjustified overconfidence that seems so prevalent in the religious domain.

Suppose that most human beings are largely in error in their views on central religious questions. In this case, it is likely that widespread adoption of rationalist weak conciliationism would do less to improve humanity's overall accuracy on religious matters than the widespread adoption of strong conciliationism. Were one to choose a disagreement policy from behind a veil of ignorance, without knowledge of who one will be and how one will reason, it might very well be rational to choose strong conciliationism. But I have argued that the disagreement policy that is rational for you to follow after thinking through some controversial matter may not be identical to the policy that your past self, who had only p-neutral considerations to go on, would rightly want to impose on your present self. If you presently have genuine insight into the matter at hand, then you are better positioned than your past self to gauge your present reliability. While it may be true that the broad process of trusting whatever *apparent* insights you might have on the matter is not an especially reliable process (since apparent insights often fail to be genuine), your present self-trust need not be based on your trust in this broad process. Your self-trust might instead be based on your trust in a narrow process involving some highly specific line of reasoning, reasoning whose cogency you are in a position to appreciate.

Many will no doubt be skeptical of the rationalism that informs my position and will endorse a more demanding policy, one that imposes not only agent impartiality (which I affirm) but reasons impartiality as well. This more rigorous impartiality requirement satisfies the hope of those who want to undermine religious zeal of various sorts by appealing only to epistemic principles of higher-order defeat and noncontroversial facts about religious disagreement.

There is, I concede, something attractive about this position. But are strong conciliationists really prepared to embrace the radical impartiality they commend? Consider some difficult questions that arise for a prospective strong conciliationist. What would epistemic impartiality have required of early opponents to slavery, or of early advocates of women's suffrage? Does impartiality require merely that atheists and theists become agnostic, or might it require atheists to concede the greater probability of theism (or vice versa)? Does impartiality threaten to undermine the normative beliefs that bear on how people should conduct their lives in the face of religious uncertainty? Are there limits to the degree and kinds of normative uncertainty that practical rationality can tolerate? If so, does epistemic impartiality push one beyond those limits?

Some of these difficult questions were taken up in part II. The arguments of part II, which are intended to be exploratory, suggest that a commitment to rigorous epistemic impartiality may be corrosive to both epistemic and practical rationality in the religious domain. There may be no impartial way of determining which doxastic states on religious matters do well in according with the demands of impartiality. And the normative uncertainty that would be required by epistemic impartiality might make it impossible to rationally decide on what sort of religious or irreligious way of life to pursue. Impartiality threatens to leave people rudderless in their cognitive and practical lives, at least when they enter into territory that is deeply contested.

These troubling conclusions may give one reason to hope that a moderate position like rationalist weak conciliationism is correct.

References

Alston, William P. "Epistemic Circularity." *Philosophy and Phenomenological Research* 47, no. 1 (September 1986): 1–30.

Alston, William P. "Level-Confusions in Epistemology." *Midwest Studies in Philosophy* 5, no. 1 (1980): 135–150.

Alston, William P. *Perceiving God: The Epistemology of Religious Experience*. Ithaca: Cornell University Press, 1991.

Audi, Robert. *Rationality and Religious Commitment*. Oxford: Oxford University Press, 2011.

Bealer, George. "On the Possibility of Philosophical Knowledge." *Philosophical Perspectives* 10 (1996): 1–34.

Benacerraf, Paul. "Mathematical Truth." *Journal of Philosophy* 70, no. 19 (1973): 661–679.

Bengson, John. "Grasping the Third Realm." *Oxford Studies in Epistemology* 5 (2015): 1–38.

Bergmann, Michael. "Epistemic Circularity: Malignant and Benign." *Philosophy and Phenomenological Research* 69, no. 3 (2004): 709–727.

Bergmann, Michael. *Justification without Awareness: A Defense of Epistemic Externalism*. Oxford: Oxford University Press, 2006.

Bergmann, Michael. "Skeptical Theism and the Problem of Evil." In *The Oxford Handbook of Philosophical Theology*, edited by Thomas P. Flint and Michael C. Rea, 374–399. Oxford: Oxford University Press, 2009.

Bernstein, A. R., and F. Wattenberg. "Non-standard Measure Theory." In *Applications of Model Theory of Algebra, Analysis, and Probability*, edited by W. A. J. Luxemberg, 171–185. New York: Holt, Rinehart and Winston, 1969.

Bogardus, Tomas. "The Problem of Contingency for Religious Belief." *Faith and Philosophy* 30, no. 4 (2013): 371–392.

Bogardus, Tomas. "A Vindication of the Equal-Weight View." *Episteme* 6, no. 3 (2009): 324–335.

Boghossian, Paul. "Inference and Insight." *Philosophy and Phenomenological Research* 63, no. 3 (2001): 633–640.

BonJour, Laurence. *In Defense of Pure Reason*. Cambridge: Cambridge University Press, 1998.

BonJour, Laurence. "Replies." *Philosophy and Phenomenological Research* 63, no. 3 (2001): 673–698.

Bourget, David. "The Role of Consciousness in Grasping and Understanding." *Philosophy and Phenomenological Research* 95, no. 2 (2017): 285–318.

Bourget, David, and David Chalmers. "The PhilPapers Surveys: Results, Analysis, and Discussion." http://philpapers.org/surveys/.

Bourget, David, and David J. Chalmers. "What Do Philosophers Believe?" *Philosophical Studies* 170, no. 3 (2013): 465–500.

Briggs, R. "Distorted Reflection." *Philosophical Review* 118, no. 1 (2009): 59–85.

Brunner, Emil, and Karl Barth. *Natural Theology*. Eugene: Wipf and Stock, 2002.

Calvin, John. *Institutes of the Christian Religion*. Edited by John T. McNeill. Translated by Ford Lewis Battles. Vol. 1. 2 vols. Louisville: Westminster John Knox Press, 1960.

Carey, Brandon, and Jonathan Matheson. "How Skeptical Is the Equal Weight View?" In *Disagreement and Skepticism*, edited by Diego E. Machuca, 131–149. New York: Routledge, 2013.

Cath, Yuri. "Evidence and Intuition." *Episteme* 9, no. 4 (2012): 311–328.

Christensen, David. "Disagreement and Public Controversy." In *Essays in Collective Epistemology*, edited by Jennifer Lackey, 142–164. Oxford: Oxford University Press, 2015.

Christensen, David. "Disagreement, Drugs, Etc.: From Accuracy to Akrasia." *Episteme* 13, no. 4 (2016): 392–422.

Christensen, David. "Disagreement, Question-Begging and Epistemic Self-Criticism." *Philosophers' Imprint* 11, no. 6 (2011): 1–22.

Christensen, David. "Epistemic Modesty Defended." In *The Epistemology of Disagreement: New Essays*, edited by David Christensen and Jennifer Lackey, 77–97. Oxford: Oxford University Press, 2013.

Christensen, David. "Epistemology of Disagreement: The Good News." *Philosophical Review* 116, no. 2 (2007): 187–217.

Christensen, David. "Higher-Order Evidence." *Philosophy and Phenomenological Research* 81, no. 1 (2010): 185–215.

Christensen, David. "Rational Reflection." *Philosophical Perspectives* 24, no. 1 (2010): 121–140.

Chudnoff, Elijah. *Intuition*. Oxford: Oxford University Press, 2013.

Chudnoff, Elijah. "The Nature of Intuitive Justification." *Philosophical Studies* 153, no. 2 (2011): 313–333.

Chudnoff, Elijah. "What Intuitions Are Like." *Philosophy and Phenomenological Research* 82, no. 3 (2011): 625–654.

Coates, Allen. "Rational Epistemic Akrasia." *American Philosophical Quarterly* 49, no. 2 (2012): 113–124.

Cohen, Stewart. "A Defense of the (Almost) Equal Weight View." In *The Epistemology of Disagreement: New Essays*, edited by David Christensen and Jennifer Lackey, 98–119. Oxford: Oxford University Press, 2013.

Conee, Earl, and Richard Feldman. *Evidentialism: Essays in Epistemology*. Oxford: Oxford University Press, 2004.

"Cracks in the Atheist Edifice." *Economist*, November 1, 2014. https://www.economist.com/briefing/2014/11/01/cracks-in-the-atheist-edifice.

Decker, Jason. "Conciliation and Self-Incrimination." *Erkenntnis* 79, no. 5 (2014): 1099–1134.

Draper, Paul, and Ryan Nichols. "Diagnosing Bias in Philosophy of Religion." *Monist* 96, no. 3 (2013): 420–446.

Edwards, Kari, and Edward E. Smith. "A Disconfirmation Bias in the Evaluation of Arguments." *Journal of Personality and Social Psychology* 71, no. 1 (1996): 5–24.

Elga, Adam. "Lucky to Be Rational." Unpublished paper presented at the Bellingham Summer Philosophy Conference, 2008. www.princeton.edu/~adame/papers/bellingham-lucky.pdf.

Elga, Adam. "Reflection and Disagreement." *Noûs* 41, no. 3 (2007): 478–502.

Elga, Adam. "The Puzzle of the Unmarked Clock and the New Rational Reflection Principle." *Philosophical Studies* 164, no. 1 (2013): 127–139.

Elga, Adam. "Subjective Probabilities Should Be Sharp." *Philosophers' Imprint* 10, no. 5 (2010): 1–11.

Elga, Adam. "The Puzzle of the Unmarked Clock and the New Rational Reflection Principle." *Philosophical Studies* 164, no. 1 (2013): 127–139.

Elkin, Lee, and Gregory Wheeler. "Resolving Peer Disagreements through Imprecise Probabilities." *Noûs* 52, no. 2 (2018): 260–278.

Enoch, David. "Not Just a Truthometer: Taking Oneself Seriously (but Not Too Seriously) in Cases of Peer Disagreement." *Mind* 119, no. 476 (2010): 953–997.

Enoch, David, and Joshua Schechter. "How Are Basic Belief-Forming Methods Justified?" *Philosophy and Phenomenological Research* 76, no. 3 (2008): 547–579.

Feldman, Richard. "Reasonable Religious Disagreements." In *Philosophers without Gods: Meditations on Atheism and the Secular Life*, edited by Louise M. Antony, 194–214. Oxford: Oxford University Press, 2007.

Field, Hartry H. *Realism, Mathematics, and Modality*. New York: Blackwell, 1989.

Fraassen, Bas C. van. "Belief and the Will." *Journal of Philosophy* 81, no. 5 (1984): 235–256.

Fraassen, Bas C. van. *The Empirical Stance*. Rev. ed. New Haven: Yale University Press, 2004.

Fraassen, Bas C. van. *Laws and Symmetry*. Oxford: Oxford University Press, 1989.

Fricker, Elizabeth. "Epistemic Trust in Oneself and Others—An Argument from Analogy?" In *Religious Faith and Intellectual Virtue*, edited by Laura Frances Callahan and Timothy O'Connor, 174–203. Oxford: Oxford University Press, 2014.

Ganson, Dorit. "Evidentialism and Pragmatic Constraints on Outright Belief." *Philosophical Studies* 139, no. 3 (2008): 441–458.

Garber, Daniel. "Old Evidence and Logical Omniscience in Bayesian Confirmation Theory." *Minnesota Studies in the Philosophy of Science* 10 (1983): 99–131.

Goldberg, Sanford. "Does Externalist Epistemology Rationalize Religious Commitment?" In *Religious Faith and Intellectual Virtue*, edited by Timothy O'Connor and Laura Frances Callahan, 279–298. Oxford: Oxford University Press, 2014.

Gustafsson, Johan E., and Olle Torpman. "In Defence of My Favourite Theory." *Pacific Philosophical Quarterly* 95, no. 2 (2014): 159–174.

Gutting, Gary. *Religious Belief and Religious Skepticism*. Notre Dame: University of Notre Dame Press, 1982.

Hájek, Alan. "Dutch Book Arguments." In *The Handbook of Rational and Social Choice*, edited by Paul Anand, Prasanta K. Pattanaik, and Clemens Puppe, 173–195. Oxford: Oxford University Press, 2009.

Hájek, Alan. "Waging War on Pascal's Wager." *Philosophical Review* 112, no. 1 (2003): 27–56.

Hájek, Alan. "What Conditional Probability Could Not Be." *Synthese* 137, no. 3 (2003): 273–323.

Harmon, Elizabeth. "The Irrelevance of Moral Uncertainty." *Oxford Studies in Metaethics* 10 (2015): 53–79.

Hasan, Ali. "In Defense of Rationalism about Abductive Inference." In *Best Explanations: New Essays on Inference to the Best Explanation*, edited by Kevin McCain and Ted Poston. Oxford: Oxford University Press, 2017.

Hawthorne, John, and Jason Stanley. "Knowledge and Action." *Journal of Philosophy* 105, no. 10 (2008): 571–590.

Hick, John. "The Epistemological Challenge of Religious Pluralism." *Faith and Philosophy* 14, no. 3 (1997): 277–286.

Hick, John. *An Interpretation of Religion: Human Responses to the Transcendent.* 2nd ed. New Haven: Yale University Press, 2004.

Horowitz, Sophie. "Epistemic Akrasia." *Noûs* 48, no. 4 (2014): 718–744.

Howard-Snyder, Daniel. "The Skeptical Christian." *Oxford Studies in Philosophy of Religion* 8 (2017): 142–167.

Huemer, Michael. "Epistemological Egoism and Agent-Centered Norms." In *Evidentialism and Its Discontents*, edited by Trent Dougherty, 17–33. Oxford: Oxford University Press, 2011.

James, William. *The Varieties of Religious Experience.* New York: Random House, 1902.

James, William. *The Will to Believe and Other Essays in Popular Philosophy.* New York: Longmans, Green and Co., 1896.

Johnston, Mark. "The Authority of Affect." *Philosophy and Phenomenological Research* 63, no. 1 (2001): 181–214.

Jordan, Jeff. *Pascal's Wager: Pragmatic Arguments and Belief in God.* Oxford: Oxford University Press, 2006.

Joyce, James M. "Bayesianism." In *The Oxford Handbook of Rationality*, edited by Alfred R. Mele and Piers Rawling, 132–155. Oxford: Oxford University Press, 2004.

Joyce, James M. "A Defense of Imprecise Credences in Inference and Decision Making." *Philosophical Perspectives* 24, no. 1 (2010): 281–323.

Joyce, James M. "How Probabilities Reflect Evidence." *Philosophical Perspectives* 19, no. 1 (2005): 153–178.

Kelly, Thomas. "Consensus Gentium: Reflections on the 'Common Consent' Argument for the Existence of God." In *Evidence and Religious Belief*, edited by Kelly James Clark and Raymond J. VanArragon, 135–156. Oxford: Oxford University Press, 2011.

Kelly, Thomas. "Disagreement in Philosophy: Its Epistemic Significance." In *The Oxford Handbook of Philosophical Methodology*, edited by Herman Cappelen, Tamar Szabó Gendler, and John Hawthorne, 374–393. Oxford: Oxford University Press, 2016.

Kelly, Thomas. "The Epistemic Significance of Disagreement." *Oxford Studies in Epistemology* 1 (2005): 167–196.

Kelly, Thomas. "Peer Disagreement and Higher Order Evidence." In *Disagreement*, edited by Richard Feldman and Ted A. Warfield, 111–174. Oxford: Oxford University Press, 2010.

Kierkegaard, Søren. *Concluding Unscientific Postscript to Philosophical Fragments.* Edited by Howard Vincent Hong and Edna Hatlestad Hong. Princeton: Princeton University Press, 1992.

Kitcher, Philip. *Life after Faith: The Case for Secular Humanism.* New Haven: Yale University Press, 2014.

Lackey, Jennifer. "A Justificationist View of Disagreement's Epistemic Significance." In *Social Epistemology*, edited by Adrian Haddock, Alan Millar, and Duncan Pritchard, 298–325. Oxford: Oxford University Press, 2010.

Lackey, Jennifer. "What Should We Do When We Disagree?" *Oxford Studies in Epistemology* 2 (2010): 274–293.

Ladha, Krishna K. "The Condorcet Jury Theorem, Free Speech, and Correlated Votes." *American Journal of Political Science* 36, no. 3 (1992): 617–634.

Lamm, Norman. "Faith and Doubt." *Tradition: A Journal of Orthodox Jewish Thought* 9, no. 1/2 (1967): 14–51.

Lasonen-Aarnio, Maria. "Disagreement and Evidential Attenuation." *Noûs* 47, no. 4 (2013): 767–794.

Lasonen-Aarnio, Maria. "Higher-Order Evidence and the Limits of Defeat." *Philosophy and Phenomenological Research* 88, no. 2 (2014): 314–345.

Lasonen-Aarnio, Maria. "New Rational Reflection and Internalism about Rationality." *Oxford Studies in Epistemology* 5 (2015): 145–171.

Lewis, David. "Immodest Inductive Methods." *Philosophy of Science* 38, no. 1 (1971): 54–63.

List, Christian, and Robert E. Goodin. "Epistemic Democracy: Generalizing the Condorcet Jury Theorem." *Journal of Political Philosophy* 9, no. 3 (2001): 277–306.

Littlejohn, Clayton. "Disagreement and Defeat." In *Disagreement and Skepticism*, edited by Diego E. Machuca, 169–192. New York: Routledge, 2013.

MacAskill, William. "Normative Uncertainty as a Voting Problem." *Mind* 125, no. 500 (2016): 967–1004.

MacAskill, William, and Toby Ord. "Why Maximize Expected Choice-Worthiness?" *Noûs*, 2018. doi: 10.1111/nous.12264.

Meacham, Christopher J. G. "Impermissive Bayesianism." *Erkenntnis* 79, no. 6 (2014): 1185–1217.

Moss, Sarah. "Credal Dilemmas." *Noûs* 49, no. 4 (2015): 665–683.

Newman, John Henry. *Fifteen Sermons Preached Before the University of Oxford*. 3rd ed. London: Longmans, Green and Co., 1872.

Otto, Rudolf. *The Idea of the Holy*. Translated by John W. Harvey. 2nd ed. London: Oxford University Press, 1950.

Pace, Michael. "The Epistemic Value of Moral Considerations: Justification, Moral Encroachment, and James' 'Will to Believe.'" *Noûs* 45, no. 2 (2011): 239–268.

Parfit, Derek. *On What Matters*. Vol. 2. 2 vols. Oxford: Oxford University Press, 2011.

Pascal, Blaise. *Pensées*. London: Penguin Books, 1995.

Pasnau, Robert. "Veiled Disagreement." *Journal of Philosophy* 111, no. 11 (2014): 608–630.

Pittard, John. "Conciliationism and Religious Disagreement." In *Challenges to Moral and Religious Belief: Disagreement and Evolution*, edited by Michael Bergmann and Patrick Kain, 80–97. Oxford: Oxford University Press, 2014.

Pittard, John. "Disagreement, Reliability, and Resilience." *Synthese* 194, no. 11 (2017): 4389–4409.

Pittard, John. "Fundamental Disagreements and the Limits of Instrumentalism." *Synthese*, 2018. doi: 10.1007/s11229-018-1691-1.

Pittard, John. "Resolute Conciliationism." *Philosophical Quarterly* 65, no. 260 (2015): 442–463.

Pittard, John, and Alex Worsnip. "Metanormative Contextualism and Normative Uncertainty." *Mind* 126, no. 501 (2017): 155–193.

Plantinga, Alvin. *God and Other Minds: A Study of the Rational Justification of Belief in God*. Ithaca: Cornell University Press, 1967.

Plantinga, Alvin. *Warranted Christian Belief*. New York: Oxford University Press, 2000.

Reining, Stefan. "Peerhood in Deep Religious Disagreements." *Religious Studies* 52, no. 3 (2016): 403–419.

Rinard, Susanna. "Against Radical Credal Imprecision." *Thought: A Journal of Philosophy* 2, no. 2 (2013): 157–165.

Rinard, Susanna. "A Decision Theory for Imprecise Credences." *Philosophers Imprint* 15, no. 7 (2015): 1–16.

Rotondo, Andrew. "Undermining, Circularity, and Disagreement." *Synthese* 190, no. 3 (2013): 563–584.

Roush, Sherrilyn. "Second Guessing: A Self-Help Manual." *Episteme* 6, no. 3 (2009): 251–268.

Schellenberg, J. L. *The Wisdom to Doubt: A Justification of Religious Skepticism.* Ithaca: Cornell University Press, 2007.

Schoenfield, Miriam. "An Accuracy Based Approach to Higher Order Evidence." *Philosophical and Phenomenological Research* 96 (2018): 690–715.

Schoenfield, Miriam. "A Dilemma for Calibrationism." *Philosophy and Phenomenological Research* 91, no. 2 (2015): 425–455.

Schoenfield, Miriam. "Permission to Believe: Why Permissivism Is True and What It Tells Us about Irrelevant Influences on Belief." *Noûs* 48, no. 2 (2014): 193–218.

Sepielli, Andrew. "What to Do When You Don't Know What to Do." *Oxford Studies in Metaethics* 4 (2009): 5–28.

Sepielli, Andrew. "What to Do When You Don't Know What to Do When You Don't Know What to Do . . ." *Noûs* 48, no. 3 (2014): 521–544.

Siderits, Mark. *Buddhism as Philosophy: An Introduction.* New York: Routledge, 2007.

Sidgwick, Henry. *The Methods of Ethics.* 7th ed. London: Macmillan, 1907.

Sliwa, Paulina, and Sophie Horowitz. "Respecting All the Evidence." *Philosophical Studies* 172, no. 11 (2015): 2835–2858.

Smithies, Declan. "Moore's Paradox and the Accessibility of Justification." *Philosophy and Phenomenological Research* 85, no. 2 (2012): 273–300.

Smithies, Declan. "A Simple Theory of Introspection." In *Introspection and Consciousness,* edited by Declan Smithies and Daniel Stoljar, 259–294. New York: Oxford University Press, 2012.

Stanley, Jason. *Knowledge and Practical Interests.* Oxford: Oxford University Press, 2005.

Swinburne, Richard. *Faith and Reason.* 2nd ed. Oxford: Oxford University Press, 2005.

Swinburne, Richard. *Providence and the Problem of Evil.* Oxford: Oxford University Press, 1998.

Tan, Charlene. "Michael Hand, Indoctrination and the Inculcation of Belief." *Journal of Philosophy of Education* 38, no. 2 (2004): 257–267.

Taylor, Charles. *The Language Animal: The Full Shape of the Human Linguistic Capacity.* Cambridge, MA: Harvard University Press, 2016.

Taylor, Charles. "Reason, Faith, and Meaning." *Faith and Philosophy* 28, no. 1 (2011): 5–18.

Taylor, Charles. *A Secular Age.* Cambridge, MA: Harvard University Press, 2007.

Tiberius, Valerie. "Practical Reason and the Stability Standard." *Ethical Theory and Moral Practice* 5, no. 3 (2002): 339–354.

Titelbaum, Michael G. "Rationality's Fixed Point (Or: In Defense of Right Reason)." *Oxford Studies in Epistemology* 5 (2015): 253–294.

Topey, Brett. "Coin Flips, Credences and the Reflection Principle." *Analysis* 72, no. 3 (2012): 478–488.

Turri, John. "On the Relationship between Propositional and Doxastic Justification." *Philosophy and Phenomenological Research* 80, no. 2 (2010): 312–326.

Unger, Peter. *All the Power in the World.* New York: Oxford University Press, 2006.

Unger, Peter. *Ignorance: A Case for Scepticism.* Oxford: Oxford University Press, 1978.

Van Inwagen, Peter. *The Problem of Evil.* Oxford: Oxford University Press, 2006.

Van Inwagen, Peter. "Quam Dilecta." In *God and the Philosophers: The Reconciliation of Faith and Reason,* edited by Thomas V. Morris, 31–60. New York: Oxford University Press, 1994.

Vavova, Katia. "Moral Disagreement and Moral Skepticism." *Philosophical Perspectives* 28, no. 1 (2014): 302–333.

Weatherson, Brian. "Can We Do Without Pragmatic Encroachment?" *Philosophical Perspectives* 19, no. 1 (2005): 417–443.

Weatherson, Brian. "Disagreements, Philosophical, and Otherwise." In *Disagreement: New Essays*, edited by David Christensen and Jennifer Lackey, 54–73. Oxford: Oxford University Press, 2013.

Weatherson, Brian. "Running Risks Morally." *Philosophical Studies* 167, no. 1 (2014): 141–163.

Weiner, Matt. "More on the Self-Undermining Argument." *Opiniatrety* (blog), January 9, 2007. http://mattweiner.net/blog/archives/000781.html.

White, Roger. "Epistemic Permissiveness." *Philosophical Perspectives* 19, no. 1 (2005): 445–459.

White, Roger. "Evidential Symmetry and Mushy Credence." *Oxford Studies in Epistemology* 3 (2010): 161–186.

White, Roger. "On Treating Oneself and Others as Thermometers." *Episteme* 6, no. 3 (2009): 233–250.

White, Roger. "Problems for Dogmatism." *Philosophical Studies* 131, no. 3 (2006): 525–557.

White, Roger. "You Just Believe That Because . . ." *Philosophical Perspectives* 24, no. 1 (2010): 573–615.

Wright, Crispin. "Warrant for Nothing (and Foundations for Free)?" *Aristotelian Society Supplementary Volume* 78, no. 1 (2004): 167–212.

Wynn, Mark. *Emotional Experience and Religious Understanding: Integrating Perception, Conception and Feeling*. Cambridge: Cambridge University Press, 2005.

Yang, Fenggang. "When Will China Become the World's Largest Christian Country?" *Slate*, December 1, 2014. http://www.slate.com/bigideas/what-is-the-future-of-religion/essays-and-opinions/fenggang-yang-opinion. Accessed November 14, 2016.

Zagzebski, Linda Trinkaus. *Epistemic Authority: A Theory of Trust, Authority, and Autonomy in Belief*. Oxford: Oxford University Press, 2012.

Index

For the benefit of digital users, indexed terms that span two pages (e.g., 52–53) may, on occasion, appear on only one of those pages.